# METAPHOR AND FIELDS

*Metaphor and Fields* is an explanation and demonstration of the value of metaphoric processes and fields in psychoanalysis. In this book, S. Montana Katz articulates a future direction for psychoanalysis which is progressively explored, taking into account features essential to psychoanalysts of all persuasions, clinically and theoretically. In this way, psychoanalysis is brought into the postmodern future by fashioning an umbrella for the discipline. With this umbrella, the barriers to mutual understanding may be dismantled and a path permanently forged to the possibility of meaningful international, intercultural, interdisciplinary, and poly-perspectival psychoanalytic exchange.

    *Metaphor and Fields* organically merges work on metaphoric processes with work on fields. The use of a framework with metaphoric processes and fields combined exhibits the uniqueness of psychoanalysis and shows how it explores and explains human experience. The relational fields of the North American school of relational theory, intersubjective matrices, self object matrices, and the ground breaking work of Madeleine and Willy Baranger are all examples of field concepts that have been successfully employed in theoretical frameworks and clinical technique. They show how other schools of thought can be understood as using an implicit field concept.

    The chapters in this book approach the subject from diverse vantage points. Taken together, they form an intricate web of psychoanalytic thought that moves the scope of psychoanalysis beyond dispute towards the open, inclusive discussion of core concepts and technique. *Metaphor and Fields* will be of interest to psychoanalysts, psychiatrists, mental health clinicians, psychologists, social workers, and a wide academic audience drawn from the fields of philosophy, linguistics, comparative literature, anthropology, and sociology.

**S. Montana Katz** is a training and supervising analyst, and a member of faculty for the National Psychological Association for Psychoanalysis. She is in private practice in New York City.

# PSYCHOANALYTIC INQUIRY BOOK SERIES
## JOSEPH D. LICHTENBERG
### SERIES EDITOR

Like its counterpart, *Psychoanalytic Inquiry: A Topical Journal for Mental Health Professionals*, the Psychoanalytic Inquiry Book Series presents a diversity of subjects within a diversity of approaches to those subjects. Under the editorship of Joseph Lichtenberg, in collaboration with Melvin Bornstein and the editorial board of *Psychoanalytic Inquiry*, the volumes in this series strike a balance between research, theory, and clinical application. We are honored to have published the works of various innovators in psychoanalysis, such as Frank Lachmann, James Fosshage, Robert Stolorow, Donna Orange, Louis Sander, Léon Wurmser, James Grotstein, Joseph Jones, Doris Brothers, Fredric Busch, and Joseph Lichtenberg, among others.

The series includes books and monographs on mainline psychoanalytic topics, such as sexuality, narcissism, trauma, homosexuality, jealousy, envy, and varied aspects of analytic process and technique. In our efforts to broaden the field of analytic interest, the series has incorporated and embraced innovative discoveries in infant research, self psychology, intersubjectivity, motivational systems, affects as process, responses to cancer, borderline states, contextualism, postmodernism, attachment research and theory, medication, and mentalization. As further investigations in psychoanalysis come to fruition, we seek to present them in readable, easily comprehensible writing.

After 25 years, the core vision of this series remains the investigation, analysis and discussion of developments on the cutting edge of the psychoanalytic field, inspired by a boundless spirit of inquiry.

# PSYCHOANALYTIC INQUIRY BOOK SERIES
## JOSEPH D. LICHTENBERG
### SERIES EDITOR

# PSYCHOANALYTIC INQUIRY BOOK SERIES
## JOSEPH D. LICHTENBERG
### SERIES EDITOR

# PSYCHOANALYTIC INQUIRY BOOK SERIES
## JOSEPH D. LICHTENBERG
### SERIES EDITOR

# METAPHOR AND FIELDS

Common Ground, Common Language,
and the Future of Psychoanalysis

*Edited by*
*S. Montana Katz*

Routledge
Taylor & Francis Group

NEW YORK AND LONDON

First published 2013
by Routledge
711 Third Avenue, New York, NY 10017

Simultaneously published in the UK
by Routledge
27 Church Road, Hove, East Sussex BN3 2FA

*Routledge is an imprint of the Taylor & Francis Group, an informa business*

© 2013 Taylor & Francis

*Library of Congress Cataloging in Publication Data*
Metaphor and fields : common ground, common language and the
future of psychoanalysis / edited by S. Montana Katz.
     p. cm.
  1. Psychoanalysis. 2. Field theory (Social psychology)
  3. Metaphor--Psychological aspects. I. Katz, Montana.
  BF173.M38 2013
  150.19'5--dc23                        2012028007

ISBN: 978-0-415-63171-6 (hbk)
ISBN: 978-0-415-63172-3 (pbk)
ISBN: 978-0-203-07231-8 (ebk)

Typeset in Garamond
by HWA Text and Data Management, London

SUSTAINABLE
FORESTRY
INITIATIVE

Certified Sourcing
www.sfiprogram.org
SFI-00555
*The SFI label applies to the text stock.*

Printed and bound in the United States of America by
Walsworth Publishing Company, Marceline, MO.

This book is dedicated to the work of Madeleine and Willy Baranger, and to the possibilities for finding psychoanalytic common ground in field theory.

# CONTENTS

CONTENTS

# CONTRIBUTORS

**Nikaya Becker-Matero**, MA, is a Clinical Psychology PhD candidate at Adelphi University, Garden City, NY. She completed internship training at Albert Einstein College of Medicine's Bronx Psychiatric Center, Bronx, NY, and is Adjunct Assistant Professor in the Department of Psychology at Adelphi University. Ms. Becker-Matero has published in the *Journal of Personality Disorders*, *Psychoanalytic Inquiry*, and *Journal of Counseling Psychology*; she has presented her work at the Society for Personality Assessment (SPA) and Society for Psychotherapy Research (SPR). Her main research interests focus on conducting empirical studies of psychoanalytic and psychodynamic models of personality, particularly histrionic personality, and on self-concept, self-complexity, and social awareness. Additional interests include the links between assessment and clinical practice in personality disorders. She has worked on grants founded by the National Institute of Mental Health and the National Science Foundation.

**Antal Borbely**, MD, is a Board certified psychiatrist and a graduate and lecturer at the New York Psychoanalytic Institute. He is a member of the American Psychoanalytic Association. He is interested in questions regarding the centrality of time and metaphor in psychoanalytic theory and in the mind's functioning. He wrote the following papers regarding these topics: "Towards a temporal theory of the mind," *Psychoanalysis and Contemporary Thought*, 1987; "A psychoanalytic theory of metaphor," *International Journal of Psychoanalysis*, 1998; "Towards a psychodynamic understanding of metaphor and metonymy: Their role in awareness and defense," *Metaphor and Symbol*, 2004; "Metaphor and psychoanalysis," in *The Cambridge Handbook of Metaphor and Thought*, 2008; "The centrality of metaphor and metonymy in psychoanalytic theory and practice," *Psychoanalytic Inquiry*, 2009; "Metaphor and metonymy as the basis for a new psychoanalytic language," *Psychoanalytic Inquiry*, 2011. He is presently working on the comparison between the bootstrapping aspects observed in evolutionary robotics and in free association (in preparation).

**Robert F. Bornstein** received his PhD in Clinical Psychology from the State University of New York at Buffalo in 1986 and is Professor of Psychology at Adelphi University. He has published widely on personality dynamics, assessment, and treatment, wrote *The Dependent Personality* and *The Dependent Patient: A*

*Practitioner's Guide*, and co-edited (with Joseph Masling) seven volumes of the *Empirical Studies of Psychoanalytic Theories* series. Dr. Bornstein is a Fellow of the American Psychological Association, Association for Psychological Science, and Society for Personality Assessment; his research has been funded by grants from the National Institute of Mental Health and the National Science Foundation. Dr. Bornstein received the Society for Personality Assessment's 1995, 1999, 2002, and 2008 awards for Distinguished Contributions to the Personality Assessment Literature, and the American Psychological Foundation 2005 Theodore Millon Award for Excellence in Personality Research.

**Giuseppe Civitarese MD, PhD**, a member of the Italian Psychoanalytic Association and of the American Psychoanalytic Association, is in private practice in Pavia, Italy. He has published several papers in the main international psychoanalytic journals. His books include: *The Intimate Room: Theory and Technique of the Analytic Field*, The New Library of Psychoanalysis, Routledge, London 2010; *The Violence of Emotions: Bion and Post-Bionian Psychoanalysis*, The New Library of Psychoanalysis, Routledge, London 2012; *Perdere la testa: Abiezione, conflitto estetico e critica psicoanalitica*, Clinamen, Florence 2012 [*Losing One's Head: Abjection, Aesthetic Conflict and Psychoanalytic Criticism*]; *I film della vita. Il cinema e l'interpretazione dei sogni* [*The Films of our Life. Cinema and the Interpretation of Dreams*] (in preparation). He has also co-edited *L'ipocondria e il dubbio: L'approccio psicoanalitico*, Franco Angeli, Milano 2011 [*Hypochondria and Doubt: The Psychoanalytic Approach*].

**Antoine Corel**, MD, is a member of the Argentine Psychoanalytic Association where he was trained, and member of the Paris Psychoanalytic Society. Since 1976 he has been in private practice in Paris. His main interests concern the psychoanalytic process approached as a transformation in time and the formulation of constructions. His activity as a film critic has continued around the relation between psychoanalysis and the cinema.

**Antonino Ferro** is a training and child analyst for the Italian Psychoanalytic Society, IPA, and an APsaA member. He has published several books translated into many languages – the most recent being *Mind Works: Technique and Creativity in Psychoanalysis*, and *Avoiding Emotions, Living Emotions* published by Routledge/ New Library. In 2007 he was selected as a recipient of the Mary S. Sigourney Award. He is has been Chair since 2007 of the Sponsoring Committee for the Turkish Provisional Society of Psychoanalysis and Chair of the Executives of the International Appointments Committee of the *International Journal of Psychoanalysis* elections. He was editor for Europe of *IJP* for seven years and, since January 2011, a member of the editorial board of *Psychoanalytic Quarterly*.

**S. Montana Katz PhD, LP** is a training and supervising analyst and on the faculty of the National Psychological Association for Psychoanalysis. She is on the editorial boards of *Psychoanalytic Inquiry* and *The Psychoanalytic Review*. S. Montana Katz has a private practice in New York City.

**Beatriz de León de Bernardi** is a Uruguayan psychoanalyst, and full member and training analyst of the Uruguayan Psychoanalytic Association (APU). She is past president of the APU and has formerly been Director of the Scientific Committee and editor of the *Uruguayan Journal of Psychoanalysis*. She is an editorial board member of the *International Journal of Psychoanalysis*. Currently she is also a Representative for Latin America in the International Psychoanalytical Association Board. She has published papers and books in different languages on psychoanalytic topics, mainly about the patient–analyst interaction and the analyst's contribution to the analytic process, the notion of countertransference in Latin America, and the thought of Madeleine and Willy Baranger and Heinrich Racker. She has researched and published on implicit theories in psychoanalytic practice. She has received the award of the Latin-American Psychoanalytical Federation (FEPA L) in 1992 and the Training Today Award in 2009.

**Arnold H. Modell, PhD** practices psychoanalysis in Newton, Massachusetts. He is the author of numerous papers and five books. The most recent is *Imagination and the Meaningful Brain* (MIT Press). He is currently Clinical Professor of Psychiatry at Harvard Medical School and a training and supervising analyst at the Boston Psychoanalytic Institute.

**Claudio Neri MD, PhD** is a psychoanalyst and group analyst who lives and practices in Rome. He is a full member of the Società Psicoanalitica Italiana and a training and supervising analyst in its Institute; full member of the International Psychoanalytic Association, and the Group-Analytic Institute of London; full professor at the Faculty of Medicine and Psychology, University La Sapienza of Rome; and visiting professor at the University Lumière-Lyon 2 and Descartes-Paris 5°. He is chief editor of the online journal *Funzione Gamma*, and is the author and editor of numerous books, among which are: *Group* (Jessica Kingsley Publishers, 1998), and, with Pines and Friedman (eds), *Dreams in Group Psychotherapy* (Jessica Kingsley Publishers, 2002).

**Elsa Rappoport de Aisemberg** is a member and training analyst of the Argentine Psychoanalytic Association; former vice-president of the Argentine Psychoanalytic Association; member of the IPA New Groups for the Sponsoring Committee of Asunción; past Chair of Scientific Colloquiums and Advisor for the Scientific Department of the Argentine Psychoanalytic Association; Chair of the Research Group on Psychosomatics at the Argentine Psychoanalytic Association; and author of many papers and publications on sexuality and gender, psychosomatics, art and psychoanalysis and theoretical and clinical approach of the analytic field in psychoanalytic journals in Spanish, English, French, German, and Portuguese. Additionally, she is co-editor of *Psychosomatics Today, A Psychoanalytic Perspective*, London, Karnac, 2010.

**Ana-María Rizzuto MD** is a training and supervising analyst at the PINE Psychoanalytic Center, a member of the American Psychoanalytic Association and a member of the International Psychoanalytic Association. She is the author of *The Birth of the Living God. A Psychoanalytic Study* (1979), The University of Chicago Press, and *Why did Freud Reject God? A Psychodynamic Interpretation* (1998), Yale University Press. This book received in 2001 the Gradiva Award for Best Book (Religion Subject), given by the National Association for the Advancement of Psychoanalysis. She co-authored with W. W. Meissner and Dan H. Buie the book *The Dynamics of Human Aggression: Theoretical Foundations and Clinical Applications: Theoretical Foundations, Clinical Applications* (2004), Brunner-Routledge. She is the author of numerous articles on the psychodynamics of religion, language in psychoanalysis, aggression, the clinical situation, and other subjects. In 1996, she received the William C. Bier Award, given by Division 36, American Psychological Association, and in 1997 she received the Oskar Pfister Prize, given by the American Psychiatric Association. Both prizes were given to her for her outstanding contributions to the Psychology of Religion. She is a regular participant in national and international psychoanalytic congresses and a frequent psychoanalytic lecturer in the USA, Latin America, Europe, and Japan.

**Juan Tubert-Oklander MD, PhD** is a psychoanalyst, group analyst, and family therapist who lives and practices in Mexico City. Originally from Argentina, he has been living in Mexico since 1976 and is presently a Mexican citizen. He is a full member of the Mexican Psychoanalytic Association, and training and supervising analyst in its institute; additionally he is a full member of the International Psychoanalytic Association, the Argentine Psychoanalytic Association, and the Group-Analytic Society International. He is author of *The Learning Operative Group* (in Spanish), *Operative Groups: The Latin-American Approach to Group Analysis* (with Reyna Hernández-Tubert), *Hybrid Science: Psychoanalysis and Analogical Hermeneutics* (with Mauricio Beuchot-Puente, in Spanish), and *Theory of Psychoanalytic Practice: A Relational Process Approach* (in preparation).

**Robert Wallerstein, M.D.** is Emeritus Professor and former Chair of the Department of Psychiatry of the University of California San Francisco School of Medicine, and Emeritus training and supervising analyst, San Francisco Center for Psychoanalysis. He is a former President of the American Psychoanalytic Association (1971–72) and a former President of the International Psychoanalytical Association (1985–89). He graduated from Columbia College (June 1941), the Columbia University College of Physicians and Surgeons (September 1944), and the Topeka Institute for Psychoanalysis (June 1958). He was Director of Research at the Menninger Clinic (Topeka Kansas) until June 1966, and then Chief of Psychiatry at the Mount Zion Hospital, San Francisco (1966-75). He was twice a Fellow at the Center for Advanced Study in the Behavioral Sciences at Stanford, California (1964–5, 1981–2), a Fellow at the Rockefeller Foundation Study Center at Bellagio, Lake Como, Italy (1992), and given the Mary Singleton Sigourney Award for outstanding contributions to psychoanalysis in 1991.

**Robert S. White** is a graduate and member of the Western New England Psychoanalytic Society, Faculty, and Western New England Psychoanalytic Institute. He is associate editor for the Internet, JAPA 2004–2009, and founder and moderator of the JAPA online discussion group, 1997–2009. Since 2010 he has been Chair, IPA website editorial board, and is Assistant Clinical Professor of Psychiatry at Yale University. He is in private practice in psychoanalysis and psychiatry, New Haven, Connecticut, USA and publishes in the areas of intersubjectivity, interpersonal psychoanalysis and Bion studies.

**Léon Wurmser MD, PhD hc** (honorary degree in philosophy, Humboldt University, Berlin), is a psychoanalyst and former Clinical Professor of Psychiatry, University of West Virginia, with regular and extensive teaching in Europe. He is the author of *The Hidden Dimension* (1978); *The Mask of Shame* (1981); *Flight from Conscience* (1987, in German); *The Riddle of Masochism* (1993, in German); *Magic Transformation and Tragic Transformation* (1999, in German); *The Power of the Inner Judge* (2000); *Values and Ideas of Judaism in Psychoanalytic View* (2001, in German); *Torment Me, But Do Not Abandon Me* (2007); and *Shame and the Evil Eye* (in German, 2011) and co-author with Heidrun Jarass of *Jealousy and Envy— New Views on Two Powerful Emotions* (2007), a monograph in the Psychoanalytic Inquiry Book series and *Nothing Good is Allowed to Stand* (2012) in the same series. He is a training and supervising analyst for the New York Freudian Society, and recipient of Egnér and *Journal of the American Psychoanalytic Association* prizes.

# FOREWORD

*Madeleine Baranger*

I am extremely touched by the fact that Dr. S. Montana Katz considers the work of the Barangers in the psychoanalytic field an important source for her own work and that she relates it to the concept of metaphor, which she has studied in depth.

The subject of this book, as reflected in the title, is captivating: *Metaphor and Fields: Common Ground, Common Language, and the Future of Psychoanalysis.*

Its purpose is to examine and address obstacles in understanding and dialogue between different psychoanalytic authors and schools and other types of professional institutions.

She is trying to demonstrate that the concepts of metaphor and of the field are valuable for psychoanalysis.

The book is structured to progressively explore a goal for the future that takes into account all of the psychoanalytic orientations that are usually recognized as constituents of a particular science. The goal is to convince readers to immerse themselves in the project, theoretically and clinically, so that, in a postmodern future, an "umbrella field" is created for psychoanalysis.

Regarding this objective, the concepts she uses to illustrate her convictions originate from diverse sources.

This is an excellent example and model for thinkers and researchers who seek to evolve and present their own convictions and want a way to recognize the different concepts that have contributed to their development.

As a whole, the book is a project to present the psychoanalytic research and thought of a variety of current authors whose perspectives are considered building blocks of psychoanalysis. This is not just my definition; it is demonstrated by the variety of themes and developments that are presented.

So far, I have only made reference to the statements and intents of the book's editor. I would also like to focus on the most remarkable parts that manifest her conceptual way of thinking and expressing herself.

The book is organized and presented in an original manner. In the relevant portions, the editor/contributor clearly indicates her own theories, which are referenced in the title. With a sense of flair and generosity, in addition to the usual quotations, she offers the reader complete texts from analysts she recognizes as influencing her work or from those who have made remarkable contributions to topics of her interest.

There is a lesson to be learned from the contributions of so many different points of view. It is not about adopting one wholeheartedly—declaring ourselves disciples of some fellow scientist—or about rejecting a point of view because of its maximal or minimal differences about the same topic.

It is necessary to have a very precise knowledge of one's own thinking, to feel it, and to want it to be in constant evolution around the same issues. This requires modesty alongside creativity. It does not involve a search for final certainty but eternal revisions and possible disillusions in order to acquire new knowledge.

It was wonderful to be able to compare many of the authors mentioned, along with the author.

In my case, I would like to mention the work of Léon Wurmser, with which I was not very familiar, and of other authors about whose valuable contributions I was not so aware.

We can deepen our own thoughts by recognizing the importance, whether major or minor, of an influence from or similarity with a colleague. Readers can learn a way to get to know themselves better, accepting or rejecting other people's concepts. This is a great example—and a model—for analysts committed to an endless education, as for any thinker or researcher with the same eagerness to learn and develop.

The book's richness and scientific rigor make it an essential resource for readers—who will undoubtedly experience the same interest and pleasure I felt in discovering it.

# 1

# INTRODUCTION

*S. Montana Katz*

As the editor, I have multiple expectations for what can be accomplished with this book. For the reader unfamiliar with the use of either metaphoric processes or fields in psychoanalysis, I hope that this book will offer an explanation and demonstration of the use and value of these concepts. For all readers, I have striven to arrange the contents of this book such that a potential future direction for psychoanalysis is articulated and progressively explored, taking into account features essential to psychoanalysts of all persuasions. I have attempted to build a convincing case for readers to become immersed in the resulting framework, clinically and theoretically. In this way an attempt is made to bring psychoanalysis into the postmodern future by fashioning an umbrella field for psychoanalysis.

A common language is constructed in this framework through which all psychoanalytic perspectives can find faithful expression. It is hoped that conference and dialogue among the different analytic perspectives about psychoanalytic theory and practice will be possible without ineradicable loss or confusion of meaning. It is further anticipated that, ultimately, the result could be an expanded potential for the integration of concepts, principles, and techniques across analytic positions. Construction of the shared core concepts that underlie analytic perspectives constitutes a significant clinical and educational tool and may thus have an impact on psychoanalytic training.

There are other potential and far-reaching consequences to a common base for the psychoanalytic perspectives. Under this umbrella, analysts may reach across the interdisciplinary divide on firm ground. Psychoanalysis may become more accessible to disciplines in the humanities. Its irreducibility to other sciences is also clarified. The model exhibits what is unique to psychoanalysis and how it cannot be subjected to a reduction to a physiological or any other kind of inquiry. A possible outcome is enhanced and genuinely interdisciplinary cooperation, discussion, and research. This may afford a way to describe the discipline of psychoanalysis across perspectives for quantitative research. It is, moreover, an umbrella through which psychoanalysis may have expanded exposure in higher education and other kinds of professional institutions.

This book will thus address the current situation, in which not only are there multiple branches of psychoanalysis—each reflecting a different theoretical and

1

clinical perspective—but also there is also a dearth of understanding among the branches. This situation is due to several historical and other factors, which have been written about elsewhere and in some of the chapters here. Such a project is of contemporary relevance and perhaps urgency. In the current climate, psychoanalysis has endured diminished status and recognition, as well as reduced educational outlets.

Combining these factors with the lack of communication amongst the multiple branches of psychoanalytic theory and practice, it is unclear whether there is currently a discernable integrated field of psychoanalysis. This situation is unacceptable if psychoanalysis as a body of theory and as a clinical set of techniques for addressing issues in mental health is to thrive. Over the past decades, there have been repeated calls to find a common ground and to open genuine discourse and understanding among the various analytic perspectives.

Most of the work for this book grew out of two issues of *Psychoanalytic Inquiry* for which I was the editor (31[2] and 33[3]). Many of the chapters in this book were written for one or the other of those issues. The first issue brought the psychoanalytic use of metaphoric processes up to date, with a particular eye toward forging a common ground amongst different schools of thought in psychoanalysis. The chapters in this book from that issue are 4, 5, 6, 7, 8, and 9. Together, these papers form a compelling discussion of how common ground might be achieved.

Taking an overview of the work on metaphor, I felt that something was lacking in the structure such that the emerging umbrella framework was not entirely cohesive or complete. The missing piece was supplied by the formulation of a generalized notion of the psychoanalytic field. This concept arose from a process of abstracting from specific kinds of fields used in different psychoanalytic perspectives. This was part of the subject of the second issue. The chapters in this book that appeared in the second issue of *Psychoanalytic Inquiry* are 11, 12, 13, 14, 15, 16, and 17.

In the issue on fields, the discussion taken as a whole demonstrates the essential nature of this emerging family of field concepts and of the idea of a generalized psychoanalytic field in particular. That issue brought the discussion onto the cusp of a potential future direction for an integrated discipline of psychoanalysis. There a double language barrier was broached. First was the barrier of natural languages, in that much of the vast, important, and highly stimulating work on fields in psychoanalysis was just beginning to be translated into English. Second was the barrier of the difficulty of translating the specific languages of the different psychoanalytic perspectives; this situation was partially addressed in some of the papers in the first issue.

Field theory has emerged as an international psychoanalytic concept that may help bring not only a coherent underlying structure for disparate psychoanalytic perspectives, but also a way of fostering interactive exploration of the various uses of psychoanalytic concepts and techniques. Field concepts are not new to psychoanalysis. Since at least 1960, Madeleine and Willy Baranger have elucidated their formulations of analytic fields and have shown how they work with them clinically. The relational fields of the North American school of relational theory, intersubjective matrices, self object matrices of self psychology, and recent developments in Italian psychoanalysis resulting in a modified form of the field work of the Barangers are all examples where field concepts have been employed in theoretical frameworks and clinical technique.

Other perspectives can be understood as using some form of field concept at the base of their theoretical structure, as well as underlying their clinical approach. In this way, the contents and process of what occurs in sessions conducted by an analyst of each perspective can be described in what will be explored in general field theory terms. In fact, each clinical way of working can be described as employing a specific kind of field. Thus, a general field structure that encompasses individual field configurations supplies an essential component for the psychoanalytic framework with which to move the new paradigm forward.

This book thus furthers the exploration of a merging of work on metaphoric processes and that on fields. The use of a framework with metaphoric processes and fields combined exhibits the uniqueness of psychoanalysis and shows how and with what concepts it explores and explains human experience. An umbrella for psychoanalysis may not dissolve disagreements amongst psychoanalytic schools of thought, but it may permit the schools to be more clearly rendered and more explicitly understood. Formulating an umbrella for the discipline does not have the objective of eradicating differences among perspectives, but rather to be able to understand, explore, and learn from each of them. Both similarities and differences amongst the different psychoanalytic perspectives may be clarified with such a model, which also shows how psychoanalytic perspectives are related and how they are more like each other by far than like any other discipline or clinical technique.

With this umbrella, the barriers to mutual understanding may be dismantled and a path permanently opened to the possibility of meaningful international, intercultural, and poly-perspectival psychoanalytic exchange. Thus, this book contains an attempt to shine a light on a possible future direction for psychoanalysis by building a framework that can be used to structure clinical work and the theoretical constructs of psychoanalysis. This framework builds on the complex and rich history of psychoanalysis and takes fundamental psychoanalytic principles and concepts as a foundation. The framework allows an exploration of what it means to thoroughly probe core psychoanalytic insights.

In particular, this book can be viewed as an exploration of building from the fundamental premise of the existence of unconscious processes and the discovery of the complex affective meaning of human experience. Every analytic perspective accepts the existence and influence of some form of unconscious processes. Following from this, each perspective can agree to the use of a psychoanalytic conception of unconscious metaphoric process. From this, a general concept of unconscious fantasy emerges.

Pursuing the premise of multiple affective meanings embedded in every experience leads to the development of what is here called a general psychoanalytic field structure of human experience. Some analytic schools of thought explicitly employ field concepts. Others can be understood as having an operative, implicit field concept, each specific to and uniquely formed by the particular analytic perspective. What evolves from the multiple field concepts in use in psychoanalysis is the employment of metaphoric processes and a generalized understanding of psychoanalytic fields utilized as a way of comprehending and speaking about psychoanalytic processes, theory, and human experience, such that a psychoanalyst from any school of thought can engage with and speak a common language. With these building blocks, psychoanalytic work on metaphoric processes is united organically with the use of field theory.

The chapters in this book approach the subject from diverse vantage points. Taken together, they form an intricate web of psychoanalytic thought that moves the scope and frontier of psychoanalysis beyond the format of dispute and toward the open, inclusive discussion of core concepts and technique, in an era in which psychoanalysis is coming to terms with the conclusions and implications of postmodernism.

In Chapter 2, I discuss the first principles necessary to build a base for psychoanalysis in which all schools of thought can participate. In this brief chapter, I discuss the consequences of adopting the fundamental psychoanalytic premise of the existence of unconscious processes. Included in this chapter is a discussion of the implications of dualism and holism for psychoanalysis. Interpretation and fantasy processes emerge as essential to human experience. The multiple affective meanings of human experience are also explored.

In Chapter 3, I discuss the evolution and use of the concept of metaphoric processes in psychoanalysis. I describe a model of metaphoric processes by breaking them down into component parts and subsidiary concepts. The ingredients of metaphoric processes are then used to express fundamental psychoanalytic concepts. Psychoanalytic perspectives are characterized according to this model in order to display similarities and differences among the different perspectives within a single common base and resulting common language.

In Chapter 4, Robert Wallerstein revisits a pertinent aspect of psychoanalytic history in his discussion of the attempts to eliminate the use of metaphor in psychoanalytic theory with the purpose of rendering psychoanalysis more on a par with other sciences. Citing the work of Lakoff and Johnson, Wurmser, and others, Wallerstein discusses the ubiquity as well as the inevitability of metaphor in general, in all scientific theory and in psychoanalysis in particular. He cautions against the current trend to spread the concept of metaphor so widely as to render it devoid of content. Wallerstein calls for some way of drawing a distinction between the metaphoric and the literal, locating the latter in the data of clinical experience. Different theoretical perspectives are then viewed as employing different scientific metaphors, which serve as heuristic devices to guide clinical work. Common ground is located in the clinical concepts of transference, countertransference, defense, conflict, and compromise.

In Chapter 5, Léon Wurmser provides a philosophical and psychoanalytic discussion of metaphor. He locates metaphor in the tension between the realms it brings together. In this way, metaphor is discussed as uniquely suited to portray inner conflict in the widest sense. Building on his previous work, Wurmser finds common ground for psychoanalytic perspectives in the study of cultural historical metaphors for conflict, complementarity, and harmony. Both ancient Greek and Chinese traditions are discussed in this connection.

Arnold Modell, in Chapter 6, describes the evolution of his thought on the use of metaphoric processes in psychoanalysis. He locates the motivation for the genesis of different psychoanalytic perspectives alongside the rise in popularity of ego psychology. Modell identifies with Freud's early emphasis on the unconscious processing of memory and feeling, through which meaning making takes place. Modell elaborates and argues for his proposition that metaphor is the currency of the mind. In so doing, he refers to a potential common ground in psychoanalytic concepts rather than in psychoanalytic technique. Metaphoric processes, then, are the subject matter of both psychoanalytic theory and clinical work.

In Chapter 7, Robert White focuses on the concept of the *nondynamic unconscious*, and in particular on three psychoanalytic perspectives in relation to this concept. The three theories are found in the work of Wilfred Bion, Cesar and Sara Botella, and Donnel Stern. White discusses these theories in detail and emphasizes the metaphors contained in them. The three perspectives are then compared on this basis.

Antal Borbely, in Chapter 8, envisions the possibility of forging understanding among different theoretical psychoanalytic perspectives and between psychoanalysis and cognitive science. He discerns closer alignment in practice among various schools of thought in their use of metaphoric process and temporality. Borbely characterizes the fundamental psychoanalytic concepts of transference, defense, and interpretation in terms of a conception of temporal metaphors. That is, the common ground amongst psychoanalytic perspectives is here identified in core aspects of psychoanalytic process. These are modeled in terms of temporality, metaphor, and metonymy.

In Chapter 9, Robert Bornstein and Nikaya Becker-Matero discuss the role of metaphor in psychoanalytic process, psychoanalytic research, and interdisciplinary discussion. They show how psychoanalysis has and can make use of metaphors from other disciplines, and how psychoanalytic metaphors have been translated and transformed in the language of other disciplines. Included is a discussion of the use of metaphor in both the design of psychodynamic research and in understanding the results.

In Chapter 10, I describe extant field concepts in contemporary psychoanalysis. I then provide a structure for what I call *general psychoanalytic fields*. This structure is designed to express the principles and concepts of different psychoanalytic perspectives and afford a neutral language in which to be able to compare and discuss the concepts of each perspective.

In Chapter 11, Antoine Corel describes the conceptual, social, and psychoanalytic antecedents to the development of the field concept by Madeleine and Willy Baranger. He describes the intellectual atmosphere in Argentina preceding their work and explains the development of psychoanalytic concepts in that time and place that led to the concept of the analytic field.

In Chapter 12, Giuseppe Civitarese and Antonino Ferro discuss the central role of metaphoric processes in analytic field theory, as both a clinical tool and a core component of a model of human experience. They explore the genesis and meanings of the field metaphor in Bion's work and in field theory in general. Civitarese and Ferro discuss the paradigm shift that occurred in psychoanalysis as a result of Bion's work and the development of field theory. The authors then offer rich clinical examples of work with metaphoric processes in a field theory context, expanding their discussion with retrospective reflections.

Ana-María Rizzuto, in Chapter 13, explores the analytic process from the perspective of the Barangers' work, with attention to the use, function, and evolution of the meaning of words and other forms of expression. She then reviews neuroscientific, psychoanalytic, and other literature concerning communication, including verbal communication. Rizzuto argues that communication is fundamentally embodied. She further draws out the psychoanalytic implications of the embodied nature of word meaning, with emphasis on understanding the nature of the intersubjective. Rizzuto locates word meaning in experiential and affective interpersonal meaning.

In Chapter 14, Juan Tubert-Oklander adds to the working concepts of this book—metaphor and field—two other concepts to be taken into account: process and analogy. He makes use of Matte Blanco's concept of *bi-logic* to describe the differences between primary and secondary process, and he reformulates the objectives of psychoanalytic process. Tubert-Oklander offers a fundamentally holistic account of human experience that integrates the concepts of field and process.

Beatriz de León de Bernardi, in Chapter 15, reviews the development of field theory in Latin America. She then explores the role of metaphoric processes implicit in analytic process within field theory. De León de Bernardi discusses the influence of Lacan's work and of the use of metaphor on field theory. She further discusses the psychoanalytic conceptions of *temporality* and *spiral process,* illustrating her discussion with clinical material.

Next, in Chapter 16, Claudio Neri discusses working within a field theory model with groups in psychoanalysis, and how this differs from field theory work with individuals. Neri discerns other kinds of fields that analysands experience. He describes working with what he calls the *shadow* of such fields in which the analysand is immersed. It is in the analytic field, Neri argues, that these other fields can be detected. He also explores how to analyze such fields by gradually bringing them into the work within the analytic field.

Elsa Rappoport de Aisemberg's contribution, Chapter 17, describes the history of the evolution of the concept of countertransference, and then of the Barangers' field theory. She describes a crucial element in clinical work: the movement from the intrapsychic to the intersubjective and then back to the intrapsychic. She discusses working with countertransference within contemporary field theory and offers clinical material in which this work was salient.

These chapters discuss and demonstrate different ways of understanding and working with metaphoric processes and with fields. They also suggest a language and a structure through which to express and ground each of the various psychoanalytic perspectives. As we move into the future, there may be a way to experience psychoanalysis as an integrated discipline and practice in which internal as well as interdisciplinary discussion and debate are fruitful. Greater familiarity with field concepts may help foster an interest in articulating other kinds of fields associated with schools of thought that are not currently expressed in terms of field work. Some of this work has begun on the following pages. The more that psychoanalytic education includes a framework such as the metaphor and field structure presented here, the more students will be able to readily grasp the connections between their institute's theoretical and clinical perspective and other perspectives. In this way, interperspectival understanding may come to be a matter of course in the future.

These chapters implicitly indicate another way in which the umbrella framework of metaphoric processes and fields opens an avenue into the future of psychoanalysis. This consists of drawing from a full exploration of the oneiric in everyday processes. That is, working with metaphor and fields as the basis of psychoanalytic work undermines the distinction that has at times been drawn between dream states and waking states in analytic process. In this way of looking at human experience, all communications in an analytic process are, in a general sense, infused with fantasy products. This makes explicit a fundamental aspect of psychoanalytic understanding: that in clinical work, there are no communications that are outside the process. Neither are there communications that can be understood solely on the manifest level. Psychoanalysis and postmodern thought together belie the possibility of such an utterance in any context. This framework brings this and other psychoanalytic working principles to the fore.

In conclusion, I wish to thank my colleagues and co-contributors who read or wrote and discussed different parts of this book. Joseph Lichtenberg offered the initial idea, encouragement and motivation for the book. Kristopher Spring helped me to develop the initial conception of the book and Kate Hawes and her assistant Kirsten Buchanan saw the project to completion. Gina Atkinson was a thoughtful and invaluable reader, commentator and editor for Chapters 1, 2, 3, and 10. Laurie Erskine skillfully edited and prepared the manuscript. I would also like to thank *Psychoanalytic Inquiry* for the permission to reprint most of the chapters in this book and *The Psychoanalytic Review* for the permission to reprint excerpts that contributed to two chapters.

2

# PRELIMINARY
# FOUNDATIONAL CONCEPTS[1]

*S. Montana Katz*

In this chapter, I will explore some core principles of psychoanalysis from which the concepts of metaphoric process and of psychoanalytic fields (both general and specific) may be developed. These principles are ones that all psychoanalytic schools of thought could accept and make use of. This discussion revolves around neutral ways in which to understand and articulate human experience. In particular, some implications of what can be generally agreed upon amongst analytic perspectives— that is, the existence of some form of unconscious process—are explored. In this way, an underlying base for a neutral psychoanalytic umbrella framework is articulated.

A conclusion that emerges from this chapter is that psychoanalytic conceptions of some form of fantasy process are essential to understanding human experience, and this conviction about fantasy grows out of the idea of unconscious process. This is integral to formulations both about metaphoric processes and about all kinds of fields. To reiterate, this belief in the central role of fantasy is not one specific to any particular school of thought; rather, fantasy is seen as a general process that transcends and transforms experience.

A crucial aspect of the development of the concept of fantasy in psychoanalysis has been present from the beginning and has been emphasized in the postmodern era. This is the matter of the origins of and the potential for a foundational basis for human experience. That is, if unconscious processes in general and fantasy processes in particular are at the foundation of psychoanalysis, then it remains to be determined from where they derive: the body, the mind, or somewhere else.

To an extent, this remains an as-yet unresolved issue in psychoanalysis. The question involves consideration of the mind–body dilemma. Discussions and disagreements about the relation between mind and body have endured in multidisciplinary contexts. It is a question about which a resting place is crucial to psychoanalysis and to the potential for forming an integrated discipline from disparate perspectives. The resting place outlined here is located in a holistic model.

## The Psychoanalytic Subject and Process in a Holistic Model

For more than a century, psychoanalytic thought and practice have changed the way humans understand themselves—their thoughts, feelings, motivations, and behavior. Psychoanalytic constructs are used in ordinary discourse and have had a substantial impact on the creative arts and on many other disciplines and professions. Psychoanalysis has also been influenced by historical and social trends. Many of the psychoanalytic perspectives developed over the last half century have arisen hand in hand with a sense of disillusionment with unified and reductionist theory. This same disillusionment has led to formulations of postmodern thought.

Classical Freudian theory became identified with reductionist, positivist science and was therefore the subject of a range of critiques and, at moments, wholesale rejection. While a thorough understanding of the application of postmodern principles to psychoanalysis was lacking, postmodernism was used to support the development of new psychoanalytic conceptualizations and practices. Unnecessarily rigid camps were formed. While there have been erroneous conclusions drawn from postmodern principles, psychoanalysis as a discipline has yet to reconcile one way or another with what has become established contemporary thought. For example, the rejection of absolute forms of truth and reality can be incorporated even into a classical psychoanalytic approach (in fact, with Freud's notion of *nachträglichkeit*, amongst others, this has been implicit all along).

With the advent of the structural model and its underlying vision of human development, psychoanalysis was set on a path to favor the transferential, intrasubjectively shared, present moment. A common belief in postmodern thought and some contemporary psychoanalytic perspectives is that there is no subject, but instead it is the interactive nexus that creates an individual; consequently, the psychoanalytic subject has been purported to exist only as it emerges from a relationship. But it turns out that, for postmodern psychoanalysis, this is not an appropriate conclusion. In the postmodern framework, there is no unstructured, presymbolic, or prereflective state. It follows, then, that there is also no state of fusion. Thus, in this framework, a possibility exists from the beginning of a psychoanalytic, individual subject and structured, idiosyncratic experience.

The analytic experience for each participant has begun by the time initial contact is made between analysand and analyst. Already at that point, metaphoric fantasy processes are being brought to bear on the initial and subsequent contact and on the ongoing analytic process. At the point of initial contact, there is the beginning of a shared language with which to express the underlying intrapsychic meanings of each member of the dyad, especially the analysand. There is also initial input from each, necessarily understood by each in a different way. The analyst attempts to explore with the analysand the analysand's understandings. These inputs, verbal and otherwise, give rise to a complex set of affects, meanings, and understanding. For every communication, there is a potential for multiple, layered, and complex affective understandings.

Each communication contains conscious and unconscious components, the understanding of which by the other then incorporates both components as filtered through the conscious and unconscious structures of the listener. Each step of communication in the analytic process is filtered through the preceding communications and understandings. A complex language is built by the analytic couple in which all terms have rich meanings. That is, the ongoing interaction between the two intrapsychic subjects is part of building a language of the psychoanalytic process that attempts to explore and express the experience of the analysand and is part of the experience of both. From the beginning of an analytic process, there are two imperfect, idiosyncratic translations or interpretations operating; it could be said that part of the analytic process is about understanding, exploring, and modifying the psychoanalytic subject's translation function.

A goal of this process is to arrive at constructions that conceptualize, express, clarify, and elaborate the analysand's experience. These constructions, which may be understood as co-constructions, arise out of the analytic material originating in the analysand and interpretations from the analyst, both understood in the sense of the Barangers (2009) as having content only when each participant finds meaning in them and can make use of them to further the analytic process. An analytic goal is for the constructions to be ever more similarly understood by analyst and analysand— that is, to be utilizing the terms of the analytic language in more similar ways toward a fuller expression of the analysand's idiosyncratic structures.

Counterintuitive to postmodern psychoanalytic discussion, postmodern principles afford the possibility of a model of psychoanalytic process that is intrapsychic and co-constructed. The individual psychoanalytic subject, the analysand, naturally exists as an individual prior to the psychoanalytic process, but he or she also develops through the process of precipitating the idiosyncratic elements of experience into the process via co-constructed structures and the specific, unique language of the psychoanalytic process. Thus, the umbrella framework for psychoanalysis that is both nonreductive and allows for intrapsychic experience is compatible with contemporary, postmodern thought.

## Dualism and Reductions for Psychoanalysis

In Western culture at least since Descartes, theoretical and clinical discourse has assumed and made use of a separation and severability between each individual's mind and body, to the extremes of portraying persons as mindless bodies and as bodiless minds. In recent decades, this has often been expressed as the problem of mind–brain. The debate has evolved into various camps of more complex or more articulated forms of dualism and of monism, including but not limited to the forms that involve reductions of mind or body, one to the other. There have also been models that include the outright elimination of mind or body—often, most recently, the elimination of mind. There has also been an opposite trend: to implicitly correlate meaning with mind and to diminish the salience of the body.

Some neuroscientists view the mind as reducible to the brain. Some psychoanalysts, including those who focus on one strand of Freud's thought, view the mind as emerging from the body during the course of development. One of Freud's postulations has been called a *dual-aspect monism* (Solms, 1997a). His position is more complex than that, however, due to his sense of the individual's long-range development that reaches back through past generations to seed the components of the structural model. Overall, there has been an emphasis on the body as the base or foundation from which the mind is either derived or built. This is in part the case because it is difficult to refute the idea that humans are born with bodies. At the same time, some feel that sufficient evidence is lacking for the presence of mind at birth.

The discussions about adopting dualist or reductionist frameworks make use of many premises, some of which rely on heuristic principles about human nature involving survival instincts and adaptation hypotheses (Fonagy & Target, 2007). Developmental theory begins with bodies and builds minds, language, and individual persons from the base of bodily sensation. This is a contemporary version of the empiricist theories of past centuries. The body has been taken to be that which provides a containment schema for the self (Modell, 2007). Humans are characterized as embodied minds or bodily minds (Rizzuto, 2001).

Part of the motivation for considering the body as basic and as that from which mind grows is the quest for an answer to how it can be that humans—with everything that operates privately and internally in each, together with unique idiosyncratic experiences—may nevertheless share languages, meanings, and be largely predictable in agreeing on a multitude of factors. One point of view holds that it is the overall similarity of bodies, despite differences, and the strong similarity of bodily development and experience that affords communication and overall likeness among ourselves. As Lakoff and Johnson (1999) describe the situation—a description that many psychoanalysts accept—meaning stems from commonalities among bodies and environments. There is a compelling argument that underlies this thought process, but one that warrants attention to its assumptions and presuppositions. Alternative conceptualizations that also address the theoretical requirements of this model diminish the need to accept a reduction to the body.

Relevant to this question and of central importance to psychoanalysis are affects. As Modell (1978) has said so clearly, the communication of affect is the perceptual base of psychoanalysis. The formulation of a psychoanalytic theory of affect may be the litmus test for a characterization of mind, brain, and body, whether a dualist one, a monist one, or something else. To have a model of mind, brain, and body that allows for a rich understanding of affect would be to have the framework for a model of human experience.

Affects do not fare well in dualist or reductionist monist models of mind, brain, and body. Problems arise as a result of situations reminiscent of Freud's assertion that the drives are located at the frontier of the psychic and the somatic. Unless affects are characterized as squarely on one side of the fence or the other—which at times they have been—the interactionist problem of joining or linking the two sides becomes crucial. Using affect to provide links does not redress the problem, unless affects themselves are characterized without embedding the issue there (Pally, 1998). Heidegger graphically observed in his Zollikon Seminars that tears cannot be adequately described in a fundamentally dualist or reductionistic monist framework. To give another example, the internal perception of a sinking feeling in the stomach cannot be fully understood as body or mind alone, or as body plus mind, without some organic way of joining the two. This is the very problem posed by dualism.

A tendency to adhere to Western dualism may be partly the reason why the formulation of a theory of affects has remained obdurately intractable. Neuroscientists have characterized affects as emerging from the neurodynamics of brain circuits. One way that psychoanalysts have characterized affects is as bodily experiences of drive derivatives or representations—or, alternatively, as the basis of drives (Kernberg, 2001). As yet there is no articulated model of affects that exhibits their nature as neither solely of mind nor body, but as essential to both, and, further, as an integral part of a nondualist model of human experience. Also lacking at present is a model that recognizes the fundamental role of affects in psychoanalytic theory and in clinical practice (Arlow, 1977). More generally, an adequate theory of affects requires a different sort of framework than the ones we have been working with to date.

Beginning from either side of the traditional dualism, either mind or body, engenders the serious liability that it is likely that either an irreducibly dualist position or a reductive monism will follow. Meissner (2006) provided an extensive and comprehensive discussion of this, noting the unsatisfactory nature of any form of either reductionist monism or dualism. Meissner developed a unified position that does not explicitly involve reduction. His language, however, is very much steeped in the dualist tradition, and thus it is difficult to assess the degree of success of this unification; he seems to have accepted what he called a *methodological dualism*.

Nearly one hundred years ago, Heidegger noted that the division between mind and body is embedded in our very language. To speak of the problem or the issues involved is to use a language that renders expression fundamentally dualistic. Thus, dualism is the default position when using language to discuss the issues, with reductionistic monism a close second. Reductionistic monisms can be readily described in dualistic terms by noting that one of the two recognized categories is reducible to the other. Terminology is not lacking to make this kind of statement. But such a bias built into the language makes it very difficult, if not impossible, to formulate genuine alternatives to dualism that attempt to undercut the very way of thinking that lends to dualism.

## Immediate versus Interpreted Experience

An implicit and crucial assumption of forms of dualism and of reductionistic monism concerns the possibility of unmediated access—for example, direct access to the body, including self experience. The assumption of the existence of direct access arises organically from the separation of mind and body, whether by dualistic or reductionistic means. If the body is a severable entity in itself, then it must have at least a degree of independence. The body would thus be able to do something apart from performing automatic functions such as breathing. That is, it can also have sensations, at least in some sense of the word. This means that there is a possibility of the body taking in both the raw data of sensation and direct affective experience, without the use of the mind and without the use of concepts. This would also hold true in monisms that effect a reduction to the body. However, the assumption of direct access that would be entailed is untenable, as will be presently discussed, and without it, dualism and reductions to the body are undermined.

A relevant distinction related to this question involves a clarification of what sorts of things humans experience and which have priority. Relevant are two possible kinds of experience. The first kind is the direct experience of things, without the necessity of intermediary identifying concepts. To have this kind of predicative experience would be to have an experience of that thing, that something holds of or pertains to it. The second kind of experience, on the other hand, requires some sort of conceptual background in order to have experience involving the thing. This is propositional and contextual experiencing that something holds of the thing.

Both Heidegger (1953) and Meissner (1997) have argued that there can be no independent immediate experience—that is, experience of the first kind described above. Schafer (1993) and Solms (1997b) have also argued to similar conclusions, and related discussions can be found in Bruner (1986, 1990), Grossman (1992), and Katz (2001). In practical terms, it is evident in clinical work that no experience is purely such—free from conceptualization, interpretation, or being laden with unconscious meaning.

This means that a degree of interpretation or conceptualization is present in all human experience at all times. Specifically, there is no such thing as a pure, direct bodily experience. Even were there to be the possibility of direct sensory experience, it would have no human meaning.

Similarly, there is no direct access to the internal world or to self experience. All experience, including affective and sensory experience, is perceptual. This means that it proceeds by means of progressive interpretation, impacted by the environment and by idiosyncratic experience. A nondualist, nonreductive, holistic framework of human experience is thus essential for psychoanalysis.

## Fantasy Processes as Essential and Transcendent

Given that there is no direct access, what is left for the umbrella framework for psychoanalysis is a way of understanding human experience as operating via holistic processes from the beginning. Transcendent and transformational processes are crucial to the psychoanalytic base. Without unmediated experience, mental processes must primarily make use of some form of transcendent concepts. Transcendence may be understood in a sense akin to phenomenologists' usage, in that it concerns going beyond what is given in experience, beyond what is accepted as relatively real. What is transcendent is not sensorily conferred by experience. The transcendent is constructed by rendering portions of the stream of experience meaningful, and this occurs by means of interpretation in a general sense.

Thus, transcendence is a process that goes beyond particular experience to conjecture to or posit conceptualizations. In this sense, concepts and constructions are transcendent. A concept that collects and organizes, perhaps sharpens or clarifies, disparate previous experiences and perceptions is transcendent. The concept acquired then becomes part of the cadre of what might be called the *relatively real*. The relatively real can be used to predict and shape the future, the experience itself, and memories of the past.

For example, a transcendent process could be said to proceed via the psychoanalytic notion of fantasy. Fantasy activity operates on prior experience, prior conceptualizations, and prior fantasy products, and arrives at perception and belief that are not and cannot be wholly derived from experience. A psychoanalytic example of a transcendent process in this sense is a transference interpretation. The analyst conjectures and posits a transcendent conceptualization of the analysand's communications.

In psychoanalytic terms, perception of an object proceeds by means of a transcendent process. An object is not experienced as such in itself, but only on the basis of relatively real past experience, including the involvement of prior perceptions and fantasies of the object. One is interpreting in experiencing and making predictions about the object. Friedman's (2002) discussion of symbolizing is perhaps another way of stating that a fundamental human activity is transcendence in this sense.

While abstraction, generalization, and assessments of similarity are often taken as basic human operations, each one proceeds by means of a capacity to form and acquire concepts. What must be involved in these operations is a general psychoanalytic form of fantasy activity at their base. The ability to fantasize is more fundamental than other capacities that have been taken to be basic human ones; in fact, the capacity for fantasy activity can be considered inborn and taken as fundamental and primary. Put differently, it is perhaps by means of fantasy that humans can have and make use of sensory and other experience.

Embedded in, for example, Peterfreund's (1978) paper on psychoanalytic conceptions of infancy, and also supported in Erreich (2003), are implications that something like the capacity for fantasy activity, which gives rise to concepts, must be present from birth. The world is understood by an individual via transcendent and transformational processes. Fantasy activity is a core capacity that is essential to life, and one through which the individual is able to move about in the world. Because fantasy is an essential component of life, each experience contains multiple affective, interpretive meanings. It is an objective of the analytic process to explore links amongst such multiple meanings.

Thus, a component of the psychoanalytic umbrella framework is a holistic base, and psychoanalysis highlights a fundamental aspect of human experience and life that is not reducible to any purely physiological theory or science. This theoretical framework includes the acceptance that human experience proceeds by means of fundamental transcendent processes. Such processes are, in a psychoanalytic sense, forms of fantasy processes. These are called *metaphoric processes* and are explored in the following chapter.

## Note

1 Parts of this chapter appeared in *The Psychoanalytic Review* vol. 97 (2010), "Holistic Framework for Psychoanalysis," pp. 107–135.

# 3

# METAPHORIC PROCESSES[1]

*S. Montana Katz*

The concept of metaphor was broadened beyond the verbal by Lakoff and Johnson (1980). As will be discussed in detail in subsequent chapters, the concept of metaphoric process is an extension of this broadened view through the addition of temporal, developmental, and functional dimensions. A metaphoric process can be thought of as an unfolding of an unconscious trail, which includes and encodes emotional, procedural, dynamic, and other unconscious ingredients of experience.

Metaphor is often contrasted with the literal. Similarly, metaphoric processes might be seen in distinction from direct, reality-based experience. In the umbrella framework for psychoanalysis, these are relative terms. What is experienced as real is such as a result of the metaphoric processes that give rise to the experience. Thus, what emerges from metaphoric processes may become the (relatively) real of the future.

It is argued extensively in the preceding and subsequent chapters that metaphoric processes are inborn and involuntary. Metaphoric processes are essential to human life; that is, without the continuous, ongoing stream of metaphoric processes, there would be no human world. They are the means by which each individual has experience, learns, and understands. They are the way in which humans communicate, verbally and nonverbally, intrapsychically and intervivos. Metaphoric processes are already active in early childhood (Imbasciati, 2002, 2003, 2004, 2006). These early processes persist as strands in processes throughout life. We might consider the unthought known to be involved in such strands.

Modell (2009a) describes metaphoric processes as mappings that involve similarity- and difference-seeking activity. When similarity is salient, repetition, including transference, may be involved and may be clinically observable. When difference is salient in the activity of an individual's metaphoric processes, conceptualization and thought are relatively absent, according to the degree of difference discerned. When the degree of difference is not extreme, resistance may be clinically in evidence. When the degree of difference is high, linking is barred and conceptualization cannot be perceived.

The idea that metaphoric processes are mappings is a simplifying heuristic proposition. Mappings can be thought of as occurring in segments of metaphoric processes. A manifold of mappings could be open to view in time slices of metaphoric processes. That is, a given metaphoric process will contain multiple mappings, each of which is modified over time in form as well as in salience. It could be said that metaphoric processes may be viewed as systems of mappings during any given time segment. In their entirety, however, they are not mappings themselves. To add more complexity, a conceptualization may (and will be likely to) involve more than one metaphoric process.

For example, a subject's conceptualization of an object will in general involve segments of several metaphoric processes. Together, these segments coalesce into a temporal conceptualization of the object. This means that, at a given point in time, contained within segments of a set of related metaphoric processes, there is a conceptualization of an object. This conceptualization exists with respect to certain salient aspects. Part of the conceptualization will necessarily involve aspects of conceptualizations of other objects, including primary objects. Mappings contained in this moment of metaphoric processes could be viewed as stemming from conceptualizations of earlier objects and being transferred to aspects of one of the current object.

An inaccuracy involved in this pertains to time and where in time the mappings that make up metaphoric processes are located. During a time slice in the present, the subject does not have direct access to past conceptualizations embedded in past segments of metaphoric processes. What the subject has are current reconceptualizations of the early conceptualizations, embedded in current segments of metaphoric processes together with associated affect patterns. In that slice, these are then mapped onto aspects of the current conceptualization.

To take an extreme example for the purposes of clarity, the time slices of metaphoric processes involved in very early preverbal experiences are not accessible as such. In fact, it is not likely that the concepts that were involved are discernible in the mappings in such metaphoric processes. The conceptualizations involved may be of a radically different nature than later experiences. What carry through are associated affect clusters, including the derivatives of self experiences.

Another inaccurate shorthand is that time progresses in a measured, linear fashion. Yet it is rarely experienced or psychoanalytically understood that way. Transference is a much-discussed case of both nonquantifiable and nonlinear, lived time. Metaphoric processes can be heuristically thought of as coursing through the life of an individual in conventional time, yet one thing that is crucially plastic in such a metaphoric process is time. A past event, feeling, or experience is continually brought into the present in its rearticulation by means of newly acquired experience imported into the metaphoric process. These elements refer back to, reinvent, and restructure the experience of the past, as well as informing the experience of the present.

At every moment, metaphoric processes are based in that moment. From the salient metaphors of a given moment in the experience of a subject—including the current valences—the categories of experience, the organizing principles (Feirstein, 2009), the templates (Freud, 1912c), or the structure (Modell, 2009a; Katz, 2004) can be discerned. The early metaphoric processes of an individual, for example, may contain elements of the experience of the maternal environment. Active metaphoric processes need not form a mutually consistent set. Contradictions and paradoxes abound within the life span of an individual, and this can be represented by contemporaneous metaphoric processes containing conceptions and structures that conflict with each other. Within an individual, as with everything unconscious, a metaphoric process is lifelong. A single metaphoric process may be salient and active in and for the individual at certain points, moderately active other times, and relatively dormant at still others.

Metaphoric processes are continuously ongoing within a human being, and as Modell has described so clearly, they map from one domain to another, possibly dissimilar domain. Metaphor can be a form of transcendence, a mapping from the known, relatively real onto new conceptions of previous experience. This conception of metaphor is consistent with Arlow's (1969) discussion of fantasy in that metaphors are not only ongoing, but also provide the mental set with which humans function. Modell (1997a) states this similarly with respect to metaphor by saying that it is the *currency of the mind*. Freud, in his discussions of dreams and unconscious processes, emphasized visual components. Metaphor is multiperceptual. This includes multisensory elements as well as those of affect and conceptualization.

When a metaphoric process within which an individual is functioning can be discerned, one strand of a layer of his or her life comes into high relief. This strand can at times be perceived more or less consciously, and at others may be active solely in the unconscious. Multiple metaphoric processes are ongoing in an individual's life at all times and can merge, diverge, overlap, combine, contradict, and conflict with each other. Unlike Husserl's undifferentiated, universal stream of consciousness, there is an idiosyncratic, differentiated stream of metaphoric processes that continuously course through time.

While the concepts and constructions that an individual postulates are idiosyncratic, they are not incommunicable. A subject's experience and interpretations are unique, which is an essential premise of theoretical and clinical psychoanalysis. They are also largely unconscious. Unconscious individual heuristics are discoverable to consciousness through discourse with another (Shapiro, 2005). This is made possible from at least two directions. First, the environment has an influence in shaping an individual's conceptions, from the earliest forms of his or her protothoughts and feelings. This normative conditioning occurs as part of the way that natural languages serve to carve human experience into discrete conceptualizations of the behavior of others—especially their highly repetitive behaviors common to many individuals and present in the value systems of populations.

From at least birth on, one begins to conceive of aspects of the world through social structuring, including by means of the acquisition of language. This means that, to a large extent, an individual processes experience by means of the conceptual apparatus of the primary language learned, and begins to do so possibly even prior to achieving language competence. That is, many of the concepts acquired or formed in early experience are derived from the way of carving up the world that is implicit and embedded in the language of primary caregivers. Thus, many of an individual's concepts—and thereby his or her expectations—are learned largely through the various media the individual encounters in the world.

## Metaphoric Processes Are Essential to Human Experience

To the same degree that humans could not survive without oxygen and water, they could also not survive without unconscious fantasy activity, and therefore not without ongoing metaphoric processes. Metaphoric processes are essential for the formation, acquisition, and development of concepts within an individual, a community, and the human race as a whole. They are required for the formation of languages and other forms of symbolic representation and communication. What we are aware of and can conceive of—objects, things, self, brains, bodies, minds, etc.—are arrived at through perception and are thus interpretations. In a manner of speaking, they exist as discrete entities to the extent that they are conceptualized as falling into categorizations.

For humans, a world without metaphoric processes would not be an impoverished world; it would be no world at all. Without the ongoing capacity for metaphoric processes, human experience would not be identifiable, discernable, or even describable. All perception would devolve into discrete and unusable sensory impressions. Without metaphor, the potentially infinite amount of sensory input at any given moment would be a bombardment of particulars without any sort of filtration or conceptualization. There would be no patterns, no observations, no predications or predictions—in effect, nothing.

Modell has discussed aspects of situations in which the flow of metaphoric processes is diminished or restricted. Specifically, he has explored when and at which points the play of similarity and difference collapse into similarity-seeking processes only, resulting in a loss of the relatively free mobility of metaphor construction. Such cases eventuate in what Modell calls *frozen metaphor*—repetitions, including transference.

At the other extreme is the situation in which metaphoric play collapses into difference-seeking and discerning processes only. In this case, metaphoric processes are disabled to the same extent as the degree of the lack of similarity seeking. For example, if an analysand sees only difference between herself and the analyst or other objects, then points of reference with which to discuss this perception will be scarce to nonexistent. At the extreme end of difference discerning, with no similarities discerned overall, there are, in effect, no useful concepts to draw upon. A framework of human experience in which all concepts are singletons is not usable because of an absence of links among discrete sensations and perceptions. No patterns can be detected without categories into which things fall and in which they can be grouped together.

Affective experience under such circumstances of solely difference seeking would be unlinked as well. There would be no linking of similar affective experiences from which humans learn about the world and themselves in it. Moreover, it would not be possible to link the affective expression of others, as is so crucial for development and growth, especially in infancy. The metaphoric capacity is disabled altogether in this extreme case, and is relatively disabled in less extreme cases.

Without ongoing metaphoric processes, the beginning of life would be entirely different. One aspect of early development is that affectively linked concepts are acquired and increasingly applied. The discernment of patterns of needs, satisfactions, and frustrations; progressive recognition of others and self; increasing control over mobility—all these are in part the result of developing conceptual and perceptual apparatuses. Without this none of these developments can occur, seriously arresting maturation—for example, in the emergence of conceptualizations of space and oneself in it as three-dimensional. In extreme cases, even basic intentional mobility would not be achievable.

It is not going too far to say that human life would not be possible without some capacity to detect similarity amongst even vast differences. While the situation of living with a diminished capacity to form links is well known to psychoanalysis and is treatable with analytic processes, human life entirely without that capacity is neither survivable nor even conceivable. Virtually by definition, the state of that experience cannot be described in a language that necessarily employs linking concepts.

This exploration of the role of difference in metaphoric processes again demonstrates the fundamental nature of metaphor to human experience and to life itself. Without some presence of the play of similarity—that is, without some capacity for linking—there is no human life. Modell's (1990, 1997a) statement holds: that metaphoric processes are involuntary and inborn, that "metaphor is the currency of the mind" (2009a, p. 555). Furthermore, metaphoric processes are present from the beginning of life and are the means by which humans experience, learn about, and understand the world, including themselves and all objects. The largest element of human commonality may be metaphoric processes. What is pervasive to our processing and experience is affective and interpretive.

## Components of Metaphoric Processes

One way to articulate the concept of metaphoric process is to differentiate its components. The components are ingredients, or dimensions, of a given metaphoric process. As ingredients, each contributes to the totality of any given point or time slice of a metaphoric process. The discernment of components as various ingredients of metaphoric processes is for heuristic purposes; they may not be neatly isolable or readily observable in the flux of actual clinical experience. Four components in a given metaphoric segment are the *idiosyncratic*, *local*, *community*, and *generalized community* ingredients. Movement or influence within any one component may have ramifications and effects in each of the other components.

In normal development, the peak, active formation of idiosyncratic features of metaphoric processes will take place in the early, preverbal period. The segments of metaphoric processes that run through this preverbal period are unlikely to be retrievable with organizations or structures close to those originally involved in them. The acquisition of local and community configurations contributes to the transformation of prelinguistic, idiosyncratic elements. However, this does not mean that the latter disappear or that they have been rendered inactive.

At the other end of the spectrum from the idiosyncratic is the generalized community component. The contents of this related component are close to what have been called *primary metaphors* (Lakoff & Johnson, 1980). This component arises in structures as that portion common to all humans, across individual experience and culture. It might be that this component of metaphoric processes, while universal for humans, is relative to specific eras of human existence.

The structures from the other two components, the local and the community, lie in between the idiosyncratic and the generalized community in their influence on strands of metaphoric processes. These are configurations that revolve around perceptions of early environmental experience and those of broader cultural experience throughout life, respectively. Using metaphor as a foundation, all levels that have input into human experience can be incorporated. The idiosyncratic, the self in early relation to primary objects, the larger environment and enculturated community, as well as the level of general human experience—all these contribute to metaphoric processes across the life span.

Life proceeds along a sinew of metaphoric processes. The sinew continues for the life of the person. If the sinews of different individuals were entirely different from each other, then the individuals could not meaningfully interact with each other. While one's own sinew is what makes one oneself through time and space, many of the elements of that sinew—that is, metaphoric processes, as well as items in those processes—can be overridingly similar, more similar than not, across individuals, and this is what makes intersubjective, and derivatively intrasubjective, human interaction possible. Through early experience, the highly idiosyncratic conceptualizations embedded in the metaphoric processes give way and merge with elements of this sinew that are held in common with others. Language acquisition and exposure to wider social experience contribute to this giving-way and merging process. Even in the idiosyncratic, more private, early phase, the ingredients of metaphoric processes may be mostly shared as a result of the commonalities of *in utero* and early experience.

## The Concept of the Psychoanalytic Subject in Terms of Metaphoric Processes

A person can be represented as a sinew—a bundle of metaphoric processes. All that is identified with a person—his or her life experiences, memories, thoughts, bodily experiences, etc.—are part of the sinew of metaphoric processes associated with that person. Not all strands persist throughout the entire length of the sinew (that is, the lifespan of the individual). Some become dormant, some merge with other strands, and some may even disintegrate. Some strands commence in the middle of the sinew, while some split into multiple strands. Some segments of strands overlap with others.

20

Each strand carries valences throughout the metaphor and may become stronger or weaker at different points and in relation to valences on other strands.

A momentary cross section of an individual's sinew would display multiple metaphoric processes in that time slice. Each metaphoric process in the time segment is composed of combinations of the four categories of ingredients, together with the valences of each. In addition, each valenced time slice is impacted to some degree by any or all of the metaphoric processes in the sinew up until that point of the time slice. Valences that are the strongest at that moment give rise to a tendency to influence the individual toward movement along the components or strands to which those valences are attached.

This way of describing a self provides a structural portrayal of the complex aspect of human experience with which psychoanalysts work. Each metaphoric process in itself represents one pathway that organizes and motivates the future of the self with respect to a specific cluster of experience. In any given moment of a person's life, multiple clusters of experience, multiple metaphoric processes, all have bearing on the moment, each with its own internal set of affects. Some current elements of one metaphoric process may well stand in contradiction to, or in affect bundle opposite to, another current slice of a different metaphoric process. Thus, motivation, multiple function, overdetermination, and conflict can be understood within this framework.

In this framework, self-awareness, whether bodily or otherwise, is mediated by metaphoric processes. In principle, one has no more direct route to self-awareness than object awareness. Whether it is a self-awareness of something as basic as enjoying a certain taste, it involves multiple metaphoric processes in order to arrive at linking the discrimination of a certain taste and the experience of pleasure. This may occur without an understanding of the past experience that led to the pleasure. Awareness of objects is not different in kind, but at certain points in the lifespan, it may sometimes be more limited and at other times less limited than self-experience and awareness. It is the sinew of ongoing metaphoric processes that brings one to a moment of affective or other experience, rather than an immediate self-experience. This view of persons and personal experience is grounded in unconscious processes.

## Note

1 Parts of this chapter originally appeared in *Psychoanalytic Inquiry* 31(2): pp. 134–146 as "Unconscious Metaphoric Processes as a Basis for an Inclusive Model of Psychoanalytic Perspectives."

# 4

# METAPHOR IN PSYCHOANALYSIS AND CLINICAL DATA[1]

*Robert Wallerstein*

Since the 1980 book, *The Metaphors We Live By*, by Lakoff and Johnson, the cognitive-linguistic view of metaphor that they propound has come to be most widely accepted. Its characteristic features are that (a) metaphor is a property of the concept, not the words; (b) its function is to heighten understanding, not simply artistic or aesthetic; (c) it is often not based on similarity; (d) it is ubiquitous in ordinary language, not requiring special talent; and (e) it is an inevitable intrinsic aspect of all human thought and language. This is true of all speech, including the speech in and of psychoanalysis. Metaphor both amplifies and creates meaning. But it can also be misleading and produce conceptual errors of meaning. It should, therefore, not be reified or always taken literally, but should remain flexible and alterable, so that heuristically more relevant and more encompassing metaphor can readily be elaborated.

## The Meaning of Metaphor

Our language of discourse, daily conversation or literature and essay, has, as far back as it has been recorded, been saturated with metaphor. Zoltán Kövecses (2002), a student of, and collaborator with, the noted American linguist, George Lakoff, in his comprehensive book on metaphor—called a *Practical Introduction*—calls metaphor a figure of speech that implies a comparison between two unlike entities, though with linking common features. He states that traditionally metaphor has had five characteristic features: a) it is a property of words, a linguistic phenomenon, b) it is used for rhetorical or artistic purposes, c) it is based on resemblance, d) it is a conscious and deliberate fashioning of words that requires special talent, quoting Aristotle who called it "a mark of genius," and last, e) a figure of speech that we can well do without.

This view Kövecses declares to be dramatically challenged, and in his view superseded, by the "cognitive-linguistic view of metaphor" enunciated in the 1980 volume by Lakoff and Mark Johnson, in which five quite different—and opposed—characteristic features define metaphor: a) it is a property of the concept, not the words, b) the function is to heighten understanding, rather than simply an artistic or aesthetic purpose, c) it is often *not* based on similarity, d) it is used effortlessly, and mostly unremarked, in ordinary language, not requiring any special talent, and e) it is far from being a superfluous, though pleasing, linguistic ornament, and is rather an inevitable, intrinsic aspect of human thought, reasoning, and speech.

Though admittedly there may be strong proponents of both perspectives still continuing today, Kövecses devotes his entire volume to demonstrating, via seemingly endless examples, the clear superiority of the newer "cognitive-linguistic" perspective. The use of metaphor is so ubiquitous, and often so mundane and commonplace, that it is simply not noticed, being called in that case "dead metaphor." Two such examples are, "a local *branch* of this business" (a plant metaphor of a tree), and "the country was close to *sliding* into war" (a spatial metaphor). But these are really "live metaphors" since they frame our thinking and give it meaning; they are the metaphors we regularly live by. For example, our common metaphor of the human mind as a machine can be seen in another two of Kövecses' examples: "How could any man ever understand the *workings* of a woman's mind?" or "After my first cup of morning coffee, my brain was *ticking over* much more briskly." And this common metaphor is evident in all visions of mental activity, of mind conceived as computer for example, by scientist and general public alike.

In this perspective, metaphorical language is not arbitrary and unmotivated, nor simply ornamental, but is embedded in and central to, our entire idea-creating, thinking process, originally arising from our basic bodily (sensorimotor) developmental experiences. And when we see ideas as food ("I can't swallow that claim") or life as a journey ("We aren't getting anywhere"), we are thinking about abstract concepts (ideation, or life) in ways that are deeply facilitated by the more concrete concepts of food, or a journey. In this sense; "in the cognitive-linguistic view, metaphor is defined as understanding one conceptual domain in terms of another [more concrete] conceptual domain" (Kövecses, p. 4). Thus it creates new meaning.

Adam Bessie in his 2006 review of the literature on metaphor, also drawing centrally upon Lakoff and Johnson, states then the specific contention that "metaphor is a foundational, constructive, and natural process by which we conceptualize the world" (p. 6), and is therefore, "a process for generating ideas" (p. 5). Within this conception, "all language is, at some level, metaphoric ... not a matter for the artist alone, but a part of everyday life" (pp. 10–11), and "a way of thinking, a way to invent ideas, rather than [just] a way to clearly express thinking" (p. 11). Metaphor has been moved, powerfully by Lakoff and Johnson, from mental product to mental process.

Bessie quotes Peter Elbow (1973) on *how* metaphor generates new meaning. "When you make a metaphor you call something by a wrong name ... you are thinking in terms of something else ... [each comparison] throws into relief aspects of the [topic] you might otherwise miss. You are seeing one thought or perception in terms of another" (Elbow, pp. 53–54). "In essence... the writer discovers similarity, and between things which are at first, seemingly unrelated" (Bessie, p. 13). And it is this "discovery process [that] is generative; the writer develops new ideas atop old ones, seeing the world in new ways" (p. 13).

This is what yields new insights, activating "two separate concepts, bridging the two separate conceptual schemata" (Bessie, pp. 21–22). And, of course, it also makes for the possibility of error. As James Seitz (1999) said: "Metaphor, in other words, represents language at its most vulnerable moment, not only because it stimulates multiple, unpredictable readings, but more importantly because it risks obfuscation that can result from calling *this* by the name of *that*" (p. 42) and therefore, "the metaphoric process ... is not only one of finding comparisons between different things but [can become one of] finding contrasts" (Bessie, p. 17). And thus, can also produce conceptual errors in our process of taking "what we know, to make sense of what we do not" (Bessie, p. 14). Metaphor can also be used, deliberately or automatically, to influence, even to mislead, to further bias and advance ideology, as in political, economic, or cultural propaganda, or commercially, in product advertising. Examples are of course, everyday, and legion.

And lastly, importantly, "Given theory which suggests [that] metaphor is a matter of individual cognition 'difference' becomes contextualized within the individual, rather than universally. Thus, determining when a topic and vehicle are 'different' and thus metaphoric, is a matter of individual perception, and individual knowledge" (Bessie, p. 18). In other words; "What is metaphoric to one person, can well be literal to another" (Bessie, p. 9).

## Freud and Metaphor

Given this state of metaphor theory, with its still continuing varying perspectives, and its warning caveats on the pitfalls for the adherents of any of its perspectives, how can we situate the role and place of metaphor within psychoanalysis, both in its theory, and in its therapeutic applications, within that context? As is so often the case, Sigmund Freud can be understood on both sides of this just stated question. On the one hand his descriptive-explanatory language is drenched in vivid metaphor, in both the clinical and the theoretical realms. A very well-known and oft-remarked *clinical* example is his analogy of the psychoanalytic situation to a train ride, and the emergent free associations of the analysand to the recital of a railroad passenger seated at the window, describing the passing scenery to the companion in the adjacent seat (1913a, p. 135). An equally well-known and quoted *theoretical* statement is his effort to explain how sense-impressions relating to what he calls the perceptual system and the mnemic systems become embedded memory through analogy with the operation of the then recently introduced contrivance of the "Mystic Writing-Pad," a writing-tablet from which notes could be erased by an easy movement of the hand (1925, p. 228). Every student of psychoanalysis has many more of Freud's examples at hand.

However, given Freud's commitment—under the guidance of his neuropathological mentor, von Brücke—to the Helmholtz model of a natural science, physico-chemical basis for biological processes, he espoused lifelong his conviction that psychoanalysis, as an evolutionarily constituted, biologically grounded, psychological discipline would ultimately be firmly embedded in that same natural science framework. And, as corollary to that, would necessarily endeavor to eschew metaphorical language in favor of a more scientific mathematical language (a language direction in which Bion sought later to move, while himself, at the same time creating new metaphoric concepts like "container-contained").

At the same time Freud himself famously created numerous compelling metaphors, like those just indicated, to describe his advancing theoretical conceptions, such as id, ego, and superego, used to describe differing mental activities—and to justify their heuristic use, as well as mark out his strong awareness of their provisional, and non-literal, nature. I cite two of his best-known cautionary expressions. In his 1914b paper, *On Narcissism,* he said:

> I am of opinion that that is just the difference between a speculative theory and a science erected on empirical interpretation. The latter will not envy speculation its privilege of having a smooth, logically unassailable foundation, but will gladly content itself with nebulous, scarcely imaginable basic concepts, which it hopes to apprehend more clearly in the course of its development, or which it is even prepared to replace by others. For these ideas are not the foundation of science, upon which everything rests: that foundation is observation alone. They are not the bottom but the top of the whole structure, and they can be replaced and discarded without damaging it. The same thing is happening in our day in the science of physics, the basic notions of which as regards matter, centres of force, attraction, etc. are scarcely less debatable than the corresponding notions in psycho-analysis.
>
> (Freud, 1914b: p. 77)

In this pivotal paper, Freud clearly defended the necessity of metaphoric conceptions to the advancement of psychoanalytic theorizing—and cited the quintessential natural science, physics, as also governed by comparable needs and strategies—while expressing the implied hope that this might be only a way-station on the road to more scientific, i.e., mathematical, precision.

And in his final years, in his 1937 paper, *Analysis Terminable and Interminable,* he still made the identical point, even more dramatically, when discussing the instincts and their relation to the ego, "if we are asked by what methods and means this result is achieved, it is not easy to find an answer. We can only say: 'So muss denn doch die Hexe dran!'—the Witch Metapsychology. Without metapsychological speculation and theorizing—I had almost said 'phantasying'—we shall not get another step forward. Unfortunately, here as elsewhere, what our Witch reveals is neither very clear nor very detailed" (Freud, 1937 p. 225). And here is clearly stated the presence of—and the use of—metaphor as central to the fabric of psychoanalysis from its very beginnings as an emerging science, but also, its limitations, and its possibility for obfuscation.

## The Struggle to Expunge Metaphor From Psychoanalysis

Ever since, different theoreticians have thrown their weight on one or the other side of this struggle over the proper place, for better or worse, of metaphor within psychoanalytic conceptualizing. In the first decades after World War II—and prior to the path-changing Lakoff and Johnson volume—major theorists, concerned to make psychoanalysis more "scientific," sought to progressively eliminate metaphor from its language. For example, Else Frenkel-Brunswik (1954), schooled in Vienna in the logical positivist teachings of Moritz Schlick, averred: "While the psychoanalytic system comes closer to a truly scientific theory than most observers realize, psychoanalysis still contains many metaphors, analogies, and confusions between construct and fact which must in the end be eliminated" (in Heiman & Grant, 1974, p. 226). And she explained away such metaphoric, and in her mind, logical, lapses that appeared in Freud's theorizing. "When Freud ascribes some of the difficulties in his speculations concerning the instincts to our being obliged to operate with 'metaphorical expressions peculiar to psychology,' we must add in his behalf that for the type of problems with which psychoanalysis deals the mentalistic (introspectionist or animistic) vocabulary constitutes the precise counterpart of the pictorial vocabulary which has been stressed as a legitimate or at least *tolerable* ingredient of the earlier stages of physical science" (also p. 226, ital. added).

And H. J. Home (1966) warned of the danger of such lapses. "If mind is not a thing then each time we speak about it as if it were a thing we are speaking metaphorically … If, however, we suppress or repress our consciousness of the metaphor and speak literally about the mind as a thing then we have created a metaphysical fact" (p. 46), something to certainly be avoided.

It was under this anti-metaphorizing banner that two major American psychoanalytic theorists undertook to expunge metaphoric language from psychoanalytic discourse, though from different perspectives, Lawrence Kubie from a theoretical vantage point, and Roy Schafer from a clinical one. Kubie (1966) undertook his campaign as the centerpiece of his effort to ground psychoanalysis within "the future development of a psychophysiology of psychoanalysis" (p. 196), in accord with Freud's own dream of this future for the discipline that he had almost single-handedly created. Kubie did acknowledge that he had as yet no methods to properly carry out this intent of a biologically grounded, i.e., truly scientific (in his sense), psychoanalysis. "Unhappily we have as yet no precise methods by which to carry on such investigations. The development of appropriate techniques will constitute a major methodological breakthrough for all psychologies, but especially for psychoanalytic psychology" (p. 196).

And in decrying both Freud's topographic and structural metaphors, Kubie did endeavor to commit himself to the effort to expunge metaphorical language from psychoanalysis. "I will make no further use of this metaphor [topographic aspects of mentation], however, nor of certain other metaphors which appear currently in psychoanalytic writings, and which are regularly miscalled 'hypotheses'" (p. 191). As an example of the ill that he felt was done by the widespread use of Freud's structural metaphor of the mind (id-ego-superego), Kubie declared; "Freud called this the 'structural' aspect of human mentation. This metaphor seems to me to have been even more unfortunate and misleading than the other [the earlier topographic model] because it does not increase the precision of our descriptions of mental processes, but blurs them by an inexact analogy, and also because it has no explanatory value itself. Indeed, the effort to use this analogy as an explanatory hypothesis has led us into a morass of anthropomorphic pseudo-explanations" (p. 192).

Of such statements, Léon Wurmser (1977), who later wrote in defense of metaphor as central to the creation of (all) science, including psychoanalysis, declared, "But is a statement referring to 'the characteristics of behavior in which preconscious processing flows freely, dominating the psychic stream and furnishing a continuous supply of processed experiences for 'symbolic sampling'… in any way less metaphorical than the points of view, the metaphors and models, attacked by him?" (pp. 468–469).

It was, however, Roy Schafer who, from a clinical, rather than a theoretical, vantage point, mounted the most intense and prolonged effort, in a major sequence of papers (1972, 1973a, 1975, and others) culminating in a book (1976), to thoroughly eliminate metaphor from psychoanalytic work by shifting concretizing nouns, and their qualifying adjectives, so often cast within a passive voice, into active verbs and their adverbs—all to be called "action language" (since the verbs would specify mental acts). This would restore the personal agency, and its inherent acceptance of personal responsibility, to personal behavior and its psychoanalytic unraveling. Schafer's battle cry was, "We can no longer afford to maintain unchallenged the belief that there can be no Freudian psychoanalysis without Freudian metapsychology" (1975, p. 41).

In this effort to rid psychoanalysis of all its spatial metaphors of the mind's various functions, and their interplay and their movements inside and outside, Schafer (1972) declared, "I have been re-examining psychoanalytic terms in the interest of eliminating from our theory confusing, unnecessary, and meaningless metaphors and the assumptions they both express and generate … I am … attempting to develop a sublanguage within the English language that will make it possible to specify mental facts in an unambiguous, parsimonious, consistent, and meaningful fashion: I refer especially to facts of interest to psychoanalysts and analysands" (p. 421).

He does this because, "we have complicated our thinking unnecessarily; we are using a pseudospatial metaphor from which it is all too easy to slip into concreteness of thought; once embarked on metaphor, we tend to develop a sense of obligation to be metaphorically consistent, and to involve ourselves in extravagant niceties of formulation, and perhaps we even introduce still another assumption into theory where none is needed. The history of the pseudoquantitative energy metaphor in Freudian metapsychology demonstrates what I mean" (1972, p. 435).

Schafer then went on to assert that, "Even though such archaic thinking is widely used as metaphor in the adaptive communications of everyday life, it *cannot* be used for exact clinical description and interpretation or for rigorous theoretical conceptualization" (1973a, p. 47, ital. added). And this is because it cannot be tested: "There is no *it* that metaphors capture and so there is no way of testing the truth of a metaphoric construction of experience when one has only the metaphor to work with. Then it is self-contradictory to assert—it is so often asserted—that certain experiences can be expressed *only* metaphorically; for if the assertion is true, then there is no way of assessing the metaphor against its referent and so no basis for making the claim in the first place" (1976, p. 369). That, in essence was Schafer's message, which he kept enlarging in a series of papers seeming to cover almost every aspect of psychoanalytic conceptualizing.

That Schafer's action language never won a significant constituency can be attributed, I think, to two reasons. First is the real ubiquity of metaphor in all our spoken language, whether in social or psychoanalytic discourse, as Lakoff and Johnson demonstrated so convincingly in 1980 (after the publication of the major bulk of Schafer's writings on the subject), so that the effort to totally expunge metaphor becomes an unending, and always failed, task. And second, because the endless sample alternatives that Schafer offered so often were strained and clumsy locutions that could not come easily into conversation. For example, in a chapter in his 1976 book devoted to the language of emotion, after giving many striking and common examples of the metaphor of the heart, used to describe emotional states (big-hearted, broken-hearted, warm-hearted, cold-hearted, and many more), Schafer offers substitutions like: "A warmhearted person is someone who deals affectionately and generously with others. A chicken-hearted person is one who fearfully avoids dealing with ordinary dangers. A hearty person is one who does a variety of things vigorously, zestfully, and good-humoredly," etc. (p. 276).[2]

## In Defense of Metaphor in Psychoanalysis

But metaphor in psychoanalysis has also had its determined, early defenders, in both its clinical and theoretical arenas. Given its conversational ubiquity, working with, i.e., understanding, metaphor has long been part of the clinical armamentarium of psychoanalysis. Rudolf Ekstein and Dorothy Wright in the 1950s made explicit what Ekstein called "working within the metaphor." In a 1952 article, they described a "schizophrenoid" child, a delusional nine-year-old, massively phobic, given to suicidal fantasying, and troubled by severe asthma, who played out his psychic turmoil as a Five Star General, commanding an armada of space ships engaged in destructive inter-galactic wars. He was labeled the "space child" because of the vast cosmological distances over which his internal wars with his all too powerful parents were presented.

Working within the metaphor was described as, "When we speak of distance we refer to it in the physical, emotional, metaphoric sense, since his way of describing the man far away, his using the metaphor of hundreds and thousands of light years seemed to be nothing but an allusion to a psychological problem which he could not present in any other way. The mode of his defense, the way his ego attempted to master internal problems rather than the content of the conflict was attacked by psychotherapeutic work" (Ekstein & Wright, 1952, p. 214). And after substantial therapeutic work the child's internal world was brought down from the distant galaxies to planet earth, where he now became Oscar Pumphandle, engaged in research in Arizona, improving the atom bomb, while his parents were also now earth-bound, but as dinosaurs (still distant in time). It was such changes, as in these mechanisms of distance, of space and of time, that Ekstein felt could be taken as indicators of therapeutic progress. It was "defense through distance" (p. 222) that was gradually undone.

In a successor paper two years later, the boy was now solidly on earth but moving time over great spans through a time machine that he had created. He could now move from our primeval evolutionary birth from a fish or reptile, through all of history, favoring William the Conqueror's 1066 conquest of England, and a trip as a tourist in Europe in 1425. His mission in going back in history was to intervene to change critical familial events, and thus by changing his past, saving his future. In this paper entitled "The Space Child's Time Machine" (Ekstein, 1954), the author stated that, "Tommy has made use of many archeological metaphors" (p. 505). Tommy's delusional states could be conceptualized as experiencing concretized metaphors, literally, i.e. delusionally.

Clearly, work within the metaphor, or with the metaphor, is not always so explicit as with this very disturbed youngster, but more or less explicitly (or implicitly) it has long been an inevitable and accepted part of imaginative clinical psychoanalysis.[3] How could it be otherwise, given the ubiquity of metaphor as an inextricable constituent of even the most ordinary language, let alone the usually more educated discourse within the psychoanalytic encounter. And it can be put to apt clinical use. When a patient expresses himself, for example, as hunting around for something, the alert analyst can at least wonder about buried aggressive connotations, hunting, hostile assaults, murderous fantasies, etc.

But the place of metaphor within the theoretical language of psychoanalysis, a discipline trying to warrant its claim to be a growing science, has always been more problematic—witness the efforts by theorists like Kubie and Schafer, intent to rid psychoanalysis of its metaphoric expressions, the one to legitimate its credentials as science by making its language ultimately more mathematical, and the other to enhance its power as therapy by making its clinical language more actively verbal and its agency more owned.

It was Léon Wurmser (1977)—also writing, like Kubie and Schafer, prior to the publication of the Lakoff and Johnson volume, which retrospectively gave powerful support to Wurmser's thesis—who impressively made the case for the inevitability and the necessity, of metaphor as a central component of developing science. Wurmser began with a systematic critique of those who saw metaphor as either a distortion of the clinical process (like Schafer) or an anti-scientific turn (like Kubie), in both ways declared to be hurtful to psychoanalysis. Wurmser's response to Kubie, who he artfully showed was actually substituting one set of metaphors for another in the language of psychoanalytic theory—since, as Lakoff and Johnson later demonstrated, there is no escape from metaphor when constructing speech or writing—has already been earlier stated.

Of Schafer, Wurmser said: "As Schafer (1975) states in a recent article, his profound criticism would sweep away all of metapsychology and most of our clinical theory and erect a new theory based on psychoanalytic phenomenology. His criticism is based on two premises: first that metaphors derived from direct experience become concretized and therefore are dangerous, indeed ultimately evil;[4] and second, that it is possible to form a theory of psychoanalysis based strictly on functional correlations which have shed all metaphorical impurities, and that he has found a key to build such a nonconcretized, nonreified theory" (p. 471). But again, "shedding all metaphorical impurities" is a fruitless task, and the substituted language proved clumsy and less attractive, and therefore never caught on.

Wurmser then went on to stake out his own "defense" of metaphor in psychoanalysis, both clinically and theoretically. Essentially his argument is that, "What is crucial is that our science, like any other science, is woven of the warp of observations and held together by the intricate woof of symbolism, of many layers of abstractions, of stark and faded metaphors, which 'interpret' for us ('explain' to us) the 'direct' facts which, as we know, are never really direct" (pp. 476–477). This led to the statement all in italics; *"All science is the systematic use of metaphor"* (p. 477). Which is further explained by: "Metaphors, taken literally, are unscientific. Metaphors, understood as symbols, are the only language of science we possess, unless we resort to mathematical symbols" (p. 483). (The latter of which, of course, Bion attempted prematurely.)

Actually, this all follows ineluctably from the Lakoff and Johnson thesis that metaphor is of the very fabric of all language usage, even though as Bessie (2006, p. 7) has stated, "Across fields there is [still] a great deal of debate over what metaphor is, and how it functions. [And] ironically, or appropriately, metaphor is an abstraction, one which it is difficult to define without resorting to metaphor … In fact, the very word metaphor, Seitz (1991) observes, 'derives from a metaphor: to transfer, to carry'" (p. 389).

Since metaphor is always there, the (scientific) interest of psychoanalysis in the use of metaphor in its clinical and theoretical discourse, "is, *whether and in what forms and on what levels we choose symbolic representations* for the specific experiences gained by the psychoanalytic method and the scientific inquiry based on this method" (Wurmser, p. 482). For, "The connection between symbol and fact is solely this functional relation … A means to predict consequences" (Wurmser, p. 473). And Freud, whose dramatic and evocative prose style earned him the Goethe Prize for Literature, was so often masterful in his metaphoric language choices. Wurmser put it thus: "What has been most *fruitful* in analytic theory formation? One has only to read the works of Freud and a few other analytic theoreticians to discover that it was the richness and the systematic, coherent use of metaphorical constructs that added so much to our knowledge" (Wurmser, p. 484).

Freud, of course, was not always clear about *how* he deployed and used metaphor. Talking about Freud's energy metaphor, designed to substantiate the economic viewpoint in metapsychology, Wurmser quoted, "Shope (1973) is probably right when he states that Freud saw the concept of energy not as metaphor, but as explanatory construct (p. 396); this should not hinder our re-evaluating it critically—accepting it as useful in the former, as most dubious in the latter meaning" (p. 487). Though the energy metaphor has been substantially abandoned by much of the psychoanalytic world, replaced now by heuristically more useful metaphor, Wurmser did try to explain its long appeal to Freud (and to many others) as follows: "The economic world in psychoanalysis is an attempt not to add yet a new physical content to those physical equivalent [energy in the natural sciences] but to establish metaphorically, by analogy, a *similar system 'of quantitative relations of equivalence'*—some novel form of lawful correlation between emotional phenomena" (p. 486). And, of course, by now much of Freudian metapsychology of which the economic viewpoint was but one component, has been abandoned and replaced with more felicitous (i.e., more useful) conceptions. What are involved are continuing issues of judgment that try to find widening collegial resonance.[5]

At the New York University Institute of Philosophy chaired by Sidney Hook in 1958, devoted to an interchange between psychoanalysts (Hartmann, Kubie, Kardiner, Arlow) and philosophers of science, the philosopher Arthur Danto was one participant who spoke to the same issues as Wurmser, and made the same comparison with the queen science, physics: "a person who demands that every properly scientific term be redeemed (without remainder) with observational equivalents, merely betrays allegiance to a superannuated empiricism. It is hardly damaging any longer, therefore, to accuse psychoanalysis of being unscientific by virtue of its trafficking in unobservables. Providing that the theoretical terms function in psychoanalytical theories the way they do in (say) physical theories, and providing that psychoanalytical theories come up to the mark on syntactical grounds, the two could hardly be contrasted invidiously. So far as unobservableness goes, there is little to choose as between castration complexes and psi-functions" (1959, p. 315).

## Current Psychoanalytic Understandings of Metaphor

By now the Lakoff and Johnson "cognitive-linguistic" perspective, quoted in most current psychoanalytic contributions to the subject of metaphor, has come to be our almost universally accepted conceptual bedrock. There have been two prior issues of *Psychoanalytic Inquiry* (2005, 2009) devoted to exploring the role, rather the centrality, of metaphoric thought to psychoanalysis, both issues edited by Alan Barnett and S. Montana Katz—with this article in this third issue, with the same co-editors. Both prior issues acknowledge the pioneering role of Arnold Modell in fashioning the current very much broadened psychoanalytic conceptions of metaphor as what has been variously called the "heart," or the "currency," of psychoanalysis—both of these words, themselves metaphors. Modell, himself, has a central article in both of those journal issues (2005, 2009a) and is referred to, as basic to their understanding, by almost all of the other authors in those issues, including even one (Fred Levin) calling Modell his muse (2009, p. 70).

Building on the Lakoff and Johnson thesis about the central role of metaphor in all thought and language, Modell expanded this framework to conceive of metaphor as the linguistic "bridge" from body to mind, from its origin in the sensorimotor biological building blocks of language acquisition, to being the lifetime "bridge" between (often unconscious) feeling states and verbalized speech (knowledge). And the whole array of fellow authors in the second issue of *Psychoanalytic Inquiry* (2009) ranging from the self-declared neuro-psychoanalyst, Fred Levin, to the prominent relationist, Donnel Stern, each in their own way, fully support Modell's conceptions.

31

Some sample quotations will demonstrate this wide concordance of seeing metaphor as *the* "royal road" to meaning-making, underlying almost every central (psychoanalytic) linguistic conception, like the understanding of the unconscious, affect, thought transference, dream, etc.; even the whole of psychoanalysis itself. For example, "Metaphor is at the center of the construction of meaning" (Modell, 2009b, p. 93); "a modern understanding of metaphor as the way we initially process and articulate new concepts" (Aragno, 2009, p. 30); "metaphor ... transfers meaning between dissimilar domains, and, through the use of novel recombinations, transfers meanings" (Barnett & Katz, 2009, p. 1). Which transfer of meanings is, of course, the essence of transference, as several of the contributors point out. And, of course, of dreams as well. "Metaphorical thought—understanding one thing in terms of another—underlies and permeates dream-formation" (Aragno, p. 40), and "Metaphor points to one thing while signifying something else, just as dreams point to their manifest content while meaning their latent thoughts" (Aragno, p. 41).

Which brings us to the practical equation of the use of metaphor as the practically total explanation of the entire analytic process, in Modell's words, "the currency of the emotional mind" (2009a, p. 6); "it is fundamentally embodied and is not simply a figure of speech" (2009a, p. 68). Which leads to the full equation: "In summary, contemporary analysts of all connections agree that analysis *is* a metaphoric process, and that the patient's and the analyst's metaphoric processes and verbalized metaphors are essential for the transformations the analysand must undergo. This theoretical issue seems indisputable" (Rizzuto 2009, p. 20). And even more encompassing is a summarizing statement by Aragno "With respect to metaphor, psychoanalysts are indisputably privileged. We dwell in the realm of metaphor; of tropes, synecdoche, and metonymy: of irony, hyperbole, allusion, and illusion; of vital enactment and corresponding dream; of symptom, demonstration, meaning, and story as metaphoric *events*. Metaphor fills the space and the situation (even before the meetings have begun!); it permeates the process, its stages, phases, and exchanges ..." (p. 32).

Contrary voices in psychoanalysis, like those of Kubie and Schafer, seem to have died away. And nowhere are the cautionary notes, like those of the cognitive-linguists, or among analysts, like Wurmser, that metaphors can be poorly constructed, can point to irrelevant or false meanings, can thus obfuscate and derail psychoanalytic understanding, can even lend themselves to harmful interventions—whether in clinical interchange or in theoretical construction—at all mentioned. Nor is much specific attention paid—aside from conventional metaphors that are broadly based, quite universally self-evident, and with consensually agreed-upon meanings—to the specific individual contextualization of metaphoric meanings, that though clearly central to understanding individual therapeutic interchange, may create real difficulties in facilitating theoretical advance that is meant to be universally applicable and consensually understood.

And beyond all this, what the contributors to *Psychoanalytic Inquiry* (2005, 2009) have done, is to push the by now quite well accepted conviction that our language, in all its dimensions, is (almost) automatically and inextricably, saturated with metaphor (both conventional, and in more creative minds, quite idiosyncratic), pushed this to the contention that all of abstract thought, is necessarily metaphoric, that abstraction cannot be conceptualized except metaphorically. Thus metaphor could become properly declared by Modell the "bridge" from the latent unconscious thought to verbalized speech. This carries the risk, to me, of making every thought and every speech act, other than the exactly literal, into metaphor, and, in so doing, making metaphor itself, lose its special distinctness of meaning. To me, this can be beyond the Lakoff and Johnson thesis, and it strips metaphor of an essential element, that metaphor makes an *abstraction* more understandable in terms of something more *concrete*—with all the potential dangers then, of course, of leading to reification, to potential risk, and also to possible misunderstanding, because of individually different contextualization. To me, this overall broadening trend both overburdens the conception of metaphor and conceals its limitations and hazards.

## Where Do I Stand?

I first became explicitly involved in considering the place and the meaning of metaphor in psychoanalysis when I gave my Presidential Address to the International Psychoanalytical Association in Montreal in 1987, and chose as my topic the issue of our increasing psychoanalytic diversity, or pluralism as we had come to call it, a pluralism of theoretical perspectives, of linguistic and thought conventions, of distinctive regional, cultural, and language emphases; and what it was, in view of this expanding diversity, that still held us together as common adherents of a shared psychoanalytic science and profession.

After reviewing in some detail Freud's own lifetime strenuous efforts to define the parameters of his new science of the mind, and to hold it together as a theoretically unified enterprise, against both destructive or diluting pressures or seductions from without, and also against fractious human divisiveness from within, I outlined how this effort broke down, even in Freud's lifetime, with the emerging Kleinian movement in Great Britain, and then spread with other new theoretical perspectives emerging around the world, leading to the multiple competing metapsychologies we were facing at the time of my address in 1987—and continuing still today.

To respond to the question of what, in the face of this, still held us together that I had posed, I took as my starting point the distinction posited for psychoanalysis by George Klein (1976), between the low-level and experience-near clinical theory, dealing with the actual observables in the interactions within the consulting room, and the more encompassing, more generally explanatory, and more causally developmental accounting of mental life from its earliest fathomable origins, the experience-distant general theories (or metapsychologies) which seek to "explain" the clinical phenomena described by the clinical theory. Though Klein declared the clinical theory to be eminently testable, he stated that the canons of correspondence between the clinical theory and our varying general theories were too tenuous to be able to claim any possibility of establishing utility or validity for any of the general theories, and that indeed, the general theories were anyway all unnecessary to psychoanalytic understanding, and should therefore be severed and cast out by an action he dubbed "theorectomy." This, of course, was our entire realm of differing metapsychologies, the Freudian ego psychological (now, modern conflict theory), the British object relational, the Kleinian, Bionian, Lacanian, Kohutian self-psychological, relational, etc.

I illustrated this contention with a vignette, described by Kohut, of a specific clinical interchange where three theoretical explanatory systems, the Kleinian, the ego psychological, and Kohut's own self psychological, could each be invoked and could each be used to differently causally "explain" that same clinical interaction, each putting the clinical specifics into a different framework of plausible meaning, within an overall theoretical explanatory context. And each of these general explanatory systems would indeed be persuasive to the adherents of that viewpoint who in fact would look at it as *the* most useful and natural way in which to understand the described clinical interaction.

What Kohut made of this was that the described clinical context was insufficient to decide which of the three "interpretations" would be in this instance closest to the mark, and so he called all three of them examples, potentially, of "wild analysis"— until proven otherwise. What I was differently suggesting was that our *data* are the clinical events of the consulting room, and that their interpretation, that could carry consensually agreed meaning, was embedded only in our clinical theory, the theory level of transference and countertransference, of resistance and defense, of conflict and compromise, in fact, the original fundamental elements of Freud's 1914 definition of psychoanalysis.[6] This I stated to be our common psychoanalytic clinical ground that united us within our shared discipline.

I also suggested that our pluralism of theoretical perspectives within which we try to give overall meaning to our clinical data in the present, and try to reconstruct the past out of which the present developed, represent the various scientific *metaphors* that we have created in order to satisfy our variously conditioned needs for closure and coherence and overall theoretical explanation. Joseph and Anne-Marie Sandler had earlier (1983) approached this same conception in their statement that deep interpretations into the infantile past could be viewed as but metaphoric reconstructions. For example, "It is our firm conviction that so-called "deep" interpretations can have a good analytic effect only because they provide metaphors that can contain the fantasies and feelings in the second system [what they called the "present unconscious"]. The patient learns to understand and accept these metaphors, and if they provide a good fit, both cognitively and affectively, then they will be effective. This view gives us a way of understanding the interpretive approach of some of our [Kleinian] colleagues" (p. 424).

I broadened and extended this thinking to the conception that all our general theoretical perspectives, Kleinian, but also ego psychological, and all the others, are but our varyingly chosen explanatory *metaphors*, heuristically useful to us in terms of our varying intellectual value commitments, in explaining, i.e., in making sense of, the primary clinical data of our consulting rooms, the realm of the "present unconscious" in the Sandlers' terms, or the realm of our "clinical theory" in George

Klein's terms. Put most simply, this conceptualization makes all our grand general theory (and all of our pluralism of general theory), nothing but our individually chosen array of metaphor.

Put this way, my conception of the place of metaphor in psychoanalysis, though within the framework propounded linguistically by Lakoff and Johnson, of its inextricable ubiquity in all our thinking and verbalization processes, is less broad than its equation with the totality of the psychoanalytic process—itself very refractory to consensually agreed definition, with so many stating that, in judging case presentations, they find it hard to try to define the process, but they just know it when they see it—and is rather something less automatic, less totalistic, but rather something more personal, more individually constructed, more idiosyncratically determined, by our own developmental and personality dispositions, and the outlooks on life that they embed.

A similar view that life values are distinctly involved in our choice of theoretical perspectives, i.e., our scientific metaphors, was clearly articulated by John Gedo (1984), though perhaps not in a form with which we would all agree. He said on this issue:

> Each of these conceptual schemata [the various psychoanalytic theoretical systems] encodes one or another of the primary meanings implicit in human existence—unfortunately, often to the exclusion of all other meanings. Thus, the view of man embodied in the libido theory, especially in the form it took prior to 1920, attributed primary significance to the satisfaction of the appetites. By contrast, Melanie Klein's psychoanalytic system teaches the need to make reparation for man's constitutional wickedness ... In the 1970s, Heinz Kohut promulgated views that give comparable emphasis to the unique healing power of empathy while acknowledging man's entitlement to an affectively gratifying milieu ... Let me hasten to add that I am emphatically in agreement with the need to satisfy appetites, to curb human destructiveness, and to provide an affectively gratifying environment for our children. And I am for other desiderata to boot! Isn't everyone?
>
> (Gedo, 1984: p. 159)

Which is exactly my point extended to the role of metaphor. Our chosen explanatory metaphors are not inherent and automatic in our thought and speech construction, but are to significant extent chosen (and so often, very thoughtfully and deliberately chosen) in terms of the personality predilections that we have—individually and differently—come to live by.

This same point of Gedo's, that our theoretical positions in psychoanalysis, i.e., our chosen scientific explanatory metaphors, are inevitably embedded in our fundamental social, political, and moral value dispositions has been made strongly as the closing statement in Greenberg and Mitchell's 1983 book on object relations perspectives in (American) psychoanalysis, which they traced developmentally and historically through critical discussion of the work of the various major object relations theorists starting with such diverse contributors as Melanie Klein, W. R. D. Fairbairn, and Harry Stack Sullivan. The summarizing point that they make at the end of their book is that the drive theory perspective and the relational theory perspective are linked to differing views of the essential nature of human experience and acquired world view.

Drive theory they linked philosophically to the positions of Hobbes and Locke, that man is an essentially individual animal, and that human goals and satisfactions are fundamentally personal and individual. The role of the state rests on the concept of "negative liberty," that the state adds nothing to individual satisfaction as such, but just ensures the possibility of personal fulfillment. Relational theory they linked philosophically to the position of Rousseau, Hegel, and Marx, that man is an essentially social animal and that human goals and satisfactions are realizable only within an organized community. The role of the state rests here on the concept of "positive liberty," to provide an indispensable "positive" function by offering its citizens that which they cannot provide for themselves in isolation.

Greenberg and Mitchell stated in relation to this that, "The drive/structure and the relational/structure model embody these two major traditions within Western philosophy in the relatively recently developing intellectual arena of psychoanalytic ideas" (p. 402). And in this context they quoted Thomas Kuhn, the well-known philosopher and historian of (natural) science, that "communication between proponents of different theories is inevitably partial ...What each takes to be facts, depends in part on the theory he espouses, and ... an individual's transfer of allegiance from theory to theory is often better described as *conversion* than as choice" (1977, p. 338, ital. added). Which is my own overall point, that we can and do choose different, and conflicting, explanatory metaphors to explain the same phenomena, the same facts, even what we take to be the facts, that we are endeavoring to explain.

Within this overall context, I see our present day theoretical pluralism, our, to this point, diversity of explanatory metaphors, arising out of our different life experiences, our different personality predilections, and our different psychoanalytic trainings and allegiances, as an expression of our current state of development as a credible science. Each metaphoric explanatory system represents, for its adherents, the best possible current understanding of the phenomena displayed in our consulting rooms, and is therefore heuristically useful, even essential, to the followers of that system. In that sense, these varying explanatory metaphors are vital to the current position of psychoanalysis as an evolving science, seeing the place of metaphor, of course, in a less totalistic way than others who view it more broadly as the vital coin of the entire psychoanalytic process, as in fact, the indubitable engine of all of psychoanalysis. That argument I leave aside, as I affirm what I regard as the central and essential role of metaphor in all scientific theory construction.

I don't, of course, expect that psychoanalysis will simply remain in this current state. Psychoanalysis is rather a continually evolving scientific endeavor. I have in two previous publications (Wallerstein, 2002a, 2002b), the first, talking about the growth and transformations over time of American ego psychology, and the second, an effort to prognosticate what I saw to be the continuing course of evolving converging trends within our currently pluralistic metapsychological (metaphoric) international psychoanalytic world, recounted in both the efforts of many clinical and theoretical contributors (most explicitly Kernberg and Sandler, but also Chodorow, Gabbard, Gill, Loewald, etc.) to reconcile—even creatively amalgamate—disparate metapsychologies and their dominant metaphors. These efforts, anchored at the clinical level, but aspiring "upward" towards the general explanatory level of metaphor, represent unifying trends, which to the extent that they mature, in consensually acceptable ways, will necessarily also lead to increasingly more encompassing (and, hopefully, more precise) explanatory metaphors. (The reader is referred to my two 2002 articles, for a detailed exposition of the development, the then current status, and the expected near-future developments of these converging psychoanalytic perspectives.)

How far such unifying tendencies—with the concomitantly enlarging explanatory metaphors—will progress, is unclear, but they are similar to the unifying thrust of all science, even the paradigmatic science, physics, where an entire current generation of theoretical physicists, are pursuing, via the promise of (super)string theory, the effort to create T.O.E. (theory of everything). T.O.E. would finally unite two current major theoretical structures, Einstein's relativity theory which explains so well the very large world of cosmology (galaxies, the expanding universe, space and time), and quantum mechanics, which explains equally well the very tiny world of subatomic particles (quarks, mesons, gluons, etc.), with the dilemma being—somewhat akin to that of psychoanalysis—that the two theories, of the very large and the very small, though each presumably valid in its own domain, stand in total opposition to each other, with—in physics—the situation, that if the one theory is correct, the other must be false.[7]

How far psychoanalysis will progress in this direction is clearly not at present knowable. Sciences do, incrementally, evolve, though at different rates, and varyingly towards a more precise (non-metaphorical) language of mathematical equations and symbolisms. It is certainly an open question as to how far each science can (or should) evolve from the language of metaphor to the language of mathematics. Certainly none are wholly there now, and psychoanalysis is very far, indeed.

Finally, in terms of the whole tenor of the argument that I have been advancing through this article, the question in my title seems somewhat misplaced. Since metaphor is an integral component of the construction of language, all language, even the language of science, the issue is rather that though metaphor can indeed be misleading, and a bane, if it is concretized and reified and taken literally, it is indeed (most often) a blessing when aptly created, in the sense of imparting (and explaining) new meanings which advance our scientific understandings. And, as Freud counseled us at our very beginning, metaphor is intrinsically both flexible and alterable, so that heuristically more relevant and more encompassing metaphor can readily be elaborated. Thus scientific propositions advance towards greater explanatory comprehensions, and ultimately, testability.

# Notes

1 This chapter originally appeared in *Psychoanalytic Inquiry* 31(2): pp. 90–106 with the title, "Metaphor in Psychoanalysis: Bane or Blessing?"

2 Schafer's cause did achieve significant literary support when Susan Sontag (1978), caught up with her own cancer, published a polemical essay decrying the dangers caused by the all too ready willingness to make "mysterious" and dreaded illnesses, like tuberculosis and cancer, and also others (leprosy, syphilis, and insanity) into "morally, if not literally contagious" (p. 6) happenings. With bountiful references from world literature, Sontag described the long romanticization of tuberculosis into an ailment of talented aesthetes, "the sign of a superior nature" (p. 34) (like Shelley and Keats), or cancer as a failure of expressiveness, reflecting the repression of violent feelings by life's losers. "Contrariwise, my point is that illness is *not* a metaphor, and that the most truthful way of regarding illness—and the healthiest way of being ill—is one most purified of, most resistant to, metaphoric thinking" (p. 3). Rather than being the bearer of secret (and often shameful) taboos, disease is an "ineluctably material reality" (p. 56). And in a wholesale assault on any hint of psychosomatic thinking, "Psychological theories of illness are a powerful means of placing the blame on the ill. Patients, who are instructed that they have, unwittingly caused their disease are also being made to feel that they have deserved it" (p. 57). And that, of course, can be a danger of metaphor!

3 For further striking examples of the use of flagrant metaphor in clinical psychoanalysis, the reader can consult Aleksandrowicz (1962), Reider (1972), and Voth (1970). For somewhat more theoretical conceptualizations, see Lewin (1970, 1971) and Sharpe (1940).

4 The risks in concretizing metaphor, and taking it literally, can be very real and can do great harm. When I entered psychiatry in 1949, the lobotomy operation was still being employed for the mitigation of the psychotic structure in instances of severe, and chronic, paranoid schizophrenia. At a hospital "lobotomy conference" that I knew, the lobotomy was "explained" and justified by the conception that the ego resided in the frontal cortex, and the turbulent id in the thalamus, so that surgically severing the thalamo-cortical projections, would release the weakened ego from the tyranny of the overpowering, chaotic id. This formulation was advanced by the psychoanalytic consultant. An extreme and tragic instance of the risks of concretized metaphor!

5 The earlier widely noted 1964 article by William Grossman and Bennett Simon made essentially the same argument as Wurmser, but under the more narrowly focused conception of anthropomorphism in psychoanalysis, rather than Wurmser's umbrella of metaphor.

6 Freud stated there, "[T]he facts of transference and of resistance. Any line of investigation which recognizes these two facts and takes them as the starting point of its work has a right to call itself psycho-analysis, even though it arrives at results other than my own. But anyone who takes up other sides of the problem while ignoring these two hypotheses will hardly escape a charge of misappropriation of property by attempted impersonation, if he persists in calling himself a psycho-analyst" (1914a, p. 16). Of course we must add here that the key words "transference" and "resistance" also imply the concepts of the unconscious, of psychic conflict, and of defense and compromise formation, the key building stones of our shared psychoanalytic edifice. And, of course, modern conceptions of the place and use of countertransference must be included. Further along in this *History*, Freud elaborates this same definitional statement, using much the same words (1914a, p. 50).

7 For a detailed explanation of this situation in physics, I refer the reader to the two general explanatory books by the Columbia University theoretical physicist and string theory researcher, Brian Greene (1999, 2004).

5

# METAPHOR AND CONFLICT[1]

## *Léon Wurmser*

The chapter deals with a double idea: Metaphor itself, by bridging two domains of experience, lives in the tension, even contradictoriness, of what it brings together, and in that way may be uniquely suited to present a theory of mental life that centers on inner polarities and antitheses, i.e., inner conflict in a wide sense, not necessarily bound to the drive or structural metaphors. In turn, the concept of "conflict" itself entails a spectrum of warlike or violent metaphors, like defense, antitheses, clashing values or forces, being torn or broken apart, inner part personalities fighting with each other, etc. The history of the metaphors for various forms of inner conflict is traced back in Western and Eastern literature (Homer, Plato, Bible, Talmud, St. Augustine, Confucius, and Lao Tzu), thus broadening the search for a common ground for psychoanalytic perspectives.

The concept of "symbol," encompassing that of metaphor, is itself derived from a striking and ritualized metaphor of fitting together what has been broken apart, a ritual that is very similar in ancient Greek and Chinese tradition.

In 1977 I published my paper in the *Quarterly* defending the use of metaphor in psychoanalytic theory formation against the attacks by Schafer, Holt, Kubie, and others (Wallerstein, this volume). This paper does not repeat what has been presented there but is based on its main ideas.

### "The Seal of the Mind"

Since I wrote my paper defending the use of metaphor in theory formation in the sciences in general, in psychoanalysis in particular (Wurmser, 1977), there have been several pertinent developments. They have been ably summarized and examined in various perspectives in the previous issue of *Psychoanalytic Inquiry* (2009, Vol. 29, no. 1). The most important step, it seems to me, was distinguishing metaphoric processes from metaphor proper. The latter is bound to language and is one form of symbolic formation. The former is a biologically deeply anchored process of cross modal equations which can already be observed in newborns (Stern, 1985; Wurmser, 2000, p. 27; Aragno, 2009, p. 31). The new, broader view is simply put: "The essence of metaphor is understanding and experiencing one kind of thing in terms of another ... most of our normal conceptual system is metaphorically structured;

that is, most concepts are partially understood in terms of other concepts" (Lakoff & Johnson, 1980, pp. 5, 56). It goes beyond words and deals more generally with concepts, understanding and action: "Metaphor is primarily a matter of thought and action and only derivatively a matter of language" (Lakoff & Johnson, 1980, p. 153). Aragno (2009) speaks of "metaphoric thought as a primary activity of mind" (p. 33). Quoting Borbely, she refers to the *metaphorical process* as being situated between primary and secondary process (ibid.). "It is a fundamental *law* of ideation, a principle of synthesis and integration" (p. 36).

I asked therefore (1989, p. 33): "Is not all conceiving of truth [Erfassung der Wahrheit] lastly founded in the metaphoric action of the human being?" More specifically and summarizing, I wrote in the same work:

> Natural science does not rest until it has resolved everything into mathematical relations. The humanities trace back their phenomena to formal stylistic relations. Could it be that psychoanalysis has to put everything into relations of polarities? Is the idiom specific for it that of metaphors for paradoxes, for multiple refractions of conflicts and polarities? Does it live in the spirit of Socratic irony, like creativity in general, forever questioning all knowledge anew, disquieting, constantly on the way? "Restlessness and dignity—this is the seal of the mind (or spirit)" [*Rastlosigkeit und Würde—das ist das Siegel des Geistes*, Thomas Mann, *Joseph und seine Brüder*, 1933/1966, p. 50]. And doesn't it therefore show, more than all the other symbolic activities of man, the dominating double principle of conflict and complementarity?
>
> (Wurmser, 1989, pp. 499–500)

There is hardly any moment in psychoanalytic work where we are not aware of voices of the personality that contradict each other, of parts that struggle with each other. Such inner splits are the hallmark of the mind when studied with our method, an *a priori* starting point for our systematic efforts to understand our inner life and our dialogue with others: "We seek not merely to describe and to classify phenomena, but to understand them as signs of an interplay of forces in the mind, as a manifestation of purposeful intentions working concurrently or in mutual opposition. We are concerned with a *dynamic view* of mental phenomena. On our view the phenomena that are perceived must yield in importance to trends which are only hypothetical" (Freud, 1916, p. 67). "It is important to begin in good time to reckon with the fact that mental life is the arena and battle-ground for mutually opposing purposes or, to put it non-dynamically, that it consists of contradictions and pairs of contraries. Proof of the existence of a particular purpose is no argument against the existence of an opposite one; there is room for both. It is only a question of the attitude of these contraries to each other, and of what effects are produced by the one and by the other" (ibid., pp. 76–77).

The central concern for us as psychoanalysts is the consistent, systematic exploration of inner conflict, especially of unconscious inner conflict. No matter how we try to define our work, it always comes down to the fact that the focus, the center of our interest during our analytic work at its best, lies on inner conflict. Everything else moves to the periphery; it is not irrelevant, but our inner orientation is so that we notice it as part of the surrounding field, not as the beacon that guides us. In this way our inner life becomes the most prominent example for the word of Heraklitus, the pre-Socratic philosopher, that "war is the father of all things—*polemos pater panton.*" "Polemos" can certainly be translated as conflict.

As I described in 1977 in more detail there are other approaches to an understanding of the mind, especially those that look for the inner growth towards harmony and the full development of what Aristotle dubbed "entelechy": that try to achieve the indwelling essence of being, and correspondingly to rectify deviations from such a path and hence deficits and defects. But our approach centers on the vision of conflicts of contradictory forces or parts or values and their possible complementarity, i.e., that such opposites do not exclude each other, but complement them: "*Contraria sunt complementa.*"

The notion of inner conflict did not originate with Freud; its systematic use as explanatory device par excellence did. In his and even more so in our work, relevant *explanation* more and more moves away from the short cut attempts at reducing our inner life to certain large factors, like trauma, stages of libido development, narcissism, masochism, repetition compulsion. If these concepts are taken as explanations of causality, the clinician soon discovers that their usefulness stops precisely there where the problem begins. They are the beginning, not the end of the search. Instead, the stopping point of such exploration is the concept of a specific inner conflict, specifically inner preconscious conflict that stands for, is derivative of, long range unsolved unconscious inner conflicts in multiple layerings. Thus psychoanalytic explanation rests in an understanding of *conflict causality*: the causes of what we observe are seen in many layers of inner conflict. Conflict does not simply refer to that between drives and ego, drives and superego, ego and outer reality, but also between opposite ego aspects, between discordant superego parts, as between different ideals and values, between sharply split loyalties, even between opposing drives, between ideas and affects, between conformity and self-loyalty, etc. It is also not so that conflict psychology is synonymous with the exploration of Oedipal issues or even with the structural model, as important both are for conflict psychology; both of them deal with special forms of conflict. Nor does conflict understanding, including the analysis of unconscious conflict, have to be tied to drive theory (Modell, this volume). There are very many levels of inner conflict: between ideas, values, affects, entire "subpersonalities" within the self, as it were different selves, "the soul as multitude of subjects, as community building of drives and affects" (Nietzsche, 1885/1976, p. 20), as "dividua," as Nietzsche somewhere put it ironically.

Thus psychoanalysis is grounded in a philosophy that sees its center in *conflict and paradox, in polarity and complementarity*, and that seeks on many levels the dichotomies of knowing, acting, and feeling. This vision did not originate with Freud, but is profoundly rooted in Western literature and philosophy, and hints of it may even be traced in Chinese thought. Our classical writings for thousands of years are replete with metaphors for such inner oppositions: for inner breaks and struggles and for the abyss that opens up when such contradictions are unbridgeable and unsolvable.

## The Centrality of Metaphor

As stated earlier (Wurmser, 1977, 1989; Arlow, 1979; Sharpe, 1940; Caruth & Ekstein, 1966; Voth, 1970; Modell, 2003, 2005, 2009a), the analyst's work has to be largely *metaphorical*. Arlow spoke of the whole of psychoanalysis as a metaphorizing odyssey, it "is essentially a metaphorical enterprise" (Arlow, 1979, p. 373, quoted by Aragno, 2009 p. 45): "The patient addresses the analyst metaphorically, the analyst listens and understands in a corresponding manner. Under the influence of neurotic conflict, the patient perceives and experiences the world in a metaphorical way" (Arlow, pp. 373–374), and he quotes Empson that it is ambiguity that makes metaphor possible: "Ambiguity implies a dynamic quality to language which enables meaning to be deepened and enriched as various layers of it become simultaneously available" (Arlow, p. 373).

"The language of dreams is entirely metaphorical," says Aragno (2009, p. 42). "Metaphor is fictive, not factual; its message imaginative, not literal. Metaphors do not deliver data, but evoke *insight*; image and concept here fuse in thought" (p. 43). Quoting Goodman, she adds: "The oddity is that metaphorical truth is compatible with literal falsity" (p. 36). "Truth is always relative to a conceptual system that is defined in large part by metaphor" (Lakoff and Johnson, 1980, p. 159); there is no absolute, objectivist truth.

Primary process thinking underlying both neurosis and dream follows the logical laws of mythical thinking. Because they work with images and because they overstep the lines between perceptual categories, metaphors appeal to mythical thinking. Already the etymology of the word "metaphora" indicates the close relationship to one of the basic concepts of psychoanalysis: it means "transference" (Wurmser, 1977; Grassi, n.d.).

One of the most fascinating discoveries in the research of early infancy is the newborn's and infant's striking "capacity to transfer perceptual experience from one sensory modality to another" (Stern, 1985, p. 47). Such "yoking of the tactile and visual experiences is brought about by way of the innate design of the perceptual system, not by way of repeated world experience. No learning is needed initially ..." (p. 48). This implies "that the infant, from the earliest days of life, forms and acts upon abstract representations of qualities of perception" (p. 51). In other words, *abstraction*, i.e., the ability to transfer formal qualities between different modalities, exists from the very beginning, independent from all experience, and thus is an immediate given, is *a priori*. Metaphorical thought is only a special case of this fundamental characteristic of our mind. Metaphorical process is an inborn readiness and manifests itself independent from language.

What Aristotle (*Poetics*, 22.16/17; 1459 a) saw as the "by far greatest token of genius" (*euphyias te semeion*) in the poet, i.e., the use of metaphor (*poly de megiston to metaphorikon einai*), can by rights also be claimed for the analyst: "Seeing what is similar" (l.c.). Similes, figures of speech, are an important road that may very directly lead to what is unconscious. Philosophically, it means also a great deal that the analytic models of insight and of ordering the data are themselves of metaphorical nature.

This philosophical attitude does also greater justice to the complexity of inner life than a closed and dogmatic system of theories could do. Theoretical models as metaphorical renderings that allow approximation to "the truth," but are not absolute; models which are more useful for this purpose than others; all the models of the different schools being attempts to order smaller or larger segments of observations, some handier than others; based on such models, the technical guidelines as being more or less effective, short or long term, helpfully, yet unfortunately also often harmfully—these are the *pragmatic* foundations upon which, in my own psychoanalytic work, the concept of truth is built (Wurmser, 2000). "Each metaphoric explanatory system represents, for its adherents, the best possible current understanding of the phenomena displayed in our consulting rooms, and is therefore heuristically useful, even essential, to the followers of that system" (Wallerstein, this volume).

## Metaphor as Representation of Conflict

"If psychoanalysis is the art and scientific study of interpreting our inner life, especially those parts disguised and hidden from ourselves—that is, if it is a form of symbolically connected, meaningful wholes, patterns, strands, sequences of experience—then the science of analysis has to describe and develop as many comprehensive 'models,' 'frameworks,' 'myths' (metaphors) as are practically useful and theoretically consistent, coherent, and integrated" (Wurmser, 1977, p. 493). Today I would add: in these theoretical endeavors at explanation, metaphoric systems that center on conflict and related concepts have to assume a privileged position.

The trivial definition of metaphor is "a word *substituted* for another on account of the resemblance or analogy between their significations" (Whately, cited in Black, 1962). The one Aristotle uses is more specific and is based on the etymology of *metaphora* = transference (Wurmser, 1977): "Metaphor is the application of a strange term either transferred from the genus and applied to the species (*epiphora ... apo tou genous epi eidos*) or from the species and applied to the genus, or from one species to another or else by analogy (*kata to analogon*)" (*Poetics*, 21.7; 1457 b; Aristotle, 1927, p. 80). According to Black it is a contracted comparison (1962, p. 36). As third Black suggests the "interaction view": "In the simplest formulation, when we use a metaphor we have two thoughts of different things active together and supported by a single word, or phrase, whose meaning is a resultant of their interaction" (Richards, cited in Black 1962, S.38). He comments: "To speak of the 'interaction' of two thoughts 'active together' (or, again, of their 'interillumination' or 'cooperation') is to *use* a metaphor emphasizing the dynamic aspects of a good reader's response to a nontrivial metaphor" (S.39). "The metaphor selects, emphasizes, suppresses, and organizes features of the principal subject by implying statements about it that normally apply to the subsidiary subject" (Black, S.44 ff.). Metaphor transforms and reorganizes the view. "... the set of literal statements so obtained will not have the same power to inform and enlighten as the original" (p.46).

This idea is deepened by Beardsley (*Encyclopedia of Philosophy*) when he talks about the "verbal-opposition theory": "This theory ... rests upon 1) a distinction between two levels of meaning, and 2.) the principle that metaphor involves essentially a *logical conflict of central meanings*" (Bd.5, S.286).

This inherent difference and, I would add contradictoriness and tension, is implied, but not made explicit when Modell (1997a, p. 106) defines metaphor as "the mapping of one conceptual domain onto a dissimilar conceptual domain ... resulting in a transfer of meaning from one to the other" (quoted by Bornstein & Becker, this volume). Similarly, the latter authors describe the metaphor (metaphorically, in an inevitable circularity) as "the glue that links disparate aspects of human life, over time and across different contexts, enabling us to construct cohesive life narratives that give meaning to past and present experience" (this volume).

In contrast, White (this volume) stresses "the emphasis on collision, tension and opposition over collusion and similarity" in modern metaphor. I understand it similarly when Borbely (issue) writes about "the tension inherent in metaphor which keeps the target away from the source yet at the same time connects source and target."

I would stress the "logical conflict of central meanings" as the nub of my argument. At the end of this essay, in connection with Lao Tzu, I will talk about indirect, i.e., metaphorical presentation of conflict, by using *logical and perceptual contradiction as an indirect presentation of affective conflict*.

Taking this together we conclude that we may see in non-trivial metaphors the result of a conflict of mental contents that usually have a strong emotional significance. If the psychoanalytic method as the study of inner processes focuses above all on seeing their essence as conflict it is evident that metaphor has to be the instrument par excellence to represent conflict. Such symbolization of conflict by metaphor serves a causal understanding of mental processes and is specifically and essentially explanatory.

## "Words Have an Ancestor"[2]—A History of Some Central Metaphors

I would like to suggest that the search for common grounds for our divergent perspectives may be considerably helped if we study the metaphors that have been central throughout history for the understanding of the mind, most specifically those for conflict and its opposite: harmony.

## *Fitting Together What is Broken*

Metaphor is a special form of symbol; metaphoric processes are paramount forms of symbolic processes. But there is an inevitable circularity involved: when we talk about this we can only do so by employing metaphors as well, faded, even unconsciously deployed metaphors to be sure, but metaphors and metaphoric processes nevertheless. Etymology is largely a study of the emerging and development of metaphors.

The next question is then: What is the original metaphor standing behind "symbol"? It has a fascinating history in both world cultures, the Western and the Eastern.

The Greek word "*symbolon*" is derived from the verb "*symballein*" "to throw together." Its original meaning is that of sign, of a contract, in particular the sign by which old friends, guest and host, recognize each other. This sign consisted of a little tablet or a ring which had been broken in two at the time of farewell. Now, at the reencounter, these two pieces should fit together (Benseler-Kägi, 1931; Tzermias, 1976). Thus the "symbol" fits together two disparate realities: things and significance, concrete and what we call abstract.

It is fascinating to observe that something parallel happened in China: The ideogram for minister, Qíng, is derived from the sign for *qīng*, the image of a piece of wood or jade that had been broken in two. Here the two separate pieces have to signify and verify charge and honor: "In ancient times the Emperor, when investing the feudatories or officials, handed over to them one half of a piece of wood or of jade diversely cut out; the other half was used to make the proof, as the modern counterfoil. The two pieces gathered are the , *qīng*... When they appeared before the Emperor, or when they held the functions of their office, the feudatories or officials had this kind of scepter in their hands. It was used also as a seal" (Wieger, 1927, S.147). Astonishingly, even the modern word for symbol, *Fúhào*, uses another ideogram for the verification in front of emperor or king by such a fitting correspondence of pieces of bamboo, jade or bronze.

To return to the Greek, in Aeschylos' *Agamemnon* the fiery message of Troy's fall transmitted from mountain top to mountain top is called "proof and symbol— *tekmar ... symbolon te.*" Here the word already has our meaning: the fire has only one signification, the one that had been previously agreed upon.

On the other side we find in Plato's *Symposium* the original use in the famous myth of Eros: Zeus had cut apart the previously complete human being: "So ancient is the desire of another which is implanted in us, reuniting our original nature; making one of two, and healing the state of man. Each of us when separated, having one side only, like a flat fish, is but the indenture of man (*anthropou symbolon*), and he is always looking for his other half" (Plato, p. 158).

Just like in Chinese magical Taoism, "*symbola*" can also in Greece be used in a mythical religious sense: In the orphic tradition about the mysteries of Dionysos the story goes that the god as child was lured away by the titans with the help of such *symbola*, in particular by a mirror, then torn to pieces by them, buried or resurrected. Therefore, the mirror became the symbol for his death, to a mythically powerful, paradoxically valued, sacred object because it also meant transmigration of the soul and liberation. It became a symbol for spiritual resurrection and fulfillment (Guépin, 1968, pp. 241–251). It reappears in the mirror image of Narkissos and in our newer narcissism theories (Kohut, 1971).

> Whereas in allegory something that can be represented is replaced by something else that is expressed, in the mystical symbol something that can be presented stands for another reality that is removed from the world of presentation and expression ... A hidden life that has no expression finds it in the symbol. Symbol is sign, but more than sign.
>
> (Scholem, 1957, p. 29)

### *"Fight, But Do Not Sin"—Conflict in the Western Tradition*

The view of inner life as conflict is one that is, among others, intrinsic to the Western intellectual tradition. We find prototypes for it already in the Homeric epics: In the *Odyssey*, when Odysseus is about to stab the Cyclops Polyphemos, he stopped: "The second mind [thought] stopped me (*heteros de me thymos eryken* 9.302)," the recognition of their own inability to remove the giant boulder from the entrance. And then there is the beautiful passage in the Iliad, 11. 402 ff: Left alone by the other Greeks in the middle of battle, Odysseus "spoke to his own greathearted spirit (*eipe pros hon megalétora thymon*): 'Ah me, what will become of me? It will be a great evil if I run, fearing their multitude, yet deadlier if I am caught alone; and Kronos' son drove to flight the rest of the Danaans. Yet still, why does the heart [mind] within me debate on these things (*alla tie moi tauta philos dieléxato thymos*)? Since I know that it is the cowards who walk out of the fighting, but if one is to win honor in battle, he must by all means stand his ground strongly, whether he be struck or strike down another.'" (trans. Lattimore; cf. also Dodds, 1951/1968, pp. 16, 25, also for additional examples).

Ancient Greek tragedy revolves around the pivot of the tragic choice—the necessity to decide between the opposing commitments to two enormously important values, ideals, loyalties. Many symbols or metaphors in Greek tragedy reflect this consciousness of inner conflict—e.g., the "blue clashing rocks" or *Symplegades* of Euripides' *Medea*, the repeated use of the term *diphrontis*, "of two minds" in the *Libation Bearers* of Aischylos and in the *Hippolytos* of Euripides (I have gone into this in more detail elsewhere; see Wurmser 1981, 1989). It appears to refer with particular poignancy to what I have referred to as the shameguiltdilemma. Yet more generally, these presentations of the fatal consequences of tragic choice refer to the unresolvability of such basic, existential conflicts of conscience, i.e., that in this absolutely, extremely posed form, as it is put to the protagonists and lived out by them, it never can be resolved once and for all, that there cannot be a final, right, perfect solution, but that only the "measure" represented by the Chorus, the "moderation," the acceptance of *both* parts of conflict, and with that of the paradox inherent in human life, is compatible with the survival of individual

46

and society, of the culture and its ideals (the Gods). This "measure" however entails the insight of "wisdom" that the opposite parts of inner conflict complement each other, i.e., that the understanding of inner life as conflict has to encompass the reconciliation of the hitherto clashing forces—the drives, emotions, values, loyalties—in the form of *complementarity*. I believe it is this that Anton Kris (1984, 1985, 1986, 1987) has recently presented in the duality of convergent and divergent conflict (cf. also Rangell, 1963).

The consciousness of inner conflict accompanies Western thought and creativity throughout its history and with that the guiding metaphors for self-understanding. Speaking in the *Phaidros* of "the soul being like the combined force of the winged pair of horses and the charioteer," Plato describes how "the bad horse pulls the chariot down" and then adds: "And then there is pain (*ponos*) and extreme conflict (*agon eschatos*) inflicted upon the soul" (246/247).

In the *Talmud* we hear: "A man should always incite the good impulse to fight against the evil impulse (*le'olam yargiz adam jetzer tov al yetzer hara*). For it is written: Fight, but do not sin (*rigezu we'al techeta'u* [Ps. 4.5]). If they overcome it, fine! If not, they should study the Torah. For it is written: Speak with your hearts (*imru bilvavchem*)" (*Berakot*, 5a). Seeing a man and a woman part without engaging in anything forbidden, Abaye who had followed them, said: "'If it were I, I could not have restrained myself,' and so went and leaned in deep anguish against a doorpost, when a certain old man came up to him and taught him: The greater the man, the greater his Evil Inclination (*Kol hagadol mechavero, yitzro gadol hemennu*)" (*Sukkah*, 52a).

Before our modern age, however, such inner conflict has been, to my knowledge, nowhere more keenly expressed and reflected upon than by Augustinus in the *Confessiones*, even in its unconscious dimensions and with the very concept (metaphor) of conflict at its center: "So stood two wills of mine in conflict with each other, one old, the other new, one carnal, the other spiritual, and in their discord they wasted out my mind. *Ita duae voluntates meae, una vetus, alia nova, illa carnalis, illa spiritalis, confligebant inter se, atque discordando dissipabant animam meam* (8.5)."

"This was the controversy I felt in my heart, about nothing but myself, against myself. *Ista controversia in corde meo non nisi de me ipso adversus me ipsum*" (8.11). Here it is even the very word underlying "conflict," namely the verb "*confligere*": "clashing together, crashing, fighting."

"... it was myself who willed it, and myself who nilled it; it was I myself. I neither willed entirely, nor yet nilled entirely. Therefore was I at strife with myself, and distracted by mine own self (*Ideo mecum contendebam et dissipar a me ipso*)" (8.10). And crucially he immediately adds that there are many such inner conflicts: "For if there be so many contrary natures in man, as there be wills resisting one another; there shall not now be two natures alone, but many. *Nam si tot sunt contrariae naturae, quot voluntates sibi resistunt, non iam duae, sed plures erunt*" (ibid.). There is a multiplicity of inner conflicts which tear apart the will and hence the consciousness of the self.

He even commented upon the complementarity between these opposite parts of his self: "Hence it is that there be two wills, for that one of them is not entire: and the one is supplied with that, wherein the other lacks. *Et ideo sunt duae voluntates, quia una earum tota non est, et hoc adest alteri, quod deest alteri"* (8.9).

He gives an etiology for such an inherent inner discord—for the existential nature of man's conflict—in the *Civitas Dei*: God commanded Adam and Eve obedience because the fulfillment of their own will in opposition to that of their Creator's is destruction (14.12). It was a fitting punishment for their own disobedience that they suddenly were compelled to notice the disobedience of their own genitals, and with that the disobedience of their desires, the lack of control over their bodies; all mental activity, all reasoning becomes overrun (14.16), the entire human being is being totally taken by it. And on the other side this pleasure cannot be willed and compelled, even if one so decides and desires it (14.16). This powerlessness, this loss of control in the face of the overpowering force of the sexual parts necessarily fills man with shame, even if the sexual act is permitted and specifically engaged in for the procreation of children; even in front of one's own children it therefore has to be treated with secrecy (14.18).

In these excerpts the conflict is sharply delineated: the primary concern is the conflict between the sexual desires (and member) and the will led by reason and with that by Godly command. The loss of control over these desires and their executive organs is inherently a cause for shame. Yet this loss of control is in itself already the punishment for a deeper, prior conflict: the conflict between the wish to follow one's own will and the obedient submission under God's command. The first conflict is a shame conflict, the second, deeper and antecedent conflict is one leading to guilt, a guilt to be punished by that loss of control. The assertion of power and independence (*potestas voluntatis*) is by itself evil; it leads to the secondary evil, "the punishment" by the omnipotence of lust.

Looking back to the Talmudic sources, we see the same doubleness, although not as sharply divided: whenever there is talk about the *Yetzer haRa'*—the Evil Inclination—it always refers to sexual desire and lust; but this lust also is always equated with rebellion against God.

Yet farther back, in Platon, the negative part of human nature that pulls the soul perniciously "down" and "apart" is sensuality altogether—the attachment to the body and its desires—against the autonomous power of Reason and with that against the "vision" of the ideas.

The Augustinean view came to dominate the value system of the Western world for about one millennium: Sexual lust was the Evil par excellence, prideful assertion of will power, even in the service of Reason, ran a close second. The power of the faith in this value hierarchy is not completely broken even today.

It was Goethe who took up the concept of "inner conflict" as an explanatory metaphor when he described 1815 how Shakespeare puts in the foreground "the inner conflict" between "*Sollen*" and "*Wollen*," between what man ought to do and what he wants to do.[3] This inner conflict converges with an external one, "a wanting that goes beyond what the individual is able to, is modern"[4] (Goethe, 1961).

## *The question of conflict and complementarity in Confucius (Kong Tzu) and Lao Tzu*

What do we find in the other great and continuous tradition of thought—the Chinese world, as exemplified by these two leading thinkers (both were said to have lived around 500BCE although there is much controversy about the time of Lao Tzu)? There are a number of leading metaphors in opposition to each other that dominate the ethical, political, and metaphysical debates, centering around balance, harmony, the right path (*dao*), the uncarved block, the great flow versus strife, disorder, doubt, what we would also call conflict.

"Harmony was seen as the great norm of both the natural and social worlds; Confucianism and Taoism were equally philosophies of balance, whether man's counterpoise was society or the natural cosmos. Imbalance would have meant man against man, man against nature, in either case a separation between the self and the 'other.' But Confucianism and Taoism, each in its way, meant union, oneness, the concord and stasis of the eternal pattern" (Levenson & Schurmann, 1969, p. 113). "Conflict between Confucianism and Taoism was abortive, a) because they had a common theme, harmony, and b) because that common theme, harmony, implied a philosophical deprecation of conflict" (ibid., p. 116).

"By now it should be evident that basic among Chinese thought patterns is the desire to merge seemingly conflicting elements into a unified harmony. Chinese philosophy is filled with dualisms in which, however, their two component elements are usually regarded as *complementary and mutually necessary rather than as hostile and incompatible*. A common feature of Chinese dualisms, furthermore, is that one of their two elements should be held in higher regard than the other. Here again, therefore, we have an expression of the concept of harmony based upon hierarchical difference, such as we have already seen in the Chinese view of society" (Bodde, 1953, p. 54).

This does of course not imply that there is no awareness of conflict or that there is a relative absence of social, historical or psychological conflict. Rather it appears that there is an overriding concern to shift the focus of attention away from conflict, to the point of denying its emotional relevance. Why Chinese culture and tradition, in spite of its inner orientation, its greatly creative and expressive inwardness, seems so peculiarly inimical to psychoanalysis may very well lie in this deep and abiding antipathy to inner conflict. This means also a different approach to ethical and psychological choice.

In discussing this issue, Fingarette (*Confucius—The Secular as Sacred*, 1972, p. 22) refers to two passages in the *Lun Yü*, the "book of the discussions (or sayings)" of Kung Tse (KongFuZi, Confucius): "You love a man and wish him to live; you hate him and wish him to die. Having wished him to live, you also wish him to die. This is doubt" (*huo*—Legge: "delusion"; 12.10). "For a morning's anger to disregard one's own life, and involve that of his parents—is not this a case of doubt (delusion, *huo*)" (2.21). "In such conflict, the task is not posed as one of *choosing* or *deciding* but of distuinguishing or discriminating (*bian*) the inconsistent inclinations. Furthermore, in each passage, we have no doubt about which inclination is the right one when we have discriminated one from the other. In short, the task is posed in terms of knowledge rather than choice. *Huo*, the key term in the passages, means here 'deluded or *led astray* by an un*li* inclination or tendency.' It is not doubt as to which to choose to do" (pp. 22–23).

I interject here that the decisive word *huo* which does not appear rarely in both Confucius and Lao Tse is usually translated as "doubt, suspicion, deception." Yet as a symbol it is composed of *huo* and *xin* . *Huo* means "either, or, if," *xin* is "heart, mind," the common radical associated with any emotional, or generally mental processes. The *huo* used in this context can therefore etymologically be rendered as the "Either of the Mind," the "Or of the Mind." Fingarette is right that hardly anywhere is there an explicit formulation of inner conflict, and yet, it seems to me that the repeatedly emerging "doubt," *huo*, is something like a symbol for suppressed, hidden, veiled conflict.

This means, Fingarette continues, that "we must recognize at once that the absence of a developed language of choice and responsibility does not imply a failure to choose or to be responsible ... the task is posed in terms of knowledge rather than choice ... This Confucian commitment to a single, definite order is also evident when we note what Confucius sees as the alternative to rightly treading the true Path: it is to walk crookedly, to get lost or to abandon the Path ... it is the following of the Way itself that is of ultimate and absolute value ... The imagery in the *Analects* [*Lun Yü*] is dominated by the metaphor of traveling the road" (pp. 18–22).

He then refers to a passage which "seems ... to present a situation where the issue, as we would define it, is one of internal conflict in the moral code, a conflict to be resolved by personal choice." I quote from Legge's translation, adding some modifiers: "The duke of She informed Confucius, saying: 'Among us here are those who may be styled (*gong*, meaning personally, self, own; I think this is what Legge translates as styled; Fingarette takes this word as a proper name Gong [Kung]) upright (*zhi*) in their conduct. If their fathers have stolen a sheep, they will bear witness to the fact.' Confucius said: 'Among us, in our part of the country, those who are upright are different from this. The father conceals the misconduct of the son, and the son conceals the misconduct of the father. Uprightness is to be found in this'" (13.18).

It is the conflict between the value of *Xiao*, the loyalty and reverential commitment, the *pietas* (*Pietät*) towards the parents, versus the value of *Zhi*, honesty, sincerity, uprightness, straightforwardness (the very sign symbolizes "straightness"). Here two deep commitments stand in irreconcilable conflict. Fingarette comments:

> When two profound duties conflict, *we* must choose. And it is in this necessity to make a critical choice that lies the seed of tragedy, of responsibility, of guilt and remorse. ... Confucius merely announces the way *he* sees the matter, putting it tactfully by saying it is the custom in *Li*.[5] There is nothing to suggest a decisional problem; everything suggests that there is a defect of knowledge, a simple error of moral judgment on the Duke's part ... when we take into

account Confucius's stature as a moralist and his insightfulness into human nature, his failure to see or to mention the problem of internal moral conflict in such a case as this can only be accounted for by supposing that his interests, ideas, concerns, in short his entire moral and intellectual orientation, was in another direction.

(1972, p. 23 f.)

Zai Yü being asleep during the daytime, the Master said: 'Rotten wood cannot be carved; a wall of earth and dung cannot be covered with the trowel. This Yü! What is the use of reproving him?!' The Master said: 'At first, my way with men was to hear their words, and give them credit for their conduct. Now my way is to hear their words, and look at their conduct. It is from Yü that I have learned to make this change' (5: 9).

"Here the active disease, the fulminating wound of Augustine, is replaced by a state of mere deadness, of passivity and inherent insensitivity to moral values," comments Fingarette (p. 31). "The proper response to a failure to conform to the moral order (*li*) is not selfcondemnation for a free and responsible, though evil, choice, but selfreeducation to overcome a mere defect, a lack of power, in short a lack in one's 'formation.' The Westerner's inclination to press at this point the issue of personal responsibility for lack of diligence is precisely the sort of issue that is never even raised in the Analects" (p. 35). "Confucius's vision provides no basis for seeing man as a being of tragedy, of inner crisis and guilt; but it does provide a socially oriented, actionoriented view which provides for personal dignity. Moreover ... we see then that the images of the inner man and of his inner conflict are not essential to a concept of man as a being whose dignity is the consummation of a life of subtlety and sophistication, a life in which human conduct can be intelligible in natural terms and yet be attuned to the sacred, a life in which the practical, the intellectual and the spiritual are equally revered and are harmonized in the one act—the act of *li*" (p. 36). For Confucius man is not tragic since he is not determined by the inner crisis of choice, decision and guilt, but oriented towards action and towards the concentric circles of obligations surrounding him.

The center of gravity has entirely shifted away from the metaphors for what we would, analytically speaking, describe as the *choosing and deciding ego and to the absolutely (unconditionally) certain and commanding superego*. The side of the drives (*yü*) is not often mentioned; they have to yield to the dictates of conscience. Since the ego itself is the site of inner conflict, its complete subordination under the inner authority of conscience amounts to a kind of *invalidation of inner conflict*.

This statement is predicated on the a priori assumption, as a basic vision of existence, that inner conflict is indeed an indispensable part of human nature. It is both a philosophical premise of vision (i.e., a metaphorical system) and a methodological premise of exploration of man's nature—neither provable, nor refutable—not merely of the psychoanalytic understanding of human nature, but of the Western understanding of Man in general.

51

Now just a few references from the other great thinker who shaped Chinese culture for over two thousand years, Lao Tzu ("the Old Master" or "the Old Child").

"Nothing in the world is softer and more supple than water, yet when attacking the hard and the strong, nothing can surpass it. The supple overcomes the hard. The soft overcomes the strong. None in the world do not know this, yet none can practice it. That is why the Sage says: To accept the filth of a nation is to be lord of the society.[6] To accept the disasters (the ill omens) of a nation (country) is to be the ruler of the world.[7] Words of truth seem contradictory"[8] (trans. Tam C. Gibbs and alternate interpretations, where indicated; Ch. 78). This last sentence is: "*Zheng yan ruo fan*—*Zheng*: Straight or regular or correct—*yan*: words or speech—*ruo*: is as, follows—*fan*: to turn back, contrary, opposite, to rebel." I would paraphrase it: "The direct talk also has the opposite meaning, turns into its opposite." The outer references, like water, dirt of the country, ruler, appear like metaphors for the inner truth: that our inner life incessantly moves in contraries, in opposites.

"Words have an ancestor; actions have a lord" (Ch. 70). There is a past to one's thought; there is a context that gives it the meaning; "If they don't know this, they cannot understand me." The first reminds us of the basic premise of our genetic understanding; the latter of the coherence theory of truth; the first of Freud, the latter of Wittgenstein and of the criterion for truth stressed precisely by Freud over that by correspondence and by pragmatism.

Of special beauty is the 11th chapter (I quote from Waley's translation): "We put thirty spokes together and call it a wheel; but it is on the space where there is nothing that the usefulness of the wheel depends. We turn clay to make a vessel; but it is on the space where there is nothing that the usefulness of the vessel depends. We pierce doors and windows to make a house; and it is on these spaces where there is nothing that the usefulness of the house depends. Therefore, just as we take advantage of what is, we should recognize the usefulness of what is not." What Waley circumscribes as "the space where there is nothing," the Chinese has "*wu you*—not having, nonbeing"; the object is visible and concrete, yet its function *dang qi ... yong* depends on the absence, the void, the No, the "There is not." Is this No not also the No to consciousness, the No inherent in all defense? Are not these expressions very beautiful metaphors for the inner life we deal with in our work—clearly, metaphors of a very different kind from those we use in our theory formation, yet nevertheless metaphors that should bridge the visible world of the Yes with the invisible, but far more powerful world of the No—the *Wu* or *Wu you* or *Wu ming* or *Wu wei* (No, nonbeing, nameless, no action)?

Just as the emptiness gives the objects their ability to function, so does the silence give to the mind and to the spoken words the dimension of depth. The *Tao Te King* itself is indeed like a finely woven, and yet mighty structure built of spare words and much silence. The contradictions open up abysses of meaning.[9]

Yet what is the central concern?

"'To remain whole, be twisted (Chan: yield)!' To become straight, let yourself be bent. To become whole, be hollow. Be tattered, that you may be renewed. Those that have little, may get more. Those that have much, are but perplexed (*huo*, see above, the 'Either-Or of the heart or mind'). Therefore the Sage clasps the Primal Unity (Chan: the sage embraces the One), testing by it everything under Heaven (Chan: and becomes the model of the world). He does not show himself; therefore he is seen everywhere. He does not define himself, therefore he is distinct. He does not boast of what he will do, therefore he succeeds. He is not proud of his work (loves himself), and therefore he endures. He does not contend (*bu zheng*). And for that very reason no one under heaven can contend with him (Chan: It is precisely because he does not compete that the world cannot compete with him). So then we see that the ancient saying: 'To remain whole be twisted!' (Chan: 'To yield is to be preserved whole') was no idle word; for true wholeness can only be achieved by return (*gui* = home coming)" (Ch. 22, trans. Waley).

Here again, the contraries are seen as part of an overarching unity; the aim of the wise person (*sheng ren*) lies in overcoming what is in conflict—of what "competes," *zheng*. The most expressive formulation, however, comes right at the beginning of the *Tao Te King* (Ch. 2). I follow Chan WingTsit's translation: "When the people of the world all know beauty as beauty, there arises the recognition of ugliness. When they all know the good as good, there arises the recognition of evil. Therefore: *Being and nonbeing produce each other* (*you wu xiang sheng*); *difficult and easy complete each other*; long and short contrast (*jiao* or, alternately, *xing* compare; Waley: test) each other; high and low distinguish each other; sound and voice harmonize each other; front and behind accompany each other. Therefore, the sage manages affairs without action (*wu wei zhi shi*), and spreads doctrines without words. All things arise, and he does not turn away from them. He produces them but does not take possession of them (Gibbs: [Nature] gives birth but does not possess). He acts but does not rely on his own ability (Gibbs: It acts but does not demand subservience). He accomplishes his task but does not claim credit for it. It is precisely because he does not claim credit that his accomplishment remains with him." The first four of the six pairs of contraries are rendered by Gibbs as follows: "Is and is not are mutually arising; difficult and easy are complementary; long and short arise from comparison; higher and lower are interdependent." The accompanying commentary by ManJan Cheng calls the pairs *mutual functions, reciprocity: hu xiang*, and speaks of the *paradox of the mutual support of opposites: xiang fan xiang cheng*. In all of the six pairs the third of the fourth words is *xiang*, "mutual," translated here as "each other." Waley comments: "But, says the Taoist, by admitting the conception of 'goodness,' you are simultaneously creating a conception 'badness.' Nothing can be good except in relation to something that is bad, just as nothing can be 'in front' except in relation to something that is 'behind.' Therefore, the Sage avoids all positive action, working only through the 'power' of Tao, which alone 'cuts without wounding' *transcending all antinomies*."

Though there is no special word about or for *inner conflict*, there is thus the clear awareness of the centrality of opposites, of contradiction, and the insistence to overcome, as we would say, conflict by recognizing complementarity. SiMa Qian speaks of the *unity of spirit* as being advocated by the Taoist school (Ch. 130, quoted by Fung YuLan, 1931/1934, p. 170). We would say in our theoretical framework that there is a consistent transcendence of conflict in favor of the synthetic function of the ego that attempts to reconcile all the opposites within and without, as well as between inwardness and outside world, while letting the paradoxes stand—"the mysterious leveling" (*yüan tong*, Ch. 56, trans. Waley): "The Sage 'discards the absolute, the allinclusive, the extreme'" (Ch. 29, trans. Waley) "It is percisely because he does not compete (*bu zheng*, lit.: 'no conflict') that the world cannot compete with him" (Ch. 66, trans. Chan; cf. also 68, 72, 73, 77, 78, 81). The very last sentence of the *Tao Te King* is, I believe not coincidentally: "The Way of the sage is to act but not to compete—*Sheng ren zhi Dao—wei er bu zheng.*"

If we assume now in all these references that *zheng* does not merely refer to outer conflict in the meaning of "competition," but that it expresses, with the consistent equation of inwardness and outwardness, equally inner conflict, then we can conclude that one of the major aims of Lao Tse is the overcoming of all conflict, inner and outer, in favor of a great unity (e.g., "embracing the one," *bao yi*) or synthesis. It is what is called in Ch. 68 *bu zheng zhi Dé*—the power of no conflict (Chan: the virtue of noncompeting, Gibbs: the Teh of noncontention, Waley: the power that comes of not contending).

Instead of the social virtues of Kong Fu Zi to deal with inner and outer conflict, Lao Tzu postulates something that appears to be radically different: "Banish learning, and there will be no more grieving" (Ch. 20, trans. Waley). In the place of these societal concerns, of the loyalty towards outer norms now internalized, there is the loyalty to what Waley translates as the Uncarved Block, *bo*, to an inner truth (*chang*, the "constant"), to spontaneity (*ZiRan*, the "SelfSo") and creativity (*sheng*, "life, birth") beyond all contraries, transcending all strife (*zheng*). Putting it positively, he speaks of the "three treasures: the first is deep love, the second is frugality, and the third is not to dare to be ahead of the world" (Ch. 67, trans. Chan).

Most explicitly the Confucian virtues appear to be disavowed in Ch. 19 (Chan trans.): "Abandon sageliness and discard wisdom; then the people will benefit a hundredfold. Abandon humanity (better: human solidarity) and discard righteousness; then the people will return to filial piety and deep love. Abandon skill and discard profit; then there will be no thieves or robbers. However, these three things are ornaments and are not adequate. Therefore, let people hold on to these: manifest plainness, embrace simplicity, reduce selfishness, have few desires." Waley suggests for the latter portion: "If without these three things they find life too plain and unadorned, then let them have accessories; give them Simplicity ['raw silk'] to look at, the Uncarved Block to hold, give them selflessness and fewness of desires." Gibbs translates: "I believe these three statements show that words are inadequate. The people should be made to adhere to these principles: 'Look to the origins and maintain purity; diminish self and curb desires.'"

I think all these translations struggle to approximate the original's interweaving of inward and outward, its deft, yet bewildering use of metaphors bridging both worlds, e.g., in the concluding sentence: "Diminish 'self,' make desires scarce" involves the symbol for self, *si*. It is derived from *si*: "a cocoon. It represents a silkworm that coils itself up and shuts itself in its cocoon. By extension, selfish, to care only for one's self, separation, private, particular." The compound used means: "my share of grains. By extension, private, personal, partial, selfish" (Wieger, p. 224).

For this kind of emphasis on the synthetic ego function—especially in the sense of bridging resolutely the gap between inner world and outer world in spite of their disparate laws—learning and reeducation, in the sense of Kong Zi, can evidently not be as desirable, as a complete retreat from the entanglements in *zheng*, in conflict, would be. Instead of dealing with conflict by subordinating oneself entirely to a superego modeled after the magical power of the SageKings of hoary antiquity and their impersonal representatives in the shape of rules and forms (*li*), Lao Tzu suggests a much more determined withdrawal from choice, decision, will, wish, and action, especially, however, from all ambition and competition, in behalf of an ideal of the unity of opposites and of the power of yielding to "the spontaneous Becoming" (*ZiRan*, often now translated as Nature)—a "passivity," very akin to what I alluded to before as the stance of the analyst. It is very much a "feminine superego," even far more pronouncedly so as the Confucian superego (which, after all, also suggests submission, renunciation of self and of competition): "The good use of people is by putting oneself below" (Ch. 68, my translation). "The female always overcomes the male by tranquility, and by tranquility she is underneath ... Thus some, by placing themselves below, take over (others), and some, by being (naturally) low, take over (other states)" (Ch. 61, trans. Chan). "Therefore 'the weapon that is too hard will be broken, the tree that has the hardest wood will be cut down.' Truly, the hard and mighty are cast down; the soft and weak set high" (Ch. 76, trans. Waley). "The original power (*yüan Dé*) is so deep, so distant; it makes things so paradoxical (*fan*). Thus one goes back until one reaches the Great Flow (*Da Shun*)" (end of Ch. 65, my translation).

One removes conflict by undoing knowledge and desire; yet therewith something else is veiled: Culture and society are themselves expression of human nature, conflict itself is human nature, an indispensable basis of the *conditio humana*. It is the same dilemma as the one later on faced by Rousseau. That unity is only attained at the cost of denying such conflict. With social and cultural reality, with knowledge and social virtues, an entire part of the inner world is bypassed too—the fidelity to the need to know[10] and to curiosity, the deep need for activity and symbolization—all in favor of that overriding longing for synthesis. In our frame of reference, in our metaphorical system: the executive side of the ego—the deciding and distinguishing function—is sacrificed at the behest of the synthetic side. With that the attempt at synthesis appears to be itself subverted, undermined." If one desires to be in front of the people, one must speak as if behind them" (Ch. 66, trans. Gibbs). Yet can this be done without deception? Does not thus the very split to be avoided recur, the conflict reemerge as inner and tragic reality, as outer isolation and estrangement?

Wildly, endlessly, all men are merry, as though feasting upon beef or sitting on the veranda in the spring sunshine. I alone remain uncommitted, like an infant who has not yet smiled. I alone seem as mindless as one who has no home to return to. Everyone else has enough and more, yet I alone seem to be left with nothing. What a fool's mind I have! How muddled I am! Most people seek brightness and clarity. I alone seek dullness and darkness. Most people are imaginative and observant. I alone am stifled and mum; I am as unmoved as the ocean, as ceaseless as the wind high in the sky. Everyone else has something to do; I alone am ignorant and dull. I alone am different from the rest in that I value taking sustenance from the Mother.

(Ch. 20, trans. Gibbs)

In contrast to this supreme identification with the Maternal as ideal in Lao Tzu we have the equally strenuous identification with the idealized Paternal in Confucius— yet both in the service to avoid any power struggle and competition, be that of an anal or oedipalphallic nature. Clearly, however, the *Tao Te King* is by no means a pamphlet dedicated to the overthrow of the superego altogether. Rather it is, as I would postulate, *the overcoming of an archaic, mostly "anal" superego in favor of the positing of a new ideal.* It is a revolutionary superego, a protest against a value system that at least for us has become associated with Confucius. It is a superego that aspires to reach back to the "origin" (*yüan*), a superego living from a new vision, a very different metaphorical system. There is, as already noted, clearly a radical shift in valuation, compared with the Confucian ethos, regardless if Lao Tzu preceded Confucius, as the tradition presumed, or followed him by centuries, as is assumed by many today—a shift without requirements of faith, without a belief in a divinity in any customary sense, yet a deep spirit of reverence, a kind of "philosophical belief"— using a wonderful spectrum of metaphors without the fixation into any dogma.

What does that new vision entail? The great connectedness of life is seen, the advice given that the encompassing cohesiveness of what we know never be lost. Purposive and ambitious doing interferes with such knowing of the whole context of Being. All forms of external power destroy such awareness and should be avoided. It is a grand vision of existence that treats all the external entities—realm, war, ruler, plants, and animals—as metaphorical help to formulate such inner truth. The most important, however, of all the insights of such an inwardness is that of *mutually conditioning* attributes and actions, instead of the *absoluteness* of any one thing, subject or object, its EitherOr. Nothing that is being put into words can claim unconditional truth:

There was something undifferentiated and yet complete, which existed before heaven and earth. Soundless and formless, it depends on nothing and does not change. It operates everywhere and is free from danger. It may be considered the mother of the universe. I do not know its name; I call it *Dao* (Way). If forced to give it a name, I shall call it great. Now being great means functioning everywhere. Functioning everywhere means farreaching. Being farreaching means returning to the original point. Therefore *Dao* is great. Heaven is great. Earth is great. Man is also great. There are four great things in the universe, and man is one of them. Man models himself after Earth. Earth models itself after Heaven. Heaven models itself after *Dao*. And *Dao* models itself after Nature.

(ZiRan, Waley: the "SelfSo"; Ch. 25, trans. Chan;<br>except that I follow the reading "Man" ren, not "king")

Still the most fascinating question remains: What about the seeming merging of opposites, that what has been called *fan yan*, the speaking in paradoxes—that big is small, small is big, full is empty, old is new, strong is weak, weak is strong? How can that be understood?

The immediate response is: Speaking and knowing are impotent. It seems to imply an advocacy of a return to the preverbal, to the all encompassing and global affects. Then we think of such "absurd" reversals in dreams, that may imply: "This is incredible, ridiculous!"

What does it entail? I believe it expresses a deep doubt on the perception of reality and on the validity of everyday logic. Thus, by its very movement from one opposite to the other, it gives metaphorical expression to the profound quandary: What is truth?

And yet it goes deeper still: This is the language of the soul, the discourse of the inner world where we discover layer upon layer, where we can tear off mask behind mask. It represents the depth dimension of inner reality. This is its hallmark, in Dickens' expression: "... things are not always as they seem ..." (*Our Mutual Friend*, 1971, p. 321) and "But seeming may be false or true" (*The Mystery of Edwin Drood*, 1961, p. 262). The layering is laced with anxiety, it is a layering of defenses and of dangers.

Could it therefore be that we deal here, in the *fan yan*, with an indirect presentation of conflict, in the sense of using logical and perceptual contradiction, as an indirect presentation of affective conflict—in our terms: of intrasystemic and intersystemic conflict (whereby it is, I would think, mostly the former)?

It is evident that in the *Tao Te King* metaphysics, ethics and politics are united, even amalgamated (Jaspers); but it is also clear how everything points back to the one central and original issue: that of the insight in the inner reality, of its manylayeredness and multiplicity of meaning, of its contradictoriness, and, ultimately and inevitably, of its roots in conflict and complementarity. However, at the same time, that insight says: Inner and outer truth manifest each other in mutually reflecting mirrors. Therefore its discourse has to be eminently metaphorical: truth can only be approached with the help of images; it cannot be "grasped" and "held." Proceeding, it has to be "cautious like crossing a frozen stream in the winter—majestic in appearance—yielding, like ice on the verge of melting ..." (Ch. 15).

## Notes

1 Originally published in *Psychoanalytic Inquiry* 31(2): pp.107–125 under the title "Metaphor as Conflict, Conflict as Metaphor."

2  Lao Tzu, Ch. 70.
3  "Die Person, von der Seite des Charakters betrachtet, soll: sie ist beschränkt, zu einem Besonderen bestimmt; als Mensch aber will sie. Sie ist unbegrenzt und fordert das Allgemeine. Hier entspringt schon ein innerer Konflikt, und diesen läßt Shakespeare vor allen anderen heraustreten."
4  "ein Wollen, das über die Kräfte eines Individuums hinausgeht, ist modern."
5  *Li* is variably translated as propriety, beauty, holy ritual, sacred ceremony, used as metaphor for "the entire body of *mores,* or more precisely, of the authentic tradition and reasonable conventions of society," as Fingarette defines it, p. 6/7.
6  Better by Waley: Only he who has accepted the dirt of the country can be lord of its soilshrines; Chan WingTsit: He who suffers disgrace for his country is called the lord of the land.
7  Waley: Can become a king among those what dwell under heaven.
8  Waley: Straight words seem crooked [seem, as we would say, to be paradoxes]; Chan WingTsit: Straight words seem to be their opposite.
9  "Diese mannigfachen Gestalten der Gegensätze benutzt nun Laotse, um im Widerschein das Unsagbare sagbar zu machen, das Sein im Nichtsein, das Wissen im Nichtwissen, das Tun im Nichttun" (Jaspers, 1958 p. 926).
10  Aristotle's insight: "All men naturally desire knowledge," the beginning sentence of the *Metaphysics*.

# 6

# METAPHOR, MEANING, AND THE MIND[1]

## *Arnold H. Modell*

Metaphor and metonymy are the primary and crucial cognitive tools of unconscious thought. Acknowledging this function of metaphor and metonymy might provide a unifying bridge between the disparate schools and factions of contemporary psychoanalysis. I suggest that we are more likely to find common ground, both within psychoanalysis and neighboring disciplines, if we view the unconscious mind as the area within which meaning is processed by means of metaphor, rather than the locus of a battleground between repression and instinctual forces.

The [original] title of this chapter refers to a judgment attributed to the quantum physicist Wolfgang Pauli. A friend showed him the paper of a young physicist which he suspected was not of great value but nevertheless wanted Pauli's views. Pauli remarked sadly, "it's not right it's not even wrong." To claim that a scholarly or scientific paper is "not even wrong" suggests that the author and the critic do not share the same conceptual system so that a judgment is not even possible. I'm afraid this can be said of the sorry state of affairs that separate the various "schools" and factions of psychoanalysis at this time. A "classical" Freudian ego psychologist, a Kohutian self psychologist, a Sullivanian interpersonalist and a Lacanian cannot communicate with each other as they do not share in common a set of conceptual assumptions.

Conceptualizing the unconscious in terms of the Freudian instinctual id is unacceptable to most of us and is certainly incompatible with contemporary neuroscience. I will suggest that a revised concept of the Freudian unconscious, where metaphor is the cognitive tool, might be a starting point that will provide some shared basic assumptions. If we can agree on fundamental assumptions perhaps we can begin to talk to each other.

## Why I Am Not an Ego Psychologist

In our field, at the start of our careers, our basic assumptions and beliefs usually follow from our identification with an idealized mentor, hence we describe ourselves as Freudians, Kleinians, Kohutians, Sullivanians, Lacanians, etc. But as we gain clinical experience we should begin to question those assumptions that we have uncritically adopted from our mentors. Although I would still describe myself as a Freudian, I would more specifically claim to be an early Freudian inasmuch as I reject Freud's instinct theory and many aspects of ego psychology, especially the idea of defense mechanisms. Of course I don't reject the idea of defense but I do reject the impersonal concept of mechanism. The machine metaphor is totally incompatible with the highly individualized, self-organizing, self-selecting function that unconsciously chooses a specific mode of defense at any given point in time. What I fully embrace, and identify with, is the Freud of *The Interpretation of Dreams* (1900). As I shall describe, Freud's early concept of the unconscious processing of memory and feeling as illustrated by the formation of dreams is significantly and radically different from the concept of the unconscious that he later elaborated in *The Ego and the Id* (1923a). If we return to Freud's early idea of the unconscious as a meaning making process and not a battle ground between instinctual wishes and those agencies that oppose their expression, we have, I believe, a better chance of finding a common conceptual ground between the various disparate schools that characterize contemporary psychoanalysis.

I believe that ego psychology has proved to be a major divisive force that has separated the various schools of psychoanalysis. Freud's conception of the id has prevented us from viewing "the unconscious" not as that area of the mind in which instinctual forces are held in check by repression, but as that area of the mind concerned with the unconscious processing of meaning.

Not surprisingly, the development of my beliefs and conceptual assumptions were influenced by the impact of my clinical experience. After my graduation from the Boston Psychoanalytic Institute in 1961, I tried to test the limits of the psychoanalytic method by accepting patients for psychoanalysis who were seriously ill such as the so-called borderline case as well as some patients who were diagnosed as schizophrenic. I soon discovered that their relationship to me was central to their treatment and that interpretation of their unconscious thoughts and feelings was not always useful and at times was counterproductive. Such an observation is today self-evident. I would think every clinician knows that with the sicker patient the effect of the therapeutic relationship transcended the result of interpreting unconscious content. But at that time this two-person relational understanding could not be easily integrated into Freud's third person concept of the mind as a mental apparatus. Nor could this two-person relational understanding be reduced to or understood simply under the rubric of transference. We know of course that this gap between clinical observation and Freudian theory was subsequently filled with the emergence of various "relational" and inter-personal schools of psychoanalysis.

To continue with this account of my conceptual development, I discussed this issue of a two-person psychology and its relation to Freudian theory in *Psychoanalysis in New Context* (1984) (Modell, 1984) where I stated: that Freud essentially oscillated between a one person stance, for example, dream interpretation, and a third person "scientific" account of human psychology. In that volume I wrote: (p. 11) "The process that occurs between two people, between the subject and the object in psychoanalysis is referred to the mind of the subject, who is the patient. This produces in us a certain intellectual unease when, for example, we describe dependency, a process occurring between two people, as an event in the mind of one person. Traditional psychoanalysis has not yet acquired theoretical language that would enable it to describe process occurring between two separate personalities in terms encompassing the events in both individuals."

Freud of course was not unaware of a two-person dialogical perspective as such a perspective is implicit in Freud's recognition of the unconscious communication that occurs in transference and in the process of free association. For example in his encyclopedia article Freud (Freud, 1923b) understood free association to be a "means to catch the drift of the patient's unconscious with his own unconscious." But this implicit two-person system could not easily be fit into his instinct theory or his structural ego psychology. Furthermore, Freud thought that the third person perspective, of a "mental apparatus," a concept central to ego psychology, supported psychoanalysis' claim to be a scientific discipline.

To find mentors whose work was consistent with my clinical experience I turned to Winnicott as I did in my 1968 book *Object Love and Reality* (Modell, 1968). There I applied Winnicott's concept of the transitional object to certain aspects of the relationship that one experiences in the treatment of borderline and schizophrenic patients. The concept of the transitional object can be thought of as a conceptual metaphor that is a shared imaginative construction, present in the minds of both parent and child. In a transitional object relationship the person of the analyst is treated as a protective magical agent that is interposed between the individual and one's existence of the world. There is a clear analogy here to the child's creation of the transitional object, where a real object, a blanket or teddy bear is, by means of the imagination, magically transformed. In a broader context this process can be thought of as an interplay between the real and the imagined. The transitional object illustrates the interplay between the real, the actual object, and its transformation by means of metaphor. This interplay reflects the synergy between metonymy and metaphor. The real object, blanket, etc., is a metonymic object, in that the part substitutes for the whole—the whole being the mother. This "real" object is then magically transformed by means of metaphor. This interplay of metaphor and metonymy, the real and the imagined, is a crucial process that determines the unconscious construction of the other person. As this process is not limited to the therapeutic relationship, this can be described as the transference of everyday life. In our imaginative transformation of the other person we invariable respond to actual perceptions, something that is "real." Metaphoric process always requires the "real" of metonymy (Jakobson, 1995). This formulation is consistent with a broader view of the perceptive process, including other species, where a distinction is made between raw sensations and their subsequent interpretation by the unconscious self (Pincus, et al., 2007).

## Reconstructing the Freudian Unconscious in the Light of Neuroscience—Hoping to Find Common Conceptual Ground

Anyone who identifies themselves as a psychoanalyst would, I imagine, unquestionably accept the idea of unconscious determinism. But how unconscious processes are conceptualized is a subject of much discord and disagreement. How one understands unconscious process is linked to several other theoretical controversies. One such controversy is the extent to which one believes that unconscious processes are neuro-biologically determined. Another is the extent to which one believes that unconscious processes are determined by the past unconscious, that is to say, memory, or the extent to which one believes in the importance of the present unconscious that is embedded in the inter-subjectivity of the present moment. As you know there are analytic schools of thought that minimize the importance of the past and therefore the significance of unconscious memory in determining the meaning of current experience. Some claim a certain autonomy for the present moment. I am thinking, for example, of the Boston Change Process Study Group (2008) who seem to have ignored the Freudian concept of unconscious process although they do acknowledge the significance of metaphor. It is not that I deny the importance of the present moment, which I take to be an aspect of the real, but this view omits a consideration of an unconscious metaphoric process that organizes the affective memories of the past through which the present moment interpreted. I will suggest, as I described in *Imagination and the Meaningful Brain* (Modell, 2003) that an unconscious metaphoric process, analogous to dreaming, occurs in the waking state.

It is my belief that Freud went down the wrong path when he reframed human psychology in terms of instinct theory. Originally, in *The Interpretation of Dreams*, Freud (1900) viewed the unconscious as a knowledge processing system that gave metaphoric expression to the unconscious wish. This view of the unconscious was radically altered with Freud's elaboration of instinct theory and the development of ego psychology. This is I believe one of the root causes for the divisions that separate the various schools of contemporary psychoanalysis. Freud never disclaimed his description of unconscious processing in dreaming, but he viewed it as special instance and put it aside when he re-characterized the unconscious, not as an area in which knowledge is processed, but as an area of the mind in which there is a conflict between instincts seeking discharge and the forces of repression that prevent, instinctual derivatives, thoughts, feelings and fantasies, from being from becoming conscious. The primary function of this revised unconscious was not the processing of knowledge but to prevent unacceptable impulses, wishes and fantasies from becoming conscious. In his introduction to his 1915 paper *The Unconscious* Freud (1915b) states that everything that is repressed must remain unconscious, but he also noted that the unconscious has a wider compass, that the repressed is only one part of the unconscious and does not cover everything. But Freud does not say what this part consists of. Freud writes in that paper "the nucleus of the unconscious consists of instinctual representatives which seek to discharge their cathexis; that is to say, it consists of wishful impulses." In his 1915 paper Freud further states that "the content of the unconscious may be compared with aboriginal population of the mind. If inherited the mental formation exists in human beings—something analogous to instincts in animals—these constitute the nucleus of the unconscious" (1915b, p. 186). At the end of his life, when he wrote *An Outline of Psychoanalysis* Freud (1940a) now viewed unconscious process not as potentially adaptive but as a danger to the self. The id was seen as the ego's internal enemy he said: "[I]mmediate and unheeding satisfaction the instincts, such as the id demands, which all would often lead to perilous conflicts with the external world and to extinction." Had Freud retained his earlier view of the unconscious as a knowledge processing system, there would today be fewer theoretical divisions amongst psychoanalysts.

Let me now turn to another conceptual area that has contributed to the divisions that exist between various schools of psychoanalysis. There are those who claim that psychoanalysis should have nothing to do with neuroscience because of the problem of reductionism (Blass & Carmeli, 2007). As a consequence those psychoanalysts who were interested in neuroscience have of necessity formed yet another separate school. In 1976 Merton Gill in his influential paper "Metapsychology Is Not Psychology" observed that "metapsychology deals with neurology and biology, with the physical substrate of psychological functioning while clinical psychoanalysis is a 'pure' psychology which deals with intentionality and meaning." Gill's belief that intentionality and meaning, the heart of psychoanalytic understanding, is a subject that is divorced from any biological substrate is no longer true. Some neuroscientists (Freeman, 1999), but I grant you not many, describe neural events that serve the function of meaning construction and intentionality. It should be noted however, in Gill's defense, that his paper was written in 1976 prior to the expansion of cognitive science and neurobiology. However, I believe that there are many psychoanalysts today who still wish to keep psychoanalysis "pure," that is uncontaminated by neuroscience. There are even some analysts who have recently argued that being influenced by neuroscience is actually dangerous for psychoanalysis (Vivona, 2009).

One of the aims of this paper is to show that this problem of reductionism can be avoided if we recognize that there are separate and different levels of unconscious processing so that unconscious psychological processes are not to be confused with neurophysiological events.

As unconscious processes cannot be observed directly they can only be noted by inference and analogy. As Freud famously noted, the dream is the royal road to the unconscious. We can be conscious of the dream itself, but the process that created the dream is undeniably unconscious. You will recall that Freud understood that the metaphoric processes observed in dream formation was the same unconscious process that contributed to symptom formation in hysteria (Freud, 1923b). The physical symptoms of hysteria Freud interpreted as the metaphoric expression of an unconscious wish. The dream was also interpreted as a metaphoric expression of an unconscious wish. *Metaphor is therefore a fundamental cognitive tool that is central*

63

*to unconscious mental process.* Freud described dreams as a factory of thought, but to follow the analogy of a factory, the basic machinery that this factory employs is predominantly that of metaphor. The transfer of meaning between different domains and the multiplicity of different meanings that can be attributed to a single dream element, what Freud described as condensation, attests to the ubiquity of the metaphoric process in dreaming. As I have repeatedly maintained: metaphor is the currency of the (unconscious) mind (Modell, 2003). This means that unconscious thoughts, whether in the dream or whether in response to sensory inputs in current time are cognitively organized through the medium of metaphor.

## Unconscious Metaphoric Process and the Meaning Attributed to Past Experience

In my book *Imagination and the Meaningful Brain* (Modell, 2003) I suggested that a metaphoric process analogous to dreaming is operative in the waking state. In that book I quoted the critic and novelist Cynthia Ozick (Ozick, 1991) who observed that "Metaphor, like the Delphic oracle is a priest of interpretation, but what it interprets is memory." According to the Nobel Prize laureate Gerald Edelmam (Edelman, 1998) memory carves both the inner and outer world into categories. Further, these categories are recontextualized through experience. What I have observed is: that emotional memory is categorized by means of metaphor. In health these memorial metaphoric categories oscillate between similarities and differences. In the face of trauma, however, this play of similarity and differences is lost and the metaphoric transfer of meaning is invariant.

In health, metaphoric process facilitates the recontextualization of autobiographical memory. We assume that old memories are constantly re-interpreted in the context of new experience. This is the process that Freud termed *nachtraglichkeit*, the meaning of old memories are re-interpreted in the light of subsequent experience. (I discussed this process in greater detail in Modell, 1990.) Metaphoric matchings play a crucial role in this process. Traumatic memories may represent a failure in the transformative power of metaphor. In this example memory was not recontextualized by means of metaphor. Metaphor was used not to transform memory but to simply transfer memory so that an unyielding similarity is experienced between the past and the present.

My patient reported the following incident. Because his airline went out on strike, my patient was stranded in a distant city and unable to return home. He did everything possible to obtain passage on another airline: he cajoled and pleaded with the functionaries of other airlines, all to no avail. Although my patient was usually not unduly anxious and was in fact a highly experienced traveler, in this particular situation he experienced an overwhelming and generalized panic. He felt as if the unyielding airline representatives were like Nazis and that the underground passages of the airline terminal resembled a concentration camp. The helplessness of not being able to return home, combined with the institutional intransigence of the authorities, evoked the following memory, which had been unconscious.

When this man was three years old, he and his parents were residents of central European country and, as Jews, were desperately attempting to escape the Nazis. They did in fact obtain airline passage to freedom, but until that point, the outcome was very much in doubt. Although my patient did not recall his affect the state at that time, his parents reported that he seemed cheerful and unaffected by their anxiety. And as in this example, this helpless inability to leave a foreign city, combined with the intransigence of the authorities, evoked a specific affect category that remained a potential memory of an unassimilated past experience. In this example, unconscious memory was metaphorically interpreted with the help of a metronomic association. His helpless inability to leave a foreign city combined with the intransigence of the authorities served as a metonymic trigger. The metaphoric process can be defined as the transfer of meeting between different domains in this case the different domains are that of unconscious autobiographical memory and the present moment. This example also illustrates my hypothesis that an unconscious metaphoric process operates in the waking state. It is a process that interprets the meaning of current experience in a manner that is analogous to the way a dream utilizes metaphor.

The similarity between dream process and the unconscious process that occurs while we are awake has received some support from neuroscience. The neurophysiologists Llinas and Pare have also seen an analogy between the dream state and waking unconscious process. They provide some experimental evidence that points to a similarity of the neural process that supports the unconscious mentation of dreams and an analogous unconscious process that occurs while awake (Llinas & Pare, 1991). As a consequence of their experimental observations they made the following statement: "[T]hese observations indicate that mentation during dreaming operates on the same anatomical substrate as does perception during the waking state." This means that my suggestion that an unconscious metaphoric process, analogous to dreaming, occurs in the waking state is not physiologically implausible.

I shall attempt to further spell out this analogy between dreaming and a waking unconscious process. Neuroscience believes that dreaming is initiated by a self-generated excitatory process within the brain. The anatomical site of this process is correlated with the various stages in the sleep cycle (Llinas & Pare, 1991). Let us label this as the deepest level of unconscious dream process; it can be thought of as the physical or the neuro-chemical dream. Let us further consider that the dream of which we are conscious, is the product of a higher level of unconscious processing as compared to the initiating neurophysiological events. This higher level unconscious process interprets the excitory signals, what may be described as the raw neurophysiologic dream. This higher level represents the functioning of the unconscious self. The functioning of the unconscious self encompasses many tasks of the dream that Freud described. These functions would include the classical Freudian dream wish, the defensive functions in accord with internalized moral values of the self as well as intentional thoughts directed towards future actions in response to specific elements from the previous day's residue. In contrast to the deeper neurophysiologic level of unconscious processing, which like other physiological processes are shared by all, the functions of the unconscious self are highly individualized.

I recognize that these ideas are speculative and undoubtedly controversial. But I firmly believe that a revised theory of "the unconscious," or more properly speaking unconscious processing, is a useful starting point. It is a theory that recognizes the ubiquity of the metaphor process that is active both in dreaming and in the waking state. I suggest that we seek common ground in concepts rather than in matters of technique. Those analysts who favor one aspect of technique over another will find it impossible to prove their case. For the uniqueness and variability of selves are such that generalizations are nearly impossible. Controversies concerning menace of technique ultimately prove to be irresolvable.

It may be a Quixotic hope that some agreement regarding the nature of unconscious process and recognition of the ubiquity of metaphor will enable a dialogue between the various factions of contemporary psychoanalysis. But the alternative, the absence of dialogue is unacceptable. We should welcome conceptual controversies for without controversy a discipline lacks vitality. But in order for controversies to be fruitful there must also be some basic shared assumptions. If the various psychoanalytic factions accept the idea that metaphor is the cognitive tool of unconscious processing, it is possible that we may then be able to establish other areas of conceptual agreement.

## Note

1 Originally published in *Psychoanalytic Inquiry* 31(2): pp. 126–133 with the title, "Not Even Wrong."

# 7

# METAPHOR IN THREE PSYCHOANALYTIC PERSPECTIVES[1]

## *Robert S. White*

Adopting the Lakoff and Johnson view that conceptual systems of the mind are inherently metaphoric and embodied, I examine theoretical metaphor in psychoanalytic theory as an example of the use of metaphor more generally in the mind. I have chosen concepts of the non-dynamic unconscious to explore representative metaphors. These include the theories of W. Bion, C. and S. Botella, and D. Stern. This chapter first outlines recent interest in the non-dynamic unconscious and then examines the theories of Bion, the Botellas, and Stern in detail. Differences and similarities among the theoretical metaphors are explored. I suggest that theoretical metaphors progress both through the attempted destruction of existing metaphor and reshaping of existing metaphor into new meanings. I am interested in finding among the metaphoric collisions that there may be hidden collusions that can potentially lead to unifying concepts.

## Metaphor

The modern view of metaphor was introduced by Lakoff and Johnson (1980a) in the now classic, *Metaphors We Live By*. In this work, our conceptual system is thought to be fundamentally metaphoric. All degrees of abstract thinking are built up of layers of metaphor. Conceptual metaphors consist of a mapping from a more concrete source domain onto a more abstract target domain. Meaning is created from such mappings. Lakoff and Johnson (1999) went on to claim that the mind is inherently embodied. Thinking is mostly unconscious and is built up out of sensori-motor experiences. This cognitive-linguistic approach is now widely accepted in psychoanalysis (Wallerstein, Chapter 4). Wurmser (1977, Chapter 5), Modell (1968, 1990, 2003, Chapter 6), Borbely (1998, Chapter 8) and Katz (2010a, 2011b) have been most instrumental in arguing for the centrality of metaphor. Wurmser believes that all scientific thinking is the systemic use of metaphor. Modell, drawing from Lakoff and Johnson, proposes that metaphor is the currency of the unconscious mind. Katz and Borbely believe that meaning, created out of metronomic and metonymic processes, can be the primary organizing concept and bridge among disparate psychoanalytic schools.

I would like to add a dialectical dimension found in the modern metaphor. In addition to unity, there is an emphasis on collision, tension, and opposition over collusion and similarity (Harries, 1978). He suggests that, in modern poetry, metaphors become weapons directed against reality, to break the referentiality of language, to find a magical presence, a godlike self-sufficiency. It is a refusal to owe anything to the world. Out of the destruction of the world, the poet creates his own poetic world. Inherited metaphor must be removed for the poet's more daring combinations. The poet seeks a presentness and instantaneousness, a perpetual creation of self. Transcendence means a world that would be truly objective and transparent, free from all perspectival distortions. In a poem, there is an invitation to leave familiar ground for the sake of a more profound transcendental vision of what is, to throw into relief and destroy beloved reality. A new predicative meaning emerges from the collapse of the literal meaning. It is the destruction of ordinary reference and the projection of new possibilities.

Using collusion over similarity gives another modernist twist. Collusion is defined as a secret agreement between parties for fraudulent or deceitful purposes. So even when there is apparent similarity and agreement, we see just beneath the surface the emergence of deceit and hiding of secrets. The collusion quickly shades into collision.

Another way to view this tension is the difference between a fox and a hedgehog (Berlin, 1951). These metaphors come from the Greek poet Archilochus: "The fox knows many things, but the hedgehog knows one big thing." The fox pursues many ends even if unrelated and contradictory. This is a centrifugal vision that is scattered, diffuse, moving on many levels, finding the essence in many things. The hedgehog relates everything to a centripetal vision or system, a single and universal organizing principle. The major figures in psychoanalysis have been hedgehogs (Strenger, 1997). They favor the development of a single, organizing system that guided the interpretation of every phenomenon. Hedgehogs provide magnets that shape possible voices into integrated visions. They push ideas to their logical extremes. Beauty, coherence, and nobility are prized above all others. Harries' modern poets are hedgehogs. Freud, Klein, and Bion are all hedgehogs. They attract schools and apostles. They wish to destroy in order to build a pure system. I think there is a universal human need to build pure systems. It is a fantasy of being uncontaminated and of being controlled by no one. Most people who write theory take one or more organizing principles and then see all of phenomena through the lens of these principles. Another theorist comes along and sees what is missing, then builds his or her theory around that. Freud's (1919a, p. 168) famous statement speaks to this: "The large-scale application of our therapy will compel us to alloy the pure gold of analysis freely with the copper of direct suggestion; and hypnotic influence, too, might find a place in it again, as it has in the treatment of war neuroses." The pure gold of analysis has a magical draw in psychoanalytic theory.

Most clinical practitioners are foxes, borrowing and using whatever theory seems to fit. In the real world of clinical work, the pure gold does not work. In thinking of the metaphor of gold and copper, we should note that pure gold is beautiful and precious, yet it is too soft to be useful in practical life. It must be alloyed with copper or other metals to make it useful. It is a pragmatic approach, a craft to serve people and fit local reality. The map must never be confused with the territory. Theory is a tool and not a map of reality.

We could think of psychoanalytic metaphor in three levels, metaphors of human nature, metaphors of psychoanalytic theory and metaphors in clinical practice. In this paper, I plan to concentrate on theoretical metaphors. Out of this, I will develop the following categories to use in analyzing psychoanalytic metaphor:

1 What reality does the new metaphor attack and attempt to destroy?
2 Is there preserved any continuity and similarity between the new metaphor and existing reality?
3 What is the mental space that the new metaphor inhabits?
4 To what extent does new metaphor aim for a transcendence of a unity of vision?
5 In destroying existing reality, can a new unity be found that provides a new coherent vision?

In this project, I will choose a common psychoanalytic space, which can be described from several theoretical points of view. From the different theoretical points of view, I will select representative technical metaphors. Each theoretical school had developed metaphoric labels to reflect their core assumptions (Bornstein and Becker-Matero, this volume). These metaphors will be compared and contrasted, using the categories outlined above. The psychoanalytic space that I will use is non-symbolic codes. This will also give us a chance to examine the limits of metaphor when we examine non-linguistic mental space. The three theorists are all hedgehogs, who attack existing psychoanalytic metaphor and seek to organize psychoanalytic reality using new assumptions. This paper is written by a fox who admires hedgehogs but finds they do not fit the everyday reality of psychoanalytic work.

## Non-Symbolic Codes

There is now widespread convergence among a number of psychoanalytic theories of the existence of dual codes in the mind, the symbolic and nonsymbolic (Lecours, 2007). Symbolic codes are the characteristic targets of classical psychoanalytic theories. This would include mental conflict, signal affects, intrapsychic mental structures, unification of self identity, links between affects and representations, networks of unconscious wishes and pathological beliefs, and networks of defenses and compromise formations. Defenses based on repression are characteristic of symbolic conflict.

The persistence of non-symbolic codes in adult life can result from deficits in early development, from borderline and psychotic functioning and from severe trauma. The lack of symbolization results in the use of primitive defenses, organized around splitting and projective identification, and the compulsion to repeat in actions.

Affects are unmodulated and eruptive. Mental structures are split into dissociated areas or fragmentation.

Theorists from a number of traditions have articulated versions of non-symbolic code. Freud (1915a) developed a second theory of the unconscious; conscious ideas could be split into word-presentations and thing-presentations. In repression, the word-presentation is stripped off and only the thing-presentation is retained. The thing-presentation is the raw material of the sensory experience. Loewald (1978) argues that word-presentations are not a higher organization than thing-presentations. At the beginning of mental life, words are part of the undifferentiated total experience of the infant, a primordial density. Busch (2009), from American conflict theory and building on Loewald, describes action-language, where words become concrete acts. Green (1998, 1999a, 1999b) speaks of the work of the negative: disavowal, splitting, and foreclosure. Bucci and Maskit (2007), from an empirical orientation, suggest multiple coding systems in the mind: symbolic codes either verbal or non-verbal, and subsymbolic coding system which can occur in motoric, visceral or sensory modes.

## Three Theorists

I will choose three theorists, each coming from different analytic cultures, to compare and contrast. Wilfred Bion comes out of the English Kleinian school with its roots in object relations. César and Sára Botella come out of the French school, with its roots in early Freud, Lacan and philosophy. Donnel Stern comes from the American interpersonal school with its roots in H. S. Sullivan and interaction.

### Wilfred Bion

Bion (1957, 1962a, 1965, 1989, 1995b) aims for a radical attack and recasting of basic Freudian and Kleinian metaphors. He used Greek letters for his major metaphors because he wanted to start fresh, without any pre-existing meanings. This is the opposite of Freudian theorists, such as Loewald (1978) who aimed to extend existing metaphor and maintain a tradition. Bion's key metaphors would include β-elements, α-function, α-elements, reverie, K-link, and container/contained.[2]

Bion recasts Freud's metaphor of primary process into a more modern theory of thinking, where there is a progressive increase in complexity and integration of thinking and transformation of preverbal into verbal thoughts. Bion is dissatisfied with the primacy of libidinal and aggressive drives. While he does not deny the existence of these drives, he postulates that human growth occurs primarily through the emergence of truth in knowledge. Drives are recast as links, L (love), H (hate), and K (knowledge). For Bion, these are not drives but emotional activities. The ability to think is born out of the ability of the person to tolerate frustration. The movement is from evading pain to the acceptance of painful truths. Thinking does not reduce psychic tensions but manages them. Bion discards the polarity of conscious/unconscious in favor of the metaphors, finite and infinite. Primary and secondary process is discarded and replaced with β and α-elements. The structural model is replaced with the metaphor of container/contained (♀♂).

Bion postulated a psychic space that precedes and underlies the dynamic unconscious. It would correspond with Freud's (1915b) thing presentation and the repressed that never achieve consciousness (Freud, 1915a). For Bion (1995b), the mind starts out in catastrophe. Mental space cannot be represented, leaving an immensity that is accompanied by violent and psychotic fear. This space is filled with what Bion calls β-elements.[3] They are fragments and debris of the mental catastrophe. While for Freud, these objects are a form of thought, for Bion β-elements are the matrix from which thoughts can arise. β-elements can be stored and clog up the mind or can be evacuated by projection or through acting out. The only link possible with the analyst is projective identification because β-elements can only be evacuated by projection (Bion, 1959).

For use in thought, β-elements must be transformed by α-function into α-elements. α-elements are comprised of visual, auditory and other sensory patterns that are now available for dreaming and unconscious waking thought, what Ferro (2005b, 2005c) calls visual pictograms. Dreaming, for Bion, is a form of psychoanalytic work (Ogden, 2004b), in which pre-conscious thoughts are pressing toward awareness. Attacks on α-function, from envy or hate, destroy the person's ability to make contact with herself or others. The self and objects become inanimate, lifeless, dead.

Bion uses the metaphor of a container to understand the communicative aspects of projective identification. In the metaphor of container and contained (♀♂), the infant projects β-elements into the containing mother, who at first provides the α-function to transform the contained β-elements into α-elements and feed them back to the baby at an appropriate moment (Bion, 1965). The mother must be in a state of reverie, a dreamlike state, in order to receive and contain the infant's β-elements. Over time, the infant can acquire his mother's α-function and perform his own transformations. The capacity for α-function makes possible the development of thinking and the possibility of thoughts.

### *César and Sára Botella*

The Botellas (2005) propose another view of the non-verbal. Unlike Bion, they do not want to destroy existing theory but extend it. They would understand their project as completing an aspect of Freud's thought that was left unfinished at his death. But metaphors of the traumatic dream are bent and shaped into a much larger theory of trauma, so we end up much as in Bion with a completely new theory. Key metaphors include figuration, perceptual axis, and non-representation.

They suggest we conceptualize the psyche space as having two axes. One axis is familiar to psychoanalysis. It is the system of representations, the familiar world of drive – repression – fantasy. It is located in the Pcs and Cs. It encompasses all of what we ordinarily think of psychoanalytic technique: conflict, defenses, transference, the return of the repressed, memory and interpretation. Even primitive defenses such as splitting and projective identification utilize the representational system. It is the act of giving form, of developing linguistic and symbolic forms. The object representation is not just a memory but it also contains the meaning for the subject.

What is new in their psychic space is the second axis, the perceptual system. This is drawn from Freud's metaphor of perceptual identity (Freud, 1900) and the unconscious work of representability (what the Botellas translate at figuration). They wish to emphasize that what is nonverbal cannot be understood by the same processes of normal representation. If progression of the sequence of drive to object-representation is blocked, the result is negating of representation, leading to disavowal. In this void, the mind has the capacity for creating the sensation of reality to fulfill a wish with a materialization through an hallucinatory actualization. It is transient, dazzling, and instantaneous. It is what will not go into words. We have a traumatic plunge into the loss of representation and the sudden emergence of hallucinatory phenomena. The Botellas call this the act of figuration. Freud had found in the experience of the uncanny, animistic thinking and the experiences of traumatic neurosis hints of this traumatic loss of inner objects (Freud, 1913a, 1919a, 1933b, 1939). It is ordinarily only found in night-time dreams but will emerge under traumatic conditions. Figurations carry the conviction of having grasped the truth, a hallucinatory experience of continuity projected onto the sensory realm. They are created to banish what is unfamiliar and disturbing. Perception of the object must be disavowed so that belief can be maintained as representation.

In psychic trauma, there can be a sudden experience of the loss of representation, either because of a lack of internalization or a traumatic rupture of the chain of representations. The trauma cannot be represented and can only be experienced as a negative, a violent and abrupt absence. There is a violent excitement. This is experienced as a negative, a void, an implosion, a psychic death. It completely erases the negative and provides a presence. This zone of non-representation exists at the heart of the psyche.

### Donnel Stern

If Bion and the Botellas are both revising the basic Freudian canon, D. Stern (1983, 1990, 1997) has more of a radical revision. This goes back to a basic distinction between repression and dissociation. In *Studies on Hysteria* (1895), Breuer explained Anna O's hysteria as two states of consciousness existing side by side while Freud formulated repression, that of erecting a barrier that prevents emergence into consciousness. Traditional psychoanalysis is founded on the defeat of dissociation and the primacy of repression.

Eagle (2000) points out the key differences between repression and dissociation. In repression, certain mental contents are excluded from a unified ego or self. The repressed is constantly driven by drive pressure toward consciousness and requires continual repression to maintain unconsciousness – the return of the repressed. In dissociation, mental contents are split into sections that each are potentially accessible to consciousness.

Stern, coming out of the Sullivanian tradition, proposes dissociation as a primary defense and the unconscious as the "natural state of experience" (1997, p. 85), where experience is outside awareness. Action and effort are then required to bring experience into consciousness. This reverses the Freudian theory of repression as a pressure to force out of consciousness. To make something conscious is to construct the experience in words. Consciousness is not a passive container but an active shaping and representing. What are dissociated, then, is differences in function, between formulated, largely verbal experiences and unformulated murky and poorly defined experience and images. Stern proposes that unformulated experience is the primary matrix of all thinking. Unformulated experience is mentation characterized by lack of clarity and differentiation, familiar chaos. It is experience that has never been articulated enough to enter into defensive operations. To be unconscious is something that is so much present that we live it rather than see it or understand it. Key metaphors include unformulated experience, construction, and dissociation.

Action, an interpretive construction, is necessary for consciousness. The basic metaphor is of seeing, turning our eyes toward. Rather than forcing meaning and risking stereotyping, we let meaning come to us, to just appear directly. Language must be authentic and creative, bringing thoughts alive. The basic defensive process is one of prevention of interpretation in reflective awareness. It is a restriction on the experiences we allow ourselves. Instead of repressed content, we have familiar chaos and the refusal to allow prereflective experience to attain full-bodied meaning. Clinically we look for absences, gaps, contradictions, stereotypes, repetitions, and dead spots. Dissociation is a selective inattention, an avoidance of certain unformulated experiences, so they never reach reflective consciousness.

## Collisions

All of the theorists aim to attack and destroy existing psychoanalytic theory and metaphor, while preserving what they consider pure metaphor. Bion attacks Klein's extension of object relations to birth and her extensive use of the death instinct, while wanting to preserve and enlarge on Freud's later thinking on primary and secondary process. The Botellas attack the Freudian unconscious while preserving and extending Freud's ideas about dream work. Stern attacks Freudian defense and the unconscious while preserving Freud's early work on dissociation and hysteria.

The most fundamental division among the theorists is the contrast between the model of Stern and the models of Bion and the Botellas. Stern's unconscious is non-dynamic, a "natural state of experience," having never become conscious. The post-Freudian unconscious remains dynamic, a depository of the repressed or fragmented, what once had been conscious and now excluded from consciousness. For Stern, the primary defense is dissociation, a selective including or excluding contents from consciousness. The main action of defense is not seeing, an unconscious shaping of what is allowed into consciousness. The flip side of defense is creativity, the active shaping of unconscious mentation into new and surprising forms. For the post-Freudians, the primary defense is repression, a force preventing the movement from unconscious to conscious. The unconscious is always forcing its way into consciousness and must be continually resisted. Creativity comes from a relaxation and reshaping of the defensive structures.

A second division among the theorists would contrast Bion and Stern against the Botellas. Bion, although he retains a Freudian dynamic unconscious, postulates a second non-dynamic unconscious with many similarities to Stern. Both are unformulated and require a translation to move toward consciousness. Both non-dynamic unconsciouses are filled with experiences and affects of early development, that both must be defended against and potentially provide creativity and life. The Botellas do not have a concept of the non-dynamic unconscious. At the bottom of the dynamic unconscious is the ultimate consequence of repression, non-representation. Non-representation is then covered over by the flash of figurability.

## Collusions

All of the theorists would broadly fit into Modell's model of unconscious metaphoric process (Modell, this volume). In this view, all unconscious thoughts are cognitively organized through the medium of metaphor. Metaphor is crucial in creating more complex and more organized meaning states. The unconscious is not just a repository of repressed instinctual derivatives.

Both Bion and the Botellas have a dual unconscious. They postulate a psychic space that underlies and forms the dynamic unconscious, a second unconscious. Bion speaks of processing of β into α elements. The β elements represent the concrete source domain and the α elements the target domain. The mappings between domains are called links. The Botellas speak of a perceptual axis. The work of figurability is the act of giving form to what is unrepresentable. There is a similar mapping from the unrepresentable to the form of the hallucination.

Both Bion and the Botellas conceive of spaces of trauma and terror. For Bion, it is the space of β elements. He speaks of "an intense catastrophic emotional explosion" (Bion, 1995a, p. 14) with immense fear and violence. The explosion results when either the contained blows up the container or the container cannot contain the explosive nature of the contained. This explosion destroys links and the resulting fragments are dispersed into an infinite space. The metaphor is of debris and fragments from the explosion floating in a vast space. For the Botellas, it is the perceptual axis. In the perceptual axis, there is the presence of animistic thinking in which representation, perception and motor activity become equivalent as a continuous universe. Rather than the terror of fragmentation, it is the terror of non-representation, of the metaphor of nothingness. There is a violent and abrupt collapse into nothingness. In the violent excess of excitation and distress, the ego murders the object and its meaning. The shadowy equivalent of the perception has disappeared, and the persecuting perception invades the scene. The metaphor is of a deep and dark hole that is patched out and hidden from view.

Both Bion and the Botellas talk of hallucinations yet they differ phenomenologically. Bion describes hallucinations among other types of fragmentary experiences. The mental event is transformed into a sense impression. They provide only pleasure or pain and a failure to yield meaning. This is a transformation into a β element which can only be evacuated. There is a vicious cycle in which the patient continues to hallucinate to compensate for the missing meaning. Greed increases the hallucinations. Hallucinations are "a state always present, but overlaid by other phenomena, which screen it" (Bion, 1995a, p. 36). For the Botellas, the hallucination is a figuration, a defensive operation in which the hallucination is potentially reparative and integrating.

Stern and Bion have a concept of dissociation in common. Bion, in the Kleinian tradition, would understand β elements as split off fragments, a type of dissociation. Stern enlarges the concept of the non-verbal to include the entire unconscious. He privileges dissociation as a primary mechanism over repression. For both of them, dissociation is the natural condition where the β space or the unconscious contain elements that are widely separated and not linked.

Both Bion and Stern are constructionists. The β elements have to undergo a construction, what Bion calls α process, before they can access consciousness. Stern postulates that all unconscious elements are unformed and undergo a construction to become conscious.

Both Bion and the Botellas think of this psychic space as containing fragments that cannot enter the dynamic unconscious. Both conceive of these elements as subject to projection. Both think of projection as a mean of communication. Both think of reverie as a receptive state. Yet these elements are quite different. For Bion, β-elements are a basic sensori-motor level of organization that directly incorporates the traumatic elements. For the Botellas, figuration is a hallucinatory experience that covers over and defends against the loss of representation.

There is a difference about the direction of psychic movement. For Bion and Stern, the movement is forward, originating in the non-verbal unconscious and proceeding forward, achieving greater complexity and symbolization in the process. The movement is toward consciousness. For the Botellas, the movement is regressive and backward. Unacceptable psychic elements are repressed and regress backwards toward the perceptual and the void. In contact with the void, there is a violent and defensive push forward again in the figuration.

## The Limits of Metaphor

Borbely (this volume) provides a model of psychoanalytic process that uses metaphor as a basic template for framework language that is relevant for all the psychoanalytic schools. Source and target domains are separated by two dimensions, time and form. Defense, for example, is understood as a temporal metaphor. The defending part is associated with the present time and the defended against is associated with the past time. The repressed then becomes an interpretation of the present based on the past. The second dimension, form, is the domains of metaphor and metonymy. In trauma and neurosis, there is a loss of metaphoricity and replacement with metonymic relationship. This is the movement from abstract to concrete and rigid relationships. The defending part stands for, in a metonymic way, the defended against part.

This model works well to explain key dimensions in the traditional Freudian unconscious where the linguistic forms of metaphor and metonymy are maintained. In the non-verbal unconscious, there are no such forms. In addition, in a dissociative process such as splitting, there is not a temporal present and past relationship. The split off fragments are both in present time but kept separate. Or one might say they are both in the past but contemporary to each other. Borbely's model of temporal metaphors is a good fit for repressive defenses but not splitting defenses. Wurmser (this volume) suggests an answer. He distinguishes metaphorical processes from metaphor proper. Metaphoric processes are a biological aspect of the brain and a deep principle of the mind: "processes of cross modal equations." Metaphor proper is the verbal and linguistic aspect of this larger process, bound to language and symbol formation. This would imply an inherent and biologically based process of progressive organization of mental functions. Could we think of metaphor proper as only the final stages of a larger process of progressive symbolization and differentiation of mental structures?

Bion implies such an organizing principle. β-elements are unmentalized fragments that have no links to each other or to more organized forms. Bion postulates a separate α-process, at first in the mother and later internalized, that transforms the β-elements, at first into more complex α elements or pictograms and in a further process, into proto-symbols or metaphors. Bion does not specify how this α process might work but it fits well with Loewald in a progress toward linkages and symbolization.

The Botellas also imply a progressive organizing function of the mind. In the trauma of nonrepresentation and nothingness, the figuration is a binding together into a sensory whole. It erases the negative and provides a presence. Representational thinking is a higher level of organization, arising out of the mirroring and doubling of mother and child. Like Loewald, they see a linking and symmetry of word and think presentation.

## A Unifying Proposal

Stern asks the question, how can we refuse to spell-out an experience without first having spelled it out? (1997, p. 123). His answer is that the self has a consistent sense of coherence. What is not me is disavowed, not formulated. Yet does not this act of disavowal depend upon the self having some recognition of what is alien and erecting some sort of barrier?[4] It is not logically possible for the unconscious to formulate its own barrier. Does this not bring repression and dissociation closer together conceptually? Both would have barriers between the unconscious and conscious. We could postulate different elements, some of which represent excluded conscious contents that retain a linguistic mode, while other elements are unformed and have never risen to full consciousness.

Is there here a possibility of a unified theory of defense? Defense could be conceptualized with two basic dimensions. One dimension is force. There is a variable degree of force that maintains access to consciousness of a mental element. The other dimension is separation. There is a variable degree of separation of mental elements as a means to control access to consciousness. Pure repression emphasizes the maximum degree of force to prevent consciousness and a minimum of separation. Pure dissociation emphasizes a maximum of separation and a minimum of force. Freud (1927, 1940c), late in his life, was trying to grapple with such complexities. In his concept of splitting of the ego, he finds an intermediate position between repression and dissociation. Freud's example is castration but we could read these papers as a theory of trauma. Under traumatic danger, there is simultaneously a recognition and a disavowal of the danger. When the danger is recognized, repression occurs; the instinctual pressure is forced out of consciousness. When the danger is disavowed, instinctual pleasure is allowed into consciousness but displaced or separated by placement in a new object, the fetish. Thus, for Freud, there are two types of defense that operate together, repression and displacement, a type of dissociation. Both originate in the ego. I think the Kleinians have come up with a different middle view. Repressive defenses are characteristic of higher level mental operations. More developmentally primitive defensive operations are based on splitting and dissociation. In the Kleinian view, all patients have a mixture of repressive and splitting defenses. There is a greater predominance of splitting in borderline and psychotic personalities.

Bion fundamentally changes the idea of splitting. Instead of a primitive defense originating in the ego as a pressure, splitting is a fundamental property of the non-dynamic unconscious in which mental content exists as unlinked fragments. Yet there is also a sense of defense in which these unlinked fragments are further separated through evacuation via projective identification.

While the Botellas do not directly address Freud's concept of the splitting of the ego, they refer to another type of splitting, that of the two axes of representation and perception, in which animistic and formal thinking exist side by side. Animistic thinking is a kind of dissociation, in which pleasure is allowed to attach to hallucinatory objects.

Freud's concept of splitting also differs from both Bion and Stern, for which dissociation is the natural state of the unconscious. Yet Bion and Stern also differ in the origin of the dissociation. For Bion, β-elements are a result of the catastrophe of being born, of dangers that cannot be contained because there is no container. For Stern, the mind is also born in a state of dissociation but he lacks the sense of danger. It is just the natural state of the unconscious.

## Conclusions

1   I have focused on theoretical metaphor in psychoanalytic theory to illustrate how we can conceive of theory through the eyes of metaphor.

2  Psychoanalytic theory and its theoretical metaphors are born out of an attack and murder of existing theory and the erection of a new pure theory and metaphors.

3  Psychoanalytic practitioners take aspects of pure theory and metaphor, and mix them pragmatically in their clinical work.

4  In the formation of new theoretical metaphor, we can see the use of new metaphor that is thought to be uncontaminated with old meaning and the shaping of existing metaphor into new meanings.

5  In the development of conflicting theory and metaphor, we can see a complex of similarities and differences.

6  Examining such theoretical metaphors may provide insight into unifying concepts. I have given such an example in the differences and unities of splitting and repression.

## Notes

1  Originally published in *Psychoanalytic Inquiry* 31(2): pp. 147–158 with the title "The Non-verbal Unconscious: Collision and Collusion of Metaphor."

2  Of course, over time, Bion's Greek letters have become metaphors in themselves. In this paper, I treat his Greek letters as metaphors.

3  This account of elements and functions is taken from what Ogden (2004a) calls early Bion, up to and including *Learning from Experience,* where he does not depart significantly from Klein. Only in the later papers (Bion, 1995b) does he move beyond Kleinian theory (Symington & Symington, 1996).

4  The Freudian definition of "disavowal" would include an active force coming from the ego that pushes the disavowal.

# 8

# METAPHOR AND METONYMY AS THE BASIS OF A NEW PSYCHOANALYTIC LANGUAGE

*Antal Borbely*

Metaphors are "in terms of" relationships whereas metonymies are "stands for" or "belongs to" relationships. These relationships are basic on the linguistic, mental, and developmental level. They are therefore suitable for a psychoanalytic framework language capable of uniting the psychoanalytic schools and achieving a rapprochement to those cognitive sciences which already see the mind's functioning as based on metaphor and metonymy. Psychoanalysis with its dialectic between past, present, and future yields a temporal dimension to metaphor: Mentation at one time is understood in terms of mentation at another time—therefore metaphorically ("in terms of"). If metaphoric "in terms of" flexibility is lost, a metonymic (neurotic) "stands for" or "belongs to" relationship holds between issues rooted in different times. It is this temporal dimension of metaphor and metonymy which can conceptually bridge the cognitive sciences with psychoanalysis. The main psychodynamic concepts *transference, interpretation,* and *defense,* if slightly reformulated, become relevant within and without the treatment setting. They all can be seen as relating issues from different times flexibly (metaphorically) or neurotically (metonymically) with each other. This leads to conceptualizing transference, interpretation, and defense as having two variants: A metaphoric (healthy) and metonymic (neurotic) one. Psychoanalytic theory was burdened by a one-sided focus on clarification at the expense of enigmatization, both being important aspects of metaphor. The enigmatization, not understood in its theoretical centrality, was therefore collectively enacted as a Babel-like confusion between psychoanalytic languages. The central importance of metaphor and metonymy was not theorized.

Why, after more than a century, are the penetrating insights of psychoanalysis underappreciated—and largely ignored—outside the field? Why isn't psychoanalysis more of a participant in the important discussions about the mind's functioning that have been going on within the cognitive sciences (Barcelona, 2000; Borbely, 2004; Sweetser and Fauconnier, 1996; Gibbs 1994, 2008; Kittay, 1987; Lakoff and Johnson, 1999)? Finally, why has there been such disagreement among the many competing schools within psychoanalysis about basic terms and concepts (Wallerstein, 2002b)? These questions are not unrelated. They deserve further inquiry.

To a large degree, psychoanalysis will continue to be a bystander to the great scientific and cultural debates, and psychoanalysts will continue to misunderstand or talk past one another, until a metaphor-based framework language can be formulated that could accommodate the divergent psychoanalytic schools, traditions, and languages. When intelligent, highly educated, and well-trained psychoanalysts find themselves to be adherents of so many divergent schools without being able to account for their choice, we should think of the possibility that we are witnessing a collective enactment of something suppressed. This deserves an inquiry.

Before I begin my argument, let me make a few obvious points. First, unlike the cognitive sciences, which are primarily focused on understanding the mind's normal functioning, psychoanalysis was developed as a way of understanding psychopathology. Although there was originally an expectation that psychoanalysis could serve as a basis for a general personality theory, the main psychodynamic concepts—namely, transference, defense, and interpretation—remained almost exclusively connected with what occurred in the therapeutic setting. Even today, these terms generally do not apply to the individual outside the consulting room.

Seeing temporality, metaphor (Wurmser, 1977), and metonymy as central to all psychodynamic notions (Borbely, 2008, 2009) allows us, as we shall see, to comprehend transference, interpretation, and defense deeper, namely in their intrinsic, rather than only in their extrinsic, functional, relatedness. The fact that in psychoanalytic theories, the main psychodynamic concepts remained only extrinsically related to each other is, in my opinion, the main reason for the stagnation of psychoanalytic theory and for the splitting of psychoanalysis into different schools, as well as for the isolation of psychoanalysis from other cognitive sciences. Psychoanalysis, freed from such stagnation, could and should take its rightful place among the "sciences of surprise" (Casti, 1995, p. 15): theories of creativity, chaos, fractals, and complexity.

## Metaphor and Metonymy

To begin, let me be clear about terminology. Metaphor is defined (Ricoeur, 1986) as seeing or understanding one thing *(the target)* in terms of something else *(the source)*. In "Juliet is the sun," the two objects or ideas that are being related belong to different semantic domains, namely the domain of human beings and the domain of celestial bodies. A nonlinear—that is a complex, nonadditive, evocative, open-ended—relationship exists between source and target located in these different domains.

Another noteworthy fact about metaphor: It is sensitive to the context in which it occurs (Stern, 2000). For example, when Romeo exclaims, "Juliet is the sun," we understand his meaning: As a lovesick young man he considers Juliet of supreme importance. If we were to consider the same statement in a different context—say, as a remark made by a member of the Montague family—it might have a more sinister quality. In that case, we might be invited to see Juliet as the sun that is blinding Romeo, making him unable to assess the danger he is in.

Metaphor entails some features that are especially relevant for psychoanalysis and are labeled by us as *psychodynamics.* For the remainder of this article, I propose to focus among psychodynamic terms on the three important notions: *transference, interpretation,* and *defense.* The connection between psychodynamics, metaphor, and metonymy is, at first, not easy to understand, but will later become clearer. Metaphor entails interpretation because the source interprets the target: In "life is a journey," *journey* interprets *life.* One aspect of such interpretation is what could be called transference, in the sense of the source transferring selectively, attributes to the target: In "Juliet is the sun," some attributes of the sun get transferred; others concealed. The source, the sun, not only interprets the target, Juliet, but endows it with new attributes and, thus, changes its meaning. We can thus talk of a mutative interpretation. Another of metaphor's features can be called *tension* or *defense:* Metaphor invites us (Ricoeur, 1987) to consider a new mental organization of source and target remaining in tension with the previous organization of source and target. Metaphor thus also entails memory. The target, now understood in a temporal way as this new organization (of source and target), defends itself against undue intrusion by the source, now understood as the previous and subsequently transgressed organization. Through the remembrance of these mental organizations, narrative coherence can be maintained. Consider the following example: When Freud metaphorized hitherto independently understood concepts such as motivation and the unconscious by proposing to understand one in terms of the other, the newly suggested organization of the two concepts, namely "unconscious motivation," remained in temporal metaphoric tension with the familiar one. Because of this tension, a new metaphor in science can be both interesting and controversial. The new organization *defends itself* against the old one by holding the latter in abeyance; the old one *defends itself* against the new one by trying to maintain its staying power through an appeal to familiarity.

To summarize, metaphor entails, among many others features, the psychodynamic concepts interpretation, transference, and defense. We will later see the surprising fact that interpretation, transference, and defense are not only features of metaphor but have themselves a metaphoric structure. The point here is that the two concepts "metaphor" and "psychodynamics" can be metaphorized: One is seen in terms of the other.

In a metonymy, the name of one object or idea (the source) stands for or belongs to another (the target). We ask, "Have you read the latest Philip Roth?," thereby equating the writer with his work. We use the term "the White House" as a stand-in for United States policy, and the term "the Crown" for the person of the English king or queen. In a metonymy, unlike a metaphor, both the source and the target are seen as located in the same domain. Unlike metaphor, a metonymy expresses a linear relationship—direct, one-to-one, literal, and closed—between the source and the target.

In summary, we can say that metaphor articulates *in-terms-of* relationships, where source, target, and context change relative to one another; whereas metonymy articulates *stands-for* or *belongs-to* relationships. The former could be likened to a storyline's plot, the latter to one of its scenarios. Obviously, plot and scenario are specific viewpoints focusing on transfiguration versus configuration of narrative elements. The narrative process is, itself, as we shall see, a metaphoric process. Such a process reassigns in an ongoing way what should be seen as part of a metonymic configuration, thus belonging to each other, and what as part of a metaphoric transfiguration, thus interacting with each other.

A further point has to be made to understand the functioning of metaphor in health and of metonymy in neurosis. Metonymy, as used by linguists, gives access to something that belongs to it or for which it stands (Langacker, 1993). Consider, for example, the phrase: "They went out for a drink." This phrase gives access to many other possible but not articulated phrases such as, "They went to a bar," "They had a good time." Thus, linguistically speaking, in metonymy one mental entity gives access to another mental entity.

For psychoanalysis, I introduced the concept of *negative metonymy* (Borbely, 2004) to describe what happens when access to a mental entity is not given but barred, as in a neurotic defense. The defending mental entity (e.g., "I love my brother so much!") stands for a defended-against mental entity ("I hate him also quite a bit!") to which access is barred. This relationship is linear and rigid and has a *belongs-to,* metonymic, quality. For the remainder of this article, unless otherwise noted, *metonymy* will be used to mean negative metonymy.

## The Psychoanalytic Process as Metaphoric Process

Although there are substantial theoretical disagreements among psychoanalytic schools, most analysts of divergent persuasions would agree today that all schools attempt to and, in general, succeed in establishing a psychoanalytic process with their analysands. Given this consensus, we have to assume that the different schools are closer to each other in their practice than in their theories. Accordingly, as we search for a framework language within which to discuss the various theoretical conceptualizations and traditions, it is best to start with examining common elements within psychoanalytic practice.

Earlier, we defined the linguistic concept of metaphor as seeing, understanding, or mutatively interpreting something in one semantic domain in terms of something in another domain. Temporality is not a central issue here. But because psychoanalytic practice aims at increasing awareness in an ongoing way, a process that entails the fundamental notion of temporality, we must expand the linguistic to a psychoanalytic *temporal metaphor* concept. Temporality (Borbely, 1987) now becomes central within this metaphor concept as a reflection of the mind's changing in the course of time.

The psychoanalytic temporal metaphor concept relates to the linguistic one in the following way: Linguistically, as just mentioned, the purpose of metaphor is to see something, understand something, or mutatively interpret something in terms of something else. Psychoanalytically, *in terms of something else* becomes *in terms of another time*. In the enacted transference, the present is understood in terms of the past and in the interpreted transference the past is understood in terms of the present. An analysand misses a session, having overslept. The analyst's thoughts, guided by the present transference picture, move to the analysand's earlier experiences in life or in the analysis to find a possible hint for why the analysand's absence occurred. A specific problematic event in the present is, in principle, understood in terms of previous, now unconsciously reenacted, experiences. At the same time, such a present enactment can lead to new material from the past. For example, if the analysand were to experience a present vacation-related interruption of the analysis as abandonment, the analyst, drawing attention to this transference enactment, may gain access to childhood abandonment experiences, which can now be interpreted for the first time from an adult perspective.

It may turn out, for example, that what was originally experienced as abandonment was a separation due to a parent's illness. In both these just mentioned cases, the analyst will try to establish a metaphoric in-terms-of relationship between an experience in the past now resonating with an experience in the present. The aim is to overcome a sterile metonymic repetition in which the past cannot inform the present in a way that is sensitive to the new context.

Metaphor as principle, structure, and process underlies the mind's functioning. Metaphoric processes, in an ongoing way, reinterpret and change one's self and one's world (Bruner, 1987). Given the discussion so far, attempts to integrate the concept of temporal metaphor with psycho- dynamic concepts of the mind are of obvious importance. Today, metaphor is also researched as an important principle, structure, and process not only of the mind, but also on the level of the brain's neuronal functioning (see Lakoff, 2008).

### *A Temporal View of Interpretation, Transference, and Defense*

To integrate psychoanalysis and the theory of metaphor and metonymy, it is necessary to show that the main psychoanalytic dynamic concepts, namely transference, interpretation, and defense, actively structure the relationship between time domains—either in a metaphoric way in the case of health, or in a metonymic way in the case of neurosis.

Let us look at a temporal view of interpretation: in the case of health, where present and past can recursively reach each other, an interpretation is metaphorically mutative; in neurosis, where present and past are unable to communicate, an individual's self-interpretation becomes metonymic, nonmutative, and repetitious, and is in need of the analyst's interpretation.

Let us look at a temporal view of defense: According to the classic theory of defense, defending and that which is defended against are seen as discretely opposed entities assignable to the specific agencies ego, id, and superego. Yet, such a nontemporal assignment runs into logical and clinical difficulties: What serves a defending function at one moment can be defended against in the next; and what was defended against can likewise assume the role of defender. Therefore, no matter how ego, id, and superego are defined, they can be found simultaneously on the side of defending as well as defended against mentation. Only a temporal, as opposed to a content- or function-related, view can help to differentiate between defending and defended: We can assign the defending to the present domain and the defended to a past domain. It is, after all, something that happened in the past that evokes a defending in the present so as to avoid anxiety.

This temporal view of defending and defended can accommodate clinical observations where passions like perversions defend against guilt-laden phantasies. In the received, logically and clinically flawed, parlance, this would amount to the id defending against the ego and the superego.

Assertions regarding the superiority of drive theory, object-relations theory, intersubjective theories, and others, are closely connected to how the relationship between defending and defended parts of the mind are understood. A concept of defense based on temporality allows us to put aside the sterile discussions whether thoughts defend against drives or whether relationships in the here and now defend against relationships of the then and there, etc. Drives, object relations, intersubjective relations, self-objects, part-objects, are aspects of the simultaneously occurring defending as well as the defended parts of mentation, and there is, therefore, no need to play one theory out against the others. What is now relevant relates metaphorically or metonymically to what was then relevant, whatever we call it. In summary, the structure of the neurotic defense (the relationship between the defending and the defended-against aspects of defense) is a metonymic one; the structure of the healthy defense is a metaphoric one.

The point I am making here for psychoanalysis and, therefore, for the mind's temporal functioning, is this: In the optimal functioning or healthy mind, experiences have to be reinterpretable with the changing context of an individual's personal narrative. Experiences can be reinterpreted if they have been integrated in a context-sensitive, that is, a healthy way. Such integration means that the present experience can be seen metaphorically in terms of previous experiences, and the meanings of these previous experiences change in terms of the new experience (Johnson, 1987). The new experience interprets the old one, updating it and changing it so that it can become a meaningful precursor for the ever-changing narrative.

Although psychoanalysis cannot change a person's past as it occurred, it can and must change the effects the past has on the present. The past continues to mutatively interpret the present. As indicated, we can assume that such mutative change between different time domains occurs quite naturally, and mainly unconsciously, also in life outside any treatment setting. Therefore, our psychodynamic concepts, once temporally redefined, can be used to describe neurotic, as well as healthy, functioning in and outside the treatment setting.

When the mind functions optimally, present and past relate to each other bidirectionally, both forward and backward, like the source and the target in a metaphor (Borbely, 1998). In health, with the passing of time, one time domain changes its view of the other, and by informing the other of such a change, changes the other. This bidirectional, nonlinear dialogic relationship is also characteristic of the analytic situation in which the past and present are interpreted metaphorically in terms of one another and where, based on metaphor, "the interpenetration of all systems of experience" can occur (Coburn, 2002, p. 657).

Psychological trauma leads to an overly concrete way of experiencing. It leads to a loss of context sensitivity and, with it, to an isolation of the traumatic experience from the context-sensitive, ever-changing, mainstream of narrative processes. After a traumatic experience, a new experience, touching on issues sequestered by trauma, cannot be interpreted in terms of the traumatic one (that is, it cannot be interpreted metaphorically). The sequestered experience metanymically determines (rather than metaphorically informs) the present by rigidly inducing a defense in order to avoid unbearable anxiety.

For example, an authority figure elicits fear for a young man not only in the context of the original experience in which he was abused by his father, but for all contexts involving authority figures. The structure of the relationship between the defending mentation, namely the fear of authority, and the defended-against mentation, namely the fear of the abusive father, has become metonymic. In other words, the fear of authority relates in a rigid, linear way to a target as yet unknown. Even though it is unknown—in the sense that the man does not have conscious access to it—such a target exerts its power by rigidly evoking a specific defense in the present. By falsely locating the source of anxiety in the present, rather than in the past, the past cannot inform and be integrated with the present and the future. As a result, the man's ability to comprehend the present is impaired, and his creative potential in the here and now is diminished. Thus he is said to be neurotic, or, put differently, time-confused.

### The Metaphoric Process as Equivalence in Motion

To orient itself, the infant's and adult's mind has to be able to establish metaphoric and positive metonymic equivalences. This occurs within a supraordinate metaphoric *currency* (Modell, 1997b) of meaningfulness across myriads of dimensions, so that concepts, sensations, categories, values, identities, needs, and plans become commensurable and, thus, translatable into one another regarding their narrative meaning. The metaphoric process is the making of new meaning (Hausman, 1984, p. 92). It establishes a hitherto unknown equivalence in form of a meaningful anticipation. It is the currency within which changing mental organizations can be negotiated. As already mentioned, the metaphoric process reassigns, at each moment, which among the mental entities should be seen as relating in an in-terms-of and which in a belongs-to or stands-for relationship.

Let us look at some such meaningful equivalencies across different sensory registers. For the infant, mother's soothing voice in the domain of sound is the same and not the same as her tender stroking in the domain of touching. Can these cross-modal sensations be understood metonymically as standing for something, for example, as two forms of satisfying a need? Or are they to be understood metaphorically, in terms of something else, for example in terms of mother's mood at the moment? Does mother's smile metonymically stand for her approval of the infant's behavior, or does it have to be seen metaphorically, in terms of something else going on in the mother? Like the poet, the young child, to borrow a phrase from R. Posner (1982), "makes use of non-precoded properties of language" or observations (p. ix).

Immaturity or trauma can cause confusion regarding the metaphoric or metonymic connection between mental entities or relationships. The infant's immature mind might see the bottle metonymically as an extension, or stand-in, for the mother's breast. The child who has been beaten by the father may, from then on, see father—and future authority figures—almost exclusively as an authority to be feared. Father's metaphorical meanings in terms of a role model, a friend, a caregiver, or a loved-one subject to moods cannot any more be fully experienced. Both immaturity and trauma can degrade a potentially metaphoric integrative experience to a metonymic concrete one.

The fundamental importance of metaphor for understanding the mind's functioning cannot be overstressed, even though here we can only highlight a few further points. Metaphor, unlike metonymy, creates new categories that allow for learning, maturational change and innovation. Metaphor integrates the old with the new by bringing memory and anticipation into the here and now. Accordingly, it has aspects of both succession and simultaneity (Vrobel et al., 2008) and can move from discursiveness to image (Langer, 1957).

Consider a situation in which the analyst is seen in a metonymical form of transference as an authority figure to be feared. Once interpreted metaphorically, the analyst can again be experienced as the coinquirer into the analysand's way of functioning; as a result, the analysand can become more creative and able to relate to the present more realistically, rather than to live in a pseudo-present filled with unrecognized ghosts of the past.

By showing how trauma can cause an event to be experienced metonymically, transference interpretation thus allows for the possibility of upgrading such experiencing to a metaphoric integration with its open-endedness and enigmatic resilience. It can bring together the relevant elements of different times into the simultaneity of a now (Vrobel, 2006), from which past, present, and future can be recast. Interpretation as curing means metaphorization of lost or lacking metaphoricity.

The metaphoric process is comparable to a tune connecting antecedent and subsequent. It is our ability to connect the memory of the preceding note, which still lingers on in our consciousness of the present, with the note we anticipate to follow it. This ability enables us to perceive a meaningful entity, a tune, as opposed to a succession of uncorrelated, isolated notes. Therefore, we must assume the Now to be extended "in order to host retention and protention" (Vrobel et al., 2008, p. 5). The metaphoric process is the basis for narrative coherence regarding memory and anticipation.

## *Summary of the Expanded and Temporal Definition of Transference, Interpretation, and Defense*

To accomplish the integration of psychodynamics with metaphor theory as so far outlined, the notions transference, interpretation, and defense have to be conceived in a somewhat broader but also simpler way. Seeing transference, interpretation, and defense as corresponding to their temporal metaphoric or metonymic structure can accomplish the three goals mentioned at the beginning of this discussion: To find a framework language through which divergent psychoanalytic schools can express themselves and communicate with each other; to bridge the gap between psychoanalysis and other cognitive sciences where there is an increasing consensus that the mind (and possibly the brain) functions metaphorically and metonymically; and that the basic psycho-dynamic concepts become equally useful to describe the neurotic and the non-neurotic aspects of the mind's functioning.

Let us start with the expanded definition of *transference:* All influences originating in the past and targeting the present will be seen as aspects of transference. There are three aspects of transference in this broader sense: (a) transference in the narrower, received sense; (b) the defended-against mentation; and, (c) the return-of-the-repressed mentation. These three aspects are, according to this redefinition, synonyms referring to transference in a specific clinical context.

We continue now with a broader definition of *interpretation:* All influences originating in the present and targeting the past will be seen as aspects of interpretation. The three aspects of interpretation in this broader sense are: (a) interpretation in the narrow, received sense; (b) the defending mentation; and (c) the mentation holding the past in abeyance. These three aspects are, according to this redefinition, synonyms referring to interpretation in a specific clinical context.

Since the direction of influence differs between transference in the broad sense and interpretation in the broad sense, we can construct temporally bidirectional pairings of above synonymous aspects. We get the following equivalences: *interpretation of transference* is equivalent with *defending against the defended* and with *holding in abeyance against the return of the repressed.* The pair *defending and defended against* can be called *defense complex* or, briefly, *defense.* We now come to the following important and clarifying formulation: "Defense is the interpretation of transference." This formulation, with its temporal and metaphoric/metonymic implications allows for a recasting of frozen parts of psychoanalytic theory in order to achieve the goals just mentioned.

The phrase *interpretation of transference* is familiar to us from our practice, where it is one of the ways we try to promote insight. Seeing interpretation of transference as synonymous with *defending and defended against* allows us to understand that the analyst's interpreting the transference is aimed at the change of a neurotic into a healthy form of defense.

In the example described earlier, concerning the analysand who was abused by his father, the analyst's interpretation is the transfiguration of a metonymically structured defense into a metaphorically structured one. Put differently, it is a remetaphorization of a trauma-based loss of metaphoricity. At first, the analysand experienced the neurotic part of the transference metonymically: He regarded the analyst as a childhood figure without the awareness that the tension between present and past had collapsed from two temporal domains into one. We recall here that, in linguistics, metonymy is defined as articulating a source and target within the same domain.

We have described the neurotic and healthy variants of transference, interpretation, and defense. As already indicated, we postulate that at any time the mind functions, in the main unconsciously, by interpreting its transferences such that the present and past maintain the metaphoric tension allowing for mutual and mutative interpretations.

## The Enduring Enigma of the Sphinx

The process of metaphorization occurs not only within the changing mind but also within theory development. At one time, Freud metaphorized such hither to dualistically understood psychological concepts as motivation versus sexuality, motivation versus unconscious processes, personality development versus sexual development, remembering versus enacting, and many others, by seeing them in terms of each other. He discovered the intrinsic relationship between these hitherto only extrinsically related notions. His most famous metaphorization was the Oedipus complex, in which the triangular relationships between father, mother and child were seen in terms of passions conceived as incestuous sexuality and aggression.

Oedipus, according to the Greek legend, solved the riddle presented by the Sphinx, which had caused such devastation for the population of Thebes. But in doing so, Oedipus bypassed the enigma contained in what we could call the Sphinx complex: How was the Sphinx able to tempt so many young men to their death? Why did these would-be heroes perish after not understanding something of great importance, which, as it turned out, had to do with the notion of the life cycle of childhood, adulthood, and old age? What kind of creature or event was half male, half female; half human, half animal? What was the function of the Sphinx's gravity defying wings? Why did the Sphinx need to kill herself when Oedipus uncovered her secret? What was the great danger and great promise all about? (See Roheim, 1934, regarding the Sphinx as representing the primal scene.)

Oedipus had to enact what he did not understand. He made the prophecy of filial rage and lust come to pass by killing his father and marrying his mother. When the truth was revealed, his mother, like the Sphinx, killed herself. His unbearable guilt about having availed himself of mother's secret ended in self punishment through blinding himself. What one cannot metaphorize one has to enact, as is well known from clinical experience where enactments are observed when metonymic transferences remain without adequate metaphoric interpretation.

It was Freud's genius that solved the Sphinx's enigma by conceptualizing the Oedipus complex. What Oedipus understood too concretely, Freud was able to metaphorize. This is what the analyst does when interpreting. Metaphorizing means to make something more interesting by clarifying it while illuminating the ensuing enigma. But metaphorization needs to be kept up lest it becomes metonymic both clinically and theoretically.

In view of the puzzling existence of so many divergent psychoanalytic schools, we can now ask: What was it, in analogy to Oedipus, which Freud and his disciples were enacting and thus remained unaware of? It was building theory only on the level of metaphoric clarification— and leaving out the crucial second step of metaphorization, namely enigmatization. Clarification without metaphoric enigmatization leads to dichotomies, thus reducing the flexibility of even the most creative concepts. As a result of this shortcoming, psychoanalytic theory became increasingly metonymic, filled with hard-to-resolve dichotomies resisting metaphorization. I am defining dichotomies as pairs of concepts that oppose or exclude each other and are left without mediation. This can be remedied by suffusing psychoanalytic theory with metaphor theory.

### *Psychoanalytic Schools and Their Pitfalls of Dichotomous Thinking*

Metaphor mediates between two separate entities, and thus can be used as an antidote to dichotomies. The concepts *primary process* and *secondary process* can serve as an example. Mediation between these exclusionary processes is achieved with the concept *metaphoric process*. The metaphoric process, like the primary process, entails displacements and condensations of meaning and, like the secondary process, is reality-oriented. The metaphoric process, neither fully irrational nor fully rational, can be said to represent imaginative rationality. As such, it is a process occurring between the edge of chaos and the edge of stagnation. It is the creative self-organizing process that occurs on a daily basis in parts of the mind that are not neurotically impaired. Metaphorizing has to be an ongoing process in order for the mind not to become metonymic.

The theories developed by the different psychoanalytic schools, having remained insufficiently metaphorized, are therefore burdened with a multitude of dichotomies. Starting with Freud and the orthodox Freudians, we encounter the following dichotomies, most of which we have only touched upon: The just mentioned primary versus secondary process was not mediated by conceptualizing a metaphoric process; psychodynamic concepts solely pertaining versus not solely pertaining to the treatment setting remained not mediated by a theory where the interplay of transference, interpretation, and defense is seen as occurring in and outside the treatment setting; defense versus defended against was not mediated by a theory of their metaphoric or metonymic relationship; transference versus interpretation versus defense were seen in their external, functional relationship and remained not mediated through a theory of their being congruent with each other as temporal metaphors; interpretation of transference versus defending against the defended was not mediated by a theory of their being synonymous; the concepts conscious versus unconscious were not mediated through a concept of awareness that could include both.

The Jungians, perhaps sensing the dichotomy of acceptable rationality versus unacceptable irrationality, developed theories trying to integrate enigmatic aspects of life. The Kleinians sensed, perhaps, the lack of an elaborated temporal theory as they developed a theory of successive paranoid and depressive positions, where patterns of organization rather than specific contents are emphasized as relevant for the interplay between developmental and transferential issues. The Kohutians sensed, perhaps, the dichotomy of drive-based motivation versus motivation resulting from interpersonal influences and, with it, the absence of a theory mediating self-interpretation and other-interpretation—the analyst's or the parents'. They developed a theory integrating the influence of the parents' and the analysts' quality of empathy with the child/analysand.

All psychoanalytic schools use their own metaphor language to connect transferential and developmental phenomena by seeing them as mutually illuminating. Each school, in its own way, brings the present transferential issues into metaphoric alignment with issues of the past, understanding one in terms of the other.

## Review and Outlook

Although psychoanalytic practice deals with temporality and metaphor in a mainly implicit but central manner, the psychoanalytic theories do not thematize temporality and metaphor as central notions. There are several reasons for this lag in theory: Metaphor, because of its open-endedness and its enigmatic vagueness (Tuggy, 1993), was not seen as a serious scientific subject; interpretation, an aspect of metaphor, was not seen as metaphorization of lost metaphoricity and, therefore, as both clarification and enigmatization: making something interesting, rather than being limited to solving a problem. The psychoanalytic process was not seen as a special case of ubiquitously occurring metaphoric processes in the mind. The dialogic recursivity between the present and the past time domains was not sufficiently theorized. The psychodynamic concepts of transference, interpretation, and defense were, therefore, not understood as temporal metaphoric ones, and, in the case of neurosis, as temporal metonymic ones. The complexity theories' notions of nonlinearity and disequilibrium (Prigogine, 1997)—important aspects of metaphor—were not known as essential attributes of the mind's functioning and were replaced by stifling notions of linearity and equilibrium. The notion of emergence, so important in the theory of metaphor and the developing theory of complexity, was, to some extent, thematized by psychoanalytic theory as the return of the repressed, as becoming conscious, and as getting in-touch with heretofore not integrated dynamics.

Most important, transference was not generalized to mean the mutative interpretation of the present by the past and interpretation as the mutative interpretation of the past by the present. Transference, interpretation, and defense were, therefore, understood only in their extrinsic relationships. The notion of a defense complex with the two components of defending and defended was not theorized sufficiently, and their relationship as source and target of a metaphor or metonymy remained unexplored. The psychodynamic pairing of these temporally bidirectional concepts, namely interpretation and transference on the one hand and defense as defending and defended against on the other hand, were not seen in their congruence. The important formula revealing the intrinsic connections between the main psychodynamic concepts, namely that *defense is the interpretation of transference*, was not discovered. Interpretation of transference was conceptualized only as one of the analyst's activities, rather than as the mind's ubiquitous, mainly unconscious, and ongoing process in or outside any treatment setting. Accordingly, the extension of all psychodynamic concepts as relevant to the mind's general functioning, in or outside the treatment setting, could not occur because the psychoanalytic process was not seen as a special case of the mind's metaphoric processes.

To repeat, these theoretical shortcomings were the consequence of overlooking temporality and metaphoricity as the most central, albeit implicit, notions of psychoanalytic practice. The concept *metaphoric process* remained unknown and thus could not forestall the sterile, metonymic dichotomies that became entrenched in psychoanalytic theories. Charismatic psychoanalysts, sensing the impediments of unacceptable dichotomies but not understanding their source, tried to overcome the problem by creating new theories, new languages, and new dichotomies. Many of these nonmetaphorically conceived theories had, nevertheless, staying power because they were still capable of grasping the metonymic, repetitive, neurotic aspects of the mind's functioning. Repetition was thematized, creativity (metaphor!) as a central concept of personality theory remained neglected.

As we contemplate, based on this discussion, the puzzling existence of divergent psychoanalytic schools, we should resist the following two suggestions advanced by contemporary theoreticians (Wallerstein, 2005) for solving this problem: We are asked to either research what these schools' theories have in common and hope for a diminishing divergence between them over time or find an ecumenical way of agreeing to disagree and see the burgeoning number of schools as a sign of vitality with which psychoanalytic theory advances. In both cases we would clarify, like Oedipus, a riddle but continue, like Oedipus, to enact confusion, instead of getting interested in the enigma of metaphorizing. Such enactment would further increase the distance to the cognitive sciences in general and to the unfolding complexity theory of the mind in particular. The latter, as well as the neural theory of metaphor, now in early formation (Lakoff, 2008) could be greatly advanced by introducing metaphor- and metonymy-based psychoanalytic notions.

# 9

# METAPHOR AND
# PSYCHODYNAMIC RESEARCH[1]

*Robert F. Bornstein and Nikaya Becker-Matero*

In recent decades psychoanalysts have examined the role of metaphor in psychodynamic theory and therapy, but the uses of metaphor in psychoanalytic research have received only modest attention. After briefly reviewing extant psychoanalytic writings on metaphor, we discuss how research from outside psychoanalysis (i.e., studies of embodied affect-space links, mental images and prototypes, and associative networks) can inform us about the nature of metaphor. We then explore the ways that metaphor deepens our understanding of psychodynamic research and its implications, focusing on metaphoric definitions of concepts, and the metaphoric features of experimental manipulations and outcome assessments. Implications of a metaphoric perspective for the empirical testing of psychoanalytic concepts are discussed, and future directions for exploration in this area are described.

Metaphor has been defined as "the mapping of one conceptual domain onto a dissimilar conceptual domain ... resulting in a transfer of meaning from one to the other" (Modell, 1997b, p. 106). As Lakoff and Johnson (1980a) noted, metaphor is not merely a rhetorical device, but a fundamental way of thinking and understanding. Metaphoric concepts connect ostensibly separate aspects of human experience, linking body and mind, emotion and memory, past and present, unconscious and conscious. Our ability to interact and communicate effectively with others depends upon a shared metaphoric understanding of ourselves and the world; intersubjectivity is inextricably grounded in metaphor. Formal definitions notwithstanding, perhaps the most useful conceptualization of metaphor is itself metaphoric: Metaphor is the glue that links disparate aspects of human mental life, over time and across different contexts, enabling us to construct cohesive personal narratives that give meaning to past and present experience.

Although the concept of metaphor is rooted in linguistics, in recent decades psychoanalysts have noted the central role that metaphor plays in psychoanalytic theory and therapy (Borbely, 2009; Gargiulo, 2006; Katz, 2011b). Metaphor helps unify disparate psychoanalytic perspectives (e.g., drive theory, object relations theory, self psychology) and illuminates common elements of different models. Analysts have begun to explore the ways in which metaphor may be a useful tool for embedding psychoanalysis in a broader epistemological context as well, making explicit connections between psychoanalysis and other areas of inquiry (e.g., Levin, 2009;

Modell, 2005). In this respect metaphor has the potential to bridge the divide between psychoanalysis and other perspectives on personality (e.g., cognitive, humanistic), other areas of psychology (e.g., developmental, social), and fields outside psychology (e.g., art, physics).

One issue that has received only modest attention from analytic writers is the role of metaphor in psychoanalytic research—the ways in which metaphor may help researchers test psychoanalytic hypotheses empirically, and utilize research findings from outside psychoanalysis to enhance psychoanalytic theory and therapy. This paper seeks to fill that gap by examining the role of metaphor in research, to facilitate meaningful dialogue in this area. After briefly reviewing extant psychoanalytic writings on metaphor, we address two issues in detail: 1) how research from outside psychoanalysis can inform us about the nature of metaphor; and 2) how metaphor can deepen our understanding of psychodynamic research and its implications.

## Theory, Process, and Treatment Dynamics: The Three Prongs of Psychoanalytic Metaphor

Freud often relied on metaphor to describe psychoanalytic constructs and make esoteric concepts accessible to the reader. As Wachtel (2003) pointed out, many of these metaphors involved spatial and military imagery, sometimes in combination (e.g., Freud's [1923a/1961] likening of fixation and regression to an army advancing through territories but leaving behind contingents of troops at various points along the way). For the most part metaphoric concepts have been applied in three domains of psychoanalysis: theory and metatheory, psychological process, and therapist–patient interaction.

### Theory and Metatheory

A diverse array of psychoanalytic constructs (e.g., psychic energy, displacement, preconscious, repression, libido) are fundamentally metaphoric. As Wurmser (1977) noted, this situation is not unique to psychoanalysis: Novel concepts from various disciplines often emerge first in metaphoric form, eventually acquiring fixed labels as they become more widely accepted. Resistance to acknowledging the metaphoric underpinnings of psychoanalytic concepts can have myriad negative effects, however, leading to "the error of misplaced concreteness" (Gargiulo, 1998, p. 416) wherein metaphoric concepts are reified and treated as immutable entities rather than descriptive labels.

Metaphor also plays an important role in psychoanalytic metatheory. Every major school of psychoanalytic thought (e.g., drive theory, self psychology, object relations theory) is identified by a metaphoric label which reflects the core assumptions characterizing that model (e.g., behavior as shaped by instinctual drives, mind-as-map, psyche as mental representations of self and significant figures). In some respects the evolution of psychoanalytic metatheory during the past 100 years has been a search for the ideal metaphor to capture in a single word or phrase all the key elements of intrapsychic functioning and interpersonal dynamics.

## Psychological Process

Metaphoric concepts have helped shape psychoanalysts' understanding of a broad spectrum of psychological processes, being applied most prominently to trauma, symbolization, memory reconstruction, and the dynamics of emotional memories. In this context, Modell (1997b, 2005) delineated the ways in which metaphoric processes help categorize and map emotional experience, providing structure and agency during periods of intense or overwhelming affect. Consistent with Modell's view, Stern (2009) noted that dissociation occurs when this process fails, and memories of traumatic experiences are not infused with metaphor. As a result traumatic experiences become isolated and compartmentalized, and cannot take on new meaning: The patient is unable to apply new experiences to gain a more nuanced understanding of the traumatic event. As trauma gradually comes to be seen through a metaphoric lens, the patient can begin to experience the traumatic event as part of an evolving life narrative, linking the traumatic experience to aspects of the self and facilitating a therapeutic shift from knowing to feeling.

## Therapist–Patient Interaction

Seventy years ago Sharpe (1940) conceptualized free association—the grist of the psychoanalytic mill—as a metaphoric process in which preverbal events are expressed through speech. More recently Arlow (1979) suggested that psychoanalytic treatment *in toto* is inherently metaphoric: The patient provides the analyst a metaphoric expression of unconscious fantasy, and the analyst engages the patient by adopting the perspective that the patient's metaphor requires. Consistent with Arlow's view, Ogden (1997) noted that a central curative element (or "common factor") in many psychodynamic interventions is that they help the patient replace concrete language with metaphorical dialogue.

Metaphor not only provides the essential language of psychoanalytic process, but plays a key role in shaping transference by functioning as a "pattern detector so that the meaning of an old relationship is unconsciously transferred into the here and now" (Modell, 2005, p. 526). Borbely (1998, p. 933) captured nicely the central role of metaphor in these aspects of therapist–patient interaction, noting that "In order to be able to help the analyst must be in possession of a theory and technique of metaphor language, which is capable of conceptually encompassing the salient developmental stages, traumata and conflicts of childhood, as well as the events unfolding in the transference." In this respect different psychoanalytic schools may differ in the details, but they share a common goal of conceptualizing (and helping the patient conceptualize) psychological development, conflict, striving, and defense in metaphoric terms.

## How Research Informs Metaphor: Reifying the Unobservable

In recent years psychodynamic theorists have used research findings from outside psychoanalysis to explore the ways that metaphor can enhance our understanding of a broad array of psychoanalytic concepts. The most widely discussed links involve neuropsychology, wherein research on brain structure and function has elucidated the biological underpinnings of unconscious mental processes, helped trace the evolutionary roots of human behavioral predispositions, and been used to examine the interplay of neuropsychological, social, and cultural influences on affective experience and emotional responding (e.g., Modell, 2005; Slipp, 2000).

Developmental studies—especially those focusing on early infant-caregiver interactions—have also garnered considerable attention. Research in this area has provided an empirical basis for distinguishing primary—or "root"—metaphors (i.e., metaphors that originate in pre-verbal bodily awareness), from metaphors that are more strongly shaped by experience (Modell, 1997b). Developmental studies have also enhanced analysts' understanding of the ways in which variations in infant-caregiver mirroring (itself a metaphoric concept) shape subsequent personality dynamics (Stern, 2009).

Cognitive science has been a third area of emphasis, with cognitive research helping elucidate the role of metaphor in contextualizing memories, and the process by which retrieval of schema-based memories inevitably results in some degree of distortion and reconstruction (Michels, 2005). These latter findings have been particularly relevant for understanding the long-term negative effects of early trauma, and the obstacles to accessing and working through traumatic memories in psychoanalytic treatment.[2]

Beyond these widely studied topics, a number of research programs from outside psychoanalysis have the potential to enhance our understanding of the psychodynamics of metaphor. Three stand out.

## Metaphorizing the Environment: Embodied Affect-Space Links

Central to contemporary psychodynamic models of metaphor is the assumption that there are inborn, pre-existing connections between affect and bodily experience, sometimes described as *embodied affect-space links*. For example, there appears to be an innate association between upward gaze or movement and positive affect (as reified in the assumption that heaven is skyward, and the common comment that "things are looking up"), and a parallel association between downward gaze or movement and negative affect (which is why hell is below us and sometimes we "feel down"). Until recently evidence for embodied affect-space links was primarily anecdotal, but research from social cognition has provided empirical support for psychoanalytic thinking in this area.

For example, Meier and Robinson (2004) found that evaluations of affectively positive words occurred more rapidly when those words were presented in the upper portion of the visual field, whereas evaluations of negative words occurred more rapidly when these words were presented in the lower portion of the visual field; presumably our tendency to associate "up" with positive affect and "down" with negative affect facilitated cognitive processing when affect and word position were concordant. In a subsequent series of studies Meier et al. (2007a) found that participants encoded God-related concepts more easily if those concepts were presented in a high (versus low) vertical position; the opposite pattern was obtained for devil-related concepts. A second study demonstrated that when participants were presented with God- and devil-related concepts and later asked to recall the physical location of each concept, they showed a bias toward misremembering God-related concepts as being high and devil-related concepts as being low. When shown pictures of strangers and asked to assess their religious beliefs, participants rated strangers as stronger believers in God when their pictures appeared high in the visual field.

Studies further suggest that these highly automatized metaphor-affect links are not limited to vertical position. For example, Meier et al. (2007b) found that people perceive positive words as being brighter in color than negative words, which appear comparatively dark (even though all the words were actually presented in the same shade). Meier et al. (2008) demonstrated that, metaphorically speaking, bigger is indeed better: Positive words were evaluated more rapidly when presented in a large font, whereas evaluations of negative words were more rapid when their font was small. These size biases occur for neutral words as well: In a follow-up experiment affectively neutral words were evaluated as being more positive when their font was large, and more negative when their font was small.

## Internalizing the External: Imagery as Metaphor

Each individual's internal world can be conceptualized as a metaphoric representation of the external world. We construct and retain mental images of significant figures (e.g., mother, father, self) that have both physical attributes and affect qualities (e.g., benevolence, punitiveness, empathy, rigidity; see Blatt, et al. 1993). We construct mental images of other features of the external world as well (e.g., common objects, familiar environments), and like mental representations of significant figures, our mental images of inanimate objects are to some degree veridical, and to some degree distorted. These distortions reflect constraints inherent in the human information processing system (e.g., external percepts are reconstructed as they are encoded in memory), and psychodynamic processes as well (e.g., affective experiences which bias the ways in which we perceive and encode object features). Some of our internalized images need not reflect external reality at all: Many mental images depict people or places we have never actually seen (which is why we can generate an image of an ideal lover we've never met, or what the stairways inside the World Trade Center must have looked like on 9/11).

Research on the metaphoric aspects of mental imagery may point toward a deeper understanding of the ways in which person and object representations shape behavior and affective responding. Like affect-space links, our mental representations of self and others reflect innate predispositions to encode images in particular ways. Thus, cognitive scientists have shown that mental images must be conceptually categorized before they can be encoded in long-term memory (Finke, 1989; Kosslyn, 1994); there is no such thing as an "uncategorized" mental image. As we form mental images we integrate objective features of the stimulus with an array of expectancy and experience variables that modify the initial percept, transferring meaning into the image (thus, a photograph of a person is encoded differently when the person is identified as a criminal than when they are identified as a scientist; see Bornstein & Craver-Lemley, 2004).

Prototypes—exemplary members of a conceptual category—also illustrate the ways in which mental images have metaphoric qualities (Corneille et al., 2004). When asked to picture a dog, few people generate an image of a dachshund, but instead generate a more prototypic dog, like a retriever. People judge retrievers to be "doggier" dogs than dachshunds, and hence more prototypic (Rosch, 1978). The same occurs with psychodynamically relevant prototypes, so that as transference occurs and an older male therapist takes on more and more paternal attributes, the therapist gradually comes to resemble the patient's "father" prototype. Metaphorically speaking, the therapist has replaced the father (see Borbely, 1998, 2009, for more general discussions of metaphoric aspects of transference).

## Metaphoric Associates: Accessing the Unconscious

Central to the definition of metaphor is that meaning is transferred among ostensibly unrelated concepts; through this process connections among different objects, ideas, and experiences are created, and associative links are developed and maintained (Fosshage, 2005; Melnick, 2000). Some of these metaphoric connections seem logical and rational (as when unfamiliar authority figures take on parental attributes); other metaphoric connections have a more idiosyncratic, primary process quality (as when smiling clowns appear threatening and malevolent).

Metaphoric links among tangentially related concepts can be quantified using the Emotional Stroop Task (EST; Riemann & McNally, 1995), a laboratory procedure designed to map an individual's associative network by determining the degree to which a concept within that network is active at any given moment. On the EST a prime word (e.g., FATHER) is first presented, following which a target word (e.g., STRONG) appears. The target word is presented in one of several colors (e.g., blue, green, red), and the participant's task is to ignore the content of the target word and name the color in which that word is printed as quickly as possible. To the extent that the prime word (FATHER) is conceptually linked with the target word (STRONG) in the mind of the participant, the target word will be activated by the prime word, and reaction time will slow because the participant must devote additional attentional capacity to deliberately ignoring the activated concept and focusing on the color—an effortful, time-consuming task (see William et al., 1996). Thus, EST response times are typically slower when FATHER is followed by

STRONG than when FATHER is followed by TABLE, suggesting that most people have a stronger associative link between the first two concepts than the latter two concepts.

The EST can also be used to examine individual and group differences in associative links (Bornstein et al., 2005; Dozois & Backs-Dermott, 2000), helping quantify the "transfer of meaning from one to the other" (Modell, 1997b, p. 106) that forms the basis of metaphor. For example, most psychodynamic frameworks would suggest stronger associations between FATHER and DANGEROUS in men than in women, so EST response times for this word pair should be longer in men. Women who have been sexually abused by their father should show longer reaction times to this word pair than women who have not been sexually abused. To the extent that the FATHER = DANGEROUS equivalence has generalized metaphorically to other male authority figures, one would expect that abused women's reaction times for HUSBAND (or MAN) and DANGEROUS would also be lengthened.

Using similar logic, the degree to which THERAPIST is metaphorically linked with MOTHER, FATHER, or PARENT can be evaluated using the EST, as can the degree to which SICK is associated with POWERFUL (if, e.g., the clinician believes that a particular patient is motivated to remain symptomatic to gain influence within the family). Finally, it is worth noting that changes in associative linkages over the course of treatment can be evaluated using this procedure. For example, EST reaction times for THIN and GOOD should decrease in an anorexic patient during the course of successful treatment, but remain unchanged in an anorexic patient for whom treatment was less successful.

## How Metaphor Informs Research: Inside the Freudian Skinner Box

Freud's liberal use of metaphor has led some philosophers of science (e.g., Grunbaum, 1984) and critics of psychoanalysis (e.g., Crews, 1996) to describe Freud's work—and much of the theorizing that followed—as unscientific. Freudians are hardly alone in their reliance on metaphor to identify and describe unobservable constructs, however. Many core concepts in physics (e.g., black holes), biology (e.g., natural selection), and chemistry (e.g., molecular bonds) are metaphoric. As Wurmser (1977, p. 483) pointed out, "Metaphors, taken literally, are unscientific. Metaphors, understood as symbols, are the only language of science we possess …." Edelson (1983, p. 56) put it more directly: "A scientific theory is a metaphor for reality … it is only through our studies of the metaphors of science that we can come to find out which is real."

In this respect a focus on metaphor may help inform psychodynamic research, and illuminate the ways in which the empirical testing of psychoanalytic hypotheses overlaps with and differs from the empirical testing of hypotheses in other domains. In the following sections we discuss the role of metaphor in delineating scientific concepts, developing useful experimental manipulations, and quantifying the impact of these manipulations on thought, emotion, and behavior.

## Naming the Unobservable: Metaphoric Concepts

Naming the unobservable is invariably metaphoric, and because all theories of personality invoke unobservable theoretical constructs, all rest upon metaphor. The left column of Table 9.1 lists some widely used psychodynamic constructs, many of which are clearly metaphoric in nature (e.g., repression, ego, repetition compulsion). The right column of this table lists parallel labels for these concepts that were developed by researchers in other, more "scientific" areas of inquiry. Perusal of these alternative labels confirms that they too are metaphoric (e.g., cognitive avoidance, central executive, nuclear script). As Bornstein (2005) pointed out, even though operational definitions of the psychoanalytic and non-analytic versions of these constructs typically differ in certain respects, in every instance there is considerable overlap between the two versions of a given construct.[3]

It is important that psychoanalysts become familiar with the operational definitions of key psychodynamic concepts, and with the operational definitions of parallel non-analytic concepts, for two reasons. First, by doing this our theoretical frameworks will become more rigorous, and more firmly embedded in an appropriate nomological network of related constructs: Researchers in other areas have much to teach us if we attend to their ideas and findings more closely. Second, by becoming familiar with the various definitions applied to a given concept we will be in a better position to prevent these concepts from being co-opted by researchers in other disciplines. Myriad seminal constructs originating in psychoanalytic theory (including those listed in Table 9.1) have been renamed and reinvented by non-analytic psychologists, who gradually assumed intellectual ownership of the co-opted constructs (see Bornstein, 2005, 2007b). This process has contributed substantially to the decline of psychoanalysis within mainstream psychology in recent years.

*Table 9.1*   Revisions and Reinventions of Psychoanalytic Concepts

| *Psychoanalytic Concept* | *Revision/Reinvention* |
| --- | --- |
| Unconscious Memory (1900/1953a) | Implicit Memory |
| Primary Process Thought (1900/1953a) | Spreading Activation |
| Object Representation (1905/1953b) | Person Schema |
| Repression (1910/1957a) | Cognitive Avoidance |
| Preconscious Processing (1915/1957b) | Preattentive Processing |
| Parapraxis (1916/1963) | Retrieval Error |
| Abreaction (1916/1963) | Redintegration |
| Repetition Compulsion (1920/1955) | Nuclear Script |
| Ego (1923/1961) | Central Executive |
| Ego Defense (1926/1959) | Defensive Attribution |

*Note*: Original Freudian sources are identified by year of original publication/date of corresponding Hogarth Press *Standard Edition* volume.

ROBERT F. BORNSTEIN AND NIKAYA BECKER-MATERO

## Operationalizing Phenomenology: Metaphoric Manipulations

Every experimental manipulation is a metaphor for in vivo experience; the more closely the phenomenological impact of a manipulation approximates that of the real-world experience we are trying to evoke, the more effective the manipulation. This principle can be restated in empirical terms: The external validity of an experimental manipulation is a function of the degree to which that manipulation produces the intended psychological impact in participants (e.g., evokes the desired emotional response, initiates a thought pattern, alters a motivational state).

Thus, when examining the impact of affect state on self-report and free-response measures of interpersonal dependency, Bornstein et al. (1996) asked participants to write brief essays regarding traumatic events, joyful events, or neutral events to induce a corresponding mood. In a subsequent investigation examining the impact of the presence (versus absence) of an authority figure on dependency related behavior, Bornstein (2006) employed an experimental manipulation wherein some participants were told that a psychology professor would soon arrive at the laboratory to evaluate their performance in the study, and other participants were told that no one but the undergraduate experimenter would have access to their data. In this instance the unseen professor was a metaphoric stand-in for authority figures in general.

Similar logic holds for other psychodynamically relevant research programs. For example, Subliminal Psychodynamic Activation (SPA) researchers frequently use the subliminal message MOMMY AND I ARE ONE to evoke pleasurable feelings associated with Mahler's (1968) symbiotic stage, when infant and caregiver were psychologically merged (Weinberger & Hardaway, 1990). Conversely, I AM LOSING MOMMY has been used to induce feelings of helplessness and abandonment (Patton, 1992). Along somewhat different lines, Pennebaker (1997) has documented the positive effects of cathartic unburdening of negative affect by asking participants to write essays regarding traumatic events and experiences. In these studies essay writing replaces more traditional verbal disclosure (e.g., free association) as a method for accessing heretofore unexpressed thoughts and emotions.

## Quantifying Impact: Measurement as Metaphor

Just as experimental manipulations are metaphoric replacements for in vivo experiences, the outcome measures used in most studies are metaphors for in vivo responses. For example, the Rorschach inkblots are just that—inkblots—but descriptions of these inkblots are taken to represent respondents' perceptions and experiences of self and other people (see Exner & Erdberg, 2005). Put another way, when a respondent's descriptions of inkblots are filled with malevolent imagery, we assume (and data confirm) that these malevolent attributions taint the respondent's perceptions of actual people as well (Blatt, 1990; Lerner, 2005). Simply asking someone if they see others as dangerous is likely to produce a defensive reaction at best, and at worst outright hostility; asking someone to describe inkblots allows them to make malevolent misattributions without acknowledging (or even recognizing) their source (Bornstein, 2007a).

The notion that measurement is metaphor for in vivo response is not limited to inkblots, but occurs for a broad array of psychological assessment tools. Following Milgram's (1963) groundbreaking obedience studies there have been dozens of experiments examining conditions that exacerbate or inhibit people's willingness to behave aggressively toward others. But none of these investigations measured actual aggression (nor did Milgram): In every case aggression was operationalized metaphorically and assessed indirectly (e.g., willingness to shock another person during a "learning study," severity of prison sentence assigned to a mock trial defendant, number of personal fouls committed during a hockey game).

It is important to recognize the metaphoric aspect of measured outcomes, because if we do not we risk erroneously equating the measurement with the underlying variable it is intended to represent. Such equivalence errors—akin to Gargiulo's (1998, p. 416) "error of misplaced concreteness"—are surprisingly common in psychology. For example, a survey of five leading personality disorder (PD) journals revealed that 80% of all PD studies published between 1991 and 2000 relied exclusively on self-reports to assess both personality pathology and its correlates; no behaviors were ever measured in these investigations (Bornstein, 2003). Such patterns would be troubling in the best of circumstances, but are especially problematic given the topic being examined. After all, a distinguishing feature of PDs is limited insight and distorted self-awareness (Kernberg, 1984; Millon, 1996). It is ironic (to say the least) that the vast majority of PD studies rely exclusively on questionnaires, when we know *a priori* that the questionnaire responses of PD patients are almost certain to be unreliable.[4]

## Reconnecting Psychoanalysis to Mainstream Psychology: Can Metaphor Glue the Person Together Again?

Psychoanalysts' historical reluctance to embrace traditional empirical methods has had numerous unintended negative effects, including the co-opting of psychoanalytic ideas by researchers in other areas, and the marginalization of psychodynamic treatment in an increasingly cost-constrained managed care environment (Bornstein, 2001, 2005). Reconnecting psychoanalysis to mainstream psychology is crucial if psychodynamic principles and therapies are to regain the stature they had during the early part of the twentieth century. Although metaphor is essentially idiographic in nature (see Arlow, 1979; Gargiulo, 1998), it has the potential to contribute to a fruitful integration of psychoanalytic and non-analytic perspectives, and to nomothetic as well as idiographic research efforts. In this context the parallels between metaphoric and nomothetic understanding of internal and external reality, though subtle, are noteworthy. One function of metaphor is to contextualize emotional memories, tagging them with a sort of affect label that facilitates retrieval of these memories when similar situations arise in ostensibly unrelated contexts years—even decades—

later. Nomothetic research serves a similar function: It contextualizes discipline-wide principles ("scientific memories") to facilitate retrieval of these principles when similar results emerge in new, ostensibly unrelated contexts (see Bornstein, 2009, for a discussion of this process in the evolution of personality assessment, quantum theory, and nonrepresentational art).

Psychoanalysis is in a unique position to conceptualize and study metaphor in the laboratory, as it has in the consulting room. Continued efforts in this area represent an opportunity to strengthen the empirical base of psychoanalysis, and increase the relevance of psychoanalytic research for clinicians. Equally important, a focus on metaphor may provide one of the best opportunities to identify those psychoanalytic constructs that have been co-opted, renamed, and reinvented by researchers in other disciplines. In this respect understanding the contrasting metaphoric labels used by psychoanalysts and others to identify similar psychological constructs represents a unique opportunity for us to reclaim what is ours.

Understanding scientific metaphors is key, but scrutinizing the pseudo-scientific metaphors that are sometimes used to describe psychological constructs is important as well. Oftentimes patients have internalized misleading metaphors to understand mind and brain, leading them to develop inaccurate beliefs about psychological difficulties and unrealistic expectations regarding psychological treatments (e.g., that the effects of early trauma will dissipate immediately if repressed memories of the traumatic events can be accessed). Worse, countless patients have been harmed by well-meaning clinicians who internalized misleading metaphors (e.g., memory as film or computer hard drive rather than sketchpad, dissociative identity disorder as literally reflecting multiple personalities rather than a fragmented ego/self). Understanding how research informs metaphor (and vice versa) can help correct the distortions associated with reliance on pseudo-scientific metaphors in our patients, and in ourselves.

A similar process of self-scrutiny may be useful in understanding the limitations of the *Diagnostic and Statistical Manual of Mental Disorders* (DSM) as a tool for classifying psychopathology. Many DSM category labels have become metaphors for the syndromes they are intended to identify, and we find ourselves describing patients in metaphoric terms (e.g., "a flaming borderline," "a toxic narcissist"). Exacerbating the problem, DSM category labels have become so widely used that many are now dead metaphors, having lost their metaphoric qualities. In this context one important contribution of the *Psychodynamic Diagnostic Manual* (PDM) is that it calls our attention to the fact that DSM categories represent only one of many possible metaphoric frameworks for describing psychological syndromes. To the extent that the PDM helps clinicians see the metaphoric qualities of DSM labels more clearly, it can enhance the rigor of both diagnostic systems.

Finally, as the study of metaphor moves forward, it may be time to shift our focus from general principles of metaphoric process to individual differences in metaphor use. Beyond emphasizing the fundamental role that metaphor plays in thinking and understanding, Lakoff and Johnson's (1980a) work illustrates how different groups (e.g., liberals and conservatives) differ in their use of metaphor to conceptualize various issues. Although initial research in this area focused on individual differences in political attitudes and beliefs, the same principles hold for other individual difference variables as well (e.g., gender, age, ethnicity). Examining differences in metaphoric process in different types of patients (e.g., histrionic versus borderline) may allow us to tailor our interventions more precisely and enhance the effectiveness of psychodynamic treatment.

Thus, in addition to elucidating the role of metaphor in psychoanalytic theory, and the ways in which metaphor may deepen our understanding of research and its implications, it is time to explore differences in metaphor as a function of gender, culture, personality style, and other psychologically relevant variables. A truly integrative twenty-first century psychoanalysis must not only combine clinical wisdom with empirical data, and embed its ideas and findings in the broadest possible epistemological context, but it must also refine its interventions to maximize treatment effectiveness for patients with a broad array of backgrounds and diverse life experiences.

## Notes

1  Originally published in *Psychoanalytic Inquiry* 31(2): pp. 172–184 with the title "Reconnecting Psychoanalysis to Mainstream Psychology: Metaphor as Glue."
2  Although numerous analytic writers have drawn upon studies from cognitive science to test and refine psychodynamic concepts, Michels (2005) pointed out that many constructs in contemporary cognitive science are flexible enough that they can be incorporated into extant psychodynamic frameworks without altering these frameworks in substantive ways (cf. Bucci, 1997).
3  Behaviorists might argue that behavioral models—especially radical behavioral models—are metaphor-free, but they would be wrong. Myriad behavioral constructs (e.g., generalization, discrimination, unconditioned stimulus, avoidance learning, intermittent reinforcement) are to varying degrees metaphoric.
4  PD researchers are not alone in their implicit equating of self-reports with the underlying variables assessed by self-report measures. Although the Five Factor Model (FFM; Costa & McCrae, 1997) is far and away the dominant model of personality in scientific psychology today, the vast majority of FFM studies rely exclusively on self-reports to assess personality as well as its correlates.

# 10

# PSYCHOANALYTIC FIELD CONCEPTS[1]

## *S. Montana Katz*

Field concepts currently in use in psychoanalysis may be viewed as special cases of general psychoanalytic fields. Existing field concepts include the fields of relational, intersubjective, and interpersonal psychoanalysis, self object matrices, the analytic situation of Donnet, Green's thirdness, Ogden's thirdness, fields resulting from Faimberg's listening to listening, and the fields originated by the Barangers and elaborations of them. Each particular kind of field serves as a core concept of the psychoanalytic perspective in which it was created or implied. It is useful to parse clinical process as evolving within an environment that could be called a "field." The specific kind of field employed depends upon several factors, including the psychoanalytic orientation of the analyst. This chapter describes the fields employed in different psychoanalytic perspectives and also the concept of a general psychoanalytic field.

### Relational, Self Psychology, and Constructivist Fields

Forms of relational psychoanalytic perspectives have used field terms such as *relational field, intersubjective field, interactional field,* and *interpersonal matrix* to describe the medium in which the analytic process unfolds. The emphasis is on the here and now of the interaction between analysand and analyst. This real-time interaction is what constitutes the relational field. The clinical interaction between analysand and analyst is the medium in which meaning evolves. This meaning of, for example, the analysand's enactments with the analyst is construed and understood within the dyadic interaction in which both participate. Enactments are understood as the means of expression of unsymbolized affective experience, primarily of the patient but also of the analyst (Bromberg, 2008). Unconscious intersubjective patterns are live in the transferential matrix. Once lived through in the analytic setting, there is a potential for understanding transferential elements. The individual is understood to emerge from the relational process of co-constructed meanings.

In contrast, in a classical model the individual enters the psychoanalytic process, is the focus of it, and leaves the process the same individual, albeit ideally deeply affected by the process. In relational models, the two-person field is posited to constitute the analysand through the analytic process. In forms of relational models, there is a varying degree of tension concerning the individual roots of the meanings of enactments. That is, the degree to which repetition is involved varies in relational perspectives. The psychic structure said to emerge from an interactional field is considered a co-construction based on the unfolding understanding of the analysand's historical, relational patterns that come alive and are potentially modified in the field (Hirsch, 1995). Analyst and analysand are both considered fully present and active, albeit asymmetrically, in the process.

Self object matrices of self psychology could be described in terms of relational fields that include—and, in the transference, emphasize—developmentally early relational fields of the analysand as experienced in the present analytic process. Constructivism expands the relational framework. It emphasizes that the progressive understanding arrived at is a collaboration between the processes of both participants—that it is original, that it necessarily leads to change in both analyst and analysand, and that each emerges from the field as a result of what transpired there (Hoffman, 1991).

## Thirdness

The relational and constructivist perspectives indicate the possibility of a complement to the concept of the here and now (Green, 2004). In this regard, concepts of thirdness could be viewed as widening the psychoanalytic relational field. In its most general form, the third points to other significant influences beyond the dyad that are involved in the analytic interaction. A specific concept of the analytic third could be viewed as launching from a relational matrix to posit another subjectivity beyond that of the analyst and analysand within analytic processes. The analytic third is considered to be generated by the dialectic of the subjectivities of the analysand and the analyst. This third is both created by and creates the subjective experience of analysand and analyst (Ogden, 2009). The necessarily unique matrix that evolves from the interplay and creation of subjectivity and intersubjectivity within the analytic process becomes an aspect of the object of psychoanalytic study.

A further widening of the concept of the psychoanalytic field derives from an emphasis on the impact of the analytic setting itself on the process, as described by Donnet (2001). Donnet's conception of the analytic situation recognizes the interaction of the analysand with the analytic site, which includes the analyst, the analytic process, and what it offers. This interaction includes the activity of the intersubjective third.

## Faimberg Fields

Faimberg (2007) refines the concept of *nachträglichkeit* and in so doing in effect constructs a kind of field. In the model that arises from the work of Faimberg, a central part of the analytic process is the analyst's attention to how the analysand listens to the analyst's interpretations and to the unfolding exchange within the dyad (Faimberg, 2005; Sodré, 2005). That is, the analyst is attending to the conscious and unconscious ingredients in the analysand's understanding of the meanings of the analytic exchange.

In effect, a kind of field is created by this attentive analytic listening to listening. This field contains a detailed expansion of the metaphoric processes from within each expression in the analytic exchange. The expansion includes an ever-branching articulation of derivatives of the analysand's unconscious processes that are involved in her or his experience of the analytic exchange.

The intrapsychic is modeled as constructed and reconstructed within the intersubjective exchange in a Faimberg field. The construction of the intrapsychic in this model is related to that posited in relational and other fields. As a part of the field, neither participant can survey the entirety of the field nor make sound, general statements about it. The analyst thus cannot be considered an authority concerning herself, the analysand, or the field.

In most psychoanalytic perspectives, analytic fields are said to be asymmetrical. As Baranger (2009) points out, it is only the analysand who speaks associations aloud, not the analyst. This creates asymmetry. The training and objective of the analyst to attend to understanding the derivatives of the analysand's unconscious processes strengthen the existence of asymmetry in the process (Katz, 2011b).

With Faimberg's concept of *listening to listening*, the assertion that the analytic process is asymmetrical can be understood and given more precise meaning. That is, it is the analyst whose focus is primarily to listen to the analysand's listening to the analytic process. The analysand may also engage in this, but it is an essential role of the analyst to do so.

## Baranger Fields

The foregoing field concepts lead directly to a further elaboration that yields another conception of an analytic field. This concept of the analytic field was introduced by Madeleine and Willy Baranger (1961–62). The Barangers' work, based on Kleinian and especially on Bionian thought, has multiple influences, such as the Gestalt theory of Kurt Lewin, Merleau-Ponty's work, Pichon-Rivière's contributions, and Racker's work on countertransference. The Barangers developed a structure with which to describe and guide clinical work (de Leon de Bernardi, 2000; Lewkowicz & Flechner, 2005; Silverman, 2010; Zimmer, 2010). The analytic field concept is used to describe another conception of the analytic situation as a whole. The analytic field encompasses all aspects of the analytic situation, including the spatial, temporal, and functional. Employing such a conception of the analytic field broadens the understanding of the analytic relationship and process to explicitly include all these dimensions (Ferro, 2005a).

While there are said to be asymmetries in the field between the participants, the analyst is not considered to have authority in the process. In the Barangers' model, as in the relational, constructivist, and Faimberg models, the analyst is not considered to be self-contained or solely an observing interpreter. Rather, the analyst is viewed as an active contributor to and participant in the production of what is called the *basic fantasy of the field*. Thus the analyst is also an immediate part of the object of analytic study within the psychoanalytic process.

The individuals participating in an analytic process are considered to be derivative from the field, as are their unconscious processes. Unlike what is seen in relational models, the analytic field itself is posited to contain an unconscious dynamic that is more than and different from the sum of the unconscious dynamics of each participant. In this model, the unconscious of the field and the concomitant fantasies, called basic fantasies, are the immediate objects of interest and exploration in the analytic process. The analytic object of interest is thus neither the analysand nor the two-person interaction.

The quality of the analytic field is described as oneiric and as a dream membrane (Grotstein, 2009). The field is conceived in important ways as atemporal and as embodying a virtual reality. The fantasies of the field arise within the field and are not simple or direct imports from either participant.

Similarly, the presences found in the field are the results of and take shape in the fantasies of the field, and are thus neither solely from the past nor from the current experience of either participant. Derivatives of the metaphoric processes of the analyst and of the analysand are in the field, as are multiple virtual presences of analyst, analysand, primary objects, and others, as well as combinations and permutations of the participants' metaphoric processes.

The field and its fantasies are viewed in this model as novel creations that could not have arisen or been constructed in any other circumstance. This means that there will necessarily be different fields associated with different analytic couples and therefore different analytic processes. The intrapsychic is considered to be derivative from the intersubjective creations of the field. The individual participants are understood as emerging from the field rather than as components of it. By observing and understanding the basic fantasy, the intrapsychic processes of the analysand can be understood. The intrapsychic is viewed as a precipitate of the basic fantasy of the field.

## Comparison of Field Concepts

In the following, common labels for psychoanalytic perspectives will be used only to locate classes of perspectives and without the precision of specific instantiation. That is, none of the names of different perspectives—such as classical, Kleinian, relational, and so forth—here specifies a theoretical and clinical position, but rather points to a general orientation within which there are variations.

It can be asked what work in one kind of field looks like from the vantage point of another. It might be that viewing an alternative perspective involves the diminished emphasis or erasure of certain components of metaphoric processes, or possibly understanding them as something else. Each analyst views clinical material through the filter of the chosen form of field implied by the psychoanalytic perspective used. For example, classical Freudian and relational filters are different in important respects that render understanding and clarity between them difficult. That is why general psychoanalytic fields in their broad inclusiveness of elements can help bridge gaps in understanding and meaning.

As has been elaborated above, the contents of analytic fields of different psychoanalytic perspectives vary. Psychoanalytic perspectives can be differentiated as well as linked in terms of the kinds of fields employed, together with which components of metaphoric processes and their derivatives are emphasized within each model. The kind of field associated with classical theory takes shape as a result of the transferences that develop. This means that, while there are two persons in a consulting room, there is in effect one subject recognized, and the focus is on action and change for that subject, the analysand. The components of metaphoric processes that are emphasized are the idiosyncratic and the general community. What could be called early metaphoric processes and thereby early fantasies are not emphasized in a classical analytic process. The phase of peak idiosyncratic development of metaphoric processes and early local experience is not the principal focus in a classical perspective. Because of the centrality of oedipal issues in a classical perspective, at least some of the salient poles in a classical field will necessarily have prominent features of sex and gender identifications and will involve oedipal-configuration derivatives. The analytic process is understood as steeped in the timelessness of the unconscious metaphoric processes and emphasizes repetition in the transference.

In Kleinian theory, while the environment is acknowledged, the focus is on phantasy and objects, which are always internal. In terms of the language put forth here, as described above, early segments of metaphoric processes—particularly from the idiosyncratic and general community inputs—and the objects extracted there from are salient to analytic processes. The field contains the derivatives of the analysand's metaphoric processes and evolves with the projective identifications of the analysand. While a Kleinian perspective could be represented in this model as having much in common with a classical perspective, the positions differ in that a Kleinian perspective significantly emphasizes the peak idiosyncratic as well as the universal, general community input to the analysand's metaphoric processes.

The field associated with a self psychological perspective also might be described as placing an emphasis on the local component of metaphoric processes, and to some extent on elements of the general community. A self psychology field, or self object matrix, will have self object poles and will contain derivatives of the metaphoric processes of the analysand. Rather than emphasizing transference repetition, the self object function complements or supplements early object experience. Repetition is considered to be present and as what motivates and formulates the self object matrix.

Forms of relational perspectives view the action of an analytic process as taking place within relational fields that emphasize the local and community components of metaphoric processes. The metaphoric processes of an individual in a relational perspective consist of unconscious organizing principles that have evolved intersubjectively (Stolorow & Atwood, 1996). Analyst and analysand bring the contents of their prereflective unconscious and its derivatives and share an ever-expanding field containing the intersection of their structures and derivatives, and in which transference and countertransference are the means by which the intersubjective field is woven together and takes shape. This field is a functioning whole and is the object of the psychoanalytic process (Stolorow & Atwood, 1989). Individuals coalesce as precipitates of the field. The field functions in present, real time. Repetition, strictly speaking, does not occur. Where organizing principles are activated, it is within the intersubjective intersected nexus, and these are not attached to an individual.

The notion of the unconscious developed in Baranger models is a departure from the understanding of it found in classical and most other psychoanalytic perspectives. The central unconscious is that of the field and is not associated with an individual. In this conception of the unconscious, repetition in a traditional or even a relational-theory sense does not occur. As a result, there is a potential for—and, in fact, a certainty of—creativity and novelty. In other models, accounting for creativity and novelty is problematic. When the main action in analytic processes is, for example, intrapsychic and transferential, repetition of the analysand's past experience is a major focus. From repetition, there is no clear route to the creation of genuinely new meaning. Similarly, if the emphasis is on the enactment of amalgams of historical ingredients, repetition remains at the center of the analytic process. Experience in both cases is thus considered to proceed on the basis of transference and fantasy, which are understood to derive, ultimately, from previous experience and meaning. This can lead to a reconfiguration of what was already experienced but not necessarily to creation.

In some relational models, it is not repetition of the analysand but the real-time interaction of analysand and analyst, including the contribution of transferential elements of each, that is the focus of clinical process. In this case also, the available ingredients to work with are the union of the experience of the two participants. The potential for the emergence of something novel is not significantly different from the classical, one-person-focused situation. In this regard, a constructivist model does not introduce the possibility of something genuinely new beyond relational or intersubjective models.

The tension between repetition and the possibility of creativity is a core psychoanalytic issue. This tension and the problem of accounting for genuine creation in the analytic setting are sometimes believed to be, but are not addressed in the concept of *nachträglichkeit* as understood as involving retranscription. That is, the understanding in the present of experience from the past, through the lens of accumulated further experience, involves the rearrangement of existing ingredients, including the emergence of derivatives of unconscious processes and the reconnection of affect with memories. Still, while new understanding of experience may be evocative or transformative, it does not necessarily afford the emergence of something new.

## Psychoanalytic Process and Creativity in Fields

A general psychoanalytic field consists of bundles of metaphoric processes that potentially include all four elements: the idiosyncratic, local, community, and general community. An initial translation occurs when the idiosyncratic elements of an individual's experience become infused with those shared by the individual's local and extended communities, through natural language and other shared structures.

A second level of translation involves the language built by analyst and analysand in the course of the analytic process. This language is unique to the couple. These two levels of translations are interpretations in a general sense and are necessarily imperfect and incomplete. This consequence lends weight to the associative method of psychoanalysis. Free association is the tool that allows for the translation and interpretation of the multiple systems of structuring by and with which an individual experiences. The way into these unconscious processes is by means of free association, which taps into and allows for the expression of the individual's metaphoric processes. The psychoanalytic process and the language built by the analytic couple seek to reverse the processes of the first level of translation with the acquisition of shared natural language and the socialization of the individual. That is, the analytic process attempts to precipitate idiosyncratic elements of the analysand into the constructs, understanding, and language of the couple, and bloom them in the analytic process in order to lay bare as much as possible of the analysand's unconscious idiosyncratic motivators.

When two people come together to enter into an analytic process, a dialogue ensues. An utterance of either participant contains and potentially conveys multiple meanings. Included are the consciously intended meanings and derivatives of unconscious contents from the utterer. Once spoken, the utterance may take on other meanings, including those in the mind of the utterer. This is a commonly known event within analytic process. The one listening to the utterance may attend to some or all of these three sets of meanings. In addition, the listener will attach idiosyncratic meanings to the utterance, deriving from both conscious awareness and the listener's unconscious processes. The listener now takes in four potential sets of meanings at conscious and unconscious levels, all filtered by the listener's metaphoric processes.

When a participant in the analytic process makes a contribution to the dialogical process, the utterer does not have control over the meanings of the utterance. In addition, when the utterer is the analysand, the analyst is explicitly attempting to attend to the derivatives of unconscious communication embedded in the utterance. Like all forms of perception, both participants are taking in more meanings of the utterances than they are consciously aware of. Such meanings taken in are the results of individual filtering and elaborations. What is absorbed by a participant will then impact on that participant's future contributions to the dialogical process. In this way, meanings associated with utterances necessarily give rise to their permutations.

Understanding between the participants, given the multiple sets of meanings associated with any given utterance, can have several senses. When analyst and analysand have developed enough of a common language in which to work and understand each other well enough to have what is called *bipersonal understanding*, several factors must be present. For an utterance of the analysand, for example, to be understood at least in some aspects by the analyst, there must be significant overlap in the conscious, intended meaning of the utterance by the analysand and the conscious understanding of the utterance by the analyst; there must be a significant overlap in the analysand's unconscious communication of the utterance with the conscious understanding of the utterance by the analyst; and there must also be a significant overlap in what the analysand understands of the utterance after having said it with what the analyst understands of the utterance. More will be absorbed by both parties in light of the utterance, and possibly other overlaps will emerge, but the foregoing is a minimal standard for mutual understanding of an utterance.

Within general psychoanalytic field theory, the lack of control over the meanings of utterances on the part of the participants in the analytic process gives rise to the possibility of the emergence of new meanings. The possibility of new meaning is not modeled on the interpretive understanding of its transferential repetition. Perceived repetition of the analysand's patterns in the present moment of therapeutic process is understood as the analytic pair's jointly fabricated pattern. This contains derivatives of the experience of the analysand. Such derivatives pertain to previous experiences, which correspond to what the current joint product appears to refer to in the analysand's past.

Because of the loss of control of meanings within the dyad and because two sets of derivatives of idiosyncratic unconscious processes are intermingling, patterns within the dyad are necessarily hybrid affairs. New meaning may emerge in this process of intermingling. In models in which transferential repetition is a straightforward concept, such as forms of classical theory, and in models that do not include idiosyncratic elements, such as forms of relational theory, genuine creation of new meaning can only be a premise.

## Ontological Commitments of General Psychoanalytic Fields

The idea that the field is an object of psychoanalytic interest, that there is an unconscious process of and in the field that is different from and independent of the participants, has heuristic value clinically. It serves to focus the work on the unconscious derivatives present in the analysand's communications. It highlights the fact that the utterances of each participant convey more than is in the awareness of either party. The field concept is a way of modeling unconscious communication within an analytic process. Nevertheless, an ontology is potentially being posited by field models that bear understanding. The concepts of *thirds* in their various formulations posit entities; for example, Baranger fields posit the third entity of a field, not a person, which has its own unconscious processes and fantasies.

In order to have more than heuristic value, the field concept and its ontological commitments need specification. A third, independent, nonhuman entity with its own unconscious process is not necessary to general psychoanalytic field theory. Rather, it is the conscious and unconscious transformations and permutations of elements in the analytic process that inform and are informed by the metaphoric processes of each participant. When a segment of a set of these meanings converges and coalesces, an insight has formed within one of the participants that may lead to an interpretation. Due to the factor of the lack of control over meanings, the unconscious processes and resulting fantasies are as independent of the participants as the Baranger or relational field models require. There is no loss of power to the model in paring down the ontology.

Ontological questions reemerge in further specifying the contents of fields. Psychoanalytic discourse proceeds as if persons, offices, thoughts, feelings, derivatives, and unconscious processes may all be elements of fields; thus, fields contain an ontological hybrid of ingredients. While there is heuristic value in this, it is also necessary to make explicit what is being posited underneath this manner of speaking. Psychoanalytic theory posits the existence of unconscious processes. The existence of individual humans and of space-time locations, such as consulting rooms, are further assumptions. All such entities are conjectured (Katz, 2010a). Just as there is no direct contact with the unconscious, neither is there with humans, couches, or other items purported to be in the world. The ontology of fields is relatively uniform and consists of derivatives.

## Two Kinds of Derivatives in Analytic Processes

A thread in an analytic process may be identified by the persistent presence of certain derivatives. Such a process could be considered constructive if it involves the articulation, elaboration, or connecting of these derivatives. A constructive process might culminate in the introduction of a construction. This would be a coalescing of derivatives into a formation that conveys emotional and other meanings to the participants, especially the analysand. A construction is an interpretation in the wide sense; an analytic interpretation proper is a special case. The latter consists of an interpretation that leads to the revealing or inciting of further derivatives and thus changes in the field.

What can be worked with in general psychoanalytic fields are two kinds of derivatives, the first- and second-order derivatives of the participants' experience. Second-order derivatives are derivatives of derivatives. What are in evidence in the consultation room are linguistic and other expressions of the participants. Second-order derivatives consist of the meanings of expressions. These are derivatives of aspects of the participants' experience with embedded emotional valences attached to experience. First-order derivatives are the aspects of experience. These are themselves derivative of underlying unconscious metaphoric processes.

When thinking in terms of field concepts, derivatives could also be thought of as precipitates. Every expression contains derivatives of both orders. Different psychoanalytic perspectives have different points of emphasis and goals in analytic processes and so make different use of derivatives to widen the scope of understanding the analysand. Different perspectives also emphasize different kinds of derivatives. For example, relational and constructivist theories in the United States rely on second-order derivatives. Classical models and those that use Baranger fields employ both orders of derivatives and emphasize first-order derivatives.

Derivatives relate to aspects of the participants' experience and coalesce into different formations at different times. Derivatives are not perceived singly but as derivatives in coalesced states within constructions. Coalesced derivatives of either order are interpretations in the wide sense. First-order derivatives consist of aspects of experience and coalesce into interpretations (constructions) of metaphoric processes. Second-order derivatives consist of the meaning of the participants' expressions and coalesce into interpretations (constructions) of aspects of experience.

## Poles and Neighborhoods in Fields Represent Object Formation and Consolidation of Experience

On the one hand, a field can be thought of as atemporal, as has been discussed throughout the history of psychoanalysis concerning the unconscious. Since multiple presences of the same person at different points of lived time can inhabit a given field and even be in contradictory relationship to each other, atemporality seems to describe fields. On the other hand, an analytic process is steeped in time (Birksted-Breen, 2003). What it has to work with is the present experience of the past and present predictions about the future. Thus, what an analytic process at any given moment has is what is contained in the field. It is not outside of it or located in the past of the analysand. In being wholly in and of the present, aspects of the field itself are both the subject and the object of analytic study. Interpretation and other aspects of analytic processes necessarily occur within and about aspects of the field.

A field can be said to be inhabited by all kinds of presences. In terms of elements of fields, presences consist of coalescences of derivatives of segments of metaphoric processes. This includes a potentiality for multiple presences or aspects of experience of certain objects. These include the analysand and the analyst, primary objects—especially of the analysand, and acquaintances of each of them, as well as public figures. All these presences inhabit the field, bearing multiple and possibly incompatible relationships to each other. In this medium, derivatives of the unconscious processes of both analysand and analyst co-mingle and combine.

A field has poles that are consolidations of aspects of experience. Each pole could be thought of as having a *neighborhood* or space around it, which consists of compact clusters of metaphoric processes. Derivatives of a metaphoric process within such a neighborhood have elements that pertain to the experience of the construct at the center of the pole. A field will contain poles of aspects of experience of objects, including at least one for the analysand and another for the analyst. A transference situation could be represented, for example, by the convergence or significant overlap of the neighborhoods around poles of a primary object and of the analyst.

## Field Representation of Change in an Analytic Process

It is possible to filter a field for indexical items in aspects of experience and their derivatives. An indexical item of relevance in an analytic process is the temporal one. The filtering pertains to neighborhoods of poles. This might proceed in some way analogous to the way in which specific statements with indexical elements can be filtered out of a larger set of statements. In other words, it might be possible to compare aspects of experience and neighborhoods, making use of the filtering of certain kinds of indexical components. Derivatives and constructions might be considered congruent if they agree once they have been filtered for indexicals. When there is a change in a neighborhood across time, then there will also be concomitant change in aspects of experience, and therefore also change in the pole around which the neighborhood centers.

From one point in time to another, nontrivial change might be described as a *nonindexical* change in the elements within a neighborhood. That is, change could be said to take place if a neighborhood around a given pole is filtered for changes, from one time to another, that involve purely indexical item difference, while other differences remain. Change of this sort reflects movement in the sense of Faimberg (2005). When neighborhoods around a pole change, it follows that the pole itself within the time span has also been altered. When a neighborhood is stable, so is the pole within it. It could then be said that when there has been change in a pole, something has happened in the analytic process; there has been some therapeutic action. When there is no change, there is some sort of block, or *bastion* in the sense of Baranger fields.

Psychoanalytic perspectives place the locus of therapeutic action in various locations. In a model that uses Baranger fields, for example, the locus is in the unconscious of the field. In self psychological models, models implicit in Faimberg (2007), and classical models, the locus is in the unconscious process of the analysand. In Spezzano (2007), it is in the unconscious process of the analyst.

The use of unconscious metaphoric processes and psychoanalytic fields allows for a description of the increased complexity of psychoanalytic models. Within a psychoanalytic perspective, the specific kind of field used is posited to provide the medium of analytic process and a model of human experience. In the latter is a potential claim that human functioning inherently proceeds according to the structure of the elements of the kind of field used in that perspective. A series of debates in the history of psychoanalytic discussion can be rephrased to contain assertions that humans operate in one kind of field rather than others, and thus the analytic medium must be the designated kind of field.

## Perspective of Psychoanalytic Process From General Fields

A still greater increase in complexity emerges when we step back from specific perspectives to the vantage point of general fields. This affords a broader view and allows for a way of reflecting on what is being modeled by the different forms of field. Within general psychoanalytic field theory, each field model is to be viewed as a possible model of human experience that is related to and interconnected with other possible models. From this vantage point, it can be asked whether the different field models necessarily apply to the analytic pair, or instead to the individuals in the pair. That is, within general field theory, the question naturally arises whether it is possible to have more than one form of field operative at the same time within an analytic perspective. From within perspectives, this question is not intelligible.

From the general field view, this can be further elaborated to the question of whether participants in an analytic process might each make use of different aspects of the process in such a way that each is active in a different field. The analysand, for example, might be understood as working in a Baranger field, while the analyst is working within a classical field. If this is conceivable, issues arise concerning communication between analyst and analysand.

It may make sense to wonder whether some of the impasses within a therapeutic process or misalignments between analyst and analysand may be understood as the result of a lack of awareness of the possibility that analyst and analysand are operating under different sorts of fields. A Pandora's box, so to speak, opens up here, of possibilities for understanding what is happening in the course of an analytic process. For example, it may make sense to understand the nature of the analytic field within a specific analytic process as determined by the analysand's state of mind rather than by the analyst's theory. It may also be plausible to view the form of the field as shifting throughout the course of a specific analytic process, either as the work progresses over time or session by session, or even possibly from moment to moment. More complex still, it may make sense to understand the kinds of fields operating as variable according to the different layers of unconscious processes at work. In this case, more than one kind of field is operating at the same time.

Psychoanalytic fields may be used to model and describe what sort of experience is occurring at a given point in the analysis for the analysand. This might be effected in several ways. One is to determine which aspects of the field the analysand can make use of at that point. Another is to understand the analysand's experience of the field at that point—that is, to appreciate what kind of field it is for the analysand. While the analysand's and the analyst's experiences of and in the field are necessarily different, the degree and kind of discrepancies also pertain to the analysand's experience. This is a way of expressing a generalization of Faimberg's (2005) concept of the distance between the analyst's understanding of an interpretation and how the analysand processes and understands it.

Analytic progress might be measured in some cases by the analysand's expansion of the kinds of fields within which the analysand is able to function. An eclectic perspective might entail the analyst changing the kind of field over the course of the analytic process, in tune with where the analysand is, as understood by the analyst. The analyst's assessments are made from the vantage point of the analyst's field. That is, there are choices to be made about whether a field model is considered to apply to what is occurring for the analytic pair, or for each individual of the pair, and by whom in the pair the field options are determined.

Each analytic perspective, even an eclectic one, operates with a model of mental processes that is the foundation of that perspective's theory. This model then determines what kinds of fields can be used clinically within that perspective. That is, the field is a technical, psychoanalytic tool, and this points to another asymmetry of the field. The field is the field of the analyst, and it is determined and justified by the choice and assumptions of the psychoanalytic perspective within which the analyst works. Thus what is relevant is the analyst's field working with a specific analytic perspective, not that of the analysand. The analysand comes to treatment with a mass of experiences and active unconscious processes. The analyst works with the analysand progressively, making use of the field. Only general psychoanalytic fields include all possible elements. This is by design, in order that all perspectives may be included.

## Note

1  Some of the material for this chapter derives from *Psychoanalytic Inquiry* 33(3) (May 2013) "General Psychoanalytic Field Theory: Its Structure and Applications to Psychoanalytic Perspectives."

# 11

# CONTEXT FOR THE BARANGERS' WORK ON THE PSYCHOANALYTIC FIELD[1]

*Antoine Corel*

This chapter evokes the intellectual atmosphere and the ideas developed within the psychoanalytical movement in Argentina during the two decades that preceded the formulation of the concept of "psychoanalytic field" by Madeleine and Willy Baranger in 1961.

However brief its existence, a magnetic field organizes forces that may carry powerful effects—as happens in a dynamo. Nearer to our analytic domain, with F. de Saussure we speak of the semantic field that organizes meaning in language.

These associations to the word "field" would be met by Madé Baranger (and would have been met by Willy) with one of their characteristic, wise, and meaningful bursts of laughter. I am pleased to imagine this, as I set out to evoke the intellectual atmosphere in which they coined the concept of psychoanalytic field. It was a fruitful soil that met them in the Rio de la Plata after World War II.

In the decade that preceded their arrival in Argentina in 1947, a dynamic group of psychoanalysts had gathered, coming from a variety of backgrounds. Angel Garma, a Spanish physician born in 1904, had obtained his psychoanalytic training in Berlin, where he was analyzed by Theodor Reik and had been accepted as a member of the Society with a paper on "Reality and the Id in Schizophrenia"—a remarkable subject matter for the times, which we shall see reappear in the membership papers of Pichon-Rivière and Racker. Besides an interest in psychosomatic symptoms characteristic of those years, Garma insisted throughout his life on the traumatic origin of dreams.

As a consequence of the Fascist takeover of his country, Garma was unable to settle in Spain. In Paris, he met Celes Cárcamo (an Argentine physician analyzed by Paul Schiff who had become a member of the Paris Psychoanalytical Society). They both went to Buenos Aires, where, as the only two formally trained analysts, they joined several persons from various horizons and frames of mind who shared a passionate interest in the science created by Freud. Among them was Marie Langer, who had interrupted her analysis with Richard Sterba in Vienna to take refuge first in Montevideo (Uruguay), then in Buenos Aires in 1942. And in December of that same year, the Argentine Psychoanalytic Association was founded by Cárcamo, Garma, Langer, Enrique Pichon-Rivière, Arnaldo Rascovsky, and G. Ferrari Hardoy. With the exception of G. Ferrari Hardoy, who left to settle in the United States, they all became training analysts in 1943. Also in 1943, the *Revista de Psicoanálisis* was founded; in the first years of its existence, papers by Fenichel, M. Klein, Sterba, Reik, Tausk, K. Abraham, Frieda Fromm-Reichmann, Ferenczi, F. Alexander, H. Deutsch, and G. Róheim appeared, together with articles by the local members.

Enrique Pichon-Rivière is the personality who should interest us most in retracing the intellectual environment in which the "field" concept grew. Born in 1907 in Geneva to French parents who eventually settled in the subtropical northeast region of Argentina, Pichon-Rivière began to develop his original ideas on mental illness as a psychiatrist at the Hospicio de las Mercedes in charge of admissions. For him, the mentally diseased patient is the spokesman of the family group. This led him to take innovative initiatives in terms of family and group therapies, and to consider the conditions under which the sick member might be reintegrated (or not) into a family who would attempt to keep the disease "frozen" upon him. Pichon-Rivière described two essential types of anxiety: fear of losing and fear of being attacked. Asserting that a person falls ill "for love, of hate," in his dialectic way of conceiving of psychic functioning he came to consider there to be only *one* mental disease—while at the same time maintaining refined nosographical distinctions. He described the interplay of three areas: mind, body, and the external world; and he pointed out, for example, that the persecuting object is located, in melancholia, hypochondria, and paranoia, respectively, in each of these three areas. In a study devoted in 1938 to delusions according to the German and French schools, he declared that the future lies with a structural approach.

These concepts provided the basis for the psychoanalytic treatment of schizophrenics within a rigorous frame. His paper on becoming a training analyst in 1943, "Contribution to the Psychoanalytic Theory of Schizophrenia," draws on these experiences. One of Pichon-Rivière's favorite metaphors refers to a "spiral process," a dialectical way of thinking applied both to the therapeutic process and to the process of learning: the spiral consisting in meeting similar conflicts or configurations at successively upward, growing levels. Another of his ideas that he carried to practice is "the operative group," whose members learn within a model that includes solving the psychic conflicts that preclude learning.

Pichon-Rivière resorted predominantly to the oral transmission of his ideas. He published sparsely, or late. Among the exceptions we could mention: the aforementioned paper on schizophrenia published in 1946; another on the same subject in the *Revue Française* (1952); and a study on the poet Lautréamont. Many of his papers were collected in 1970 in two volumes under the title *Del psicoanálisis a la psicología social*. But the series of conferences he gave in APA in 1956–1957 on his original theory of linking—which has inspired many authors who have later elaborated on the topic—for example, was published posthumously, in 1980, as *Teoría del vínculo*.

With the group who gradually gathered around his teaching and practice (and in which the non-medical, such as Racker and the Barangers, also benefited from the contact with psychotic patients), Pichon-Rivière founded in 1960 the School of

Dynamic Psychiatry, where the psychoanalytic ideas were presented and discussed in a four-hour-per-week course of three years. José Bleger, D. Liberman, E. Rolla, and F. Taragano contributed to this space of psychoanalytic thinking that appeared, as we must recall, at a moment of democratic rebirth of the society at large.

José Bleger (born in 1922) was perhaps the most brilliant exponent of that group, and certainly the thinker who carried the fruitful dialogue with Pichon-Rivière to its most achieved methodological and philosophical foundations. Perhaps Bleger's most widely internationally known contribution is "Psychoanalysis of the Psychoanalytic Frame," where he purports that, parallel to the frame proposed and established by the analyst in terms of space, time, and method, there exists a frame (tacitly, unconsciously) conceived by the patient that explodes to light at moments of change or crisis and should be the object of interpretation. Bleger shared with many of his colleagues in Argentina a peculiar sensitivity to the elements that may thwart the process—we could say an "ear" to understand secret, stealthy forms of resistance.

In *Symbiosis and Ambiguity*, José Bleger gave the largest and most systematic expression to his ideas. He there describes the psychotic part of the personality (Bion) as linked to a phase of indifferentiation in psychic development, which he terms "glischrocharic" (meaning an agglutinated nucleus), that logically, not chronologically, preceding the paranoid-schizoid position (M. Klein) may manifest itself throughout life in the phenomena mentioned in the title. Though couched in Kleinian terms, both his clinical examples and his conceptual formulations in *Symbiosis and Ambiguity* go far beyond M. Klein. They may be linked to ideas of Ferenczi and Winnicott and, of course, Bion, without detracting from their originality.

José Bleger is no exception in this sense. Arminda Aberastury, in collaboration with Marie Langer, translated and published in 1948 *The Psychoanalysis of Children*; contacts were established in supervisions, by letter and personally; Emilio Rodrigué went to London to be analyzed by Paula Heimann and participated in *New Directions* with the paper "The Analysis of a Three-Year-Old Mute Schizophrenic": these may suffice as examples that the ideas of M. Klein were widely known and accepted within the Argentinian group—which nevertheless kept the width, originality, and elasticity of its views in accordance with the teachings of Pichon-Rivière that had also included the ideas of W. R. Fairbairn and of French authors—among them, Lagache.

One more point about José Bleger. He himself considered one of the rare antecedents to the ideas he presented in *Symbiosis and Ambiguity* to be the article by Madeleine Baranger titled "*Mala fe, identidad y omnipotencia*" (1963), in which a form of ambiguous personality is described: by means of the "Proteus defense," the subject aims at maintaining omnipotence by presenting a succession of internal divided characters.

David Liberman (b. 1920) gave a systematic slant to his formidable clinical intuition when he described the phenomenon of "stylistic complementarity" that, unawares or deliberately, may be produced by the analyst in relation to the patient's style; for example, to a discourse in the obsessional mood, the analyst would tend to respond in a "hysterical/dramatic" style. Liberman later carried his developments into the field of structural linguistics—another way of inscribing, we might say, the analytic dyad into a larger "third" frame.

At this point, we should recall that in 1954, Luisa Alvarez de Toledo's paper "Analysis of 'Associating,' of 'Interpreting,' and of 'The Words'" made a long-lasting, fundamental contribution to this topic.

Another essential participant in the intellectual atmosphere of the 1950s in Argentina was Heinrich Racker. A non-medical, trained in music and philosophy, analyzed by Jeanne Lampl de Groot until he was obliged to flee Vienna in 1939, and then by Marie Langer, Racker became a member of the Argentine Association with a presentation on "Aspects of the Psychoanalysis of a Schizophrenic." From 1948 to 1959, he gave a series of papers on countertransference that had deep resonance in the thinking of that group. The fact that the analyst relates to the patient, contributes to the process with his own psychic functioning, including his conflicts, and is in absolute need of knowing this in order to help the patient and modulate the process: all these ideas so thoroughly developed became essential acquisitions both at the clinical and the theoretical level. Together with the contemporaneous papers by Winnicott and Paula Heimann, Racker's essays (gathered in Spanish as *Estudios sobre técnica psicoanalítica* and published in English under the title *Transference and Countertransference* in 1968) gave systematic bases to accepting countertransference as an element that cannot be neglected in the process. Racker died in 1961, at age 50.

Finally, we should consider another author, Jorge Mom. With the seminal papers on phobias he published from 1956 on, Jorge Mom appears more concomitant than antecedent to the concept of field formulated by the Barangers. They had trained in the same milieu and kept up a lively scientific dialogue, as evidenced by the contributions the three of them later brought to international congresses (e.g., "Process and Non-Process" in 1982, "The Infantile Psychic Trauma From Us to Freud" in 1988). But in the middle, there was another period in which they worked in close association.

In 1954, Madeleine and Willy Baranger settled in Montevideo with the task of developing the Uruguayan psychoanalytical movement. They organized the training system counting with the regular visits and contributions to seminars by Jorge Mom, Pichon-Rivière, David Liberman, and José Bleger. The Barangers took in analysis the candidates who would constitute the Uruguayan Association. It was in that stimulating atmosphere in 1956 that they founded the *Revista Uruguaya de Psicoanálisis*, to which they gave numerous papers—among them, in the first issue of 1961–1962, a certain "The Analytic Situation as a Dynamic Field"—but that, as the saying goes, is another story.

## Note

1 Originally published in *Psychoanalytic Inquiry* 33(3) (May 2013).

# 12

# METAPHOR IN ANALYTIC FIELD THEORY[1]

## Giuseppe Civitarese and Antonino Ferro

*... as I lay in bed, with my eyes shut, I said to myself that everything is capable of transposition ...*

Marcel Proust

Each of the principal psychoanalytic models is underlain by certain key metaphors. For example, the archaeological and surgical metaphors, as well as that of the analyst-as-screen, all throw light on some of Freud's basic concepts. In classical psychoanalysis, however, metaphor still tends to be an illegitimate or secondary element. Analytic field theory, on the other hand, reserves a completely different place for it, both as an instrument of technique in clinical work and as a conceptual device in theoretical activity.

Metaphor and the field are linked in a chiasm: the field metaphor transforms Kleinian relational theory into a radically intersubjective theory, which in turn places metaphor at a point along the spectrum of dreaming—to paraphrase Bion, it is the stuff of analysis.

For the sake of illustration, we shall examine first the origins and meaning of the field metaphor in analytic field theory; we shall then consider the mutual implications of this particular development of post-Bion psychoanalysis and the modern linguistic theory of metaphor; and, finally, we shall put the theoretical hypotheses discussed in the first part of this contribution to work in the clinical situation.

## Origins of the Analytic Field Metaphor

Madeleine and Willy Baranger developed the notion of the analytic field on the basis of Gestalt theory; the ontology of Merleau-Ponty (1945, in turn influenced by the dialectic of Hegel and by Kojève's reading of it); Klein's concepts of projective and introjective identification; Isaacs's (1948) concept of unconscious fantasy; and Grinberg's (1957)[2] notion of projective counteridentification (Etchegoyen, 1986). The Barangers' basic idea is that patient and analyst generate unconscious field fantasies, or couple fantasies, which may even become actual obstacles ("bastions" or "bulwarks") to the psychoanalytic process. These are bipersonal fantasies "which cannot be reduced to [their] habitual formulation—as, for example, in Isaacs—that is, as an expression of the individual's instinctual life" (Bezoari & Ferro, 1991, p. 48).

Among the nonpsychoanalytic sources, let us briefly consider Merleau-Ponty, because he furnishes a philosophical foundation for the field concept, which he emphasizes to such an extent as to make it the cornerstone of his own theory, and because his conception of corporeality is extraordinarily modern. By the metaphor of the field, Merleau-Ponty conceptualizes the rigorously interdependent relationship that comes into being between subject and context, the reciprocal and constant influence of self and other, and the dynamic continuity arising between consciousness and the spatiotemporal parameters of experience of the world (time and space not being containers within which the individual moves, but instead being born together with him[3])—the intersubjective determinants of identity.[4]

The subject is formed on the basis of a substrate of anonymous, prereflective, and prepersonal intersensoriality/intercorporeality even before any actual self-reflective capacity exists. An albeit still obscure precategorial background which, however, does not lack meaning, paves the way for the entry of the transcendental ego on to the world stage.

In this phase (which then remains as it were one of the constant dimensions of experience, given that the ego will never be able to free itself from the environmental context and from the contingency of a certain life situation), subject and object are not distinguished from each other—that is to say, they are dialectically correlated. Rather than existing as positive entities, pure presences-in-themselves, except in an abstract sense, they mold each other in an incessant, fluid to-and-fro traffic of sensations regulated by the "porosity of the flesh." Subject and object "co-originate" in a primordial medium to which both belong. Touching something is at the same time being touched. Our sense of the world is not only an intellectual content, and cannot dispense with our experience of our bodies; it stems from our *fleshly* existence and is present even before a consciousness of self forms. Hence Merleau-Ponty's assertion: "I am a field, an experience" (1945, p. 473)—that is, *a system of relationships*.

The Barangers' essay in which the French philosopher's vision is subsumed, "The Analytic Situation as a Dynamic Field," dates from 1961–1962. Significantly, in the same years Winnicott and Bion were laying the foundations of a radically intersubjective psychoanalytic theory of the birth of the psyche. The dialectic that underlies subjectivity—which could in Bion's sense be formulated in terms of the binary couple *narcissism/socialism*—seen as an ongoing process, is the same as that which Winnicott sought to apprehend by his famous gerunds, such as *coming-into-being, a going concern, holding, handling, object-presenting, realizing*, or *indwelling*. In this way, as Ogden (1992, p. 620) explains, Winnicott

> captures something of the experience of the paradoxical simultaneity of at-one-ment and separateness. (A related conception of intersubjectivity was suggested by Bion's [1962a] notion of the container-contained dialectic. However, Winnicott was the first to place the psychological state of the mother on an equal footing

with that of infant in the constitution of the mother-infant [relationship]. This is fully articulated in Winnicott's statement that "There is no such thing as an infant [apart from the maternal provision]."

(Winnicott, 1960)

For an ideal genealogy of the field metaphor in psychoanalysis, Bion is an unavoidable reference. While the Barangers do not quote him in their now classical paper, Madeleine Baranger[5] (2005; Churcher, 2008) acknowledges his influence on her from the early 1950s on. At that time, Bion was already developing a highly original theory of the analytic field, although he did not use that metaphor.[6]

In his contributions on the "basic assumptions" (1948), which date precisely from those years (Ferro & Basile, 2009, p. 92f.), he develops the concept of unconscious fantasy within the group. The analytic couple is in fact already a group. In Bion's view, individuals are endowed with "valences"—the term, borrowed from chemistry, denotes the propensity of atoms to bind together into molecules—that is, the spontaneous and instinctive (unconscious, automatic, and inevitable) capacity to establish mutual emotional bonds, "for sharing and acting on a basic assumption" (Bion, 1948, p. 153), "behaviour in the human being that is more analogous to tropism in plants than to purposive behaviour" (ibid., p. 116f.). The basic assumption, whether Pair, Fight-Flight, or Dependent, gives rise to "other mental activities that have in common the attribute of powerful emotional drives" (ibid., p. 146). It is "the 'cement' that keeps the group assembled" (López-Corvo, 2002, p. 39).

Valences and basic assumptions express the psychological function of an individual as dictated by the "proto-mental system." The proto-mental system is one of Bion's more speculative concepts, in that it "transcends experience" (1948, p. 101). He coined it to explain the tenacity of the emotional bonds that keep the group together, linking its members in a common psychological situation, and to denote a dimension of the psyche in which the basic assumptions that are for the time being inactive can be accommodated. The proto-mental system is

one in which physical and psychological or mental are undifferentiated. It is a matrix from which spring the *phenomena which at first appear*—on a psychological level and in the light of psychological investigation—*to be discrete feelings* only loosely associated with one another. It is from this matrix that emotions proper to the basic assumption flow to reinforce, pervade, and, on occasion, to dominate the mental life of the group. Since it is a level in which physical and mental are undifferentiated, it stands to reason that, when distress from this source manifests itself, it can manifest itself just as well in physical forms as in psychological.

(Ibid., p. 102, our emphasis)

The absence of a distinction between the physical and the mental in the proto-mental system is of course reminiscent of the ambiguous status of the drives in Freud, as a "concept on the frontier between the somatic and the mental," just as the valences call to mind the concept of libido (Fornaro, 1990, p. 55); the point here, however, is that "proto-mental phenomena are a function of the group" (Bion, 1948, p. 103). *The individual's proto-mental system is merely a part of a larger whole, namely the proto-mental matrix of the group, and cannot therefore be studied in isolation from it.*

It will be seen that, already for Bion—who is here absolutely in unison with Merleau-Ponty—the subject cannot be thought of except on the basis of the intrinsic intersubjective dimension of the proto-mental system, of the area of "initial biopsychic emergence" (Fornaro, 1990, p. 20, translated). Mental life extends beyond the physical boundaries of the individual; it is "transindividual" (ibid.). Hence the (relative) absence of a distinction between mind and soma in the individual is in some way correlated with the background of a substantial (relative) absence of distinction between individuals.

With regard to Merleau-Ponty's postulate of the ego-as-field and Bion's of the proto-mental area, the concept of projective identification now assumes powerful explanatory force, because it so-to-speak confers "tangibility" on the communication channels through which this common, unconscious psychological area can establish itself, as well as on the *way* in which it can do so. It imparts "visibility"—in Greek, *theorein* means to see or contemplate—to the concrete and indispensable points of contiguity whereby the processes of interindividual mental influencing take place.

These theoretical foundations show that, already with Bion, and even more with the developments that came after him and the transition to an analytic field theory, psychoanalysis underwent a change of paradigm of the kind described by Kuhn (1962). For example, it may be misleading to define the characteristics of the analytic field in terms of the use of the classical concepts of transference and countertransference, because these presuppose a configuration in which analysand and analyst "face each other" as two positive, pure, complete, and separate subjectivities, each somehow totally "external" to the other. Ogden comments:

> I believe the use of the term *countertransference* to refer to everything the analyst thinks and feels and experiences sensorially obscures the simultaneity of the dialectic of oneness and twoness, of individual subjectivity and intersubjectivity that is the foundation of the psychoanalytic relationship.
>
> (Ogden, 1994a, p. 8, n.)

In a theoretical framework inspired by a one-person psychoanalysis, the concept of projective identification too would assume an a-dialectic and substantially solipsistic meaning. If, however, subject and object are thought of as places in an intersubjective field, it will be realized, as Ogden (2008) writes, that when a patient goes into analysis, he so to speak *loses his own mind*. He reconnects with the reestablished proto-mental area. He initiates a communication which involves him in depth and can be channeled in such a way as to repair dysfunctional places in his internal group configuration, to restart the conversation that the various parts of the mind incessantly carry on among themselves, while always seeking better ways of thinking about his current emotional problem (however, terms such as unconscious thought, dreaming, thinking, and the like must be seen as virtually equivalent).

## Elements of Analytic Field Theory

Analytic field theory fruitfully combines the contribution of the Barangers with the developments of post-Bion thought and certain ideas derived from modern narrativity known in the English-speaking world by the labels of *critical theory* and *reader-response criticism*, and developed in Italy by, in particular, Umberto Eco (Ferro, 1999b). Another important component, on the other hand, stems, via Luciana Nissim Momigliano (2001), from Robert Langs and his original conception of the spiraling progression of the unconscious dialogue between patient and analyst. Other significant notions are the emphasis by Ogden (1979) on the concept of projective identification in a strongly relational sense, and that author's more recent idea, avowedly inspired by Kojève's lectures[7] on Hegel (!), of the "intersubjective analytic third" (1994a). Nor must one disregard the fundamental contribution of Bleger (1967) on the "institutional" nature of the setting and on everything involved in the formation of the individual's so-called *meta-ego* (Civitarese, 2008).

These initial remarks already point to the reason for the central position of the metaphor—and with it the "philosophy"—of the field, perhaps because no other lends itself better to the construction of a radically intersubjective psychoanalytic model, which we consider to be most suited to a psychoanalysis for our time. By virtue of a whole set of theoretical increments, the metaphor of the field has succeeded in expressing all its theoretical and clinical potentialities, such as grasping/casting, characters of the session, narrative derivatives of waking dream thought, transformations in dream, weak or unsaturated interpretation, and the like (Ferro, 1992).

The field metaphor is of course borrowed from electromagnetic or gravitational field theory. Its essential properties are that it represents a *dynamic* totality, and that it is *inclusive, invisible* (but deducible from its effects on its constitutive elements), and *delimited* (even if constantly in the throes of contraction or expansion).

The field is intrinsically unstable and subjected to continuous displacements of energy. The forces concentrated at a given point in the field can have effects on other forces in locations remote from that point. Hence all the elements in a field are structured as a differential system in which each term is defined in relation to the others in a process of constant, mutual cross-reference. This is not very different from de Saussure's conception of the structure of language, Lacan's of the system of signifiers in the unconscious, or Derrida's of the text. Perhaps only chaos theory could offer an effective representation of the dynamism of the field, because it can model the complex vectorial manifestations that give rise to turbulence, catastrophic points, and ultimately changes of state.

Furthermore, the field is delimited. It is a container. This does not of course mean that it is a closed system; instead, by causing itself to be contained, it is itself in a dialectical relationship with what is outside it—that is, with other, broader containers (social groups, institutions, ideologies, etc.). However, the fact that the field is relatively closed permits account to be taken of what may be defined as *inclusiveness*. This is an aspect given an original interpretation by Antonino Ferro, who radicalizes the model of the field already outlined by the authors mentioned above, and invites us to see *any* element within the fictional frame of the setting as (virtually) a function of the analytic field.

In clinical psychoanalytic work, the field concept effectively supports the extension of the dream paradigm of the session, to which it imparts rigor, because it puts to work in the couple Klein's concept of projective identification (albeit as revised and corrected by Bion and Ogden) and Bion's of "waking dream thought" (we dream not only at night but also during the day). There is no point in the field (whether an event, a memory, a dream, an enactment, a reverie, an association, an emotion, a sensation, or whatever) that is not touched by the "electromagnetic waves" of the intersecting projective identifications of patient and analyst, and that does not correspond to the recordings made of it by their respective alpha functions; it might in fact be better to invoke the alpha function of the field (or its *gamma function*, as Francesco Corrao called it). This function represents the capacity of the couple, outside the rigid framework of a subject/object dichotomy, to narrate, dream, think, and construct metaphors or myths in order to attribute a specific meaning to their joint experience. The field takes the form of "a system dedicated to the transformation of sensory and emotional experiences into thoughts and meanings, [and confers life on a] theory of treatment centered on the transformations and developments of the psychoanalytic field (which includes the analyst, the patient, and theories) rather than on individuals and contents" (Neri & Selvaggi, 2006, p. 182, translated).

A limitation of the field metaphor is that it might suggest a two-dimensional situation. This may indeed be the case when a quasi-autistic type of mental functioning arises. Instead of actual characters, there are only flat, emotionless "picture cards." The patient draws the analyst into an exclusively concrete world. Play is impossible. There are no metaphors, no dreams, and no reveries. If, however, these possibilities can gradually be introduced, that will be tantamount to adding new dimensions or worlds to the field. Moreover, except in these situations the field *is* as a rule multidimensional—it is a *pluriverse*.

Each of the characters in the analytic dialogue, "including those called the analyst and the patient" (Ferro, 2010, p. 428, translated), and their internal worlds (!), represents a specific place in the analytic field. However, the following can also be places in the field: its scenic component (the ongoing formation and transformation of the characters); the analyst's mind; the countertransference; the place of formation of images (waking dream thought) and its derivatives; the analyst's actual countertransference dreams; his reveries; the internal worlds of the analyst and the patient; their histories; their relationship; enactments; projective identifications and all their vicissitudes; and the transgenerational elements of both protagonists (Bezoari & Ferro, 1991; Ferro, 2006a). The art of the analyst is to apprehend the patient's point of view, using the restrictions imposed from time to time on the field by the viewpoint that can be assumed by dwelling in one of its many different places.

It would of course be misleading to think of this situation in terms of a process of constant, hyperwakeful monitoring of the field, which would be mechanical and unproductive. The metaphor of virtual reality (Civitarese, 2008), which is basically an extreme form of the concept of the transference neurosis, can be used to show how a clinical and theoretical field model aims to keep two aspects in balance—namely, the usefulness for the actors in and authors of the analytic dialogue of *losing themselves* in the fiction established by the setting (which means intimacy, closeness, spontaneity, emotional intensity, and authenticity), and the need to *reemerge from it* in order to gain access to the plurality of the possible worlds in which they are simultaneously living.

In this way it is possible to satisfy, on the one hand, a poetics and an aesthetics of emotional involvement (how to allow oneself to be captured by the text of the analysis, and why), and, on the other, a poetics and an aesthetics of disenchantment (how to achieve the insight that the text is a fiction, and in view of what effects). The analytic field might then perhaps be definable as a medium—a means of communication—in which the analyst seeks to achieve the best possible balance between immersion and interactivity, between semiotic transparency and self-referential demystification (like dreaming and waking from a dream, both of which are necessary for the definition of a dream). Unless the oscillations between these poles are made explicit, the result will be narrative interpretations or, in other words, transference interpretations (which are in fact nothing but metanarrations).

When Ferro attributes an innate transformative capacity to the field and to the narrativities it expresses, he is on no account invoking some kind of magical virtue inherent in it, but rigorously articulating the intersubjective implications of the field metaphor and of analytic field theory. The mere fact of being in a room already modifies the chemical composition of the air breathed by its occupants. Likewise, any change in the medium in which they are immersed influences both patient and analyst, even if the change is coincidental and peripheral to the points of concentration of the system of forces in the field that correspond to the two subjectivities involved. If a cellphone rings, the field is modified. The modification is even greater after a significant exchange in the analytic dialogue. Between the two "places" represented by the patient and the analyst, there occur interactions that are to a greater or lesser extent direct and of variable intensity and to a greater or lesser extent differentiated in terms of the continuum from metonymy to metaphor, from sensoriality/intercorporeality to the exchange of concepts or to the vicissitudes of the unconscious projective and introjective processes.

The field, seen as a dynamic system that identifies with the analytic couple and interweaves narrations that tell instant by instant of its own functioning, is a viewpoint very different from that of an analyst acting as a screen for the patient's projections. If three "negative" characters appear in the first analytic session after the summer break, they may be regarded as three areas of emotional congestion, lumps of nonthinkability waiting to be narrated and broken up (like the crime featuring at the beginning of a traditional thriller)—but without any need to be made explicit by interpretation, unless the actual psychoanalytic game of interpretation itself becomes a place in the field, or a character in the text of the analysis. If one of the three "baddies" were an incompetent lifeguard or a rude barman, the narration could develop along the lines of understanding why he behaves in this way, of making hypotheses, of getting to know them, of considering them from a number of different possible points of view, and of trying to guess the reasons for them—in a word, with a view to seeing if it is possible to bring about a transformation that can rid the field of the initial atmosphere of persecution. Of course, the patient could perfectly well signal the change in the plot by allowing a new character to take the stage. Beneath the new mask, however, the analyst would have no difficulty in recognizing the same tangled ball of emotions in the process of transformation.

## Metaphor as a Rhetorical Figure and as a Basic Cognitive Mechanism

Metaphor, in the sense of a rhetorical figure, is a schema (a "configuration" according to Mortara-Garavelli, 2010) that serves to model the expression of thought. A synonym of a rhetorical figure is a "trope," which means "turn," denoting an effect of "deviation and transposition of meaning." When the "deviated use" becomes habitual, the metaphor turns into *catachresis* (this Greek coinage means "misuse"). The irregularity receives the sanction of law and even becomes the norm. A catachresis, like certain state pardons granted for especially common offenses, is the fruit of a "necessity": it provides a name for an object that did not previously have one. The institution of a catachresis is therefore governed by a principle of economy which is applied at the cost of a certain imprecision, while also involving an effect of polysemy, or expansion of meaning. It is only when a catachresis is awakened from its sleep—as often occurs in analysis by virtue of the attention devoted to the play of the signifier, for example in the case of a parapraxis or a joke—that its primal nature as a metaphor is revealed. The memory of the underlying abuse then comes to the surface. A catachresis is usually seen as different from *extinct* or lexicalized metaphors, which are now completely unrecognizable as such except by exploring the derivation of the word concerned (for example, the Italian word *testa* [head] comes from the identical Latin word, which originally denoted the shell of a tortoise—ibid.).

Metaphor is deemed the queen of tropes, "the easiest to recognize and the most difficult to define [...] a mechanism that is so universal and so within everyone's reach has resisted every attempt to explain it completely and homogeneously" (ibid., p. 9, translated). After all, metaphor is not always the contraction of a comparison or a simile that is abbreviated or described as such. The analogy is in fact often not recorded but *created*. Metaphor is the invention of an intelligence that is "sympathetic" (de Beistegui, 2010, p. 35, translated) to the matter of the world, a way of assigning a personal meaning to it, and of impressing one's own "style" on it. It is not the fruit of an analysis of the similarities and differences between two terms/objects thought of as always identical with themselves, but itself *generates* the relationship. Establishing a metaphor is tantamount to the use of a kind of violence, to causing a slight shock; in this respect, it is more consonant with a psychoanalysis understood as a *development of narrations or opening up of possible worlds*, and less with a psychoanalysis that translates the unconscious into the conscious and is inspired by a cold, distant, and objective intelligence, as, for example, Freud's surgical metaphor might suggest.

It is at any rate clear that, on the one hand, language is composed of a gradient of abusive acts (cf. de Saussure's notion of the arbitrary nature of the link that joins the signifier to the signified, the word to the thing, or separates them from each other, or Aulagnier's idea of the "violence" of interpretation, 1975), while, on the other, it is nothing but a "cemetery of tropes" (Mortara-Garavelli, 2010, p. 11, translated): violence and mourning would appear to lie at the origin of language and culture. Be that as it may, metaphor's constant "transportation" of heterogeneous terms remote from each other, like the subterranean cars of a subway train between stations, serves the purpose of *seeing reality*—of seeing it for the first time, as children do; and children of course produce highly original metaphors. They also make it possible to see again with new eyes, a capacity possessed by poets in greater measure than anyone else. For this reason it is indeed the case that "metaphors can be the ghosts of ideas waiting to be born" (Bion, 1977, p. 418). They are ultimately the royal road to reality, because they express the functioning of what we sense to be a basic cognitive mechanism of the psyche—an actual "principle of knowledge rather than of recognition" (de Beistegui, 2010, p. 44, translated).

In a famous passage from *Totem and Taboo*, Freud discusses the way in which magic thought treats past situations as if they were present:

> It is further to be noticed that the two principles of association—similarity [Ähnlichkeit] and contiguity [*Kontiguität*]—are both included in the more comprehensive concept of "contact" [*Berührung*]. Association by contiguity is contact in the literal sense; association by similarity is contact in the metaphorical sense. The use of the same word for the two kinds of relation is no doubt accounted for by *some identity* [*Eine ... Identität*] in the psychical processes concerned which we have not yet grasped.
>
> (Freud, 1913b, p. 85, my emphasis)

Freud here identifies an essential, albeit problematic, quality of the mind that makes the creation of meaning possible. He postulates the existence on the infralinguistic level of a central psychic mechanism, albeit as yet indeterminate, and does so by invoking linguistics and rhetoric. He thus subordinates similarity (metaphor, from the Greek *metapherein*, "to transport") and contiguity (metonymy, from the Greek *metonymia*, "exchange of name"—although what is involved here is not so much the classical definition of the figure as the type of semantic relationship, based on its implication of coexistence/proximity) to "contact." But when we say "contact," are we not in fact still referring to an idea of contiguity? In other words, are we not stating that the second of the modes of relating, contact *in the direct sense*, is primary? It is no coincidence that the English words, as well as their Italian equivalents, have a common root in the Latin *contingere*.

Freud here seems to be alluding precisely to the relationship between metaphor and metonymy, a figure (of "contiguity"—Mortara-Garavelli, 2010, p. 23, translated) that is no less important and no less difficult to define. The debate is ongoing in the linguistic field: some hold that metaphor can be reduced to metonymy because it is the fruit of a twofold metonymy ("'two metonymies short-circuited,' or, as it were, the product of two synecdoches"—ibid., p. 24, translated). From this point of view, metonymy is the only transformational device, or trope, that can be thought of both as a general function of semiosis, and as something that entails a strategy of thought *which cannot be further broken down.*[8]

Ordinary usage of course relies on traditional definitions and customary practical distinctions. However, this hypothesis will facilitate the tracing of thought, and the huge gulf it can bridge in joining even the most diverse of objects in metaphor, back to their bodily and sensory roots (as Merleau-Ponty teaches); to the cheek-breast interface (a relationship of contiguity), an "area of sensations of a soothing sort" that is the first nucleus of subjectivity (Ogden, 1994b, p. 174); and to the first (the most elementary) "translation," which Freud may have had in mind in 1895 when he wrote in the "Project" that, for an infant at the beginning of life, the object is his own cry. Metonymy would then in effect be metaphor in its ground state, and thought an extension (virtualization) of the concrete and direct interbody contact that acts as a matrix for a child's nascent psyche (or for the development of the rudimentary subjectivity/alpha function with which a child might already be endowed at birth). *"Transferred contact" (i.e., contact at a distance) would then be referred to "direct contact," the intellect to its sensory and bodily roots, and the isolated subject to the intersubjective field.*

However, as (mostly verbal) rhetorical figures, do metaphor and metonymy not correspond, as Lacan maintains, to the two key dream mechanisms discovered by Freud, namely condensation and displacement? *So in trying to define metaphor and metonymy, are we not actually referring to the meaning of dreaming? After all, did Bion not say that we dream not only at night but also during the day, and that to dream is to think?* Here, then, linguistic theory and psychoanalysis, although starting from different vertices, are seen to converge in formulating the idea that *in order to name things (to think), it is necessary to construct metaphors or to dream (to displace/to condense)*, and that these are two modes of expression, albeit on different levels of abstraction, of one and the same basic psychological process.

This meeting between a new theory of dreams (and of reverie) and narratology (and the modern theory of metaphor) underlies the model of the mind that serves as a framework for analytic field theory. Let us therefore briefly consider this model before turning to clinical examples.

## A Model of the Mind

In psychoanalysis, the realm of the image is the dream. Perhaps we should say "was" rather than "is," at least since Bion provided us with a model of the mind involving the continuous production of images (that could be called pictograms) by a function (described as the alpha function) on the basis of the sensoriality that pervades us from whatever source. The sequence of images somehow soothes and pacifies the mind whenever the transformation is successful. The result is a sequence of such images or pictograms, called "dream thought of the waking state." These images are normally unknowable in themselves. Given, for example, a sequence of powerful sense impressions such as relatively undefined proto-emotional states of rage → relief → longing, a possible sequence of pictograms might be:

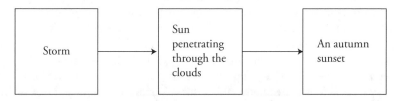

Of course, the choice and construction of an individual "pictogram" and of sequences of pictograms are extremely subjective. It is like one and the same "subject" painted by Degas, and then by Caravaggio, Monet, Chagall, Picasso, etc.

This, then, is the mind's first locus of creativity. In Bion's terms, it would be the transformation beta (via the alpha function) → alpha.

There is also a second locus of creativity in the mind. In a manner that is again extremely subjective, the sequence of pictograms (waking dream thought) is "narrated"—that is, put into words. Here too, an infinite number of narrative genres can be used to perform this transformation. In any case, *narrative derivatives* of the pictograms (or of the alpha elements, or of waking dream thought) are the outcome.

The sequence in the above example could generate a set of stories differing in style but all characterized by one constant—namely, the succession rage–relief–longing. A "memory" of infancy leads to a "diary entry," a chronicled event, a fantasy, and so on.

We can also come into contact with a pictogram of the sequence that forms in our mind in (and outside) an analytic session, by the phenomenon we call reverie. Reverie enables us to make contact with the image synthesized by the alpha function—for example, that of a "storm."

Another situation in which a pictogram of the sequence originating in waking dream thought is "seen" is when the patient projects one of these images to the outside, thus endowing it with a strongly sensory character; this is not a true hallucination, because the meaning it conveys can easily be guessed. A telling example is that of the patient who responded to a request by one of the present authors for an increase in fees by exclaiming: "Good heavens, I can see a chicken being plucked on the wall opposite!"

According to this model of psychic life, throughout the day an enormous number of pictograms (alpha elements) are constantly forming and being transferred to memory. These are acted upon by an "alpha-megafunction" (Grotstein, 2007, p. 271)—a mental device that performs a kind of second pressing or weaving of this material, eventually giving rise to dream images. These are the most "digested" elements which our apparatus for thinking thoughts is capable of producing.

It is no coincidence that Ogden holds that a psychoanalyst's work consists of dreaming—that is, of undertaking the transformations of sensory "storms" into images which the patient cannot perform by himself. It follows, too, that the aim of analysis is to develop in the patient the capacity to "generate images," to create dreams out of the forms of concrete thought represented by symptoms.

O'Shaughnessy (2005) distinguishes Bion's notion of waking dream thought from Klein's conception that the infant mind possesses from the beginning a rich unconscious fantasy life manifested in sensations and affects. Both of these processes confer meaning on experience, even if waking dream thought entails something new—namely, the idea of a primary process (situated upstream of unconscious fantasy) of transformation/"alphabetization" of the crude data of experience.

Let us try to describe what happens in the analyst's consulting room. The patient arrives with a variously sized bottle of ink (his anxieties and proto-emotions—in the jargon, his beta elements), which he keeps pouring on to the special kind of blotting paper represented by the field. The field absorbs the ink and becomes thoroughly soaked in it. Analyst and patient dip their pens into this ink in order to write down the text of the session. What was previously a mere formless blot is transformed into stories, narrations, and constructions. In this way, what at first had a "soiling" effect becomes susceptible to thought, narration, and sharing.

Another image of the patient's problem might be that of a big horse, with "*ferri*"(!)[9] on its hoofs, which, as it gallops, clip-clop back and forth like the types of an old-fashioned typewriter. However, eventually the horse finds a groom to take care of it, and as its hoofs flail back and forth, it begins to write at first fragments of stories, and then complete stories. Moreover, in the process of writing it calms down, grows ever smaller, and ultimately ceases to be a problem.

## The Aesthetics of Metaphor and the Analytic Field

So far we have considered the significance of the field metaphor as the organizing schema of a particular psychoanalytic model.[10] Examples include the use of the archaeological, military, and chess metaphors in Freud's theories; Bion's digestive and sexual metaphors; or the gastronomic or cinematographic metaphors employed by Ferro (1992, 1996). We then proceeded to examine metaphor as a rhetorical figure and an elementary psychological mechanism (cf. also the now classical studies of

Lakoff & Johnson, 1980a); *and, on the basis of a passage from Freud and certain cues from the linguistic theory of metaphor, we postulated the substantial identity of metaphors and dreams (and visual images)*. Last, we come now to the meaning and use of metaphor in both the broad sense (referring to the level *of* discourse) and the specific sense (of an image or rhetorical figure involved *in* discourse), as a technical device in clinical psychoanalytic work within a field model.

### *Playing with Metaphors*

#### *Not Just Herbivores*

Paolo begins his analysis as the good boy that he is. In his first session, he tells me about his attempts to fix his "Vespa," which has been lying about, forgotten for years. After a number of sessions devoted to this subject, I venture to suggest that "sometimes a *vespa* [Italian for wasp] will sting." A prolonged silence ensues.

In the next session Paolo, who has hitherto always come along with a laptop, tells me: "My computer has been struck by lightning and it is literally completely burnt out." So I mitigate the pressure of my interpretations, which was intended to demechanize certain aspects of the patient, but when I later return to a more pungent interpretative regime, there appears "the neighbor who collects weapons and who seemed to be aiming a threatening submachine gun." When I return to a more "playful" style of interpretation, Paolo mentions the neighbor again, saying that his gun—now he has had a clear view of it!—has a red plug on top of it. It is manifestly a toy weapon, so there is no reason to be worried.

As the analysis proceeds, he tells me about his grandmother's farm, which is populated by a whole menagerie of chickens, ducks, hens, sheep, cows, and so on—until one day I ask him if he is not fed up with all these herbivores (!). Paolo at first reacts as if struck by a wave of persecution, but in the final session before the summer vacation, I am surprised to be given a present of little toy wild animals. On returning from vacation, he discovers, carved into the beams of the ceiling of my consulting room, a five-pointed star, the symbol of the Red Brigades—which neither I nor the patients on the couch had ever noticed in thirty or more years.

I now realize that rage and revolution have entered the room. However, when I try to find the carving again, I cannot focus on it: these aspects of Paolo tend to disappear. On another occasion when he shows me the five-pointed star and the mark of the Red Brigades, I take the opportunity of telling him that he has the eyes of a hawk. In this way, I am substituting the hawk for the lost little sparrow he kept in a cage, about which he had told me at length.

These more intensely passionate aspects make their entry into the sessions, albeit in "bleached white" form, when he receives a letter from his girlfriend, from whom he has heard nothing for a long time; after a prolonged silence on my part, he comments: "I didn't know whether to tear it up or to open it with the letter opener."

It will thus be seen that metaphor in the strict sense of the term (as a word-related fact) belongs to the order of the narrative derivatives of waking dream thought, but also that the process whereby it comes into being is the same as that of unconscious thought. The transformations from sensoriality into narrative derivatives are "metaphorical," and conversely the metaphors are narrative derivatives.

## Metaphors Living or Dead?

### The Check

Andrea tells me of the climate of anxiety into which he was plunged by a friend who made him fear that he would no longer receive his monthly check for his new job. In fact, it would not be very serious even if he did not receive this check, as that would enable him to look for a more satisfying, better paid job. However, his friend has succeeded in making him feel persecuted and threatened, as well as open to the envy of others.

The "friend" of course represents a kind of functioning in the patient himself which, in the absence of analysis at the weekend, manages to undermine his (wavering) basic level of confidence, plunging him into a climate of discomfort and distrust, and causing him to lose sight of the progress he has made.

I now make a metaphorical intervention. I tell him that he reminds me of a competent swimmer who is told that his lifejacket might be removed or that he will not be given one, because he doesn't need it and it would get in his way. My point is that this image, however, is not a preconstituted metaphor, because it arises in me, with him, there, in real time, for the first time and simultaneously with his communications. It is a reverie produced on the spot, or rather, one whose discursive formulation arises out of a reverie—which is not directly communicable in itself, in its visual form, just as a dream is not communicable except by a kind of intersemiotic "transmutation"/translation; that is, after being transferred from one system of signs to another, different system of signs.

## Introducing the Patient to the World of Metaphors, or the Resumption of Dreaming

### Lucio's Grease Gun

I tell Lucio that I shall be away for a couple of weeks (for professional reasons). He begins the next session by saying that *he has not had any dreams.* He then tells me that he took the cat along to be neutered and that he feels quite calm. He adds that he has met with one of the leaders of a pacifist association, who has been abandoned by his wife and weeps inconsolably. His wife cheated on him, taking up again with a female fellow student with whom she had already had a relationship.

*I tell him that, if we were to look at these two communications as if they were two dreams* (that is always one of my listening vertices when a patient speaks to me), we might think that he was worried that, if the cat had not been neutered, it might perhaps scratch me. What is more, who knows what might happen if the member of the pacifist organization who cried because of *my* cheating on him, even if the cheating was in a way "justified" (for a congress, as he tells me he has discovered on the Internet), was actually the Mexican revolutionary Pancho Villa or simply the Italian national hero Garibaldi.

Lucio immediately gets my drift, and says that he has nevertheless begun to make some progress. He has not yet become Garibaldi, but has at least taken on some of that worthy's boldness of character. He has, for example, plucked up the courage to go to the pharmacy to buy a vaginal lubricant for his girlfriend, who suffers from a dryness in that region. In the past he would never have exposed himself in this way, but this time he felt no shame. He asked for a "nonspermicidal vaginal lubricant." He then remembers the film *Kill Bill*, in which a male nurse gave a jar of Vaseline to someone about to have sex with a woman whose vagina was so dry that "without the Vaseline it would have been like sticking his penis into a can of sand."

I tell him he has been quite Garibaldi-like in managing to show his needs to the "pharmacist," but at the same time, it seems to me that he feels the need to lubricate his relationships because he wants to avoid any friction with others. Yet he is still leaving something "alive," he is not eliminating everything. Lucio confirms my interpretation, telling me of some episodes from his childhood in which, so as not to upset his parents, he always avoided any "friction" with his classmates, in what was in fact a pretty turbulent class. In the same session, he makes a slip, when he tells me of his "fear of not being able to stop" (he meant to say the opposite), and then wonders whether he should see himself as a bull dressed up as an ox or an ox dressed up as a bull. We then work on these themes of containment/noncontainment, referring also to the Michael Douglas movie *Falling Down*, and Lucio returns to the subject of lubrication as the end of the session approaches. As a boy, he tells me, he already enjoyed using a grease gun to lubricate the gears of his bicycle; it was a sort of elongated contraption with a nozzle that made a very good job of lubricating. I now tell him that it seems obvious to me that a bull likes making women grow fat,[11] and what better way could there be of making them pregnant (referring to a wish to have children that cannot be made fully explicit).

We thus observe an entire spectrum of shades of defense concerning the "bulls," the feared and uncontainable proto-emotions that extend from the production of autism to that of a bonsai, of a mechanism, and of lethargy. In particular, however, we see how, little by little, a space for dreaming is regained by a series of metaphorical openings—in fact, amounting to a kind of *ongoing metaphor*.

### Negative Reverie

The analyst's mind should be receptive and capable of absorbing and containing the patient's emotions—that is, of transforming proto-sensory and proto-emotional states into images and hence into thought, and then of imparting the method to the patient. Any narration, however seemingly realistic, always tells us as analysts (and only as analysts) of something else: of the patient's internal world and, in particular, if we are able to listen, of the appropriateness or otherwise of his instruments (for feeling, dreaming, and thinking). In substance, analysis has to do with all the methods whereby these instruments (and apparatuses) can be developed (and sometimes created).

A symptom often takes the form of a "stopper" to prevent the emergence of something unknown both to the patient and to ourselves, but about which we ought sooner or later to become capable of "dreaming together." At the beginning of an analysis, and at the beginning of each session, we should deploy our "negative capability" (a PS without persecution), and be able to wait for a meaning to slowly take shape. Every hypothesis of meaning that we formulate, and every misused metaphor that we employ, should be rapidly set aside, so as to put ourselves into a mental state open to the new and unpredictable.

Things do not always turn out that way. Our functioning is sometimes affected by various degrees of negative reverie (– R), partially or totally blocked reverie— perhaps even a situation of reversed functioning, in which the mind that is supposed to receive and transform projects things into the mind that wants and needs to evacuate and find a space and method to manage proto-emotions. These forms of mental functioning—these traumatic facts (trauma is basically exposure to more beta elements than one can receive and transform, either by oneself or with the other's help)—are then, as always, narrated in an infinite number of scripts.

### Gino

In one of his sessions, Gino takes out a Barbie Doll and says: "How's the dancer today?" The therapist interprets the question as directed to herself and answers: "Very well, and how are you?" "I'm at the cemetery," he answers (this seems to be something that has actually happened; it is the only way Gino can deal with the despair he has felt in the interval between sessions). He says the girl he likes most was not in class and the teacher was not listening. Gino is immediately noticing that the therapist has failed to pick up his depression, and adds that he would like to touch the long, bushy hair of his female classmates. Disoriented by the concreteness of the communication, the therapist (whose hair is cut short almost to her scalp) fails to grasp his wish for a gentle, soft touch, and says: "Does it turn you on?" Now also disoriented, Gino mentions a girl in his class who removed the hand he had placed on her hair, and then tells the therapist that he saw a boy blowing on a girl's hair. The feeling of being repelled makes Gino puff, but the warm, emotional component of puffing is lost in the blowing.

He goes on: "Our teacher came to school wearing an undershirt, so can the boys wear a T-shirt on top of their sweaters?" He adds: "They're speaking German." There is a coded message here; restoring the freeze-dried emotion that has been sucked away, the communication becomes: "You told me something about yourself (being turned on), so can I reveal intimate things too instead of covering them up?"

*Gino is in effect constantly sucking in the emotional sap of metaphor, and what the therapist ought to be doing (but cannot because she is in –R) is to restore sap and emotional and affective solidity to what (seemingly) has to remain totally neutral in order to be expressed.*

Gino begins another session as follows: "Do you have a short-sleeved T-shirt? Take off your sweater!" His meaning seems to be: "Uncover yourself, show the emotions you have underneath!" He then adds: "Is my hair clean?" He is afraid the therapist might think there is something dirty in his communication (the "turning on" mentioned by the therapist), whereas Gino's communication is innocent! He adds: "I want to grow a pigtail; I also like people with a crest on their heads." Although this too could be seen as a sensualization or erotization of the communication, I do not think that is correct. Until not long ago, in his sessions Gino used to lean over the desk with his face as close as possible to the therapist's. It was like the tropism of a plant toward the light, a kind of "vegetable" behavior (but previously, locked up in his mute amimia, his behavior had been mineral in nature for years on end!). Unable to say "I feel attracted by you," he *moves toward* the other, like a climbing plant. He now feels that the next stage in his evolution is the leap from the plant world of *concrete metaphor* to the animal world of proto-emotions, the pigtail, and the crest as representatives of a no longer vegetable world. This development could also be seen as possessing a sexual element, as a transition from pollination to a more sexual form of functioning of minds. An emotional thread is indeed beginning to form, binding the two minds together, even if it is still wrapped in thick layers of sweater/insulation/German.

### Metaphor, Reverie, and Free Association

The dichotomy of living vs. dead metaphor is reflected in that of reverie vs. free association. There are differences between a free association and a reverie. The latter is characterized by direct contact with the pictogram that constitutes the waking dream thought. It comes into being upstream of interpretation, and in some way inspires or suggests it. It is an image (which is usually communicable to the patient only in exceptional cases, but would then come under the heading of self-disclosure) that is created in the mind—spontaneously and not "to order"—whose difficulty lies in organizing it in a pertinent, explanatory communication. Rather than in effect being taken from an encyclopedia (that is, from the harvesting of preformed metaphors present in language), this communication should be created there, in that place, for the first time, like a small fragment of a dream triggered by situations permeated with projective identifications or, if you will, beta elements. The only possible approach for bringing out this stratum of thought processes is a negative one (Bion's "negative capability").

Any reverie could also be said to be a free association, but the opposite is not the case, even though the boundary is sometimes blurred. An association may share the nature of reverie if it is spontaneous and is received in a state of passivity. Mostly, however, it emerges among the entities that can be described as "narrative derivatives"

(Ferro, 2006a) of waking dream thought. Unlike reverie, a free association can also be "forced." A free association—which may be a metaphor already recorded in language, either because it is banal or because it has become a catachresis—arises at a less early stage of thought, downstream of waking dream thought, when the level of narrative derivatives has already been reached. It is, rather, a widening of narration.

Giovanna's analysis has reached an impasse with no obvious way out, when I come into contact with—I actually SEE—a "sailboat in a bottle," which provides me with a visual description of what is happening in the analytic field: the sailboat of the analysis is bottled up. Hence the interpretation: "It seems to me that we are stalled, and I find myself imagining a sailboat in a bottle—a boat made like the analysis for sailing ..." and so on.

The corresponding metaphor, on the other hand, would be if I were to use an example taken from one of Conrad's typical tales in which a sailboat is "becalmed." I could then more readily describe a situation of which I am already aware, to which the image of the "sailboat in the bottle" belongs; indeed, it suggests, triggers, and inspires the interpretation.

## Transformations of the Field and Narration

As these vignettes show, in an analytic field theory, the analyst's reveries and affective and visual transformations based on the patient's narration, together with any metaphors that stem from these, are the actual factors of growth. The analyst transforms anxieties and persecution feelings into affective images; he has a dream about the patient's communication. He shapes the alpha elements and passes them on to the patient—but, in particular, he puts the patient in touch with his own functioning (his alpha function), which governs these transformations. It is not so much metaphor in itself, as a living metaphor, arising there and specific to that patient at that time, that bears witness to the oneiric functioning of the analyst's mind and supplies him with the method for performing this act (paradoxically, in some cases, even if he does not say or do anything). The same can be said of the situation in which the analyst "reawakens" one of the now lexicalized or extinct metaphors used by the patient or by himself.

With patients who are more seriously ill (or with the more seriously ill parts of all patients), only this level can permit the development of the alpha function—that is to say, of the patient's own capacity to dream, both while awake and while asleep, because a more explicit offer of meaning might arouse a sense of persecution.

The session proceeds by a kind of oneiric reciprocity, both when the patient "dreams" (if he can) the analyst's intervention and mental state, and when the analyst "dreams" the response to give to the patient (Civitarese, 2006; Ferro et al., 2007). The more this response is "dreamed"—that is, the fruit of unconscious thought—the more it will be a factor in shaping the patient's alpha function or in mending any defects in it.

However, what we have described for the sake of simplicity as belonging to the analyst and the patient actually takes place in a *dimension that transcends both, which is that of the field.* This situation could therefore be redescribed from this other complex viewpoint in terms of turbulences and the alpha function of the field. The idea is that, if we creatively transform the field constituted by the two subjectivities, each will benefit—in particular, the patient, because, by definition, he comes along with less capacity to dream experience, or, in other words, to assign a personal meaning to it, and hence to contain emotions.

If the drama undergone by a character in the tale comprising the analytic dialogue is resolved, the positive turn of the plot is a narrative form that reflects profound emotional transformations occurring in the common psychological area of the analytic field, which are therefore bound to be relevant to both members of the analytic couple, albeit as a rule asymmetrically (because, after all, the analyst should also be capable of a certain detachment). Of course, whereas this situation is in our view more correctly described in intersubjective or field terms, there is no reason why it could not be portrayed more abstractly or with its complexity simplified, for example by the fiction of two completely separate subjectivities, or indeed using less radical relational models.

The vignettes show that, from a field vertex, rather than "giving interpretations" or "making interventions" *directed to* the patient, the need is to *attune oneself to* the emotions that are not yet thinkable for the patient and to help him to give shape to them. Attention will then be paid more to the development of the container—that is, to facilitating the growth of the capacity to think—than to its contents. In order to be in unison with the patient, the guiding principle is to reach him at the point where he is, and to take account of the degree of truth about himself that proves *tolerable* to him—that is, as Eco (1984) says in connection with metaphors, of his *limit of acceptability*. For this reason, the analyst must pay attention to the derivatives of waking dream thought, as a basis for constantly attempting to apprehend the signals addressed to him by the patient about where he is and how he reacts to what he says (or does not say) to him. The essential aim is to weave together the emotional threads making for growth of the patient's capacity to dream/think/symbolize. To this end, the conversation often proceeds on a twofold level, in which the manifest text *metaphorizes* the latent text of the unconscious/field dimension of the relationship— the invisible "electromagnetic waves" that establish it, exactly as in the case of play in the therapy of children.

As rhetorical figures involved in the text of the analysis, metaphors appear to us as *transformations* (A becomes B; the real appears to us, on the phenomenal level, as a given reality) which are *narrative*—that is, expressed in words: there is a temporality, a becoming. Felicitous metaphors have a containing effect (the frightening and unknowable "O" is "cooked"). By virtue of their metonymic basis, they represent a point of equilibrium between emotions and thought, because they are pervaded with sensoriality (i.e., they retain the mark of things), while at the same time distancing themselves from things (which they symbolize). They are *sensible ideas* (Carbone, 2008)—that is to say, they combine emotion and thought. They therefore restore a bodily element to the mind; they reunite psyche and soma; they reforge the "psychosomatic collusion" (Winnicott) that is the foundation of subjectivity; they are dreams that *create* reality and give it a personal meaning.

It will therefore be understood that, in order to live, rather than knowing how the mechanisms of the unconscious work or receiving logical or rational types of explanations, patients need good metaphors. As in the case of aesthetic experience in art, there is nothing like a good metaphor to give someone a feeling of truth about his existence. An apt metaphor is an image of which we can never have too much; it is an inexhaustible source of meaning. To be apt, however, in analysis a narration must be attuned to the patient; it must contain his most anxiety-inducing emotions at their point of urgency. The analyst must be capable of reverie, have a well developed alpha function, and be in a receptive state. Reveries give birth to living metaphors, while, conversely, metaphors are an excellent, if not the only, way of using reverie.

In the dialogue, priority is given to the clear text furnished by the patient, because the metaphorical discourse as a whole is open and unsaturated, conveys emotions, and creates meaning. In our view, analytic field theory is the approach that places the greatest possible emphasis on metaphors and on metaphorical discourse, because, by virtue of its strict inclusiveness (at least in principle), there is nothing that cannot refer to the field and to the transference, and hence nothing that is present only for itself, like a lexicalized or extinct metaphor. As Proust writes in *The Captive*, and as quoted in the epigraph to this contribution, "everything is capable of transposition." There is no fact, event, memory, account of a dream, and the like, that cannot stand for something else. If we accept the suggestion of one of us (Ferro and Basile, 2009) that we should precede everything the patient says (as well as everything that we say) with the words "I dreamt that ...," in order to recover an "internal setting" (Civitarese, 2011, in press), the frame of reference is immediately shifted, thus saving his (or our) words from running aground on a realism lacking in personal significance, reopening the way to the play of meaning, and revealing to the patient (and to ourselves) the path toward the resumption of dreaming one's interrupted or undreamt dreams— i.e., one's very existence (Ogden, 2005).

Translated by Philip Slotkin MA Cantab. MITI

## Notes

1 Originally published in *Psychoanalytic Inquiry* 33(3) (May 2013) with the title "The Meaning and Use of Metaphor in Analytic Field Theory."
2 The Barangers also took inspiration from Kurt Lewin, Heinrich Racker, and Enrique Pichon Rivière (de León de Bernardi, 2008). Churcher (2008) points out that Lewin's name is replaced by that of Merleau-Ponty in the second, revised version of the Barangers' 1961–1962 paper as republished in 1969.
3 [Translator's note: For convenience, the masculine form is used for both sexes throughout this translation.]
4 The lectures delivered at the Sorbonne in the 1950–1951 academic year, "The Child's Relation With Others" (published in English in 1964), demonstrate Merleau-Ponty's familiarity with Klein's works. Klein used the concept of projective identification as the basis of an intersubjective theory of the psyche that was both extraordinarily advanced

and in some respects complementary to that of Merleau-Ponty. According to Angelino (2005, p. 374, translated), Melanie Klein fascinated Merleau-Ponty "because her writings are rich in highly concrete, indeed brutal, and quite shocking descriptions of our relations with others and with things, which bear out what he thought about the role of corporeality and the drives (libido and aggression) in our relationship with the world." As we know, Klein studied in detail, to a degree bordering on obsession, the mechanisms of the first introjections/projections and identifications of a child when still immersed in a state of partial nondistinction from the object. Klein admittedly accepts the existence of a primitive ego from birth, but, as Kristeva (2000, p. 62f.) notes, "the fragile ego is not truly separated in the sense of a 'subject' separated from an 'object,' but it incessantly consumes the breast from within and ejects the breast into the outside world by constructing-vacating itself while constructing-vacating the Other." The point, however, is that Klein's model proves valuable not only for representing the relationship between the subject and his environment at the stage described by Freud as that of primary narcissism, but *also when the subject is no longer in such an elementary phase of constitution of the ego*. Like Klein, Merleau-Ponty considers that identity can be thought of only in terms of difference, of the intersection between the subject's body and the world of things and other people. A person can be himself only by projecting himself outside his own self into the other, and vice versa. The subject (S) constructs himself only by transferring himself into the object (O), which is thereby transformed (O'), and by then reintrojecting from the object what he had deposited in it, thereby in turn being modified (S'); the structure of the chiasm—the resulting notation seems to allude ironically to a kind of appeal to the other—would be SOO'S'. Hence the approaches of Klein and Merleau-Ponty can be seen as complementary. Oddly enough, because Klein was interested mainly in the unconscious and in psychic reality, she in effect disregards the "carnal"—feeling and felt—aspect of the body (even though the body is absolutely the protagonist of the subject's unconscious fantasies). Merleau-Ponty's concentration on the experience of the body, on the other hand, leads him to develop theories very close to current notions of the unrepressed, or "sensory," unconscious and of procedural, rather than declarative, memories.

5  Cf. Baranger M (2005, p. 62f.): "It was when we reviewed Bion's studies on small groups that we modified and added precision to our thinking in a direction different from transference–countertransference interaction [...] We then understood that the field is much more than interaction and intersubjective relations [...] Translating what is described as the group's 'basic assumption' to the individual analytic situation, we spoke of the 'basic unconscious phantasy' that emerges in the analytic situation, created by the same field situation [...] This phantasy is not the sum or combination of the individual fantasies of the two members of the analytic couple, but an original set of fantasies created by the field situation itself. It emerges in the process of the analytic situation and has no existence outside the field situation, although it is rooted in the unconscious of the members [...]."

6  However, consider the following passage from Bion's letter to Rickman of 7 March 1943: "The more I look at it the more it seems to me that some very serious work needs to be done along analytical and field theory lines to elucidate [...]" (Conci, 2010, in press). The article published in *The Lancet* in 1943 and signed by both, "Intra-group Tensions in Therapy—Their Study as the Task of the Group" (which subsequently became the first chapter of "Experiences in Groups" [1948]), contains what is clearly a field theory (Civitarese, 2010, in press). Lacan (1947) had no hesitation in describing this article as miraculous!

7  Kojève (1947, p. 43) concisely sums up Hegel's conception of the subject as follows: "if they are to be *human*, they must be at least *two* in number."

8  Cf. Eco (1984, p. 87): metaphor "[...] a trope that seems to be the most primary will appear instead as the most derivative, as the result of a semantic calculus that presupposes

other preliminary semiotic operations. A curious situation for a figure of speech that has been recognized by many to be the basis of every other."

9 [Translator's note: Literally horseshoes, but the Italian word is also the plural of *ferro*, the name of the analyst and one of the authors of this paper.]

10 New metaphors are among the "mutations" that cause a scientific paradigm to evolve (Kuhn, 1962).

11 [Translator's note: The Italian word *grasso* can mean either grease or fat.]

# 13

# FIELD THEORY, THE "TALKING CURE," AND METAPHORIC PROCESSES[1]

*Ana-María Rizzuto*

The Barangers field theory considers the analytic situation as dialogical, bipersonal, and at the service of the interpretation of unconscious phantasies created in the field by the shared participation of patient and analyst. They ask about the power of words to offer meaningful interpretations and their potential to return to their earlier meanings in the patient's life.

Examining the richness of the spoken word as a medium for the expression of private experiences to another I suggest that what counts in analytic work is the use of living words, linked to past and intra-analytic experiences. I suggest that in psychic life the semantic meaning of words is embedded in their experiential and affective interpersonal meaning. The words act as the medium to link the private experience of the analysand to the private experience of the analyst without a direct intersubjective communication. I illustrate my point with the example of the analyst's warm words being "savored" as warm milk by a regressed analysand.

Field theory offers a conceptual framework to describe and interpret what happens during an analytic treatment based on the therapeutic contract between two persons who have accepted to talk with each other under the conditions imposed by the analytic setting. It was introduced as a psychoanalytic conception by Madeleine and Willy Baranger in their seminal article *La situación analítica como campo dinámico* published in the *Revista Uruguaya de Psicoanálisis* in 1961–1962 and translated into English in 2008. Willy Baranger (1959) had already asserted that psychoanalysis "must accept its character as a science of dialogue—that is, of bi-personal psychology—its character as an interpretative science" (cited in de Leon de Bernardi, 2008, p. 774). Willy and Madeleine Baranger considered in their later article "that the essence of the analytic procedure is a dialogue" (2008, p. 816). The field is created spontaneously and dynamically by the participants in the analytic process and it emerges as a result of their engagement in the total situation between them, which includes the past, the present, and the future (Churcher, 2008). The Barangers had borrowed some of their concepts from the Gestalt psychologists and the work of Kurt Lewin on social field phenomena. Later, they referred to the work of the French phenomenological philosopher Maurice Merleau-Ponty without explaining their motive for the selection of the new author. Merleau-Ponty insisted on "the primacy of perception" and proposed that our knowledge of the world is dependent upon and inseparable from our bodily condition.

Based on their conception of the analytic process as a dynamic gestalt the Barangers offered their idea of the analytic field as a *heuristic model* to understand facts present in the analytic situation (Canestri, 2004–2005, p. 1511, cited by Churcher, 2008). The field they describe is ambiguous and is characterized by the emergence of a bipersonal unconscious phantasy created by the analytic couple. Such phantasy may become a "bastion" of joined resistance to the progress of the analytic process. The analytic process may also bring about a "point of urgency" calling for the analyst's to offer an interpretation to the analysand: "[W]e consider the point of urgency to be a moment in the functioning of the field when the structure of the dialogue and the underlying structure (the basic unconscious phantasy of the field) can come together and give rise to an insight. The analyst feels and thinks that he can and must interpret (formulate an interpretation to the analysand)" (M. Baranger, 1993a, p. 18).

In their original paper *The Analytic Situation as a Dynamic Field* (1961–1962/2008) the Barangers question how words acquire their interpretive power:

Our problem is therefore reduced to this: how can the interpretation reduce the "gestalt" of the manifest content to the "gestalt" of the urgent unconscious phantasy in the session? This leads us to the problem: how can the interpretation, as words, act upon the different structurings of the bi-personal field? In other words, what is the basis of the interpretative power of the word?

(2008, p. 820)

In response to their question, they mention the work of Luisa Alvarez de Toledo (1954/1996) who connects "speaking," "associating," and "interpreting" to a "doing" of the analyst with the patient based on early object relations and the maternal voice. The voice of the analyst carries not only meanings but also gratification, danger, and has the power to evoke phantasies. They believe that these considerations are not enough to understand the function of words in analysis: "It is one thing for the patient to take our words as milk or stones, and quite another for the patient to understand their meaning and for this understanding to provoke an important modification in the patient's world. The specific problem is the relation between the word and the insight that the patient acquires with an adequate interpretation" (Baranger & Baranger, 2008, p. 821). The Barangers' consider the patient's capacity for insight and change to be the final goal of analysis, achieved through "the patient's increased awareness of his or her inner world (ibid., p. 822).

They consider that "the word is equipped with three essential functions: it carries object relations and very primitive emotions, connects split off and isolated structurings in the field and differentiates the parts and aspects of the field thus reunited. Thus, the word again acquires the characteristics discovered by M. Klein (1930) in the process of symbol formation: the equivalence of symbol and symbolized, on the one hand, and differentiation between the two on the other hand. The absence or insufficiency of either of these two aspects constitutes a very great difficulty in the technique of interpretation" (Baranger & Baranger, 2008, p. 822). They believe that the question to be asked is "how words have lost their original power to reach deeply into internal life" and conclude: "The role of interpretation is to overcome the weakening of words that made them lose their original global communicational function and transformed them into mere abstract signs" (ibid., p. 823).

How do words manage to modify the field? "The word opens up the communications in the field, uniting its isolated or split off regions. But it also serves to locate, determine and differentiate its multiple aspects. It is both communication and control, and the function of interpretation can be lost if one of these aspects is exaggerated at the expense of the other" (ibid., p. 823). A modification of the field occurs when concrete words related to "primitive phantasies of object exchange" have the abstract power to make intelligible "the prevalent situation in the field" (ibid.). When this situation obtains "one of the parts of the patient that is split off and isolated or deposited in some sector of the field is re-integrated into the patient's self and recognized as the patient's own" (ibid.). As a result

> the Ego also differentiates between its own aspects that have been attributed to the object and the internal objects (different from the Ego) that contributed to the structuring of the external object. This is a double process: the Ego recovers what belongs to it as its own and also assimilates something more from its internal objects which, in turn increases the Ego's "real potential and improved contact with reality".
>
> (Baranger & Baranger, 2008, pp. 823–824)

The entire process reveals that the bi-personal field "is an experimental field" (ibid.) which in the end permits the analysand to see the analyst as the analyst and not as a projected figure. To arrive at this final point, the patient and the analyst, as participants in the field, must continuously confront ambiguity: "It is essential for the analytic procedure that each thing or event in the field be at the same time something else. If this essential ambiguity is lost, the analysis also disappears" (ibid., p. 799). The ambiguity even involves the bodily language of the patient during the analysis: "The ambiguity of the body in the analytic situation sometimes becomes quite patent at the moment when the patient abandons his 'body' of the session in order to recover the body of his daily life" (ibid., p. 801). The process affects the analyst as well who responds with "his or her own body to the patient's unconscious communications. The analyst also elaborates a body language with which to respond to certain modifications of the field" (ibid., p. 802).

The different meanings of ambiguous verbal and bodily languages converge in the field, which the Barangers call the "third configuration" where they consider that the very essence of the analytic process takes place (ibid., p. 804). The analyst strives to interpret the configuration of the field: "The analyst searches through the multiple latent situations that can be perceived in the material offered, which are also related to the manifest content and the current phantasy of the contract, to find the situation that is effectively interpretable" (ibid., p. 804). The analyst selects from the configuration the one manifestation that is most vivid to the patient, the most urgent and sees in it the "point of urgency" that calls for an interpretation capable of modifying the field" (p. 804). The analyst's interpretation and its potential to alter the analytic field reveals the asymmetry of the participation between the members of the bi-personal field.

The rereading of the Barangers' early paper and their later contributions fills me with respect and admiration for the richness of their clinical understanding and the complexity of their analytic model. I have selected out of their many conceptualizations their manner of understanding communication, verbal and bodily, as well as their key concept of the jointly constructed unconscious phantasy during analytic work with a clear intent in my mind. I believe that their ideas may find support and at the same time call for some modification if they are placed in the context of a comprehensive understanding of the function of the spoken word in human relatedness and transformative interactions. In the next part of my paper I intend to review the present-day understanding of the spoken word as a fully embodied human capability and its significance for the understanding of any human communication. Then, these concepts can be applied to the analytic process as a well-structured continuous process of verbal and bodily communicative exchanges between two individuals in the analytic setting. First, I must attend to the development process that introduces the child to the spoken word.

## The Acquisition of the Spoken Word

Children are enclosed in a speech situation before birth. The capacity to hear some sounds develops during the fifth month of gestation. Mothers seemed to know it because they speak to their babies while pregnant: One of my patients addressed her baby boy fetus who was moving inside her: "Charlie, you make me laugh. You kick so much. Be quiet now—*we* are in analysis." Kolata's (1984) research shows that babies who heard their mother's voice during gestation favor it over any other after birth. Butterfield and Siperstein (1974) have shown that four-month old babies prefer words over any other sound, even over music. Mothers seemed to know that babies experience pleasure in hearing their voice and speech because they talk to their babies to the point of keeping them "bathed in sound" (Mowrer, 1952). This is the first bi-personal situation and it involves—among the many ministrations that mothers offer to their infants—the constant accompaniment of directly speaking to the baby about them. Thus bodily care and the baby's experience of it are directly *integrated as a total situation* with the maternal voice, its prosody, affective tone, and spoken relational engagement. However, mothers—and fathers—also talk to their babies when they do not have a specific need: they want to *engage* the baby in a personal encounter, be it of playing or of describing the baby to himself or aspects of the world to the infant. It must be noticed that the tone of voice of the parents—and other adults—include modifications of melody, loudness, and pitch in order to *engage* the child in the conversation. Snow (1977) has demonstrated that mothers create for their non-speaking infants the normal turn-taking structure of dialogue. After having spoken to the baby, they use any action on the infant's part as if were a verbal response while they include the time pause typical of a conversation before entering their new spoken turn. When the child begins to use words, the parents progressively guide her to master the accurate use of language to join them in spoken exchanges. In all these developments, the child's proper name and the parent's use of the pronoun "you" (Rizzuto, 1993a) facilitates the new individual's formation of an identity, a mode of experiencing itself, and a mode of being together with others. The above description suggests that: 1) we have never been outside a context of spoken words addressed to us; 2) the prosodic component of language and its affective impact goes beyond the perception of sounds and words: it affects the individual viscerally (Fernald, 1996) and somatically (Condon & Sander, 1974) and assists him to somatically experience the affect of the other and its emotional investment during the spoken encounter; 3) the words we learn from parents and others are always richer in their associative and affective links than just giving names to things. Each person has its own affective experience of particular words in relation to the contexts of their use during development. I have called this process *the emotional history of words* (Rizzuto, 2003); 4) in ordinary life, speech is bi-personal: it involves two persons engaged with each other in order to achieve something together. In this respect psychoanalysis consists in the technical use of the richness always present in the spoken exchanges between two people; 5) language is part of the more extensive interpersonal communication between mother and child (Trevarthen, 1979) that precedes the acquisition of words. Even adults with full mastery of language cannot help but to have their spoken exchanges embedded within conscious and unconscious communications from the past; 6) bodily expressions and speech need to be organized as processes at the service of communication in the *privacy of the subjective experience* of the person who relates, speaks or listens to the bodily or spoken communication of the other. The resulting communication with its affective, motoric, expressive, and verbal components creates a bridge between the interlocutors, to facilitate access to the *private* experiences each of them is having. The aim of the communication is to find a *medium* that facilitates *some* access to the respective subjective experiences and expressions of the two people involved. This means that each participant is consciously and unconsciously (Meissner, 1993) an active intentional agent capable orchestrating—preconsciously and unconsciously—through the perception and *interpretation* of the communications of the other—its own manner of participating in the exchange. I understand this to be an interpersonal dialectic, ever present in human exchanges at the service of establishing meaningful links between two subjects whose inner reality remains *unavoidably private*. Bodily affective communication and speech create a virtual field of exchange as a *medium* to indirectly access subjective reality.

ANA-MARÍA RIZZUTO

## Recent Theories About Language Formation, Usage, and Understanding

In 1980 Lakoff and Johnson proposed that we live by bodily created metaphors. More recently, the discovery of mirror neurons mediated by visually perceived actions or acoustically presented action-related sentences suggest that embodied perception of the action of others is a mediated "embodied simulation" (Gallesse et al., 2007). Embodied simulation is a spontaneous process probably facilitated by mirror neurons. Gallese describes it: "A *direct* form of 'experiential understanding' of others is achieved by modelling their behaviours as intentional experiences on the basis of the equivalence between what others do and feel and what we do and feel" (p. 3, my italics). He concludes: "By means of a shared neural state realized *in two different bodies* that nevertheless obey the same functional rules, the 'object other' becomes another self'" (p. 3, my italics). The embodied simulation facilitates the understanding of the intentions of others: "Ascribing *intentions* would therefore consist in *predicting* a forthcoming new goal" [of an action] (p. 8, my italics). In a later article Gallese et al. (2007) says: "we employ the term embodied simulation as a mandatory, nonconscious, and prereflexive mechanism that is not the result of a deliberate and conscious cognitive effort aimed at interpreting the intentions hidden in the overt behavior of others, as implied by the theory-theory account. We believe that embodied simulation is a prior *functional mechanism* of our brain. However, because it also generates *representational content*, the functional mechanism seems to play a major role in our epistemic approach to the world" (p. 143, my italics). The authors suggest, based on numerous experiments and previous theoretical contributions, in particular Lakoff and Johnson (1980a) that we used our embodied experiences to understand the nonverbal as well as the spoken language of others.

These fascinating discoveries do add a dimension to our understanding of the function of the direct or indirect *perception* of the body, the actions, the feelings and the words of others, including their intentions. As a psychoanalyst, I consider that we must pay attention to the fact mentioned above by Gallese that the embodied simulation takes place between *two different bodies*, that can be similar in their neurological functioning, but never identical. The innumerable factors present in the simplest experience of satisfaction (Rizzuto, 2003, pp. 296–297), the variety of circumstances that affect the relational and historical life of the individual, and the never-resting process of fantasizing about them, gives each of us a *historically personalized* body to put at the service of any mirroring process. The embodied simulation seems to be an actual *neural mechanism* at the service of human relatedness. Yet, in my opinion, when we intend to understand the subliminal or obvious bodily expressions and verbal communications in analysis, we must take the mirroring processes and its *perceptual foundation* for granted, but remember that our human organism has the capacity to create a *psychical reality* based on all those phenomena plus two other functions that go beyond mirroring and embodiment: the need to interpret ourselves to ourselves by the mediation of imagery, metaphoric processes, narratives, and our untamable need to create fantasized scenarios to rehearse our wishes and fears. This brings us to the *representational content* that Gallese asserts emerges in the person involved in mirror neurons embodied simulation. In my way of understanding it, the *representational process,* includes the automatic mirror neuron registration of the perception of the action and words of others, to which the individual adds two *interpretations:* what it means for the self he conceives himself to be and what is the meaning of the *relational scene* between the self and the other in the context of the wishful and fearful expectations/fantasies elicited by them. This includes the dimension of the relational future. Green (1978) mentions scientifically well-documented transformative process in perception, in which the percept is not a simple registration of sensory input but the person's active way of organizing and decoding that input according to its own modalities of perceiving (p. 267). Gazzaniga (1995), a cognitive neuroscientist, after reviewing the large number of processes that function outside awareness introduces the notion of interpreter: "Catching up with all this parallel and constant activity seems to be the function of the left's hemisphere's interpreter module. The interpreter is the system of primary importance to the human brain. It is what allows for the formation of beliefs, which in turn are mental constructs that free us from simply responding to stimulus-response aspects of everyday life. In many ways it is the system that provides the story line or narrative of our lives" (p. 1394).

The accurate mirror neuron perception of the experiential moment, creates the possibility of analytic redressing, when the analytic process assists the patient to examine his interpretations and fantasies built around them by returning in certain global manner to the bodily memory of the original mirroring perception, that is, of the bodily state that was experienced while being with the other. This process is part of the working through, in particular of the transference.

## Freud and the spoken words

How did Freud understand the word? He presented his ideas early in his career in his monograph *On Aphasia* (1891). He considered the word to be composed of two representations: the object representation that is formed by the sensory perception of objects and the word representation, composed of the sound and the images of movement for the spoken word and the visual image for reading and writing. The replication of the sound and movements to pronounce the spoken word is a learned process resulting from the imitation of others. The object presentation originates from the sensory perceptions in the body periphery. They travel along neural pathways from the receptive sense organs on the body's surface and proceed to undergo transformative processes in their way to the cerebral cortex where they come to form the multisensory (auditory, tactile, visual, and other modalities) object representation. The neural transformative processes, Freud (1891) says explicitly, is organized to represent the body "in a manner suited to the function [of language]"(p. 53; Rizzuto, 1990). Freud makes a very strong statement about perception: "'perception' and 'association' are terms by which we describe different aspects of the same process".... "We cannot have a perception without immediately associating it ... in reality they belong to one single process" (p. 57). In brief, for Freud, object representations are not only 'embodied,' but they have the automatic capability of establishing instantaneous associations to other perceptive and mental processes. Would Freud have said that the mirror neurons associate what they mirror to other experiences? To me, this is a further confirmation that people's neural systems are unquestionably alike, but also *highly diversified* by the accumulation of private associative links. According to Freud, in normal functioning the complex formed by the object associations establishes a connection of their visual component to the sound component of the spoken word. In this manner *a meaningful psychical word* has been formed. As a learned spoken word it shares a linguistic meaning with the speaking community; as the internal representation of an object and a verbal form it combines the accuracy of sensory perception of the words learned from others with the context of the private associative networks of the individual. Freud makes another remarkable point: "all stimuli to spontaneous speech arise from object associations" (p. 79), and repeats it several times: "Every 'volitional' excitation of the speech centres... involves the region of the auditory representations and results in its stimulation by object associations" (p. 84). What is he saying? My reading is that the *wish* or the *need* to speak find their source in representational processes of associated objects in the privacy of the individual's mind. Contemporary linguist Ray Jackendoff (1988) says something very similar today: "People have things to talk about only by virtue of having mentally represented them" (p. 83). He concludes that what a person has not represented does not exist for him, even when it unquestionably exists in the world. We analysts know that our task is to assist people to represent and describe in words those aspects of their psychical or actual reality that their pathology has blinded them to. Furthermore, we can say that psychoanalysis is possible because there is always an unconscious connection between things that have been represented in the past and the subjective experience of the patient in the present, regardless of how early that experience has taken place. Assisting the patient to make that representation consciously available and namable during analysis is critical to our work.

## The Components of the Spoken Exchanged Between People

I have insisted that people talk when they have mental representations that motivate them to share them with another. Several questions emerge: To whom do I want unconsciously and consciously to talk about it? How many people am I addressing when I talk to just one person? How do I want to talk about it? What do I want to do to my listener when he hears me talking to her? What do I want her to feel for me, about herself, about us? What am I asking her to *really* hear? What kind of contact do I want to establish with her? What kind of message do I want to give? What is the context in which I want to contact her and how do I create such context? How do I phrase what I want to say so that it can be heard by my interlocutor? Or do I want to speak and not *really* be heard? The linguist Roman Jakobson (1990) created a model in response to these questions describing the six components of the functions of language and the six factors of the speech event. The latter include: the *context* [what they are talking about], a *code* [a language understandable to both partners], a *contact* [the physical and psychological connection between interlocutors], *a person who addresses* another, and *a person who is addressed*, and who receives a *message* from the addresser. As for the functions, Jakobson describes the *emotive or expressive*, that presents the speakers attitude about his words; the *conative*, that indicates the attitude towards the person addressed; the *referential,* that puts a denotation to the message; the *poetic* function that organizes the entire structure of the communication and that is manifested in the form the spoken expression takes; the *phatic* function is placed at the service of maintaining contact, as when one interlocutor asks: "Do you hear me?" Finally, the *metalingual* function serves to check the state of the communication: "Do you know what I mean?" It is no necessary to agree with Jakobson linguistic theories to accept that his description of the factors and functions present in spoken language are for real. What the description offers is a clear understanding of how many simultaneous events, actions, feelings, and relational elements are involved in the simplest of speeches between two people. Spoken language, I conclude, is closer to an orchestra than to a single instrument.

Jerome Feldman and Srinivas Narayanam (2004) outlined "an explicit neural theory of language (NTL) that attempts to explain how many brain functions (including emotion and social cognition) work together to understand and learn language" (p. 385). They propose that "one does not expect to find brain areas specialized only for language or to find language processing confined only to a few areas" (ibid.). More than a century earlier, Freud (1891) had defied the neurologists of his time by rejecting the theory of localization of language centers and proposing the involvement of large areas of the cortex in the speech function (Rizzuto, 1993a). Feldman and Narayanam (2004) assert: "The NTL assumption is that people understand narratives by subconsciously imagining (or simulating) the situation being described. When asked to grasp, we enact it. When hearing or reading about grasping we simulate grasping, being grasped, or watching someone grasp" (p. 385). We embody the words presented to us: "This ability to simulate or imagine *situations* is a core component of human intelligence and is central to our model of language" (p. 389, my italics). Their experiments argue in favor of "the embodied meaning of action words. They also provide robust biological evidence that planning, recognition and imagination share a common representational substrate. Our model of actions and their use in narrative predicts that the same structures are being exploited in understanding language about both concrete and abstract events" (p. 390). They conclude that "the basic ideas on embodied word learning, active simulation, and metaphorical interpretation appear to form the basis for a biologically plausible model of language acquisition and use" (p. 391). I conclude from these assertions that we understand language by preconsciously creating somatically based *imaginary scenes* in relation to what we are talking about. The scenes involve the multitude of interpersonal events that occur in the simplest of conversations. I have placed above a long list of questions to give concrete form to all the events that take place as a result of the factors and functions present in ordinary speech. In analysis we must add the great complexity introduce by our capacity to fantasize, to repress our fantasies, and to create with others shared fantasies, whether we are aware of them or not. When we put it all together, we can say that when there are two people talking to each other we believe that as part of their exchange they create one or several multifaceted fantasies about what is happening between them and to each of them. In other words: they place themselves in a complex interpersonal scene. It is worth noticing that although Freud did not theorize about the concept of scene, it is one of the most used words in his vocabulary. According to the Freud's Standard Edition concordance he used the term in 564 instances.

If we now connect the conceptions of Feldman and Narayanan with Jacobson description of the multiple simultaneous factors and functions that compose any spoken exchange, we have all the ingredients we need to form a conception of what the analytic field may be about.

## The Analyzing Situation and the Analytic Field

Psychoanalysis rests on a critical premise: if we are to understand the private and pathogenic reality of our patients we need to use words. There is *no other avenue* to access the patients psychic reality, the subjective experiences, beliefs, fantasies that sustain his way of relating to himself and to others. Freud said it as early as 1890: "words are the essential tool of mental treatment" (p. 283). The analyzing situation involves by definition two people speaking exclusively to each other under the specific conditions of the analytic setting or frame. The setting creates a very specific *context* for the subject matter of the communicative exchanges between them. Whatever the partners talk about is organized by the context that they are talking with each other to assist the patient to 'grasp' his difficulties, make sense of them, and overcome them. The *message*s patient and analyst send to each other, consciously or unconsciously, will be located within the context of their therapeutic relationship. The *contact* between them, mediated by spoken words, voice, bodily movements, attitude and other factors opens in analysis a much wider spectrum of experiences than in any other ordinary conversation. In ordinary circumstances the aim of establishing contact is "to enter and stay in communication" (Jakobson, 1990, p. 73). Yet, we as analysts know how many patients do their best not to communicate and *that* is their manner of communicating. We also know how frightened, ashamed, defiant, oppositional and other modalities of avoiding contact they may bring to the process. The analyst is not exempt from developing a wish to avoid hearing communications that are conflicting for her and sometimes enact the wish by losing contact with the patient's experience of the moment.

The *code* in the analytic exchanges is more multilayered than it is in ordinary circumstances. In analysis words are capable of carrying several meanings, intentions, connotations, allusions, together with the affects present in the communication. In the treatment the basic code is the actual language—English, French, Spanish—they use to communicate. The analyst, however is aware, and invites the patient to become progressively aware, that ordinary words convey in their apparent innocence and simplicity multitude of experiences and meanings. They link to memories, to the body that experienced the events of the memory, and also to wishes, fantasies, and fears, which the patient may or may not recognize, but which are present in the hearing of the analyst by the mediation of symbolic processes, unusual assonances, evoked imagery, bodily responses, and other phenomena. The analyst accesses them preconsciously by forming fleeting scenes with the assistance of nonconscious processes such as condensation and displacement. In other words, the listening analyst, who does master the spoken language as an accurate vehicle for meaning, listens to the analysand with her entire embodied being. She cannot help but transform the words heard under the guidance of the analytic context into *preconscious scenes* that involve her, directly or indirectly, with the analysand, thus registering what she has heard and sensed as a bi-personal experience, which may assist her to orient herself in the direction of understanding the analytic moment as well as non-verbalized unconscious processes present between them. The analyst is not inventing the preconscious scenes: they are somewhat present in the embodied selection of the words the patient is using to communicate what is in his mind, which in turn evokes the analyst's conscious and unconscious personal experiences. Freud (1901) was aware about the impact of the patients words upon him by noticing how: "[it] runs through my thoughts a continuous current of 'personal reference,' of which I generally have no inkling ... It is as if I were obliged to compare everything I hear about other people with myself; as if my personal complexes were put on the alert whenever another person is brought to my notice" (pp. 24–25). I am talking about the *referential function* of the words present in the patient's communications, which convey unconscious and preconscious denotations far beyond the analysand's capacity to be aware of them. Ogden (1994a) has written about the use of reverie to access the analyst's private experience of the analysand's communications. When the patient speaks, he cannot help but to address the analyst as he, consciously and unconsciously, senses the kind of person the analyst is. The universal phenomenon of transference described by Freud makes it abundantly clear that the person we intentionally address is, somehow, like a Russian doll: it contains layered one upon the other peoples of other times and circumstances, loaded with the combined affects, beliefs, and feelings of the past in the present. The analytic situation enhances and exacerbates the normal transferential situation to transform it into what we call in technical terms transference and countertransference. In analysis, more than in any other circumstances, the addressed analyst is always much more than herself. As a result, the analyst's task consists of finding in the patient's words the hidden and unconscious aspects of his communications and shared narratives, that, in one way or another, involve her as the analyst in the present. All the functions of spoken language become greatly enlarged and enhance by the analytic situation: the messages embedded in the simplest of sentences include complex affective expressions of overt and forbidden wishes, hidden or explicit demands and commands, requests to be loved—or rejected and humiliated—all of it embedded in the orchestral playing of the form (poetic function) taken by the patient's actual words, prosody, bodily posture, attitude, and gestures, in brief in his verbal and bodily communications. While listening, we, analysts, attempt to hear it all, with our embodied mind, hoping that we can achieve a sort of *free hovering attention* that excludes as little as possible. In few instances there is a single message in the patient's words. Most frequently than not conflicts, contradictions, forbidden emotions and desires appear as dissonant notes barely audible but present in the communication. This description is far from exhaustive, but it permits to glance at the extraordinary complexity of the words we hear and speak during a session.

## The Analytic Field and the Spoken Word

How does all this lengthy description of words, spoken exchanges, and their connection with the analytic situation relates to the concept of the analytic field? First I want to say that the Barangers' (2008) original article is an unquestionable precursor to all I have said about the function of the spoken word in analysis. They attended to the patient's bodily communications, his manner of speaking, and of relating to the analyst. Their concept of the bi-personal field is valid, even though, in my opinion, requires clarification and needs to be located not in the entire analytic setting but on the private and overt *interpretations* the participants make about themselves in the field. The Barangers' description of the field includes the spatial organization of the office, the temporal dimension that involves the times for meeting, the frequency of sessions, the length of the treatment, and the "basic functional configuration contained in the initial commitment and agreement" that "explicitly *distributes the roles* between the two participants in the situation: one agrees to communicate to the other, as far as possible, all his or her thoughts".... "The other agrees to try to understand the former, to provide help in resolving conflicts through interpretation and promises confidentiality and abstention from any intervention in the other's 'real' life" (p. 797, my italics). In a later definition M. Baranger (1993b) says "In speaking of the analytic field, we are referring to the formation of a *structure* which is a product of the *two participants* in the relationship but which in turn involves them in a dynamic and possibly creative process" (p. 16, my italics). She continues: "The advantage of being able to think in terms of a field is that the dynamics of the analytic situation inevitably encounter many stumbling blocks which are not due to the patient's or the analyst's resistance but reveal the existence of a pathology specific to this structure" (ibid.). The field facilitates the formation of "a basic unconscious fantasy which, as a *creation* of the field, is rooted in the unconscious of each of the participants" (p. 17, my italics). The analyst is responsible for understanding the fantasy and making sense of it. The analyst attends to three aspects of the analytic moment: "(1) the patient's explicit discourse; (2) the unconscious configuration of the field (unconscious phantasy of the field), which includes the activated aspect of the transference/countertransference; and (3) what corresponds at this point to *something unconscious in the analysand,* which must be interpreted" (p. 20, my italics). Madeleine Baranger concludes: "It is by virtue of the mediation of the unconscious configuration of the field that the analysand's unconscious can express itself and the analyst can find an interpretation. We thus avoid the risk of arbitrariness: it is not just any sense that is appropriate, and not just any interpretation that is valid" (p. 20). It must be noticed that the analyst uses the "unconscious configuration of the field" to make an analytic *inference* about "something unconscious in the analysand." That inference is conveyed in the verbal form of an interpretation. However the verbal interpretation is not based on the semantic/symbolic components of language (de León de Bernardi, 2008, p. 783), but on the understanding of the unconscious phantasy of the field. Madeleine Baranger (1993b) clarifies that "the analyst generally retains a certain distance from the field, and except in a few rare cases there is no actual blurring of the distinction between him and his patient—something that really would be an identification" (p. 1161). The field therefore is narrower than the analyst's capacity to take distance from it—as the Barangers suggested when talking about the "second look" to restore the analytic process. Analyst and patient do preserve their capacity to interpret themselves in relation to themselves and the other, the interpretive function of Gazzaniga, while still participating in the field. Madeleine Baranger (1993a) takes some notions for granted: "Let us start with intersubjectivity as a *self-evident basic datum.* Freud described one aspect of this intersubjectivity in referring to communication from unconscious to unconscious (1912a), which he stated to be bi-directional. The field is a *structure* different from the sum of its components, just as a melody is different from a sum of its notes" (p. 16, my italics). I am not sure that intersubjectivity is a basic datum. All our knowledge of the world, including of ourselves, comes from perception, intero- and exteroceptive, which as demonstrated not only by psychoanalysis, but by all the empirical studies on subliminal perception and mirror neurons among many others, needs not be conscious. The so-called direct communication from unconscious to unconscious described by Freud could today be understood as subliminal perceptual processes mediated by all the bodily and verbal exchanges that are inevitably present when two people are together in a relationship. Intersubjectivity as a concept confronts a similar problem. How can we access the subjectivity of another, except through perceptual processes? I agree with Meissner (1999b): "[T]he subjectivity of the other cannot be known directly but only inferred from objective data. Intersubjectivity comes to connote relations between persons who are known to each other as objects whose subjectivity is *inferred* or assumed" (p. 383, my italics). This notion is supported by the fact that each participant in the analytic situation has its own body—similar and different from the body of the other. They may have similar mirroring neurons or subliminal perceptions as non-conscious processes, but the non-conscious or conscious subjective associative processes and the interpretation of them in relation to the meaning to the self is private, particular, and idiosyncratic to each of them. This is the distinction Gallese makes that I mentioned earlier between the process of mirroring and the representations that emerge from it.

I am therefore disagreeing with the concept of intersubjective communication while I agree that the process it purportedly describes is in fact, as Madeleine Baranger suggests, bi-directional. We are always unavoidably registering the slightest expressions and bodily communications of others. This is not an intentional activity on our part, but the way in which our neural organization has us programmed to register what other people do with us. Only pathological defenses may remove awareness of its conscious components—in the case when the neural process, such as vision or hearing calls for awareness. All the other subliminal and non-conscious processes are perceptually registered and associated (as Freud said) with previous processes. They influence us, not by mysterious communications, but through the signals we send to and receive from the other whether we are aware of them or not. Subjectivity registers them only when I become aware within myself of my experience of those signals. Numerous non-conscious processes may accompany the moment. I may register them as subliminal perceptions without becoming consciously aware of doing it and therefore not being able to include them in my subjective experience. Meissner (1999a) attributes such actions to the self-as-agent: "Agency is attributed to the self-as-agent, encompassing all actions of the self (conscious, preconscious, unconscious) while the self-as-subject is the author of all conscious (and by implication preconscious) mental action. Self-as-agent and self-as-subject are the same in all conscious activity, but not in unconscious activity. Unconscious action has no subject, only agency" (p. 155). The conclusion seems clear to me: we cannot share our subjectivity; we must resort to a *medium* that is capable of establishing a connection between what I experience in myself and what I consciously or unconsciously want to express or communicate to another. The other has to register unconsciously or perceive consciously my communication for us to establish a *partial correlation* in his own subjectivity of what I have tried to express. In between our subjectivities there are always numerous *objective mediators*, even in the simplest of communications: words, voice, prosody, gestures, bodily posture, actions, mirror neurons registrations and all the embodied processes we use to relate to each other. And even so, the understanding of the meaning of the communication is dependent upon context and codes and the communal meaning of bodily and verbal communications. I believe that the term intersubjectivity is misleading because it gives the false impression that it is possible to share our subjective experience in a direct and unmediated form, when the truth is exactly the opposite: we all, as ordinary humans, and we analysts in particular, have to go through great efforts to ascertain what the patient is consciously experiencing, and to assist him to bring to conscious awareness what he is afraid of experiencing.

None of these considerations require that we reject the *concept* of the field as a heuristic tool to understand the extraordinarily complex events that occur in the *exchanges* between the patient and the analyst. Psychoanalysts who have adopted the concept of the field consider, together with the Barangers, that it involves the total analytic situation, including the components of the setting and some details of it such as the furniture. I believe that the setting as time, space, payment, frequency of hours, and even the fundamental rule are the *context* in which a field is created. The context *conditions* the type of communications that are suited for the analytic situation and the ones that are expected in order to achieve its therapeutic goal. The patient has to give words to all that is in his mind. We know that *that* is impossible and that what he manages to say and succeeds in concealing are at the very heart of the analytic process. His manner of interpreting and feeling subjectively what happens in the office between him and the analyst are the core of the process: not the furniture, but the meaning of the furniture for him in connection to the analyst. The Barangers understood it this way even though it is not that explicit in their papers. After having clarified my position about intersubjectivity, I want to offer my own understanding of the field.

## The Analytic Field as a Complex Emergence of Successive Converging and Diverging Interpersonal Scenes

Lakoff and Johnson (1980a) suggested in their now-classical book that "metaphors allow us to understand one domain of experience in terms of another. This suggests that understanding takes place in terms of entire domains of experience and not in terms of isolated concepts" (p. 117). They add other claims: "most of our normal conceptual system is metaphorically structured" (p. 56); "metaphor is not merely a matter of language. It is a matter of conceptual structure" (p. 235). They also assert: "Metaphor is primarily a matter of thought and action and only derivatively a matter of language" (p. 153), and: "The primary function of metaphor is to provide a partial understanding of one kind of experience in terms of another" (p. 154). They draw a strong conclusion: "*In actuality we feel that no metaphor can ever be comprehended or even adequately represented independently of its experiential basis*" (p. 19, italics in the original).

The experiential component includes the *situation* in which the metaphor is used: "Understanding a sentence as being true in a given situation requires having an understanding of the sentence and having an understanding of the situation" (p. 169). Lakoff and Johnson's conception of the metaphoric understanding of human relatedness and conceptual comprehension in language helps us see, as they say, that we live our lives metaphorically. We are like Molière's Monsieur Jourdain: we all have been speaking [metaphoric] prose for many years without having been aware of it. Today many analyst's concur that psychoanalysis *is* a metaphoric process (see *Psychoanalytic Inquiry*, 2011). How do psychoanalyst's use their experiential and spoken metaphoricity to help their patients to modify their pathogenic experiences and find metaphors they can live with and by?

The Barangers and many contemporary analysts resort to the concept of field as the medium for the analytic process. The field at times is given some ontological reality by the Barangers as a *structure* or a *third*, while at other times they present it as a virtual process. Green (1975) proposes that "the formation of the analytic object through symbolization" must take into account "the *third element*, which is the setting, in the dual relationship" (p. 21, my italics). Ogden (2009) describes the third: "This third *subjectivity*, the intersubjective analytic third ... is a *product* of a unique dialectic generated by (between) the separate subjectivities of analyst and analysand within the analytic setting" (p. 161, my italics). The many authors that use the field concept oscillate between the two positions: a virtual field or an actual third endowed with subjectivity. I want to be clear about my position: the field cannot have an *ontological reality* of its own: its virtual existence depends upon the subjective experiences of the participants and the verbal and bodily perceptual channels available to them to communicate with each other. The third cannot have *subjectivity* because it is not a subject. Only persons can be subjects.

Furthermore, the field—unlike what the Barangers and many others propose— cannot have effects caused by itself, because being a medium, the field has *no agency*. Only people have agency to carry out expressive, communicative, and understanding actions. I propose that we limit the notion of field to the extremely rich processes of simultaneous, diachronic, and synchronic verbal and somatic exchanges between the participants. The word "limit" is almost a contradiction because the multitude of events taken place between the two people who are attempting to communicate with each other is staggering. I have listed in a previous section the orchestral complexity of any verbal communication. Our present-day knowledge of embodied communication, registered preconsciously and non-consciously, barely discloses the multiple channels available to us to give perceptually registerable signals to others: think of subliminal scents and pheromones, just to talk about what we know today.

The term "field" used in analysis is itself a metaphor, most frequently than not a spatial metaphor. Freud used the metaphor of the battlefield. The Barangers (2008) describe it as the spatial structure of the entire office and setting where patient and analyst meet (p. 796). They also describe the analytic situation as one "between two persons who remain unavoidably connected and complementary as long as the situation obtains, and involved in a single dynamic process. In this situation, neither of the couple can be understood without the other" (p. 796). I fully agree with this second description. However, I want to add that for me what constitutes the analytic field, its very essence, is the personal connectedness and complementarity ever present in their daily encounters. I also want to bring back Lakoff and Johnson's (1980a) point mentioned above: "Understanding a sentence as being true in a given situation requires having an understanding of the sentence and having an understanding of the situation" (p. 169). The same applies to the understanding of any bodily communication, be it subliminal or overt. The situation in psychoanalysis is a very specific one: all that the patient and analyst do together as part of the "single dynamic process" is to use what happens between them only and exclusively at the service of making sense of the patient's experienced life and psychic reality as he presents it to the analyst. Psychoanalysis is an *intentional* enterprise on both sides: the analyst's and the patient's. Freud could not fail to observe that the patient's unavoidable difficulty in keeping his part of the intentional agreement and his inclination to seek other goals and to keep to himself what he had promised to share was at the very core of the process. Soon he would learn that the analyst must remain watchful of himself because he too might try to avoid, escape, or became entrapped in the web of demands coming from the patient to respond or to avoid them rather than making analytic sense of them.

The single dynamic process of the Barangers includes the words and bodily communications the analytic pair exchange hour after hour. I have described at length the multitude of interpersonal events present in any verbal exchange. To that we must add the bodily messages and signals ever present when two people are together. Both partners cannot help but to add almost instantaneously two *interpretations* about: 1) what it all means for the self he conceives him/herself to be, whether as an analyst/person or as a patient/person; 2) the meaning of the *relational scene* that is just occurring between them in the context of the double positioning of themselves. It is here that the asymmetry of the analytic situation becomes most obvious. The patient is immersed in the analytic process under the motivational guidance of his unacceptable wishes, fears, beliefs, in one word, his pathology. The analyst has a double task: she must be totally immersed in the process if she is to access the patient's unconscious pathogenic processes. She must also keep her distance to be able to perceive what the patient is really saying and what is actually happening between them. When this process fails and the analyst finds herself entrapped in a "bastion," the Barangers recommended that she takes a "second look" at herself and the analytic process when she is *outside* the analytic situation as a way of recovering her analytic function. What is happening between them, in their communicative field holds the clues the analyst needs in order to understand the analytic moment and the scenic roles attributed to each other. The Barangers' original article provides no clinical example but they make an allusion about the patient's perceiving the analyst's words as warm milk or as stones thrown at him. Let me play with one of them as a scenic moment. The analyst speaks calmly and warmly about something the patient has said. The scene the analyst *intends* to bring about is one of understanding in preparation for a broader insight. The patient however responds in such a way that it requires more clarifications from the analyst. At one point the analyst becomes aware of how the patient perceives the scene they are involved in: he wants more calm and warm words because they feel like warm maternal milk/words to him. A crossmodal perception of warmth has been established between the analyst's affect in her words and voice and the patient's reactivated wishes for maternal care and warm milk in the present analytic moment. It is all profoundly metaphorical and experiential. Their exchanges have revived in the patient bodily experiences that he still feels need satisfaction. How does the analyst make the transition from her scene of giving meaningful words to his scenes of "drinking" them as warm milk? The analyst arrives at that point—according to my theorizing—by observing what is *incongruous* in their share dcommunicational field: the patient should have attempted to understand her words; instead the analyst senses, through complex verbal and bodily communications, that he is not listening to her words but "savoring" them. The analyst's perception of the total situation guides her to describe to the patient what is happening between them and to access his revived wishes. After they have together recognized what is happening an interpretation is possible. If the analyst remains unaware of what is happening, perhaps because of her own maternal inclinations towards the patient, they may create a joint transient or protracted fantasy in the field that her "words" are good for him. They have jointly and unknowingly created a fantasized enactment of the good mother with the good baby she wants to feed. In this manner it must be said that enactment and fantasy/phantasy in the field go hand in hand. As the Barangers say, this very ordinary analytic event is at the core of the progress of the analysis. Now, patient and analyst together need to analyze what they have done and find a meaning that simultaneously helps them to understand their bodily and communicative stances. Let's suppose that after much work the patient "recalls" that the analyst's voice reminds him of his mother's voice when getting ready to feed the children. Then, we know that a perceptual metaphoric equation has been established between the two situations and experienced by the patient as "real" in the analytic present. The very fact that he has experienced it as "real" gives the analytic moment what it needs to give meaning to the interpretation. Perhaps this is what the Barangers meant when they say that analysis has to return to words their original meaning as the basis for their interpretation. They also questioned how the patients understand the meaning of words to achieve insight and change.

My answer is that the activation of metaphorically experienced scenes in the present moment of the analysis gives the words exchanged between them a level of meaning that goes beyond semantics and reaches the bodily experiences of the present and of the past in a single unit of perception, which connects the experienced past with the analytic present. The metaphoric experiential process is the mediatory link between life and words. Obviously the maternal care of the analyst was exclusively metaphoric, but it found its bodily incarnation in her "warm" voice duly registered by the patient. The analysand's "drinking" her words as "warm" milk was also a metaphoric process that also found its bodily form in her "hearing" him "savoring" her words. The field composed of this metaphoric processes permitted the analytic pair to revive the memory of the analysand's childhood experience and wishes that contributed to the creation of the metaphorically verbalized field of that particular analytic moment.

Joseph Sandler (1962) created the concept of role-responsiveness as a phenomenon linked to the countertransference. He describes how he felt compelled to talk more than usual in the case of a man who ended his sentences with an interrogation. It turned out that they were both reenacting an early event of the patient's life: "He would feel extremely anxious as a child when his father returned home from work, and would compulsively engage his father in conversation, asking him many questions in order to be reassured that his father was not angry with him" (p. 45). Sandler points out that the analyst may "tend to comply with the role demanded of him, to integrate it into his mode of responding and relating to the patient" and that "he may only become aware of it through observing his own behaviour, responses and attitudes, *after these have been carried over into action*" (p. 47, italics in the original). Sandler tried to differentiate role-responsiveness from a countertransference originating only in the analyst's mind. I believe that role-responsiveness *is* a component of the creation of the metaphorical field of joint experience in which somatically and verbally based signals given by the patient to the analyst have induced him to respond with a matching behavioral pattern. Sandler and his patient unknowingly recreated in analysis the childhood scene of a frightened child trying to disarm a frightening father.

## Conclusions

I would like to sum up in a concise form the main points I have discussed in this chapter.

1 Communication between subjects is never direct. It is mediated by perceptual registration of bodily and verbal communications organized as metaphorical experiences of the individuals involved in the exchange.

2 The Barangers questioned how words can return to their earlier meanings. My response is that when they do, it is through the mediation of intra-analytic experiences in the communicational field in the present between patient and analyst. I prefer to say that one could return to an experiential moment in early life in which the word was used in a particular relational context. That means to say that in psychic life the semantic meaning of words is embedded in their experiential interpersonal meaning.

3 The Barangers asked about the power of words to offer meaningful interpretations. I reflect that only *living* words have the power to offer meaningful interpretations. I call living words those that have been used and recognized as part of shared metaphoric affective experience by the patient and analyst in the present of the analytic situation. In my playful example of the analyst's "warm" words "savored" as "warm" milk by the adult/child patient, the word "warm" becomes alive between them as actual and complex metaphorical experiences they are having together, each in his own way. The word "warm" has acquired the capacity to name simultaneously, what the analyst was doing, what was happening between them, what did happened in his childhood, and what he had wished would continue to happen with his mother in the past and with his analyst in the present. In brief, the word "warm" provides access to his wishes/needs in the past and the present in the context of a concrete analytic moment and becomes a key word to interpret his metaphoric and historically revived experience of that analytic moment. The interpretation is possible because the word "warm" is a living affectively significant word between patient and analyst.

4 The Barangers search for the point of urgency to interpret. They describe how the analyst selects what "is most vivid to the patient, the most urgent" to offer "an interpretation capable of modifying the field" (2008, p. 804). I believe that in the example just discussed the word 'warm' with all its metaphoric experiential past and present meanings for both analyst and patient is the point

of urgency that will modify the field and open a new understanding of the patient's experience and assist him in the understanding of himself.

5 The Barangers also ask about how the words of the interpretation can modify the shared unconscious phantasy and the structuring of the bi-personal field. In the example of the words "warm" and "milk," patient and analyst shared for some time the unconscious phantasy that she, as a good and caring mother, is feeding him the warm milk he needs as a child/patient. The analyst's interpretation of what is happening between them instantaneously restructures the field by reorganizing the metaphorical experiential situation between them. The adult side of the patient comes to the fore to understand the child desirous of warm milk and the analyst redresses her metaphorical experiential participation as a warm mother to take up again her role as the analyst in charge of making sense of what is happening between them.

6 Finally, I want to make a brief comment about the metaphorical entailments of the word "insight" in the analytic vocabulary. It implies that real psychical life takes place in some internal locus of the individual and that the events or meanings in that place have to be seen by some psychical eye to acquire meaning for the person. This metaphorical entailment is at odds with all I have said in this presentation. We understand ourselves only through embodied interpersonal metaphorical experiences that help us to make sense of ourselves and of others. When we achieve "insight" what we actually do is to modify our embodied metaphorical experience of ourselves and the words we use to describe them to ourselves.

I hope that my presentation of how I understand the concept of field in psychoanalysis contributes to the clarification of a term that is dear to so many contemporary analysts.

## Note

1 Originally published in *Psychoanalytic Inquiry* 33(3) (May 2013) with the same title.

# 14

# FIELD, PROCESS, AND METAPHOR[1]

*Juan Tubert-Oklander*

The proposal of juxtaposing and articulating the concepts of "field" and "metaphor" is both challenging and intriguing, since both concepts are necessarily related, as pointed out by S. Montana Katz (2012). On the one hand, the very idea of the field is a metaphor; on the other, metaphors generate a field in themselves, when considered as a form of mental activity. So, this promises to be a fruitful match. To this I have added yet another metaphor, that of a "process" which complements, from my point of view, that of the field, and shall develop a juggling act, which will include yet another concept, that of "analogy," hoping that this play with ideas will clarify some of the issues raised by our present theme.

I shall, therefore, explore this problem by approaching the various concepts sequentially, while at the same time showing their mutual relations, and finally expound my own ideas on the subject.

## Analogy and Metaphor

It is clear for me, from the very start, that our interest in metaphor goes far beyond its restricted sense, as a figure of speech intended to embellish a linguistic expression, especially in poetry, but rather extends to the kind of problems studied by logic, epistemology, semiotics, and hermeneutics. It also deals with the psychological fact that a major part of our mental processes—what Freud (1900) called the "primary process"—is intrinsically metaphoric. So, I shall start from the widest possible perspective, before landing it on the more restricted purview of our discipline.

Metaphor is a particular case of a much wider concept, that of *analogy*, which has been acknowledged ever since the beginnings of Greek philosophy, even though it was Aristotle who made the first formal study of it. Unlike formal logic, which is based on *identity*, analogical thinking deals with *similarity*. To say that two things are similar implies that they have something in common, but that they differ in other aspects. Consequently, analogy is particularly useful for exploring similarities and differences between things, either physical or mental, that would otherwise seem to be unrelated. The results of this kind of reasoning are never certain, but only *probable*; this accounts for the disdain that strictly logical thinkers have always displayed towards analogy, which they consider to be an inferior and unreliable form of thought. Yet, practical disciplines such as medicine ("probable diagnosis") and law ("beyond reasonable doubt") have always relied heavily on analogy. This is certainly the case of psychoanalysis. Besides, analogy may be the only feasible way to articulate the knowledge derived from disparate disciplines, such as psychoanalysis, group analysis, philosophy, social sciences, and neurosciences, and even from the diverse theories within our own profession.

Analogy is the main tool for the interpretation of texts, so that we are now stepping on the hallowed ground of Hermeneutics, where many analysts fear to tread. This has been defined as the "theory and practice of the interpretation of texts," but "text" means here much more than a written document. *Textus* originally meant "fabric"— as in "textile"—so the term was really a metaphor for a set of words that have been woven, much as warp and woof in a cloth, to form a meaningful whole. Originally, it referred to written documents, but then extended to speech, dialogue (with Hans-Georg Gadamer, 1960), intentional action, whether conscious or unconscious (with Paul Ricoeur, 1965, who was a true Freudian scholar), and to any other meaningful human expression. Hence, nowadays hermeneutics stands for the theory and practice of interpretation of anything that might act as a bearer of meaning, and this clearly includes psychoanalytic interpretation.

Ever since its beginnings in Greek philosophy, hermeneutics has taken one of three forms: univocality, equivocality, and analogy (Beuchot, 1997). *Univocality* demands that each word, sign or text have a single unambiguous meaning; this breeds certainty, but also dogmatism—what Isaiah Berlin (2001) called "monism." Contemporary science implies a univocal conception of meaning. *Equivocality* affirms that for any meaningful expression there is an indeterminate, perhaps infinite, number of disparate possible meanings, and that they all have equal value, so that an interpreter can only choose one among them on the basis of personal taste, practical convenience, tradition or whim. This opens the way for taking into account motivation and context—both the author's and the interpreter's—but paying the heavy price of forsaking the quest for truth and proclaiming the inevitability of total uncertainty—this being what Berlin calls "relativism." Finally, *analogy* claims that there are a number of possible interpretations for any given text, though not an infinite one, but that these various interpretations may be more or less adequate in depicting some aspect of the highly complex nature of the text—some of them may be good, others not so good, poor or outright bad. Yet there may be several good interpretations of a same text, depicting different aspects of it as seen from disparate perspectives—what Berlin calls "pluralism." The result is that the path of analogy does not renounce the search for truth, and indeed attains some degree of it, even though only a partial, perspectival, and humble truth, but good-enough to continue thinking and acting rationally (Beuchot, 1997, 2003a). Such a perspective seems particularly fitting for a discipline as psychoanalysis, which was not only defined by Freud (1904) as "an art of interpretation" (p. 252) that rejects any fixed meanings, but also has to deal with the coexistence of diverse theories that seem to have a common referent, and which have probably expounded each a part of the truth about it (Tubert-Oklander & Beuchot Puente, 2008).

In contrast with formal logical thinking, which cannot create any new ideas, since the conclusion is always already contained in the premises, analogical thinking follows the drift of successive analogues, propelled by their similarities, and arrives at radically new conclusions, based on their differences. This requires, of course, a new period of rigorous thinking, in order to winnow out the less satisfactory interpretations and retain the better ones. Nonetheless, these conclusions are never certain, but only probable, or even just plausible, but in any case, something one can live and work with.

But the term "analogy" also covers several linguistic and logical phenomena that are loosely related. In other words, analogy itself is analogical (McInerny, 1971, p. 4), as it comprises three—or perhaps four—quite different types: the *analogy of inequality*, the *analogy of attribution*, and the *analogy of proportionality*, which can be further divided in two subtypes, *proper* or *metonymical* and *improper* or *metaphorical*. This classification was posed in the early sixteenth century by the Dominican archbishop, theologian, and philosopher Thomas Cajetan (McInerny, 1971; Hochschild, 2001).

It may be argued that the *analogy of inequality* is not a real analogy, since it merely states that the same word may be used to refer to quite disparate ideas. Thus, the word "body" may refer to a distinct mass of matter, the material substance of a living organism, a human being as such, the trunk of an organism, the main part of a text or document, a planet, a group or number of persons or things, the viscosity of an oily fluid, the firmness of texture of a fabric, the richness of flavor of a beverage, the fullness or resonance of a singer's voice, the import of a literary work, the spiritual presence of Christ in the bread during Eucharist, the Christian Church conceived as a mystical organism with Christ as its head, among others (Merriam-Webster, 2002, see "body"). This is a highly complex set of associated and derivative meanings, and dead, dying, and active metaphors, all as a result of the semantic shifts involved in the development and evolution of a living language. As much as univocal theories of meaning may decry the vagueness of such polysemy, both dictionaries and the actual use of language are full of it, and this certainly applies to the basic terms of psychoanalytic theory. However, it is precisely this characteristic that determines the superiority of true languages over artificial univocal ones, such as those created by symbolic logic, as tools for human thought. This is so because living words do not only have a *denotation*—i.e., they refer to some entity or other—but also a *connotation* of ramified associations, and this gives the expression a particular complex flavor, which links words by association to a whole set of related implied meanings, thus turning them into *symbols*.

For instance, the term that serves as the axis of our present discussion, "field," is most certainly analogous. It may refer to the open country, a piece of enclosed land, the place where a battle is fought, an area of land containing a natural resource, an area in which a particular activity or pursuit is carried out, the scene of actual living observation in research, the area where some sport is practiced, the empty area where visual symbols are projected (as in flags or heraldry), a battle (by extension from the battle field), a set of players in a game, a continuously distributed entity in space that accounts for actions at a distance, a complex of coexistent forces which determine human experience and behavior, a limited or demarcated area of knowledge, the site of a surgical operation, among many others (Merriam-Webster, 2002, see "field"). This multiplicity of meaning forecloses any precise definition of the term, but it is also the source of its richness, its evocative power, and the strong conviction it provides when actually used in thinking.

The *analogy of attribution* implies that there is a flow of meaning from an original primary object (idea, perception, wish, experience), called the *primary analogue*, to a series of derivative signs, called *secondary analogues*, increasingly removed from its initial term, which constitutes their final referent that gives them their meaning. For example, the term "healthy" strictly refers only to a living organism, but its use may be extended to apply to food, medicine, habits, thoughts, lifestyle, ideology, appearance or urine (as an indicator of health), all of them analogues of the primary meaning. The classical psychoanalytic theory of symbolism, as developed by Freud (1900), Klein (1930), and others, suggests that symbols are the result of a displacement from an original vital and organic experience, related to psychosexuality, to a series of substitutes that disguise and express their true meaning at one and the same time. This kind of analogy presupposes a single original primary meaning, which makes it more palatable for univocally minded thinkers.

However, the links between the primary analogue and the successive secondary analogues is something more than a matter of psychological associations, since they represent a *causal* relation. And here "causal" does not only mean the kind of active preceding cause that is the only one acknowledged by our contemporary natural science and corresponds to Aristoteles's "efficient cause," but all four Aristotelian causes: *material, formal, efficient,* and *final.* In this, the final or teleological cause is always the most important one, which is manifested by means of the other three (Beuchot, 2010). Leaving aside the possible ontological connotations of this statement, there is no doubt that psychic phenomena are always intentional, that is, that they always tend to some aim, as the young Freud soon learned in his philosophy courses with Brentano, a great Aristotelian thinker (Beuchot, 1998).

The *analogy of proportionality* represents the original Greek meaning of *analogy as proportion.* This is an assertion that follows the following logical model: "A is to B as C is to D"—for instance, "as water is to a plant, so is friendship to man." It should be noted that this statement says nothing about each of its four terms, taken in isolation, but only about their relations, and that it really compares one relation to another. When studying figures of speech, it is traditional to distinguish between a *simile*, in which the comparison is explicit ("friendship is like water"), and a *metaphor*, in which it remains implicit ("the water of friendship").

In hermeneutic analysis, this type of analogy is usually divided in two subgroups: *proper* and *improper.* A proper analogy of proportionality compares elements coming from a same semantic field; for instance, the word "semen" comes from "seed," with the implied analogy between the biological functions of two products of living organisms ("semen is to man as the seed is to the plant"). This kind of reasoning is known as *metonymy*, and remains within the realm of the literal. On the other hand, an improper analogy of proportionality, called *metaphor*, compares elements from widely different semantic fields, on the basis of a partial resemblance in structure, function or meaning, which is thus spotlighted and maximized, sometimes revealed. An example of this would be the phrase "the wings of imagination," which compares a bird's organ with a mental function, on account of their being operative in sustaining two different kinds of "flight"—physical and mental.

For the logical positivistic mood that prevails in Natural Science in our time, metaphor appears as a kind of sloppy thinking, confuse, ambiguous, and unscientific at best, but in the tradition of the Humanities it is the most approximate way of conveying and pointing at some essential human experience or complex relationship that cannot be actually said in unambiguous terms. It is therefore the very stuff of symbols. When Shakespeare puts in Hamlet's mouth the exacting task of determining "Whether 'tis nobler in the mind to suffer / The slings and arrows of outrageous fortune, / Or to take arms against a sea of troubles, / And by opposing end them" (Hamlet: III, 1), is he not using three different metaphors, including an outrageously mixed one, in order to say something meaningful about the human condition?

Psychoanalysis, as a discipline, and we psychoanalysts, as practicing professionals, are in the very same situation as the other Human Sciences. Thus we make an extensive use of metaphor in our theories, in the interpretations we offer to our patients, and in the narratives of our professional experiences, both written and oral. But here we have a wider basis for justifying this procedure, since, unlike the other Humanities, we have a special knowledge of the workings of the mind that sustain it, as we shall presently see in the next section.

## Metonymic and Metaphoric Processes

Freud's point of departure was his conviction, which he probably derived from his philosophy courses with Brentano (Beuchot, 1998), that mind and all its processes are by definition *intentional*—i.e., that they always tend towards some aim. Edmund Husserl, who was also one of Brentano's students, derived his phenomenology from the very same conviction, albeit he restricted it to the workings of consciousness. Freud, on the other hand, made the momentous discovery that *all human behavior and experience is intentional and bears a meaning, but that such intention and meaning are largely unknown and inaccessible to the subject who has these experiences and carries out these actions* (Tubert-Oklander, 2000, 2006a). They are inaccessible because the subject exerts an ongoing effort, which goes also unnoticed, to avoid their open expression; this is what we call "repression." Hence, whenever we wish to explore the unconscious dimension, we have to apply a method and work in order to neutralize this effort of repression and allow the emergence of those intentions and meanings that had been actively ignored by the subject (Freud, 1912a, 1915b). This is the work of psychoanalysis.

But Freud (1900) went even further, when he discovered that unconscious mental processes are of a different nature and follow quite another path from that of their conscious counterpart, and accounted for this with his theory of the primary and secondary processes. Ignacio Matte-Blanco (1988), who studied this problem from the logical perspective, suggests that the main characteristic of the primary process is that it is ruled by a *symmetric logic*, which allows a reversibility of all relations, this being the hallmark of unconscious thinking. This is in sharp contrast with the secondary process that rules conscious thought, working in accordance with the traditional Aristotelian logic, which deals with irreversible relations—if John is Peter's father, Peter is not John's father: this is *asymmetric logic*. But in the logic of the unconscious, all statements are reversible; thus, John and Peter have a father–son relationship, in which each of them can occupy any of its poles. This is the reason why it is easy to be alternatively a sadist and a masochist, passive and active, abuser and abused.

But with this reversibility of relations, all the other characteristics of the secondary process simply vanish. This is, for instance, the case of causal relations, which can only be thought in irreversible terms—in medicine we say that Koch's bacillus causes tuberculosis, but not the other way round. The same happens with the concept of objective time, which requires an irreversible sequence of successive moments, as well as that of space, since, if any given place can be replaced by any other, spatial relations become meaningless. Thus, in unconscious thought, a house may emerge from a fire or a mouth be turned into a nipple.

But the most striking feature of primary process thinking is the reversibility of the class-member relation. For instance, Mary is a woman and a mother, hence we may conceive her as a member of the class of mothers, but this class is not a woman, just as Humankind, conceived as the set of all human persons, is not a person. This is the irreversible asymmetrical logic of the secondary process. But in the reversible and symmetric logic of the primary process, we may say that Mary is, at one and the same time, a member—i.e., a part—of the set of all mothers, and that this set is a part of Mary. The relations between a whole and a part, and between a class and one of its members, just collapse, and we are left with a diffuse but overwhelming concept of Motherhood, in which Mary becomes the bearer of the Great Mother archetype, and the latter incarnates in the visage, the body, and the voice of a particular woman. But since every one of the members of the class of mothers participates in such reversibility, in this dimension any of them is equivalent to any other and all mothers are one. This is the basis of those two peculiar mental processes that we call "condensation" and "displacement," which, together with plastic representation and symbolism, are the instruments of the dream work (Freud, 1900).

In terms of our previous hermeneutic analysis, we may say that conscious mental processes are mainly metonymical, while unconscious ones are metaphorical. But there is yet another most significant difference, which may well account for the two types of logic: conscious thinking works mainly in terms of verbal, conventional, socially acquired, and interpersonally shared language, while unconscious thought seems to be made of idiosyncratic images derived from sensuous experiences—what we call *iconic signs*.

*Verbal signs* are conventional, in that there is no visible relation between the word "dog" and that gentle, furry, and loving mammal that sleeps happily on the carpet while I am writing these words. They are appropriate because they are shared by a linguistic community, but they could easily be replaced by others—as they frequently are, when a living language evolves—without a loss of meaning. *Iconic signs*, on the other hand, are an attempt to reproduce a part of the experience of perception of a given object or situation. An instance of this is onomatopoeia, by means of which cats *meow*, bees *buzz* or a twig *snaps* (of course, when a market *cracks*, we have concocted a metaphor out of an onomatopoeia). Another one are photographs o portraits of a person, which clearly depict her or him, but what is the status of a political cartoon that draws a caricature of its subject? The latter clearly represents a more elaborate symbol, which highlights a more general characteristic of icons: that they do not only depict, but always imply an interpretation. For Charles Sanders Peirce there were three kinds of icons, according to their distance from sensuous experience: *images*, *diagrams*, and *metaphors*. All of them are clearly ways of depicting relations, rather than things.

The icon always signals a presence, rather than an absence, and it can always be perceived simultaneously, unlike verbal discourse, which is necessarily sequential. So, the very fact that primary process operates as iconic thinking may account for its characteristic features, such as timelessness, reversibility, lack of causal relations, which are replaced by relations of meaning, and the inability for negation. But whereas words are more precise in denotation, icons have a much greater capacity for connotation, so that they have a deeper emotional impact, when used in interpersonal or social communication. In the inner workings of the individual mind, secondary process and verbal thought are the bases for reason, logic, and science—hence, metonymy. On the other hand, primary process and iconic thinking are the language of feeling, art, poetry, and religion—i.e., metaphor.

If we accept these propositions, clearly derived from the Freudian concepts of the primary and the secondary processes, as much as from hermeneutics and Peirce's conception of semiotics, we should admit that, at the unconscious level, there cannot be any discrimination between subject and object, and that they may be easily identified or interchanged. In the analytic situation, this implies that, in the unconscious dimension of the encounter, analyst and analysand are inevitably identical and interchangeable, and that this applies to the former, as much as to the latter. It is only in the conscious dimension of experience, thinking, and acting, that the analytic asymmetry can and must be understood, remembered, and preserved.

But obviously the stuff of human beings is not restricted to the unconscious and the primary process. Consciousness and the secondary process also exist and have a major bearing on human existence, so that thinking always travels along two contrasting and complementary paths. This is what Matte-Blanco calls "bi-logic," that is, the alternance and confluence of both kinds of logic, which are kept in a state of dialectic tension between them.

All this derives, not only from the Freudian discovery, but also from the Kleinian conception of an unconscious fantasy, which determines a type of experience of oneself, objects, and the world and its happenings that underlies and is quite different from ordinary conscious experience. Donald Meltzer (1981) asserts that "Mrs. Klein ... made a discovery that created a revolutionary addition to the model of the mind, namely *that we do not live in one world, but in two*—that we live in an internal world which is as real a place to live in as the outside world" (p. 178, italics added). It may be argued that Meltzer is overstating his pro-Klein case, and that this discovery really comes from Freud. This is unquestionably so, as far as clinical discoveries go, but the author develops a convincing argument for his contention that the original causal-deterministic and quasi-physiological model of the *Project* (Freud, 1950) prevented him from finding a place in his theory for an internal world, and completing his "approach to transforming himself from a neurophysiological psychologist into a phenomenological one" (Meltzer, 1981, p. 178).

This perspective brings about substantial consequences, both for our hermeneutic approach and for clinical practice. It is easy to see that any attempt to think exclusively in terms of the asymmetrical logic of secondary process will bring about a univocal interpretation and view of things, while any way of thinking ruled by the symmetrical logic of the primary process will generate an equivocal one; these would be the bases of monistic and relativistic thinking. Likewise, bi-logic would be the psychological substrate of analogical thinking. Now, according to Matte-Blanco, bi-logic is the true shape of human thought, but in most circumstances they are mutually alienated, so that conscious thinking tries to follow only the path of asymmetrical logic, while unconscious mentation takes that of symmetrical logic, generating a steady flow of *dream-thoughts* (Meltzer, 1983), thus constituting that "other scene" (Freud, 1900) of a parallel invisible world.

However, the conscious assumption and development of the capacity for bi-logic is a veritable maturational achievement, which should be expected as a result of a successful psychoanalytic treatment. This implies the assumption that the aim of psychoanalytic treatment may be framed as *the integration of the personality*, so that its various components and processes may fuse into a functioning whole—a far cry from Freud's (1933a) staunch belief that the secondary process should prevail ("Where id was, there ego shall be. It is a work of culture—not unlike the draining of the Zuider Zee," p. 80).

Now, this dual world also reflects on the very nature of the analytic relationship. In these terms, there is a conscious level in which the analyst is an analyst, the patient is a patient, and they are both together in a closed room doing something called "psychoanalysis", however, this has been defined in their initial agreement. Nevertheless, this coexists with another level in which things occur quite differently; thus the patient may feel that interpretations turn into a venom that poisons him or her, or the analyst may have the unconscious experience of being a good mother that feeds a hungry baby, or becomes the pray of the cannibalistic impulses of a starving one.

Such description is, nonetheless, insufficient, since it is trying to express an experience belonging to the domain of the symmetric logic of the primary process, in terms of the asymmetric logic of the secondary process. It is no use saying to a patient "You are having the unconscious fantasy that my interpretations are a sadistic penetration that tears you inside," since such a formulation translates the unconscious fantasy into the discriminate terms of consciousness, which are the only ones in which there is a differentiation between analyst and analysand. So, it is a metonymical framing of a valid intuition of something that can only be approached by metaphor—approached, but never fully reached or encompassed. Fortunately, the patient's metaphorical mental processes usually take hold of the interpretation and retranslate it into terms that are more adequate for the kind of understanding they are both striving to attain. In any case, the use of poetical (metaphoric) language is frequently more effective, at the time of interpreting, than that of a more concrete and precise (metonymic) one.

A more serious objection is that this way of phrasing the interpretation is tantamount to affirming that the unconscious fantasy belongs only to the patient, and that the analyst is not a part of the session's unconscious dimension—a claim that is clearly absurd and unsustainable. A more adequate formulation would perhaps be: "Something is happening to us that transforms my interpretations into a sadistic act, which may be compared to a violent and painful rape." This is the metonymic version, while a more metaphoric one would be "It seems that I am raping you with my words." Such an interpretation would be based, both on the patient's feelings of pain, humiliation or indignation, and on the analyst's experiences of guilt or sadistic pleasure, felt at the moment of verbalizing it. The concrete wording of the interpretation will obviously depend on the context and associative substrate, which would stem from the patient's dreams or associations and the analyst's countertransference occurrences (Racker, 1968), as well as from their respective personalities and communicative styles, and the history of their analytic relationship.

In this, Matte-Blanco's contribution turns out to be much more complex and nuanced than Klein's original concepts. For the former, it is not a question of us living in two worlds—that of consciousness, which is determined by reality, and that of unconscious fantasy, derived from instinctual motions—but that our relation with reality—the whole of reality, which includes both the external world facts, harvested by perception, and those of emotional life, which are experienced without any mediation—is transformed through the various thinking processes: *symmetric logic*, *asymmetric logic* and *bi-logic*. The result is a highly complex and polysemic view of the world, in which there is a confluence of disparate elements of diverse origins, which might be compared with the world of Greek mythology, inhabited by many different beings: the Titans, the major Gods of Olympus, mortals, demigods born from the coupling of the previous two, and a myriad minor gods who dwelled in the various spaces of the everyday world, such as woods, fountains, seas or crossroads.

In the previous paragraph, I have made an extensive use of metaphoric language and iconic representation, in order to convey a highly complex conception of the organization and functioning of mind. This is precisely the way in which psychoanalytic theorizing works, what Freud, in his letter to Fliess of May 25, 1895, called "fantasizing" (*Phantasieren*). The full quotation says:

During the past weeks I have devoted every free minute to such work [of theory building]; have spent the hours of the night from eleven to two with such *fantasizing, interpreting, and guessing*, and invariably stopped only when somewhere I came up against an absurdity or when I actually and seriously overworked, so that I had no interest left in my daily medical activities.

(Freud, 1895, p. 129, italics added)

So, when facing the Protean quality of human mental life, Freud felt he had to resort to a peculiar admixture of scientific and poetic thinking, which alternated between moments of imaginative frenzy ("fantasizing, interpreting, and guessing") and the more sober ones of checking these flights of fancy with actual clinical experience and the rigors of argumentation. The resulting theory is necessarily mixed, a hybrid of logical discourse and poetic language; hence the omnipresence of metaphor in psychoanalytic theory, which has been a source of vexation for many an epistemologist.

What is specific of psychoanalysis is the psychoanalytic experience, which is emotional, interactive, and cognitive, all at once. And such experience may only be conveyed by poetic language, which is mainly metaphorical. It is only afterwards that this gives rise to a conceptual discourse, as a transformation of the former, which aims at a universality that it never fully reaches; this is what we call "metapsychology."

Metapsychology is to the clinical discourse that aims to recreate in the reader or listener something of the living experience of the analytic encounter and dialogue, as metaphysics is to poetry—and this is a metonymic analogy, which follows Mexican philosopher Mauricio Beuchot's (2003b) ideas on "the intercrossing of metaphysical and poetical discourses." For him "poetry is pre-metaphysic, and metaphysics is post-poetic" (p. 143), and their mutual influence and dialogue should result in "metaphysical poetry" and "poetical metaphysics." The same may be said about the clinical-poetical and metapsychological-conceptual discourses in psychoanalysis; it is not that the latter serves as foundation for the former, or vice versa, but that they complement each other in their mutual encounter, uncovering their similarities and common ground, but without losing sight of their specific differences, not unlike what goes on in the psychoanalytic dialogue. We shall now consider how this complementarity works, in the case of the field concept in psychoanalysis.

## The Field Concept

The concept of "field" was originally introduced in physics, in order to account for phenomena that implied an influence of one object on a distant other, without any visible intermediation between them, such as gravity or magnetism. Since the type of influence the former had on the latter seemed to irradiate in all directions, as if in concentrical circles with diminishing strength, the term was thereafter used to refer to a region of space in which a given effect of these characteristics exists. But it also implied a certain organization of such region, in which any change at a given point had effects on every other point of the field. Field theories implied an epistemological revolution in science, since they replaced linear causality, as an explanatory principle, by complex interdependence. They also gave up the assumption that a cause should always precede its effects; consequently, they had the characteristic of being atemporal, since they explained the phenomena that took place in the field in terms of the latter's organization and dynamics, without any reference to its previous history (Tubert-Oklander, 2007).

These concepts were imported into psychology by Gestalt theorists, who were particularly interested in the study of "wholes," as opposed to that of "parts" (Koffka, 1935; Katz, D. 1943; Merleau-Ponty, 1942). From such perspective, *the whole was considered to be more than, prior to, and more elementary than the sum of its parts.* In other words, *the relationship between the whole and the parts constituted a field.* This meant that, in the complex organizations that characterize living phenomena—such as organisms, their structure and functions, and their interactions with other organisms and their environment—this complexity is a primary phenomenon, and its so-called parts are artificially created by our analytic activity, whether intellectual or physical. For instance, the kind of anatomical and functional dissection used by physiologists to create the "systems" they study, by means of isolating parts of the organism, falsifies the fact that the latter always acts as a whole, and generates a situation that is akin to, as Kurt Goldstein (1940) pointed out, that which characterizes pathological conditions. The same would apply to the effects of some of the research artifices introduced by Freud's technique, such as the fragmentation of the dream, in order to inquire and follow the associations forced by the analyst's questioning (Freud, 1900).

If we accept this point of view, we are bound to conclude that the results attained by an approach based on an analytic activity that fragments the integrity of an organism (or personality) in order to inquire into the nature, structure, and functioning of the "parts" that are thus created, can only be used for the understanding of normality if we identify the ways in which this isolation modifies the functioning of the whole, and take the necessary measures to compensate such distortion. This demands reintegrating this information into the functioning of the organism-as-a-whole, and restoring the organism to its normal context, from which it had been segregated when it was placed in the laboratory (or consulting room). The same applies to any study or conception of the individual in isolation. The human being always acts as a whole and is inserted in a relational and social context.

Of course, when the integrity of personality and/or its relations with others and groups is impaired by pathology, the partial aspects that result from splitting are real, and need be analyzed, in order to restore—or perhaps institute for the first time—their wholeness. In this, traditional clinical psychoanalysis has made a fundamental contribution.

But the field concept was brought to social psychology by Kurt Lewin (1951), who came, like Freud, from a natural science background, and tried to formulate his field concept in quasi-physical terms. For him, the human being existed in a "vital space," conceived as a field in which many different forces interact, thus shaping his or her behavior and experience. This concept allowed him to map the effect on the individual of a series of disparate elements, such as childhood experiences, wishes and aspirations, membership in groups and institutions, organic characteristics and transformations, physical and social climates, the geographic milieu, language, cultural values, the structure and functions of institutions and society, political events, and accidental happenings. Even though these may seem to be so different as to become incommensurable, their interaction and mutual influence turn out to be cogent, if we consider that they are all psychological events, acting within a psychological field.

This is especially evident when we consider the relation of individual psychology to interpersonal and group events and situations, which, according to Lewin, also constitute a psychological field in which the whole—the group—is more than, prior to, and more elementary than the sum of its parts—the individual members. Following the Aristotelian conception of the human being as essentially social, the individual becomes an abstraction, as the behavior and experience of concrete human beings can only be understood in terms of the organization and the dynamics of the group field.

The field approach is based on a spatial metaphor, so that it develops an atemporal theory. This implies the methodological principle of taking into account *contemporary factors* only. Everything is viewed in terms of the present, and the past and the future have a purely psychological existence, as remembrances of what has happened and expectations of what is to come. In this, it is belief and meaning, rather than actual occurrence, which determine the psychological relevance of any given event. This would seem to be in dire contradiction with the psychoanalytic approach, which seeks to explain the present in terms of the past, but this is so only in terms of Freud's ultimately unsuccessful attempt to turn psychoanalysis into a positivistic science (Freud, 1940b).[2]

Another different approach to the psychological use of the concept of field was that of Maurice Merleau-Ponty, in his books *The Structure of Behavior* (1942) and *Phenomenology of Perception* (1945). Starting from Husserl's phenomenology and the Gestalt point of view, he took a different turn, since, instead of emphasizing the experimental study of perception, as the classical Gestalt psychologists, or that of motivation, as Lewin, he adopted the phenomenological-existential perspective, thus focusing on the study of *personal experience*. This brought him into contact with one possible way of understanding psychoanalysis, as a methodology for the study of unconscious experience.

This field perspective of human existence became quite attractive for those psychoanalysts who were particularly interested in its interpersonal and social dimensions. For instance, Harry Stack Sullivan (1953) was overtly sympathetic to Lewin's field concepts, although he differed from them, as he developed his own view of human existence in terms of the individual's participation in an interpersonal field.

Field concepts also found their way into the theory and practice of those psychoanalysts who initiated the clinical analytic inquiry of groups, thus creating what became known as "group analysis." Enrique Pichon-Rivière, whose influence was acknowledged by Willy Baranger (1979a), as his analyst, teacher, and friend, explicitly referred to Lewin's concepts and techniques in his papers on his own approach to group analysis, which he called "operative groups" (Pichon-Rivière, 1971; Tubert-Oklander & Hernández-Tubert, 2004). On the other hand, S. H. Foulkes (1948; Foulkes & Anthony, 1965), the creator of group analysis in Britain, denied having a Lewinian influence, but he shared with him an origin in Gestalt psychology, which he had received from his teacher, the neurologist Kurt Goldstein (1940). The fact that Lewin's models were physical, like Freud's, while those of Foulkes stemmed from the study of human biology and social science, determined a significant difference in their perspectives.

But the true inception of a field theory of the psychoanalytic situation and process came in 1961, when Madeleine and Willy Baranger published, in the *Uruguayan Review of Psychoanalysis*, their seminal paper "The Analytic Situation as a Dynamic Field" (Baranger & Baranger, 1961–1962), which was later included in their 1969 book *Problems of the Psychoanalytic Field* (Baranger & Baranger, 1969). This seminal text has only recently been published in English translation by the *International Journal of Psycho-Analysis*, in 2008.

The Barangers' point of departure is methodological: the minimum dimension for psychoanalytic observation comprises two people, not one. In this they implicitly agree with British Independents, such as Michael Balint, who pointed out the paradoxical effects of trying to account for what happens in a bi-personal situation, by means of a one-person theory. Hence, they define the nature of the analytic field as follows:

A situation between two persons who remain unavoidably connected and complementary as long as the situation obtains, and involved in a single dynamic process. In this situation, neither member of the couple can be understood without the other.

(Baranger & Baranger, 2008, p. 796)

Here they introduce the concept of "field," which they import from Gestalt psychology, especially from Merleau-Ponty (1945), whose approach is more consistent with their whole approach to psychoanalysis, which is mainly philosophical and humanistic, in sharp contrast with Lewin's quasi-physical perspective.

But the structure and dynamics of the field include more than the two people involved; they also comprise the place and physical disposition of the consulting room, the temporal sequence of the sessions and the functional definition of both parties' roles, in sum, the analytic setting. In later papers, they also included the analyst's theories (Baranger, Baranger & Mom, 1978). What they did leave unmentioned was the participation of the social, historical, and political context in the constitution of the analytic field. This may be understood as a result of their traditional psychoanalytic focus on the intrapsychic, in spite of Willy Baranger's life-long interest on the study of ideology and its influence on the psychoanalytic situation (Baranger, 1954, 1957, 1958, 1992; Hernández-Tubert, 2005; Tubert-Oklander, 2005, 2007).

This holistic approach to the analytic situation and process led them to a reformulation of some basic concepts of the theory of technique. Insight, for instance, came to be seen as a reorganization of the field, which generates new meanings (Baranger & Baranger, 1964). The essential ambiguity of the analytic situation paves the way for a certain degree of regression in both parties, and the emergence of a *field unconscious phantasy*.[3] This is clearly derived from Melanie Klein's concepts (Isaacs, 1948; Klein et al., 1952), but with a major difference: this mental product cannot be considered as an expression of the individual's drives, but as a *phantasy of the couple*, which cannot "be considered to be the *sum* of the two internal situations … [but as] something created *between* the two, within the unit they form in the moment of the session, something radically different from what each of them is separately" (Baranger & Baranger, 2008, p. 806).

In this, there is an obvious influence of the experience and theories of group analysis, which they received from Pichon-Rivière. This they explicitly acknowledge, when they write that "we can only conceive of the basic phantasy of the session—the point of urgency—as a phantasy in a couple (in analytic group psychotherapy, the appropriate expression is 'group phantasy')" (pp. 805–806).

Another major point in their argument is that, when the patient's resistance becomes a *bastion* (*baluarte* in Spanish)—understood as "whatever the patient does not put at risk because the risk of losing it would throw the patient into a state of extreme helplessness, vulnerability and despair" (p. 814)—its analysis and final resolution shows that this was truly a field phenomenon, which included an unconscious participation of the analyst. This bi-personal bastion also includes the analyst's theories and technique (Baranger, Baranger, & Mom, J. M., 1978). In this they follow the path opened by Racker's (1958) pioneer work on the analyst's counter-resistances.

The resolution of such bastions requires that the analyst take a "second look" at the developments in the analytic situation, taking himself or herself as an object of the analytic inquiry. This happens whenever the necessary asymmetry of the analytic relation, instituted by the initial contract, has been lost and substituted by a pathological symmetrical organization, which has to be solved by interpretation (Baranger, Baranger & Mom, 1983). When this interpretive effort is successful, the result is that reorganization of the analytic field that we call "insight," and the asymmetry of the relationship is restored, thus reactivating a stagnated process, which they call a "non-process."

Now, this later formulation is more restricted than their initial statement that the analytic situation can only be fully understood as a bi-personal field. In their 1983 paper called "Process and Non-Process in Analytic Work," the Barangers and Mom were more cautious, as they seemed worried about the risk implied by taking the field concept as an affirmation of a total symmetry of the positions of analyst and patient. Perhaps this was a reaction to some misreadings of their original text that emphasized a mutuality in the analytic relationship—i.e., a relational perspective that they would be far from sharing (Tubert-Oklander, 2007). In any case, they were posing the problem of the alleged opposition between symmetry and asymmetry that emerges whenever the issue of *mutuality* in analysis is discussed, ever since Ferenczi's bold experiments in mutual analysis (Ferenczi, 1932; Aron, 1996; Tubert-Oklander, 2004a, 2004b).

## The Author's Point of View

My personal position vis-à-vis this problem is that the analytic relation needs be asymmetrical, since it is defined as a professional helping intervention; hence, the analyst's and the analysand's positions, functions, responsibilities, and rights are necessarily different and complementary. But this happens only at the differentiated level of conscious and preconscious experience, since the unconscious knows nothing about differences or professional obligations. Therefore, at the deepest level, not only are both parties symmetrical and interchangeable, but they are also completely undifferentiated, in a state of primeval unity (Loewald, 1951; Little, 1960; Bleger, 1967a; Tubert-Oklander, 2006a, 2008). This is what creates a symmetrical unconscious field, which enters into a dialectic tension with the asymmetrical analytic relation, which the analyst strives to maintain, as the only possible tool for an understanding of the field. When this difference and tension is momentarily lost, it is high time for that second look, which may come from self-analysis, personal analysis or supervision, in order to salvage the analytic process.

But the field is not a "thing," a discrete structure or event, which may or may not be present and is in need of explanation, but rather a different perspective, another way of organizing our perceptions and thinking about them. Classical psychoanalytic theory starts from the assumption that only the individual is "real," and that dyads, fields, interpersonal and transpersonal processes, or collective entities such as groups, institutions, and communities, are secondary phenomena, or even fantasies. One instance of this is to be found in Bion's (1952) assertion that "the belief that a group exists, as distinct from an aggregate of individuals, is an essential part of [the members'] regression, as are also the characteristics with which the supposed group is endowed by the individual. ... [The word] 'group' ... [means] an aggregation of individuals all in the same state of regression" (p. 142).

This brief text, which was written while the author was training as a psychoanalyst and in analysis with Melanie Klein, enters into a sharp contrast with his previous "Experiences in Groups" (Bion, 1948), in which he poses an entirely opposite position:

> In the group the individual becomes aware of capacities that are only potential so long as he is in comparative isolation. The group, therefore, is more than the aggregate of individuals, because an individual in a group is more than an individual in isolation.
>
> (Tubert-Oklander & Hernández-Tubert, 2004, p. 90)

Be it as it may, the unquestionable existence of the individual was clearly Freud's starting point, and from it he derived his research program of investigating psychic processes, considered as something "inside" the individual. The rationale seems to be that only material entities are "real," and that the isolated physical organism is the only possible true substrate of mind. But this is an assumption that stems from his previously accepted conception of the world—the materialistic metaphysics of modern science—and not a result of the psychoanalytic inquiry (Hernández-Tubert, 2004; Tubert-Oklander, 2004c).

Nonetheless, not all psychoanalysts share these positivistic assumptions, and there has been lately a sea change in a large sector of the psychoanalytic community towards holistic thinking. The idea that the psychoanalytic situation is an organic whole, whose parts cannot be understood without referring to each other and to the organized totality in which they are immersed, may be framed in more than one way ("Being is said in many ways," said Aristotle in his *Metaphysics*). If one conceives it in atemporal terms, as a complex mutual interaction and influence between a number of elements that occur simultaneously, then you have a *field model* of complexity. If, on the other hand, one looks at it in temporal terms, as a hypercomplex evolution with direction, course, and aim, this is a *process model*. Finally, if one constructs it as a model of personal relations in an imaginary group, as the Ancient Greeks did with the Olympus and Freud (1923a) with "The Ego and the Id," the result is a *dramatic or mythological model*. There is no need for us to choose between these three kinds of models, since they have an epistemological and not an ontological validity; they are something like three different lenses or recording instruments, three basic metaphors for understanding, each of which gives a different image of one and the same thing (Tubert-Oklander, 2006b). And this "same thing" is human ontology, ever present and evolving, but never fully visible or knowable. This is the Being which is said in many ways and called by many names.

Hence, the three models that I have just described are but metaphors, coined in order to describe some aspect or other of the ineffable complexity of the analytic experience. They offer a metaphoric description, more akin to the symmetric logic of the unconscious and poetry, which is to be articulated with the literal or metonymic description, in terms of the asymmetric logic of consciousness and science, in order to attain an analytic bi-logical understanding of the experience we share with our patients.

But does the assertion that human existence is a highly complex totality imply that the individual be nothing but a creation of our thinking processes, a partial metaphor used to refer to an aspect of a complex whole? I would say it is, but so are relations, the field, the group, the community, and Humankind. We are always striving to picture in our minds a hypercomplex, irrepresentable reality by building sketchy maps of our primary pre-reflective experience (Merleau-Ponty, 1945), and playing with them, like a child plays with building blocks.

In this, the group-analytic experience is the necessary complement of the traditional bi-personal psychoanalytic experience. Wilfred Bion's (1948) early incursion into groups led him to postulate the existence of *proto-mental phenomena*, prior to any dreaming or wording of them. In the proto-mental level, there is no differentiation between body and mind, self and other, individual and group, since the proto-mental system is the matrix from which such entities are formed and emerge.

In the same vein, S. H. Foulkes, the creator of group analysis, stated—in his *Introduction to Group-Analytic Psychotherapy*, published in 1948, the very same year in which Bion's "Experiences in Groups" started to appear in *Human Relations*—that:

> Each individual—itself an artificial, though plausible, abstraction—is basically and centrally determined, inevitably, by the world in which he lives, by the community, the group, of which he forms a part. ... The old juxtaposition of an inside and outside world, constitution and environment, individual and society, phantasy and reality, body and mind and so on, are untenable. They can at no stage be separated from each other, except by artificial isolation.
>
> (Foulkes, 1948, p. 10)

The obvious corollary is that the group is also "itself an artificial, though plausible, abstraction." In this, Foulkes was envisaging, just like Bion, a conception of existence as a hypercomplex undifferentiated whole, but whereas the latter conceived this as a primitive level, the former saw this systemic quality in all levels, from the apparently isolated individual through groups, institutions, and communities, up to the whole social and political reality.

The very same stance was taken by Enrique Pichon-Rivière, founder of the Argentine Psychoanalytic Association and pioneer of psychoanalysis and group analysis in Latin-America, who, as we have already seen, had a major influence on the Barangers. He also conceived both psychoanalysis and human life in general as an organic whole, although he preferred the temporal metaphor of the process to the spatial one of the field. His conception of the "spiral dialectic process" of analysis was part of the inspiration for the Barangers' concept of the analytic situation as a dynamic field (Baranger, W., 1979a).

In Pichon-Rivière's thinking, there was never an opposition between individual and collective psychology, since they are two sides of one and the same mental phenomenon—that of human existence. He used to refer to the metaphor of the island and the mainland, taken from John Donne's famous *Meditation XVII*, in which the poet says: "No man is an island, entire of itself; every man is a piece of the continent, a part of the main."

This poetic metaphor speaks for itself: neither the island, nor the continent are real entities, but only that part of a single irregular ground that can be seen over the level of the waters. Hence, the individual and the group are illusions, derived from our mind's tendency to split and splinter complex wholes, in order to be able to talk and think them through (Tubert-Oklander, 2011). Or, perhaps, rather than speaking of "illusions," we should call them, after Foulkes (1948), "artificial, though plausible, abstractions."

So, we are now back to our original problem of articulating *metaphor* and *field*. The concept of "field" is now clearly a metaphor for the analytic situation, which is complemented by two other metaphors that depict other aspects of it: the *process metaphor*, which highlights its evolution in time, and the *dramatic metaphor*, which iconizes the mental processes in the analytic relation and dialogue, in terms of that "other scene" of fantasy and dream (Tubert-Oklander, 2006b).

On the other hand, the unconscious metaphoric processes that represent the mind's basic efforts to represent its dealings with the world are the very stuff of the analytic interaction, in its three aspects of field, process, and drama. In these deepest levels of minding, there is no differentiation between self, others, and the whole environment, and unconscious experience comprises everything there is; communication does not follow the ordinary, discrete, and perceptible paths, and neither does it occur in sequence, but rather as a simultaneous mutual influence—i.e., field and process phenomena. This is what we try to depict and unravel by means of the analytic dialogue, in its double aspect of interpretation and explanation, which requires both metaphor and metonymy, which correspond to the poetic and argumentative uses of language (Ricoeur, 2008).

The end result is truly analogical, inasmuch as it finds a proportional midpoint in between the univocality of metonymy and science, and the equivocality of metaphor and poetry—"analogy" originally meant "proportion." And this requires, on the part of the analyst, an exercise of the Aristotelian virtue of *phronesis* (prudence), which is the ability to give to all parties their due. The knowledge that is thus acquired is necessarily partial, since it is based on similarity, rather than identity, but enough for the analyst and the analysand to go on thinking and working together—i.e., analyzing (Beuchot, 1997, 2003a; Tubert-Oklander & Beuchot Puente, 2008).

## Summary

The concepts of "field" and "metaphor" are necessarily related. First, because the very idea of the field is a metaphor; second, because metaphors generate a field in themselves, when considered as a form of mental activity. The mind works in terms of two logics and two processes: the secondary process, which is verbal, realistic, logical, and scientific, and the primary process, which is iconic, fantastic, metaphorical, and poetic. The logic of the secondary process is asymmetrical and that of the primary process is symmetrical; the confluence and articulation of both is bi-logical. The analogical synthesis of both logics gives the fullest integration of the human mind.

At the unconscious level, there is no individuation and no differences, but rather a primeval fusion of subject, object, and environment; this is the psychological and logical basis of the bi-personal field and process, which include both patient and analyst in an evolving dynamic whole. There is necessary complementarity between psycho-analysis and group analysis, as there was between the Barangers' concept of the dynamic field and their teacher Enrique Pichon-Rivière's concept of the spiral process. These ideas originated from the group-analytic experience and found their way into the theory of psychoanalytic technique.

## Notes

1 Originally published in *Psychoanalytic Inquiry* 33(3) (May 2013) with the same title.
2 "Psychology, too, is a natural science. What else can it be?" (Freud, 1940b, p. 282).
3 Here the unusual spelling of the word corresponds to the Kleinian usage (Isaacs, 1948), in which "phantasy" refers to the original unconscious mental processes and their iconic content, as something quite different from conscious "fantasies," akin to daydreaming, and their repressed derivatives, as described by Freud (1908).

# 15

# METAPHOR, ANALYTIC FIELD, AND SPIRAL PROCESS[1]

*Beatriz de León de Bernardi*

This chapter deals with field theory issues in the frame of Latin American thought, linking it to the subject of metaphor in psychoanalysis.

In the first part, some general developments about the theme of metaphor and about metaphor in psychoanalysis are exposed. The author presents the concept of dynamic field theory in the vision of Madeleine and Willy Baranger, the metaphoric processes implicit in this theory, and interpretations formulated over different basic concepts.

In the second part, the author develops a personal perspective of the field theory, supporting herself with examples from her clinical practice. She describes the characteristics of moments of intense communication between patient and analyst and the metaphoric processes implicit in interpretations. These metaphoric processes enable the integration of different levels of the intersubjective experience created between patient and analyst. The author postulates a dialectic point of view that allows the articulation of a situational perspective that studies the specific intersubjective moments of change in the analysis, with a vision that considers the process of analysis through time.

Conclusions are formulated regarding the role of metaphor in analysis and the future of the field theory in the context of theoretical and technical pluralism of current psychoanalysis.

## Metaphor and Theory of the Analytic Field

Metaphor has been traditionally understood as a rhetorical figure used by poets and artists. Usually, it has been defined as "a figure of speech in which a word or phrase is applied to an object or action that it does not literally apply to in order to imply a resemblance" (Collins Dictionary). Aristotle had already put the emphasis, in *Poetics* and *Rhetoric*, on the processes of transmission and extension of meaning that are characteristic of metaphoric creation. When a metaphor is created, we transfer an attribute from one subject to another subject to which it does not literally correspond. This transmission is accompanied by a figurative extension of the original meaning. From this perspective, Ricoeur (1986) considers that metaphors emerge to fill semantic vacuums. Processes of meaning extension that are present in metaphoric figures generate a new reference and new semantic pertinence that becomes impertinent with regard to the literal meaning and the usual reference of the term.

In a different posture, D. Davidson (1978) stated the pragmatic character of metaphor. From his point of view, what is relevant in a metaphor does not lie in the transmission of a meaning but in the promotion of conceptual changes and the creation of meanings in the listener. Thus, the metaphor does not create a figurative meaning, but the terms used in the metaphor keep meaning in a literal way. But the central aspect that this author highlights is that metaphors leave some degree of indetermination among related aspects, something that suggests new associations that are relevant to the listener. The way in which new connections are established, producing new meanings and emotions, depends on this listener (Quintanilla, 1999). In this approach, the function of metaphor is not mainly to give a message, but to provoke effects in the subjective experience of the listener. Following Davidson's point of view, authors such as Rorty (1989) have shown how the use of metaphors in communication also attempts to establish bonds with a strong emotional basis.

At present, the conception of metaphor does not gather only literary and philosophical reflection, but it has extended to the general processes of human cognition, the development of artistic and scientific thought, the different ways of communication and culture (Gibbs, 2008). The studies of Lakoff and Johnson (1980b, 1999) stated how metaphor is not only a figure of speech but is also part of daily expressions, being an intrinsic element of communication and of the thought processes since the origin of life.

In psychoanalysis, the subject of metaphor has been present in the reflection about the role of psychoanalytic theoretical conceptions and in elaborations about the characteristics of analytic communication. Authors such as G. Klein (1976), Schafer (1976), and Spence (1987) have understood, for example, how psychoanalytic theories may be seen as explanatory metaphors of unconscious psychic functioning. For some of these authors, this has been the reason why metapsychological constructions with a high degree of abstraction and generalization must be left aside in our practice. For others, however, this metaphoric character of psychoanalytic theory constitutes its greatest instrumental value.

Recently, Wallerstein (this volume) critically reviewed the proposals of G. Klein and R. Schafer, who considered the metapsychological contributions as metaphors that must be left aside in their clinical application. Wallerstein, on the contrary, hierarchized the instrumental and descriptive value of the different psychoanalytic theories. He also stated how this value is lost if psychoanalytic theories are taken in their literal sense when in contact with the patient, because in a contact adjusted to the richness of the clinic and to the interpretative processes, "Metaphor has been moved, powerfully by Lakoff and Johnson, from mental product to mental process" (Wallerstein, this volume).

Analytic communication may also be understood, in a broad sense, as a metaphoric process that establishes connections between the literal meaning of the analyst's expressions, those of the patient and their unconscious meaning, between manifest and latent speech. Borbely (1998), for example, stated how the metaphoric process, inherent to interpretation, establishes relationships between the present and the past as a way to re-establish the polysemic flow of experiences interrupted by the neurotic suffering. The interpretation proposes new categorizations that question old conceptions about oneself:

> All new insight leads to a greater or lesser extent, to a change to all previously established concepts. This mental change entails a re-conceptualisation of all previous concepts and their simultaneous re-categorization along new dimensions of relevance and meaningfulness.
>
> (Borbely, 1987)

As we see, considering the issue of metaphor in psychoanalysis includes different perspectives of approximation to the subject: that of metapsychological constructions of a more general and abstract character and the consideration of the specific way in which processes of metaphorization are established and the use of metaphors in the dialogue with the patient.

The perspective of the field theory constituted a model of clinical work that allowed M. and W. Baranger to establish connections between the more general and abstract levels of metapsychological constructions and the level of experience in the session. Their reflection is placed at the phenomenological level, something that allows them to rethink different general notions of psychoanalysis in relation to its way of functioning in practice. This led them, as time went by, to permanently think and reformulate their own ideas questioned by their experience.

Field theory in the vision of M. and W. Baranger was understood as a metaphor of the analytic situation, and these authors' most meaningful publication about the subject is precisely entitled "The Analytic Situation as a Dynamic Field." The different manifest aspects of the analytic field—spatial, temporal, and functional—supposed a "radical ambiguity," an "as if" that enabled the analysis of the underlying unconscious phantasies.

> It is essential for the analytic procedure that everything or every event in the field is at the same time something else. If this essential ambiguity is lost, the analysis also disappears.
>
> (Baranger & Baranger, 1961–1962a, p. 9;
> Baranger & Baranger, 2008, p. 799)

In this paper, I will first refer to the central notions of the field theory and to the vision of the analytic process of Madeleine and Willy Baranger, including references to Lacan's ideas, some of which were reviewed by these authors. I will analyze metaphoric processes in two interpretations, each formulated from a different conceptual basis.

In the second part of the paper, I develop my perspective of the field theory and of the analytic process. I describe the characteristics of moments of intense communication between patient and analyst and the metaphoric processes implicit in interpretations. These metaphoric processes enable the integration of different levels of the intersubjective experience created between patient and analyst. Starting from Pichon-Rivière's idea of the "spiral process," I postulate a dialectic point of view that allows the articulation of a situational perspective that studies the specific intersubjective moments of change in the analysis, with a vision that considers the process of analysis through time. Finally, I will consider perspectives of the field theory and metaphor in the context of the theoretical and technical pluralism of current psychoanalysis, formulating some conclusions regarding the role of metaphor in analysis and about the future of the field theory.

## The Dynamic Field Theory in Latin America

The analytic field theory emerged in Uruguay at the beginning of the 1960s with the appearance of the paper "*La situación analítica como campo dinámico*" ("The Analytic Situation as a Dynamic Field") by Madeleine and Willy Baranger (1961–1962a). This paper was published in the *Revista Uruguaya de Psicoanálisis* 50 years ago, at a moment when psychoanalytic groups were being formed and consolidated in Uruguay and Argentina.[2] That paper, which was recently reprinted in the *International Journal of Psychoanalysis* (Baranger & Baranger, 2008), had a strong impact on the psychoanalytic thought of the time and continues to have influence today, as shown in publications and congresses of the Federación de Psicoanálisis de América Latina (FEPAL).[3]

The field theory referred to the analytic situation (de León de Bernardi, 2008),[4] incorporating conceptualizations from philosophy, psychology, social psychology, and psychoanalysis developed at that time in both margins of the Río de la Plata. It also incorporated contributions from phenomenology, through Merleau-Ponty's thought, especially from "The Phenomenology of Perception" (1945); from the psychology of Gestalt and through the thought of Kurt Lewin; and from social psychology through Enrique Pichon-Rivière, psychiatrist and psychoanalyst residing in Argentina, who theoretically and clinically conceptualized the effects of the social bonds in the structuralization of psychism, favoring group treatment of different problems.

From psychoanalysis, the contributions of M. Klein, S. Isaacs, and W. Bion were central. These authors had, at that time, a strong impact on the region and meant to modify the classical Freudian points of view, centered on the role of instinct, libinal evolution, and childhood history, considered from an intrapsychic point of view. The importance given by Klein and those who continued his work to the primitive object relationships, with their anxieties and defenses when facing destructive impulses, the unconscious phantasy, and the conception of different paranoid and depressive positions along life, led to conceiving the analytic situation as an expression of primitive relationships in the "here and now" of the session.

Bion's Group Theory offered a vision of the unconscious root of certain group behaviors that went beyond individual psychology. In the same way, Kurt Lewin applied the notion of field, with its dynamism and directions, to social situations, which influenced the thought of Bion (Churcher, 2008). Enrique Pichon-Rivière (1998), from his experience as a doctor in a psychiatric hospital and later as psychoanalyst, was interested in developing group activity that would promote forms of more creative and healthier social adaptation. His experience as a psychiatrist and psychoanalyst led him to broaden the notion of object relationship, proposing the notion of bond.

> The analytic investigation of this inner world took me to broaden the concept of "object relationship," formulating the notion of bond, which I define as a complex structure that includes an individual, an object, and their interrelation with processes of communication and learning.
>
> (p. 10)

These different conceptions about the group experience influenced the analytic vision of M. and W. Baranger, which was understood as a situation of a couple.

But, in addition, the field theory had a heuristic value, offering an answer to epistemological preoccupations of Willy Baranger on the specificity of psychoanalysis and the need for validation of our interpretations.

> The systematic exam of what occurs in the analytic bipersonal situation is the only access to an ideal of knowledge validation that is truly characteristic of psychoanalysis. This ideal currently conceivable is made—without being formulated—in several writings of the last years, which offer a very exhaustive description of the analytic situation with the interpretations and modifications that occur in limited temporal groups.
>
> (Baranger, W., 1959, p. 81)

From my point of view, the field theory was conceived as a tool of knowledge and clinical investigation, representing an attempt to broaden the capacity of observation[5] and perception of the analyst to the multiple manifest and latent aspects of the analytic situation. In this regard, it was logical that they would support themselves on ideas of the Gestalt psychology, which showed how the human mind could perceive elements in globalizing structures.

M. and W. Baranger conceived the existence of a dialectic interrelation between the need for observation and the search for objectivity through acceptance and use of their own subjectivity. They considered the analyst's subjectivity as a determining factor of the field phenomena,[6] but at the same time, they found the need for the analyst to be participant and observer, an idea that was highlighted by Racker in relation to countertransference.[7]

It becomes necessary that the analyst can establish in himself or herself "a process of relative division, as an observer of the interpersonal situation" (Baranger & Baranger, 1961–1962a, p. 168), which implies questioning their own emotional reactions and interventions, evaluating their impact in the interpersonal situation, at the same time converted in object of analysis. This attitude will lead them to postulate the need of a second look after the session, which would allow the review of what was experienced and acted by both participants of the situation. We have stated (Bernardi & de León, 1993) that the second look implies the analyst's disposition to auto-analysis regarding the different ways of his or her participation in the bond with the patient. Establishing a second look during and after the session offers the possibility of testing alternative hypotheses and technical options, as we will see below.

## Metaphoric Process in the Field Theory

The approach of the analytic situation as a dynamic field led to putting the target in the present of the session and in the characteristics of the analytic dialogue established in it.

> The essence of the analytic procedure is dialogue, as Freud (1926) has defined it.
>
> (Baranger & Baranger, 2008, p. 89)

S. Isaacs's ideas about unconscious phantasy gave the conceptual basis to understanding the latent sense of this dialogue. For Isaacs, unconscious phantasies are emotional structures, primitive ways of relating in their variants of love and hate, created in the contact with the first object relationships. Still far from verbal expression, they organize the foundations of psychism, of the perception of the self and the world, and they are re-lived in the transferential bond. In this approach, what basically guides the analyst is the "logic of emotion." The point of "urgency" of the interpretation is determined by the type of anxiety, depressive or paranoid, and the defenses when facing it, captured by the analyst in his or her countertransference.

> The primary phantasies, the representatives of the earliest impulses of desire and aggressiveness, are expressed in and dealt with by mental processes far removed from words and conscious relational thinking, and determined by the logic of emotion. The unconscious phantasy condenses visual images; auditory, kinaesthetic, tactile, taste, olfactory sensations, etc.
>
> (Isaacs, 1948, p. 84)

Isaacs, as well as M. Klein, considered unconscious phantasy from an intrapsychic point of view. But the field perspective, especially influenced by Pichon-Rivière's idea of bond, integrated the intrapsychic with the intersubjective. The dialectic intergame of the individual with others modifies inner object relationships. The Subject and the Object are reciprocally constituted. It is from this perspective that the shared unconscious phantasy, in its game of reciprocal projective identifications, was placed in the center of the analytic communication in the session.

For the perspective of the analytic field, which gathers ideas of Álvarez de Toledo (1954), the words between analyst and patient acquire in the communication with the analyst a pragmatic character, being an expression of multiple actions and unconscious phantasies:

> in addition to its semantic value, the word acquires concrete value, most particularly in analytic work, in terms of fantasied action: shooting arrows, throwing rocks, poisoning, suckling, caressing, etc.
>
> (Baranger, Baranger, & Mom, 1983, p. 4)

The analytic dialogue is compared to ways of exchange from early infancy.

> In early infancy there are synaesthesias between sounds, smells, temperatures, shapes and feelings; the most frequent of these are synopsias (coloured hearing). A sensation corresponding to a given sense appears associated with one or more others, and arises regularly when the latter are stimulated ... This is particularly relevant to the process of symbolization.
>
> (Alvarez de Toledo, 1954[1996], p. 299)

I have noted (de León, 1993, 2008) proximities among these ideas with ideas emerged in investigations of early development that have shown the phenomenon of the unity of the senses and of the amodal transposition of the information in the bond of the child with his or her mother (Stern, 1985b). These phenomena are comparable to the metaphors of poetic creation, which achieve their effects of meaning when they propose analogies and correspondences among different levels of the sensorial experience. It has called my attention to how D. Stern (1985b) and Álvarez de Toledo (1954) used the same poem by Baudelaire, "Correspondances,"[8] to illustrate their ideas.

As we see, the interpretation in the perspective of the field theory, influenced by ideas of the Kleinian frame, supposed an implicit metaphoric process that attempted through the word of interpretation the symbolizing reunification of aspects of the split primitive experience, or fragmented in its emotional and bodily aspects. The word will attempt to integrate the sub-symbolic levels (emotional and bodily) with the symbolic ones (images and verbal representations).

This perspective is illustrated in an investigation about the "Changes in the Interpretation in the Uruguayan Psychoanalytic Group" (Bernardi et al., 1997). Interpretations of the decades of the 1960s and 1990s were studied in 93 papers of Associated Member Work (theoretical-clinical papers on analytic processes presented by the candidates to end their training) and 443 interpretations that made latent contents explicit. A quantitative-qualitative analysis was made of them. From that investigation we extract a paradigmatic example by Aida Fernández (1967) that shows the interpreting mode of the 1960s, influenced by Kleinian ideas and the conception of unconscious phantasy.

A young homosexual patient, with "a weak structure of the self" and with confusional states that show difficulties in the differentiation of the self and the objects, suffers intensely the separations from his analyst, experiencing them as abandonment. With great difficulty, the patient narrates that after the session he has looked for promiscuous sexual contacts, which have generated great discomfort and guilt. When referring to them, the patient describes the uncontrollable impulse of sexual contact as "a fire in my head" that had blinded him and made him lose control:

> ... then I felt as a fire in my head; it seemed that it had blinded me. I don't know what happened to me; it was amazing ...

The analyst answers, retaking the patient's expression:

> You feel fire in your head due to rage, when you believe that I stop giving you here—to give it to someone else—on weekends. That is why you go searching and giving, relating through all the holes. You go searching outside what you believe I do not want to give you. You are taking revenge brutally—leaving me alone—as you feel yourself, alone and hungry when you reject me
> (Fernández, 1967, p. 189)

In this interpretation, we see how the analyst recontextualizes the expression of the patient, giving a new meaning to it in the bond with her. The expression "fire in my head" is used as a metaphor that puts the anger with the analyst on the same level as the anger experienced when facing frustrations in the patient's primary bodily contacts.

The formation of metaphors and metaphoric processes in the analytic field shows a complex dynamism. In this case, the starting point is the feeling of the analyst of being "brutally" attacked by different actions of the patient that lead to self-destructive acts. The image of the "fire in your head" used in the interpretation contributes to the processing in the analyst of the impact generated in herself by the actions of the patient, at the same time that she attempts to facilitate processes of integration of the split emotional and bodily experience in the patient. The analyst transmits how she conceived this movement of integration and symbolization in analysis.

> The countertransferential experience is, in this regard, very important, because it can condition all the relationship between analyst and patient. My interpretative task was to translate the act at the level of verbal thought, taking each detail of his movements, of the intention, and their meaning, patiently and carefully, using the healthy parts of the transferential bond. Those of the patient and those the patient felt in me, his analyst. In this way I was able to penetrate the primitive, unreachable world of his internal reality, stopped in the primary process. I consider that he gradually came to accept his acting out and showing what he wanted to communicate to me, that he started to understand, to think.
> (Fernández, 1967)

The notion of bastion that was stated by W. and M. Baranger (1961–62a, 1983; 1983 with Mom) describes difficulties in this integration process. Splittings of the primitive self escape the flow of the verbal free association that may end up deceptive, slowing the process of analysis. In these cases, the implicit metaphoric processes in our interpretations fail. Racker's ideas on complementary countertransference (1957a) and the notion of projective counteridentification, which included the analyst's emotional and bodily reactions (Grinberg, 1956), described situations in which the analyst defensively assumed identifications with roles of objects from the inner world of the patient. If this was not understood, it could cause the formation of "types of stereotyped patterns of experiencing and behaviour," of shared phantasies acted in the analytic interaction during a long period of the analysis. In these situations, the analyst put into play his own conflicts and impulses, especially the avoidance of his own destructiveness.

## New Developments and Changes in Interpretation

The advent of Lacan's thought in the Río de la Plata at the end of the 1960s created a favorable atmosphere for the re-reading of Freud's works, introducing new ideas that differed from those postulated by the theory of object relationships. Ideas about language as the structure of the unconscious, the three registries—symbolic, imaginary, and real—introduced new metapsychological postulates.

Lacan's ideas about the influence of the other's desire in the structuring of psychism took him to first place himself in an intersubjective perspective, a position that was later modified together with the advance in his developments about the symbolic order. Lacan clearly differentiates the position of the analyst from the position of the patient. From his point of view, the ordering function of the analyst, exerted from a "third" place, is what makes restructuring the patient's psychism possible in relation to the limit of lack and castration. Lacan will question the approaches that highlight the relational or intersubjective aspects because they can cause the loss of analytic asymmetry.

The conception of metaphor had a central place in Lacan's ideas about the oedipal complex and the paternal metaphor, repression, and the mechanism of condensation. In reference to the condensation mechanism, Lacan takes up again contributions from Roman Jakobson (1956), who, based on studies about aphasia, distinguished the metaphoric axe of language, which allows the selection and substitution of linguistic items, and the metonymic axe, which allows their combination. He followed ideas of de Saussure when he considered metaphor to belong to the paradigmatic axe of *langue*, while metonymy belonged to the syntagmatic one. Jakobson linked metaphor and metonymy to the fundamental mechanisms of the dream work described by Freud: metonymy with displacement and condensation and metaphor to identification and symbolism.

Lacan takes distance from Jakobson when he links metonymy with displacement and metaphor with condensation. From his point of view, interpretation has the effect of substitution of signifiers in a new game of metaphoric meanings. The metaphoric substitution and condensation of verbal signifiers as an effect of interpretation appears in a disruptive way, and it shows in the appearance of lapsus linguae and other formations of the unconscious, provoking ruptures in the known discourse of the conscious self and new restructuring in the patient's psychism.

When it comes to hierarchizing moments of rupture, Lacan's approach is placed in the antipodes of Klein's and Isaacs's perspective, who highlighted the phenomenon of the emotional experience integration as an effect of interpretation. In the new perspective, language is what constitutes the structures of the world, as Wittgenstein would say, an outlook that prevails in structuralism influenced by Lévi-Strauss's thought. The floating attention of the analyst stops focusing on his or her own emotional reactions, to pay attention to the insistence of certain verbal signifiers in the associative discourse of the patient. This perspective necessarily made Lacan strongly question the notion of countertransference (de León, 2000).

These ideas, developed within the frame of a growing theoretical and technical pluralism, had an influence on the listening of the analyst in the session in the Río de la Plata since the early 1970s (de León, 2005). The previously mentioned paper about the changes in interpretation in the Uruguayan group (Bernardi et al., 1997) shows how interpretations become less saturated of sense and the analyst goes from an active and incisive attitude in his interpretations to an exploratory, interrogative, and expectant attitude toward the patient's associations, working on the basis of the implicit transference, differentiating from the way transference was explicitly worked into many interpretations of the 1960s.

An example of an interpretation influenced by Lacan's theory clearly appears in a more recent paper of the *Revista Argentina de Psicoanálisis*, Paulucci and Dujovne (2003), that I, myself, have commented on (de León, 2003).

The author of the paper shows how a patient complains about his relationship with his partner, saying:

> There is one *ensilladura* (a Spanish word that literally means "saddle," and that the patient here uses to mean "tight relation") between my professional relationship with J. and how mad his rudeness and the yelling he brings to the office make me.
>
> Then the analyst answers with an interrogative intervention: "*¿Ensilladura?*"
> This intervention that attempts to highlight the ambiguity and opacity of the term *ensilladura* evokes in the analysand the fragmentation of that word:
> "*en – silla – dura*" (in Spanish, "on hard chair")
> To which (the analysand) adds, intensely moved: "It looks as if I am always suffering on a hard chair."
>
> (Paulucci & Dujovne, 2003, p. 14)

The metaphoric game between *ensilladura* and on "hard" "chair" opens the patient's later associations. This allows the analyst to conclude that this interpretative modality produced a clarification in the patient about "his position of masochistic suffering."

In this case, the metaphoric process is guided by the appearance of a term in the patient's speech that is repeated by the analyst in an interrogative way. The patient transforms, substitutes, and surprisingly relocates the term in another context of meaning, linked to his masochistic identification, showing himself "intensely moved." In this case, unlike the previous example, the analyst does not make any direct reference to transference.

M. and W. Baranger reviewed the field theory in papers dated 1961–62a and 1983 (and 1983 with Mom). In these reformulations, they stated problems and limitations of the theory regarding the risk of carelessness of the patient's history, the exaggeration of the role of transferential interpretation and of countertransference that were confused, at the same time, with the mechanisms of the projective identification and projective counteridentification. These concepts could be extended in excess to explain clinical phenomena of a varied nature.

M. and W. Baranger dealt with some of Lacan's questions about the risks of asymmetry loss in a bipersonal psychology and his approach to the opaque character of the unconscious (M. Baranger, 1993a). However, they kept the notion of bastion, which would lead to articulating this notion with the one of analytic process and non-process, in their papers dated 1961–62a and 1983 (and 1983 with Mom). The second look broadens then beyond the session, to the consideration of the unconscious guidelines of interaction established between patient and analyst, in a more extended period of the analysis.

## Dialectics of Temporality: "Field" Theory and "In Spiral" Process

Although in the paper dated 1961, the subject of temporality—present, past, and future—had been introduced in regard to the patient's history, it is twenty years later that Willy Baranger (1979a), when proposing the idea of "spiral process," introduces the dialectics of temporality to the analytic process. This idea from Pichon-Rivière was developed by W. Baranger from a close exchange with Pichon that was established in Argentina and maintained in Uruguay between the years 1954 and 1958 (de León, 2008).

> The spiral process essentially aims to explain the temporal development of the analytic process, of its turns, repetitions, elaborations, in the alternation of regression and progression, of the dialectics of the history and the temporality that characterizes it.
>
> (W. Baranger, 1979a)

The notions of "dynamic field" and "spiral process" imply different perspectives. The metaphor of the "field" attempted to describe the permanent framing of the analytic work at the time that the characteristic elements that configure the analytic situation, in the synchrony of one given moment of analysis. The "spiral" metaphor used to describe the analytic process implied the vision of a succession of moments in time, from a diachronic perspective.

> The concept of "dynamic field" is a neighbour of the "spiral process" concept, though it aims to describe the structures of minor temporal units. It enables to understand the reciprocal constitution of the individual and the object, and the need to understand one based on the other. Field designates both the frame and the configuration of the analytic situation.
>
> (Baranger, 1979a)

The fertile moments of interpretation and "insight" punctuate the analytic process, described by Pichon Rivière (1998) as a "spiral process," an image which expresses the temporal dialectics of the process. "Here, now, with me" is often said, to which Pichon Rivière adds "Just as there, before, with others" and "As in the future, elsewhere and in a different way." It is a spiral, each of whose turnings takes up the last turning from a different perspective, and which has no absolute beginning or given end. The superimposition of the spiral's curves illustrates this mixture of repetition and non-repetition which may be observed in the characteristic events in a person's fate, this combined movement of deepening into the past and constructing the future which characterizes the analytic process (Baranger M., Baranger W., & Mom J., 1983, p. 9).

The idea of "spiral process" did not only introduce the issue of the temporality of the patient's life "Just as there, before, with others," but also the time in the history of analysis conceived as dialectic process.

The dialectic spiral in M. and W. Baranger's thought complements the Freudian notion of *Nachträglichkeit*, which allows understanding of how not only the analytic situation will have prospective effects in analysis, but also that while in the process, situations and analytic moments of the past history of analysis will retroactively resignify. The concept of "listening to the analysand's listening" of H. Faimberg (2006) is an example of how different interventions of the analyst only acquire their sense with the advance of the analysis, in responses the patient gives to the interpretations of the analyst in *a posteriori* time.

Together with the contributions of Pichon-Rivière and M. and W. Baranger, different authors in Latin America have differentiated situation and process (Etchegoyen, 1986), reflecting on the characteristics and the way in which they are mutually conditioned. Bleger (1967a) proposed that the analytic situation is defined from the process, because all analysis needs certain permanent conditions, as the frame and the respect to essential aspects of the analytic situation. More recently, emphasis has been given to the internal setting of the analyst (Alizade, 2002), and to the fact that the dynamics of the process gradually determine the situation and the type of setting.

These two perspectives have been integrated, attempting to both describe essential aspects of the situation and the process. Isaías Melshon (1989, pp. 57–58) stated how in the session, "the types of speech, intonation, rhythmic line, building modalities ... the expressive movements of the body ... everything, becomes ordered around nodal points of organization and disorganization" that follow one another and transform along the analytic process. Ruben Cassorla (2005), in his developments about enactment, studies phenomena of interaction over which pathological aspects of patient and analyst converge, which become chronic and prevent the advance of analysis. It is in certain moments in which these phenomena become acute that they can be perceived by the analyst in a retrospective look about the process.[9]

From an integrating approach that takes into account the situational and temporal vision, I have proposed that the analytic process is constituted on the basis of moments of mutual link, in which an intense emotional contact and an intense psychic work happens between patient and analyst. These moments imply complex dynamisms in communication in which "facilitated by regression, a tight intergame of images, affects and words happens between patient and analyst" (de León, 1993).

These moments of the analytic relationship intricately include transferential and countertransferential aspects, which, as formations of the unconscious, get installed in the field and must be unraveled in a retrospective look of the analyst, regarding the nature of his or her own participation and regarding the ways of interaction established up to that moment. In that sense, I believe that these moments constitute true neoformations of the analytic field, "interactive dynamic nuclei" that mark the history of analysis and establish "the shared substratum of interpretation" (de León, 1993).

## Situational and Temporal Perspective of the Metaphoric Processes in the Analytic Field

Pablo, aged 42, married, father of two daughters and one son, who had finished his treatment with me more than 15 years ago, recently returned for consultation. I had included a vignette of this analysis to exemplify my ideas about the characteristics of intense interaction moments between patient and analyst, in which implicit metaphoric processes take place, which allow integrating experiences expressed in different sensory registers (de León, 1993). Meeting Pablo again demanded reviewing my vision of the dynamics of these clinical moments from a situational perspective, but at the same time, the fact of Pablo having consulted me again allowed me to consider them in a temporal dialectic of effects and retrospective new meanings.

Pablo had started his analysis with me at the end of his adolescence, expressing difficulties in his relationship bonds and questions regarding his professional future. After five years of analysis, we decided, by common consent, to end it. Pablo had accomplished many objectives that he had set for himself at the beginning of treatment.

First, I did not remember a precise description of Pablo's analysis, and I preferred not to review my own written material about it, so as to be able to see the current situation with a new outlook, somehow "without memory." However, during the days before the interview, one expression came to me, which I remembered was especially meaningful in his analysis. It was the expression "¡A cucha!" (a Spanish expression equivalent to "shoo!" in English), said to dogs when we want them to get far from us. I remembered that I had referred to it in the vignette narrated in my paper dated 1993, but I did not clearly remember how that word had emerged in the analysis and who had said it.

The reunion with Pablo impresses me because of the sudden, vivid, and pleasant recovery of the shared experience that seems to have stayed intact over time. Pablo has formed a family and achieved success in his professional life. However, he returned to consult because he is going through a period of great anxiety. His wife has been promoted at her job, which revives in Pablo strong feelings of abandonment and rejection, awakening paranoid ideas. At that point, I re-read my previous vision of the patient.

### *Twenty Years Ago: A Moment in Analysis*

Almost 20 years ago, Pablo appeared to me as

> an adolescent patient who consults after moments of great insecurity in his couple relationships in which he has felt rejected. This insecurity extends to other situations. He defends himself with intellectualizations and taking distance, attempting in that way to achieve better control of his feelings. He has problems handling his aggressiveness, which is usually denied and when it appears, it generates very unpleasant feelings to him. During his childhood he had problems with sphincter control, he presents an untidy aspect and sometimes impresses me as dirty.
>
> (de León, 1993, p. 811)

From the material of the analysis, I had selected a moment that occurred in a session immediate to an unexpected interruption of the analysis. When he referred to a sexual relationship he had with a girl that weekend, the patient had used the term *acuchar* instead of the term *acostarse* (Spanish for "go to bed with"). Following is the quote of my vision of that clinical moment:

> The lapsus linguae *acuchar* provokes certain commotion to me. When exploring my countertransferential experience I admit that it is true that this patient has raised certain rejection which reason I don't get to clarify completely. His dirty aspect, his demand of proximity, certain behaviour of lack of consideration that I connect with his aggressiveness …
>
> However, at this moment his lapsus has had in me the opposite effect … I feel a special type of proximity. I have immediately related his expression *acuchar* with the exclamation "¡A cucha!," and this one with feeling rejected, taken out of my office.

The patient associates with childhood situations in which, having finished individual lessons, he waited for his mother to pick him up, feeling great anguish thinking that his mother would forget about him. At the same time he remembers episodes of enuresis and encopresis at school, in which he felt ashamed and rejected.

Then, his waits for his mother, his loneliness and his great anguish get connected in me, the image of the animal and dirt. For the first time I feel that he opens a way to the understanding of my feeling of rejection that gets partly connected to this image of something "animal," dirty, in a corner, and rejected that the patient transmits to me.

I only verbalize his feelings in relation to having felt pushed away from his sessions during the interruption of analysis, as if I had told him, "Shoo!" The patient keeps talking as if nothing had happened, but suddenly he gets quiet for a long time. Finally, when he resumes talking, he says that he can't explain why he has felt a very intense emotion, that he doesn't know how to understand it, and he associates with a poem he has read about creation.

At that time, the patient dreams with the image of an animal in a cradle. It was a "dog-fish," half dog (from the waist up) half fish (from the waist down). I recall once again the lapsus linguae of the patient and my associations.

(de León, 1993, p. 812)

At present, I agree with the characteristics that I had attributed at that clinical moment: the intricacy of the experiences of patient and analyst, the figurative character of them, and the way of multimodal functioning of the analyst's mind.

The exclamation "¡A cucha!" that had emerged in me condensed my tone of rejection and the inhibited gesture of pushing. This expression had unexpectedly revealed to me my own latent posture in the analytic situation. The halt due to the setting of the "access to motility" eased my gestures and emotions to regressively express in the image "of the animal in the corner, and far in his dirt" that imposed to me in the session.[10] This image allowed me to capture an unconscious or preconscious identification of the patient, but also to visualize the scene I myself was involved in.

It was a moment of intricacy and reciprocal link between my experiences and those of the patient. I had alternatively placed myself in a complementary or concordant way with the patient (Racker, 1957a), with a phenomenon of regressive circularity between both. From the first moment in which I had been left in a place in a complementary way, pushing the patient far from me, I came to place myself concordantly in his place, which enabled me to perceive the quality of his subjective experience and produced the feeling of greater proximity in the session.

The dynamics of the metaphoric processes that occurred in the analysis show a process that is co-built between analyst and patient. But in this case, the metaphoric condensation is not made between verbal meanings only, but among different levels of the subjective experience expressed in emotions, in images that include primary bodily representations of the bond with the others (such as my gestures in the previous clinical example), and, finally, in verbal expressions. From my perspective, the multimodal functioning and the analyst's mind capacity for reverie make it possible that the analyst, being aware of the answers of the patient, may:

> walk an alternative or simultaneously different registries of expression in himself or in the patient, attempting to give place to still unformulated phenomena. In this way, images, feelings, bodily representations and words can displace or condense in a representation, exchange themselves, re-translate themselves.
>
> Regressive understandings make possible that what is expressed in a register reaches its meaning for the patient and for ourselves in the other.
>
> (de León, 1993, p. 819)

### At Present

During the early times of Pablo's re-analysis, I find again aspects perceived at that clinical moment but now lived in an amplified and dramatic way. Pablo is afraid that the current situation will cause him to take distance from his family; he feels out of balance and overwhelmed by anguish. His painful feeling of abandonment and rejection is updated. His oedipal conflict reappears re-lived by the current situation. Intellectualizations and obsessive thoughts, uncontrollable at moments, attempt to control his jealousy and paranoid ideas toward his wife. He attempts to control his aggressiveness, which, when it gets to be expressed, does so in an explosive and sadistic way, generating great discomfort and suffering. But what called my attention most was that in certain moments, his jealousy acquired the fixing of the delirious ideas, putting his phantasies and thoughts on a level with reality. In certain moments, he lives the breaking of his couple and his family as the only possibility.

During the first months of the re-analysis, I have the impression that I am facing a crack in Pablo's psychism that cannot be reached by my words. The dimension of the "as if" is lost, and I feel that it is impossible to establish a metaphoric process that will restore it. Analysis becomes a place of catharsis, emotion processing, and prevention of his self-destructive actions.

\* \* \*

Undoubtedly, this second meeting with Pablo resignified my vision of the clinical moment previously described. I had seen Pablo as an adolescent who reproached his mother her lack of attunement and her exaggerated dedication to his father and siblings during his childhood, which at that time, I thought essentially framed in his oedipal conflicts. Although I had found little intrapsychic permeability in Pablo and great difficulties for him to become conscious of his own aggressive impulses, I had attributed it to his steely obsessive defences. Today, I see that the oedipal conflicts and their tendency to isolate his emotions is reinforced by splitting mechanisms of a more primitive self, which make the integration of different aspects of his psychism difficult.

The second dream about the "dog fish" had made me think then of the castration anguish. Today, his identification with animals shows me difficulties in the integration of his bodily image and his emotions. His movements are rigid and inexpressive at times. Today, I see his bonds little discriminated, which has made his couple relationship difficult and has caused an exaggerated identification with her, which has contributed to the genesis of the current crisis. It has been difficult for him to feel that he is not her wife, and this repeats in his close bonds, where he exaggeratedly puts himself in the others' place, taking care of their problems. His good reflexive capacity is always at the service of the others, living through them and leaving aside his own desires and personal projects. In general, he avoids, in this way, expressing his aggressiveness.

After three years of analysis, the storm calms down and Pablo recovers his stability in his family life and his working capacity. He becomes gradually conscious of his dissociations, ambivalences, and contradictions, at the same time that his bonds become more discriminate, recovering his joy. However, he has warned me that "it is better not to touch some things."

This second moment of Pablo's analysis has made me think about the limits of our task. But I have also proved how metaphoric processes established in the analytic field are a privileged way to convey the emotional communication between patient and analyst and intrapsychic modifications in the patient. The clinical situation described in the first analysis of Pablo perhaps did not have the scope that I gave it at that moment, but undoubtedly, it was a meaningful moment that enabled the understanding in the analysis of different aspects of the unconscious problematic of the patient and his integration at a mental and emotional level, something that allowed the analytic bond to sustain through time.

## Conclusions: Analytic Field and Metaphor

The central focus of the dynamic field theorization attempted to illuminate how, beyond the manifest forms of analytic interaction, unconscious interaction patterns are built and mark the dynamism of analysis. These ways of interaction are undoubtedly conditioned by the individual past of the patient and analyst but, at the same time, are specific and new in the present of the bond and context in which each analysis is established.

I think the metaphoric processes and metaphors that emerge in the analysis ease the analytic communication and the emerging of transforming moments of intersubjectivity. As the clinical moments described in this work show, these moments are dynamically co-built in a way that goes beyond the conscious will of the analyst. In that way, the relationship that is established in the analytical dialogue between the words *ensilladura* ("saddle") and *silla dura* ("hard chair") constitutes a field formation in its manifest and latent aspects that will determine the history of this analysis. This phenomenon imposes itself beyond the conceptual frame of the analyst, who apparently attempts not to get actively involved and only to participate, precisely highlighting an expression of the patient's speech.

But it is necessary to consider the limits of verbal language in our interventions and metaphors. Not only because, as in the case of Pablo, rigid defensive mechanisms can make more difficult a more permeable and fluid verbal communication of the patient with us and with himself, but also because the metaphoric processes emerged in the analysis show through language only some of the multiple phenomena (attitudes, tones, etc.) inherent to the analytic communication.

In fact, different interpretative styles also imply attitudes toward the patient that may go unnoticed at first sight. Then the explanatory style of the interpretation of the first clinical example may be accompanied by an active attitude, which may be experienced as instrusive by the patient, generating an attitude of submission to the analyst's point of view. On the contrary, the laconic style of the second case may be experienced by the patient as an indicator of a cold and indifferent analyst attitude. Pablo's case made me reflect on possible attitudes of rejection toward him that probably were present before the mentioned moment. These manifest attitudes, also in styles and voice tones, may answer to characteristics of the analyst or patient, but also to unconscious patterns of interaction that get established beyond verbal language, but which may have their meaning in the internal world of the patient. Becoming aware of them may avoid acute enactments, the installation of bastions, or impasse situations.

In psychoanalysis, interpretative processes of metaphoric character show the double function of the metaphor stated at the beginning of this paper: they transmit implicit meanings and produce unexpected effects in the patient or analyst, or in both, with the corresponding internal restructuration. One or another of these aspects, or both, may predominate along the analytical process. In this way, in the expression "fire in your head" used by the analyst, it predominates the intention of the analyst to transmit a meaning connecting the expression of the patient to different aspects of his unconscious subjective experience. In the second example, the patient is the one who, supported by the analyst's intervention, builds the connection between his own expressions *ensilladura* and *silla dura*, which allows him to become aware of his masochistic positions. In the case of Pablo's analysis, it is an expression of the patient that awakens in me a second meaning and allows me to establish the connection of the lapsus linguae *acuchar* with the expression "¡*A cucha!*" that produces in both a moment of "insight."

As we saw before, in Davidson's perspective, the emerging of novel metaphors (not the ones integrated in the conventional language) has the effect of correlating emotions and meanings linked to subjective experiences of the listeners: "Metaphor makes us see one thing as another by making some literal statement that inspires or prompts the insight" (Davidson, 1978, p. 47).

Undoubtedly, it calls to our attention the apparent coincidences between these developments and the analytic experience. In effect, the "insight" in psychoanalysis is a new and creative experience that produces similar effects to those caused by the listening to a poem or the contemplation of a piece of art, or when—as Davidson states—we feel that one metaphoric expression used in the communication makes us evoke experiences and emotions shared by those who surround us. In the Uruguayan psychoanalytic milieu, T. Bedó (1987) stated how the experience of insight in analysis can be shared between patient and analyst in an "insight à deux."

The metaphoric processes that emerge in analysis are the product of a complex dynamism that includes specific moments that have to be considered, as in a dialectic spiral, in relation to different moments of the analytic process: retrospectively—in the new meanings of previous moments—as well as prospectively, in its possible effects. Besides, these processes are guided by a therapeutic preoccupation and, in this sense, the transformation of impulses, identifications, and unconscious defenses that imply emotional and primary bodily experiences that generate suffering to the patient.

The figurative language of our interpretations evokes not only childhood experiences but also concrete experiences of the present in the life of the patient in his bonds with those who surround him or her. Pichon-Riviére had already referred to the dialectic interrelation between the internal world and the external bonds: "… all unconscious mental life, I mean the domain of the unconscious fantasy, has to be considered as the interaction between the internal objects (internal group) in permanent interrelation with the objects of the external world" (1998, p. 42). This same posture is seen in the developments of Bleger about the situational, dramatic, and dialectic perspective (Bernardi, 2009).

Pablo's analysis was done in the context of his separation from his family of origin and the search of an independent way. At present, childhood experiences are reformulated regarding his bonds at work and especially the relationship with his wife and his own children. And my current vision is also influenced by my experience, the evolution of analytic thought, and my vital situation.

The notion of dynamic field formulated within the frame of phenomenology brought up a dialectic relationship between the intersubjective and the intrapsychic, between subjectivity and objectivity. In this vision, the idea of field itself provided two aspects. It supposed a scenery in which we are immersed like actors in an immediate relationship with the other, but also a scenery-field that may be seen from a more distanced and reflective second look. In this sense, moments of intersubjectivity and of certain symmetries that manifest in regressive syntony and in the use of a figurative language get dialectically entangled with moments of intrapsychic elaboration in analyst and patient, or moments of joint elaboration.

The notions of "second look" and "participant observer" refer precisely to the possibilities of elaboration by the analyst of the different ways of his or her participation. With the notion of second look, the field theory proposed an attitude of putting off-center our own participation and the ways of established unconscious interaction. But currently, this attitude becomes necessary also with regard to the way in which our theories influence our practice, in a moment in which the development of psychoanalysis is characterized by the plurality of theoretical and technical ideas that condition in a different way our interventions with the patient.

In effect, the metaphoric processes present in our interpretations, idiosyncratic to each analytic situation, implicitly condense different "partial theories, models, or schemata" (Sandler, 1983, p. 37) that start processes of integration of the regressive experience of the analysis in the analyst, on a preconscious-conscious level.

About the expression *";A cucha!,"* in my mind converged, in a blurry and partial way, constellations of ideas belonging to different theoretical frames: implicit ideas about countertransference–transference and the mechanism of projective identification, Freud's ideas about the anal stage, and Klein's ideas about separation anxiety. But also the influence of Lacan's thought on my way of listening to the patient's speech and the formulation of open interventions, not saturated of sense. As has been noted (Sandler, 1983),[11] these groups of ideas or implicit mini-models (Leuzinger-Bohleber & Fischmann, 2006) do not look for internal coherence nor do they respect the no-contradiction principle. They emerge spontaneously in the analyst's mind, searching to adjust to the personal characteristics of each patient. This theoretical–clinical integration that is characteristic of the metaphoric processes of analytic communication seems to give the reason to F. Schkolnik's thesis (1985) that invariants exist beyond differences and Wallerstein's (1990, 2005) about the existence of a common clinical base, "a common ground," over which different theoretical approaches of contemporary psychoanalysis converge, transcending the existing differences among them.

However, it is also true that the implicit theoretical–clinical integration in the moments of greatest emotional closeness with our patients opens the space of internal differentiation processes among different alternative hypotheses, which will be available to the "attention" and "floating deliberation" of the analyst (de León, 2010). The participation and answers of the patient resignify (H. Faimberg) previous visions and hypotheses of the analyst, opening a space of reformulation, comparison, and validation of her interventions and of critical evaluation of the effects that the participation of the analyst has on different moments of the process. From the second stage of Pablo's analysis on, new hypotheses emerge. But his warning not to touch certain nuclei of his problems: Is it part of a defensive bastion that protects him from an unmanageable unbalance, or a bastion of the field that implies me somehow?

I consider it useful to hold the phenomenological and dialectic points of view on which the formulation of the field theory supported in Latin America. The phenomenological point of view broadened the possibilities of observation and perception of the analyst, making the considered analytic situation available to the floating attention of the analyst as a whole, following the perspective of Gestalt theory. The dialectic point of view complements the previous one, as it makes us consider as central the reciprocal influence of unconscious character between analyst and patient, the interrelation among different moments of the analytic process in its retrospective and prospective meanings, and, finally, the consideration of the dialectic interrelation among the unconscious aspects and the possibilities of their integration at a preconscious-conscious level (Baranger, 1993a).

If the field theory emerged within the frame of Kleinian thought, later it showed itself to have a more independent approach, which, conserving some aspects of this one, could critically reformulate them according to the phenomena of the analytic experience. In this sense, the psychoanalytic theories about the unconscious must not be considered with an ontological character but as a partial approximation to the particular characteristics of the field, in the bond with a certain patient and in a certain moment of the analytic process. In the same way, the field perspective considered the dialectic interrelation that happens in the session and the analytic process between the unconscious aspects and the possibilities of their integration at a preconscious-conscious level (Baranger, 1993a). The validity of these points of view has caused the field theory to keep its value as a tool of knowledge and clinical investigation of the analytic practice until today.

## Notes

1 Originally published in *Psychoanalytic Inquiry* 33(3) (May 2013) with the title "Field Theory as a Metaphor and Metaphors in the Analytic Field and Process."
2 Madeleine and Willy Baranger, members of the Asociación Psicoanalítica Argentina (Argentinian Psychoanalytic Association), lived in Uruguay between 1954 and 1965, helping to form the Group of the Uruguayan Psychoanalytic Association; they were founders of the *Revista Uruguaya de Psicoanálisis* (*Uruguayan Journal of Psychoanalysis*).
3 For example, the XXI Congress of FEPAL in Mexico in 1995: "Problems of the Transference and Countertransference Field."
4 The reflection about the analytic situation appeared in different thinkers of the time, as Enrique Pichon-Rivière, Heinrich Racker, Luisa Alvarez de Toledo, and Jorge Mom, among others, but we owe to M. and W. Baranger the more exhaustive study of the subject.
5 It is interesting to confirm proximities between this approach and different current experiences in working groups formed by analysts from different regions, who with different methodologies attempt to observe and investigate specific aspects of psychoanalysis based on the study of clinical materials presented by analysts (IPA Berlin Congress and Chicago Congress, FEPAL Congress).
6 "The analytic situation should be formulated by an indefinite and neutral personage—in effect of a person confronted by his or her own—but a situation between who remain unavoidably connected and complementary as long as the situation obtains and is involved in a single dynamic process. In this situation neither member of the couple can be understood without the other" (M. Baranger & W. Baranger, 2008, p. 796).
7 "The true objectivity," says Racker, "is based on a form of inner splitting that trains the analyst to take himself/herself (their own subjectivity or countertransference) as object of continuous observation and analysis. This position also trains him/her to be relatively 'objective' towards the analysand" (Racker, H. [1948/58] 1957a).
8 "La Nature est un temple où de vivants piliers/Laissent parfois sortir de confuses paroles; / L'homme y passe à travers des forêts de symboles / Qui l'observent avec des regards familiers. Comme de longs échos qui de loin se confondent / Dans une ténébreuse et profonde unité,/Vaste comme la nuit et comme la clarté,/Les parfums, les couleurs et les sons se répondent" (Baudelaire, "Correspondances") (L. Álvarez de Toledo, 1954[1996], p. 299).
9 This polarity between situation and process is present in the psychoanalytic reflection of different schools, which stress one of these aspects or the other. B. Joseph (1985), for example, from a Kleinian perspective, defines essential aspects of transference understood as total situation. From another theoretical posture, D. Stern (2004) analyzes the characteristics of "present moments" of the analytic relationship that show meaningful

changes in the relating patterns. The already-mentioned perspective of Haideé Faimberg, although it studies specific moments of analysis, also studies its effects in the process development. Thoma and Kachele (1989) referred in their interactive model of the analytic process to "thematic nodal issues" or "interactive foci" that happen one after the other along the analysis.

10 Different authors have stated that the analyst's mind operates with similar mechanisms to those described by Freud in relation to the dream work, as shown Ferro and Cevitarese in this número. W. Bucci (2001), in her theory of multiple codes, has shown how the interpretative activity allows to integrate the analogic subsymbolic, emotional, and bodily levels with the discrete, symbolic elements of image and word. The image or sequences of those which are characteristic of dreams and the expressions of the analyst or patient appear as intermediate nexus that allow integrating emotional and bodily experiences, several times split in the process of symbolization achieved by the access to the word.

11 Sandler (1983) differentiated the public, official, or explicit theories, exposed in the scientific exchange with colleagues, from the theories used in the individual clinical practice, which he called private theories or implicit theories. This perspective has given origin to different contributions. Latin American thinkers also marked differences between the way in which theory works in the psychoanalytic session and in the field of scientific discussion with colleagues, such as Pichon-Rivière (1998), Liberman (1970), and Bleger (1969). Bleger was one of the first who, in the Río de la Plata, talked about implicit theory, noted that the "theory developed and made explicit does not always coincide with the implicit theory in practice" (288). He also notes "the divergencies between psychoanalytic theory and implicit theory [in practice], not completely formulated nor assimilated—this last one—in the theoretical body of psychoanalysis" (p. 289).

# 16

# OTHER FIELDS WITHIN
# THE ANALYTIC FIELD[1]

*Claudio Neri*

The main point of this chapter is the recognition that the patient doesn't create a field only with the analyst but also with other important people, with his workplace, and with some Self-Objects. The analyst may perceive how the patient's moods, feelings, and self-esteem change when entering each of these different fields. The analytic field created between the analyst and the patient is an important tool, a sort of Geiger counter, through which the analyst may detect the presence and the activity of these other fields. Isabel's brief case history illustrates a useful approach to deal with the negative effects of a very disturbing and confusing field she established with the company she worked for.

An original "field theory" has been developed in Italy, and many colleagues have contributed to this collective intellectual achievement. I will mention only a few here: Corrao, Ferro, and Gaburri, and in 1994, the Società Psicoanalitica Italiana dedicated its X Congress to "The Transformations in the Analytical Field."

The field theory that was elaborated by Italian psychoanalysts differs from that of Madeleine and Willy Baranger in many ways. I will briefly mention only three here. First, in Italy the field theory was connected to Bion's Alpha function and the idea of transformation of emotions in narration and vice versa (Emotions ⇔ Narrations). Second, the field was not considered to be a product of exchange of projective identifications between the patient and analyst, and its existence was put into a relationship with the presence and pressure of "thoughts without thinkers" that can be taken on board and thought through by both the analyst and the patient. And, finally, the most important rules for the analyst—during the session—are the maintenance of a mental setup that is characterized by "negative capacity," and the practice of "unsaturated interpretation."

## Psychoanalysis and Group Psychotherapy

I used field theory in my practice as a group psychotherapist. In 1988, at Didier Anzieu's invitation, I presented a paper on the difference between field theory and transference theory in Paris at the historical Salpêtrière auditorium, the hospital where Freud had followed Charcot's lessons. In my opinion, this conceptual tool is of critical importance in group psychotherapy work.

Afterwards, I tried to use field theory in the traditional psychoanalytic setting. In this case, however, I came up against great difficulty. It was immediately clear for me that not only a group but also the "analyst–patient couple" produce and are immersed in a field; however, when I tried to use this theory extensively in psychoanalytical sessions, I was often dealing with the impression that it was not quite the right choice. There certainly were some advantages compared to the use of the relationship and transference concepts. For example, I managed to obtain an overall picture of the situation more easily. I was also more inclined to give a value to everything that in the sessions was non-verbal. However, the dialogue and the contact between the patient and me lost some spontaneity. In the back of my mind, the unpleasant perception that something was not working in the right way kept coming out. Discouraged, I sometimes thought about letting it drop. It could have been as in music: symphonies are for big orchestras, sonatas for two or four musicians.

## Other Fields That Influence the Patient

I don't wish to concentrate all the attention on the theme of the difference between the group setting and the psychoanalytic setting. Instead, I would like to speak about the first clinical circumstance when I used "something similar to field theory" with a patient and felt that it was something appropriate and effective. It happened when I put an idea I had to the test. What was important to pay attention to was not only the field that was established between the patient and me, but also, and above all, the "shadow of other fields" that the patient set up with other people with his self-objects, both positive and negative. The idea of using the field theory in this way came from the sudden appearance of a memory of the life of a comic-strip character, Superman.

Superman was different from other superheroes such as Spiderman, Batman, and Robin, for one main reason. These latter heroes were normal people who became superheroes when they took on a secondary identity; Superman's real identity was that of being someone from another planet. He was born on the planet Krypton and possessed all the abilities and powers of a Krypton inhabitant. When this planet was on the point of exploding, his parents put him into a spaceship and sent him to Earth. Then, after the explosion, some fragments of the planet Krypton struck Earth. I will now come to the key point. When Superman, the superhero, enters a room or an area where there is also a sliver of Kryptonite, he becomes weak, feels ill, and loses all his powers.

Some of my patients have to face up to a similar catastrophic transformation that occurs not only in the presence of their mothers but also when they perceive something that makes them remember even the most distant existences of their mother. They become confused, afraid, exhausted as if they were under the effects of the powerful rays of the "kryptonite minds of the mothers." Their faces would become dull, and they would become almost unapproachable for me (and for anyone else) during the time that they found themselves under the influence of the toxic mind-of-the-mother field. Thinking about these patients to myself, I realized that

I was using the expression "field created by the mother's mind." Thus, I was using the term and the concept of field to refer to something with which the patient had come into contact, I wasn't using it instead—which usually happens—to indicate something that was between myself and the patient, between the analyst and the patient.

## Field and Non-Places

The successive step in my process of reflecting was to recall other conditions in which a patient was under the influence of a "field" that was not produced by an imaginary figure (such as the "toxic mother") but by a social situation—for example, a field that corresponded to working in a certain company. The summary of my analytical work with Isabel illustrates this situation and explains which clinical approach I honed to deal with the problem.

I will mention a few facts. Six months after beginning the second part of her analysis, Isabel had begun to speak at length about a strong disturbance she felt regarding anything to do with work. I listened with great interest. For Isabel, her company was not an object that was totally differentiated from her. It was something that she was submerged in and, at the same time, something that pervasively occupied almost her whole life and thoughts.

At this part of the analysis, I also saw some changes that concerned the "analytical field." I noticed difficulties on both our parts in not being able to perceive personal feelings. It was as if the "analytic field" was occupied by a silent and invisible force that was restraining and imprisoning it. Everything was flat and painfully the same, hour after hour, day after day. The heavy atmosphere in Prague after the occupation by Soviet tanks that had retreated to the outskirts of the city came to mind.

For Isabel, what did the company world correspond to? Who were the tanks? Her father? Her mother? The family? Had her life been divided into two by a traumatic break that had left a feeling of emptiness? For the moment, I left these questions in the background. I wanted to concentrate on that which seemed to present a more pressing need, the sharing of Isabel's concrete daily life. So I took the problem of living the company as a very serious problem indeed. I considered it to be a real situation. However, I didn't take it at face value, but rather as something that Isabel didn't really know, even though she did say that she knew about it, and that—in a conventional and factual way—Isabel did know. At the beginning, the difficulties and uneasiness that she felt appeared, both to me and to her, comparable to the experiences, the psychic processes, and the changes that a person who has entered into an organized group has to face (in Isabel's case, the company-group).

In analysis, speaking about the "social field" of the company and its dynamics, little by little, we managed to see the existence of a "psychological field" that corresponded to the "social field" only in part. This "psychological field," which was characterized by something hazy and uncertain and waves of engulfing and discharging spurts, was fundamentally not suitable for taking on board any autonomous form of intellectual and affective life of an individual. This first knowledge of the nature of the "psychological-company field" didn't come about through a representation but through a sharing that occurred because my attentive and interested listening to her long accounts was like accompanying her to her place of work.

After a few months, the picture changed once more. Loneliness, disorientation, the lack of a guide, and affective proximity for which Isabel had suffered during her infancy appeared with great force. Isabel didn't have anyone who was really close to her. Above all, she was lacking someone who could have given her some confirmation of being right about her perceptions. Immediately after the emergence of these painful memories and experiences, two positive things happened to her. The first was her discovery of a talent for writing short stories. She read me some during the sessions. The first one she read was about a little girl who comes out of school and sees the mother chatting among the other mothers. Listening to her, I thought that she could finally see herself with her mother. I also thought about some changes I had noticed in the analytical field. It was no longer rigid and immobile. On the contrary, it was possible to see the slight presence of a "narrative field" inside it—that is, a place in which the experiences, sensations, and feelings are connected to words, scenes, and a narrating voice.

The second event related to the fact that Isabel, who had recognized the characteristics of the "company field," was then able to recognize the characteristics of her own feelings and experiences that were connected to the company. This, in turn, had freed her from her immobility and impotence. Soon after, Isabel was also able to find a practical solution to her problems at work.

## Conclusion

In presenting the second part of Isabel's analysis, I spoke about three different fields. The first one is the field of the company world; it is very concrete and, simultaneously, a very elusive field. At the beginning, when Isabel was under the influence of this field, she wasn't able to distinguish herself and her moods from the atmosphere and tension that were present in this field. Isabel also felt very unhappy and lonely. In Isabel's company-field, there were no feelings besides persecution and uneasiness. All the other feelings had either been ejected or inhibited. Later on, Isabel compared being in this field to "being in a concentration camp." It is also possible to establish an analogy between Isabel's company-field and a labyrinth—first, because there were no possibilities of reaching a sense of orientation, and second, because the people in this field appear and feel that they are like monsters and that other people are like monsters, like a Minotaur.

The narrative field is much less concrete and more livable than the company-field. It is a transformation of the company-field. This transformation takes place when the company-field becomes the subject of a repeated, friendly, and lively conversation between the patient and the analyst. The possibility of speaking in analysis besides the one just mentioned, the company-field also has other effects. First of all, the company-field can be seen through not just one position (being immersed in it), but from many vertices, as many as the different narratives. Second, being the issue of a human conversation, the company-field becomes a little bit more humane. Finally, the narrative field is full of images and feelings; some of these feelings may migrate and inhabit the company-field that was previously just a wasteland, a gulag.

The analytic field is governed by the rules of the analytic setting. Its characteristics are elements such as intimacy, directness, absence of intrusiveness from the analyst, and the continuity of the sessions with predetermined phases of suspension. The analytical field is not only a frame or structure. It is also a powerful detecting apparatus, a Geiger counter. The analyst may perceive the quality of other fields (e.g., the company-field, the mother-mind field, etc.), through either perturbations of the analytic field, or through non-verbal, extra-verbal, ultra-verbal, a communication from the patient such as body posture, facial expressions, unexpected breaks in the narration of a dream. It is as if a dream editor had introduced a cut and then continued with very different characters and feelings. Later on, the patient is able to glimpse the other fields from the secure base of the analytic field. Thus, he can begin talking about these fields, which in this way can be shared with the analyst and become objects of narrations.

## Note

1 Originally published in *Psychoanalytic Inquiry* 33(3) (May 2013) with the title "Isabel: Social Field, Psychological Field and Narrative Field." It was also presented to the panel "The Field Theory" at the IPA Congress (Mexico City, 5 August 2011).

# 17

# THE ANALYTIC RELATIONSHIP IN FIELD THEORY[1]

*Elsa Rappoport de Aisemberg*

I focus my presentation on the patient–analyst relationship within the frame of contemporary psychoanalysis. In order to do so, I take the Freudian origins of transference as a starting point, then move on to the evolution of the concept of counter-transference, and finally reach the essential point: the theory of the analytical field, such as it was described by Willy and Madeleine Baranger, including my own perspective of the subject.

The unconscious fantasy, common to both the patient and the analyst, the unconscious to unconscious communication, the relationship from the intrapsychic toward intersubjectivity and back, as well as neutrality, are all crucial concepts in the presentation, which ends with a clinical vignette in which my ideas are illustrated.

## Introduction

I celebrate that the Mexico Congress has stimulated us to think about the patient–analyst relationship, as we understand it today in contemporary psychoanalysis. First of all, why speak of a theory of the analytical field and of a contemporary psychoanalysis?

I think that when Freud created our discipline based on the concepts of the unconscious, infantile sexuality, Oedipus, drives, and transference, he focused on the patient's problematic. With the vicissitudes of clinical work, there appeared difficulties that gave rise, among others, to the notion of counter-transference. In 1910 at the Nuremberg Congress, he referred to it as an obstacle to the cure, the analyst's blind spot, the need of the analyst to be under analysis present in the demand to set up the law or order over the young analysts' erotic counter-transference so as to bar their acting out. The formulation of the abstinence law and that of neutrality belong to the same problematic.

After forty years of silence on this subject, only interrupted by Ferenczi's contributions, at the end of the 1940s and beginning of the 1950s there were Paula Heimann's conceptualizations in London and Enrique Racker's in Buenos Aires introducing another dimension: counter-transference can be an obstacle, but it can also be a tool for the understanding of preverbal, sensorial elements previous to the word.

In a third stage, we have broader counter-transference or the use of the analyst's mind, which was started in 1961–1962 by the works of Willy and Madeleine Baranger on the analytical field. Later, other concepts were added: de M'Uzan's Chimera, Bion's *reverie*, Winnicott's, Bollas's, Green's contributions, and César and Sara Botella's statements on regredience, figurability, and the "work by double" in the session. We should also add Antonino Ferro's interesting developments with his particular conception of the analytical field.

As Madeleine Baranger clearly stated in her presentation in Athens in 2010, all this speaks of an evolution in our discipline. Science develops by overcoming crises and inevitable obstacles that must be transformed into new knowledge, as Freud taught us with his works. The new hypotheses we build based on our clinical work must be articulated with Freudian metapsychology to maintain psychoanalytical status.

Moreover, the development and extension of our clinical work concerning the approach to narcissistic and non-neurotic functioning, added to classical psychoneuroses, has led us to an extension of our theories to account for the diversity of psychic functionings; this is what we call contemporary psychoanalysis.

## The Field Theory

Willy and Madeleine Baranger, both committed researchers into clinical work, thought their praxis articulating it with ideas from Gestalt psychology, from Merleau-Ponty's phenomenology, and from other psychoanalysts such as Racker and Heimann, which led them to formulate in 1961–1962 the first model of the analytical field, understood as a product of projective identifications between patient and analyst. In this manner, they generated a hypothesis lying between the clinical work and metapsychology, coherent with their concern, shared by our analytical world, about the gap between clinical work and theory.

In a later paper, they added the idea of an encounter between two psyches generating a common basic unconscious fantasy, in the manner Bion describes for groups. To do so, they used the concept of unconscious fantasy put forward by Susan Isaacs (1952), another Kleinian author who thinks that fantasies are the primary content of unconscious psychic processes, first experienced as sensations, which later take up the form of plastic images and scenes. They refer primitively to the body and represent the instinctive movements of the libido and of destruction, oriented toward the objects.

In another theoretical model, in Freudian semantics, its equivalent could be the purposive-idea (*Zielvorstellung*), as Laplanche and Pontalis (1967) point out. We should bear in mind that representation is the ideational component of the drive, while affect refers to quantity.

In 2004 Madeleine Baranger, after having widened her theoretical references, reformulated the concept of analytical field as a structure created between a patient and an analyst in the analytical situation—a third one, which has both a mythic and a symbolic dimension. That is to say, these repetitions in the analytical field, which have a mythic dimension, can achieve symbolic transformation in the interplay of the analytical situation.

I think that the patient–analyst encounter, which has something of the original encounter with the primary object or other significant objects, is what the patient transfers to the analyst and, in turn, gives rise to the therapist's listening, who brings into play his own counter-transference.

Instead, the symbolic level is the power of the setting, surely asymmetric, and of the interpretation that works as a third one that transforms the emotional experience shared by patient and analyst into what Green calls analytical object and what Ogden calls the analytical third one, thus paving the way for the construction of a representation in the analyst's mind, the origin of his intervention on transference.

## From the Intrapsychic to Intersubjectivity

It is important to highlight that in this model of the theory of the field, to which I fully adhere, there is circulation from the intrapsychic to intersubjectivity and back, whereas in the intersubjective model, to my mind, there is a predominance of interaction rather than an encounter between two subjects with their unconscious, their drives, and their unconscious fantasies, as both Barangers state.

This leads me to remark on another similar theme, as follows.

## Unconscious to Unconscious Communication

As Freud already wrote in his metaphor of the telephone in 1912, the physician "must turn his own unconscious like a receptive organ towards the transmitting unconscious of the patient. He must adjust himself to the patient as a telephone receiver is adjusted to the transmitting microphone" (1912b, *SE*, 12, pp. 115–116). The field theory and related formulations as well: de M'Uzan's chimera, Bion's *reverie,* and Botellas' figurability try to account for the communication from unconscious to unconscious, which would give rise to "perceived" experiences without being aware of it, which would function as the day's residues that stimulate the use of the analyst's mind and that of the analysand. Thus I think the corporal perception of the relationship with the object is the origin of the unconscious to unconscious communication, which certainly must be transformed by the analyst. who in these cases works as an "auxiliary," lending her or his mental capacity as M. de M'Uzan pointed out in 1976, since the patient is not yet able to turn it into words or representations. In addition, this helps us to understand figurability or the analyst's dreams aroused by the patient's clinical material as a complementary remembrance activity in the analytical field.

## On Neutrality

I believe that we should not give up the aspiration for asepsis and neutrality even though we know it is impossible to reach. It is one of our many paradoxes, as Willy

Baranger pointed out in 1957 in his work on "Interpretation and Ideology," since the analyst as a person and his or her presence inevitably act upon the patient, giving rise to diverse transferences, among others, idealized transference, which has to be deconstructed at one point during the analytical process to attain a good outcome. However, in the beginning, such transference favors the installation of the treatment, especially when there is a predominance of non-neurotic functioning.

I believe that we as analysts are involved in our task all the time. To achieve our work—aware of the asymmetry in the setting—we have to let ourselves be partly affectively and sensorially involved in the patient's unconscious messages, besides the verbal listening. We must admit we are not entomologists, but it is also true that we have to understand, self-analyze, and resolve those experiences belonging to the transference-countertransference field and then decide whether to include them in our interpretative or constructive approach. This view is accepted by some colleagues and questioned by others, depending on their theoretical framework as well as their scientific or personal ideology.

This affective involvement has advantages and problems. One advantage is that it helps to understand the patient, true within the limits of our own insight. The problems lie in the blind spots shared by patient and analyst, what the Barangers call bastions, which demand a second gaze, either self-analysis or supervision. That is to say, in the transference-countertransference field that inevitably is created between patient and analyst, we oscillate between empathy and the need of a second gaze.

## María

I shall illustrate my ideas with a clinical vignette.

It deals with María, a patient who had analysis on the couch four times a week during six years. When she first came to see me, she was a young woman, 35 years old, very pretty and elegant, who produced a great aesthetic impact. She was married and had two children and a high income. She was a psychologist but not happy with her profession; she wanted to become a writer. She had tried to start writing but had difficulties.

She needed me to help her to overcome the inhibitions that prevented her from fulfilling her wish; in addition, she brought a passionate story. The object of her love was a close friend of the couple, also married and with children, who was close affectively and also geographically. On the other hand, or "on the same hand," her husband was a very jealous man, a little paranoid, who for rational reasons kept a gun in their house.

María let me know about her intense and urgent sexual desire for this friend as well as his desire for her and, at the same time, the image of a husband who noticed that something was going on and voiced it through scenes of violent jealousy or falling ill.

I had the intuition that a situation out of Greek tragedy might burst out because María was ready to break up her marriage, her friendship with her friend's wife, the friendship between their children, and her financially comfortable position by defying a jealous husband with a gun. On a counter-transference level I was very worried; I had to put aside—the analysis of counter-transference and ideologies aims at that—my bourgeois ideology. I told myself: this married woman, with children, with an attractive and well-off husband is ready to sweep all this away in order to fulfill her passion! I had to elaborate all this to maintain certain analytical neutrality.

If I respected the rhythm set by her desire and her passion, we were approaching an atmosphere of Greek tragedy. She described with anxiety scenes in which she and her friend exhibited their erotic desire before the husband and how he reacted with violence to this provocation. If I stopped her, leading her to reflection, María had serious psychosomatic episodes. She had an accident with the car and also an infectious clinical picture lasting several months. Death anguish was floating in the air. Either she would destroy herself or she would be destroyed by her jealous husband.

Like María, I had to break with my own values, my ideas of a bourgeois woman, to accompany her in her growth so that she might find the way to realize her forbidden erotic desire without having to exhibit them before her husband, seeking punishment. She was able to do so; she succeeded in separating from her husband on friendly terms, taking care of the relationship with the children. She began to work to earn her living in something connected with writing and creation, and at the same time, she began to write novels.

During her analytical process, we went through constructions and histories about a very poor childhood when María used to share the bedroom with her brother, with incestuous, dangerous plays that were acted in the present passionate story. We also examined her guilt because of her present comfortable life in contrast with the poverty of her parents' home and also the fact that she was a survivor of a group of friends who had died during the years of state terrorism in Argentina.

Death runs through María's history, and she put my psychoanalyst's ethical attitude to a test—in the end with a good outcome for the shared task. I think that Oedipal conflicts in their dimensions of erotic and destructive desires and of prohibition and guilty feelings were dramatized in the analytical field constructed between the patient I call María and myself. The elaboration of such conflict, where I was able to rescue my own feelings and ideas to understand the patient's truth, contributed to constructing a new way out of her Oedipal drama.

## In Conclusion

Nowadays, we deal not only with what the patient repeats in the transference dimension, the repressed unconscious derivates, but also with what is dramatized in the patient–analyst relationship, and this enables us to create something new that has no meaning yet, the expressions of the proper or genuine unconscious.

## Note

1 Originally published in *Psychoanalytic Inquiry* 33(3) (May 2013) with the title "The Theory of the Analytical Field."

# BIBLIOGRAPHY

Aeschylus (1955). *Aeschyli septem quae supersunt tragoediae.* Recensuit Gilbertus Murray. Oxford, UK: Oxford University Press.

Ahumada, J. L. (1994). Interpretation and creationism. *International Journal of Psychoanalysis* 75: 695–707.

Aisemberg, E. R. (2008). The shadow of heritage in contemporary psychoanalysis. *EPF Bulletin* 62: 93–103.

Aisemberg, E. R. (2010). Psychosomatic conditions in contemporary psychoanalysis. In M. Aisenstein & E. R. Aisemberg (eds), *Psychosomatics Today. A Psychoanalytic Perspective.* London: Karnac.

Aleksandrowicz, D. R. (1962). The meaning of metaphor. *Bulletin of the Menninger Clinic* 26: 92–101.

Alizade, M. (2002). El rigor y el encuadre interno. *Revista Uruguaya de Psicoanálisis* 96: 13–16.

Alvarez de Toledo, L. (1954). El análisis del "asociar," del "interpretar" y de las "palabras." *Rev. de Psicoanálisis* 11 (3): 269–275. [También publicado como: The analysis of "associating," "interpreting" and "words."] *International Journal Psycho-Anal.* 77, Part 2 (1996): 291–318.

Angelino, L. (2005). Note sul dialogo tra Merleau-Ponty e Melanie Klein. [Some notes concerning the dialogue between Merleau-Ponty and Melanie Klein.] *Chiasmi International* 6: 369–381.

Aragno, A. (2009). Meaning's vessel: A metapsychological understanding of metaphor. *Psychoanalytic Inquiry* 29: 3–47.

Aristotle (1927). *The Poetics.* Trans. W. Hamilton Fyfe Loeb edition. Cambridge, MA: Harvard University Press.

Arlow, J. (1969 )Unconscious fantasy and disturbances of conscious experience. *Psychoanalytic Quarterly* 38: 1–27.

Arlow, J. (1977). Affects and the psychoanalytic situation. *International Journal of Psychoanalysis* 58: 157–170.

Arlow, J. (1979). Metaphor and the psychoanalytic situation. *Psychoanalytic Quarterly* 48: 363–85.

Aron, L. (1996). *A Meeting of Minds: Mutuality in Psychoanalysis.* Hillsdale, NJ: The Analytic Press.

Augé, M. (1992). *Non-lieux, Paris, Seuil, La librairie du XXIème siècle.* [Non-Places, An Introduction to an Anthropology of Supermodernity.] London: Verso, 1995.

Aulagnier, P. (1975). *The Violence of Interpretation: From Pictogram to Statement.* A. Sheridan, trans. Hove: Brunner-Routledge, 2001.

Baranger, M. (1992). La mente del analista: de la escucha a la interpretación. *Revista de Psicoanálisis* 49: 223–236. [Also published as Baranger, M. (1993). The mind of the analyst: From listening to interpretation. *International Journal of Psychoanalysis* 74: 15–24.]

Baranger, M. (1993a). The mind of the analyst: From listening to interpretation. *International Journal of Psychoanalysis* 74: 15–24.

Baranger, M. (1993b). Response. *International Journal of Psychoanalysis* 74: 1159–1162.

Baranger, M. (2004). La teoría del campo. In S. Lewkoicz, *El otro en la trama intersubjetiva*, Lugar-APA, Buenos Aires. [También en *Verdad, realidad y el psicoanalista: Contribuciones latinoamericanas al psicoanálisis*, Asociación Psicoanalítica Internacional, Londres, 2005.]

Baranger, M. (2005). Field theory. In S. Lewkowicz & S. Flechner ( eds), *Truth, Reality and the Psychoanalyst: Latin American Contributions to Psychoanalysis*, pp. 49–71. London: International Psychoanalytical Association.

Baranger, M. (2008). The analytic situation as a dynamic field. *International Journal of Psychoanalysis* 89 (4): 795–826

Baranger, M. (2009). *The Work of Confluence: Listening and Interpretation in the Psychoanalytic Field*. London: Karnac.

Baranger, M. & Baranger, W. (1961–1962a). La situación analítica como campo dinámico. *Revista Uruguaya de Psicoanálisis* IV, nº 1, 1961–62: 3–54. Reprint as Baranger, M. and Baranger, W. (2008). The analytic situation as a dynamic field. *International Journal of Psychoanalysis* 89 (4): 795–826.

Baranger, W. & Baranger, M. (1961–1962b). *Problemas del campo psicoanalítico* .Buenos Aires: Kargieman, 1969.

Baranger, M. & Baranger, W. (1964). Insight in the analytic situation. In M. Baranger & W. Baranger *The Work of Confluence: Listening and Interpreting in the Psychoanalytic Field* (2009). London: Karnac, pp. 1–15.

Baranger, M. & Baranger, W. (2008). The analytic situation as a dynamic field. *International Journal of Psychoanalysis* 89: 795–826.

Baranger, M. & Baranger, W. (2009). *The Work of Confluence: Listening and Interpreting in the Psychoanalytic Field* (ed. L. Glocer Fiorini). London: Karnac.

Baranger, M., Baranger, W. & Mom, J. M. (1978). Patología de la transferencia y contratransferencia en el psicoanálisis actual; el campo perverso. [Pathology of transference and countertransference in present-day psychoanalysis: The perverse field.] *Revista de Psicoanálisis* 35: 1101–1106.

Baranger, M., Baranger, W. & Mom, J. M. (1982). Proceso y no proceso en el trabajo analítico. *Rev Psicoaná* l 39: 527–549.

Baranger, M., Baranger, W. & Mom, J. M. (1983). Process and non-process in analytic work. *International Journal of Psychoanalysis* 64: 1–15.

Baranger, W. (1954). Tentativa de aproximación al psicoanálisis de las ideologías filosóficas. [A tentative approach to the psychoanalysis of philosophical ideologies.] *Revista de Psicoanálisis* 11: 479–505.

Baranger, W. (1957). Interpretación e ideología. (Sobre la regla de abstención ideológica.) [Interpretation and ideology. (About the rule of ideological abstinence.)] In *Problemas del campo psicoanalítico*. Kargieman, Buenos Aires, 1969, pp. 103–108.

Baranger, W. (1958). The ego and the function of ideology. *International Journal of Psychoanalysis* 39: 191–195. (Reprinted in Baranger, M. & Baranger, W. (2009), pp. 217–235)

Baranger, W. (1959). Métodos de objetivación en la investigación psicoanalítica. *Rev Urug Psicoanálisis* 3 (1): 26–41.

Baranger, W. (1979a). Proceso en espiral' y campo dinámico. *Rev Urug Psicoaná* l 59: 17–32.

Baranger, W. (1979b). *Spiral Process and the Dynamic Field*. In M. Baranger & W. Baranger (2009), pp. 45–61.

Baranger, W. (1992). De la necesaria imprecisión en la nosografía psicoanalítica. [On the necessary imprecision of psychoanalytic psychopathology.] *Revista de Psicoanálisis—1992 Número Especial Internacional* [1992 Special International Issue], pp. 83–97.

Baranger, W. & Baranger, M. (1969). *Problemas del campo psicoanalítico*. [Problems of the psychoanalytic field.] Buenos Aires: Kargieman.

Baranger, W. & Baranger, M. (1978). Patologia de la transferencia y controtransferencia en el psicoanàlisis actual: El campo perverso. *Revista de Psicoanálisis* 35: 1101.

Barcelona, A. (2000). The cognitive theory of metaphor and metonymy. In A. Barcelona (ed.), *Metaphor and Metonymy at the Crossroads* (pp. 1–30). New York: Mouton de Gruyter.

Barnett, A. J. (2008). Transformations in treatment: Sublimatory implications of an interdisciplinary hypothesis on the metaphoric processing of emotional experience. *Psychoanalytic Review* 95 (1): 79–106.

Barnett, A. & Katz, M. (2005). Exploring emotional memory: Psychoanalytic perspectives. *Psychoanalytic Inquiry* 25.

Barnett, A. J. & Katz, M. (eds) (2005). Analytic positions in the exploration of emotional memory. *Psychoanalytic Inquiry* 25: 409–576.

Barnett, A. J. & Katz, M. (eds) (2009). Metaphoric processes in psychoanalytic treatment. *Psychoanalytic Inquiry* 29: 1–97.

Beardsley, M. C. (1967, 1972). Metaphor. In P. Edwards (ed.), *The Encyclopedia of Philosophy,*. New York: Macmillan, pp. 284–289.

Bedó, T. (1987). Acerca del concepto psicoanalítico de insight. *Revista Uruguaya de Psicoanálisis* 22.

Beistegui de, M. (2010). Per un'estetica della metafora. In D. Ferrari & P. Godani (eds) *La sartoria di Proust*. Pisa: Edizioni ETS.

Benseler, G. E. & Kägi, A. (1931). *Griechisch–deutsches Schulwörterbuch*. Leipzig: Teubner.

Berlin, I. (1951). *The Hedgehog and the Fox: An Essay on Tolstoy's View of History*. New York: Simon and Schuster.

Berlin, I. (2001). *Dos conceptos de libertad y otros escritos*. [Two concepts of liberty and other writings.] Madrid: Alianza Editorial, 2005.

Bernardi, R. (2009). Qué metapsicología necesitamos? Vigencia de Bleger. *Revista Uruguaya de Psicoanálisis,* p. 108.

Bernardi, R. et al. (1997) Cambios de la interpretación entre 1960 y 1990 en el psicoanálisis uruguayo. *Revista Uruguaya de Psicoanálisis*, 84–85: 89–102.

Bernardi, R. & de León, B. (1993). Does our self-analysis take into consideration our assumptions. In J. W. Barron (ed.), *Self-Analysis: Critical Inquiries, Personal Visions*. Hillsdale, NJ: The Analytic Press.

Bernardi, B de L. (1999). Un modo de pensar la clínica: Vigencia y perspectivas del enfoque de W. & M. Baranger. In *Volviendo a pensar con Willy y Madeleine Baranger,* comp. L. Kancyper, Lumen, Buenos Aires.

Bessie, A. (2006). *Metaphor as Generative Process: An Exploratory Study of Freshman Writers in Process*. Unpublished thesis at San Francisco State University, San Francisco.

Beuchot, M. (1997). *Tratado de hermenéutica analógica*, 4th edn. [Treatise of analogical hermeneutics.] Mexico City: UNAM/Itaca, 2005.

Beuchot, M. (1998). Aristóteles y la escolástica en Freud a través de Brentano. [Aristotle and scholastics in Freud through Brentano.] *Espíritu* 47/118: 161–168.

Beuchot, M. (2003a). *Hermenéutica analógica y del umbral*. [Analogical and threshold hermeneutics.] Salamanca, Spain: Editorial San Esteban.

Beuchot, M. (2003b). *El ser y la poesía. El entrecruce del discurso metafísico y el discurso poético*. [Being and poetry: The intersection of metaphysical discourse and poetical discourse.] Mexico City: Universidad Iberoamericana.

Beuchot, M. (2010). *Hermenéutica analógica, símbolo y ontología*. [Analogical hermeneutics, symbol, and ontology.] Toluca, Mexico: Universidad Nacional Autónoma de México.

Bezoari, M. & Ferro, A. (1991). From a play between "parts" to transformations in the couple: psychoanalysis in a bipersonal field. In L. Nissim Momigliano & A. Robutti (eds), *Shared Experience: The Psychoanalytic Dialogue*. London: Karnac, 1992, pp. 43–65.

Bezoari, M. & Ferro, A. (1997). The dream within a field theory: Functional aggregates and narrations. *Journal of Melanie Klein and Objects Relations* 17 (2): 333–348, 1999.

Bibring, E. (1940). The development and problems of the theory of instincts. *International Journal of Psychoanalysis* 21: 102–131.

Bion, W. R. (1948). Experiences in groups: I. In *Experiences in Groups and Other Papers*. London: Tavistock, 1961, pp. 27–137.

Bion, W. R. (1952). Re-View: Group dynamics. In W. R. Bion (1961), *Experiences in Groups and Other Papers*. London: Tavistock, 1968, pp. 139–191.

Bion, W. R. (1957). Differentiation of the psychotic from the non-psychotic personalities. *International Journal of Psychoanalysis* 38: 266–275.

Bion, W. R. (1959). Attacks on linking. *International Journal of Psychoanalysis* 40: 308–315.

Bion, W. R. (1962a). *Learning from Experience*. London: Karnac.

Bion, W. R. (1962b). The psycho-analytic study of thinking. *International Journal of Psychoanalysis* 43: 306–310.

Bion, W. R. (1965). *Transformations*. London: Karnac.

Bion, W. R. (1966): *Learning from Experience*. London: Karnac.

Bion, W. R. (1970). *Attention and Interpretation*. London: Tavistock.

Bion, W. R. (1977). *A Memoir of the Future. Book 2: The Past Presented*. London: Karnac, pp. 219–426.

Bion, W. R. (1989). *Elements of Psycho-Analysis*. London: Karnac.

Bion, W. R. (1991). *A Memoir of the Future*. London: Karnac.

Bion, W. R. (1992). *Cogitations*. London: Karnac.

Bion, W. R. (1995a). *Attention and Interpretation*. Northvale, NJ: Jason Aronson.

Bion, W. R. (1995b). *Elements of Psychoanalysis*. Northvale, NJ: Jason Aronson.

Bion, W. R. (1998). *Learning From Experience*. Northvale, NJ: Jason Aronson.

Birksted-Breen, D. (2003). Time and the après-coup. *The International Journal of Psychoanalysis* 84: 1501–1515.

Black, M. (1962) *Models and Metaphors* Ithaca, NY: Cornell University Press

Blass, R. & Carmeli, Z. (2007). The case against neuropsychoanalysis: On fallacies underlying psychoanalysis' latest scientific trend and its negative impact on psychoanalytic discourse. *International Journal of Psychoanalysis* 88: 19–40.

Blatt, S. J. (1990). The Rorschach: A test of perception or an evaluation of representation. *Journal of Personality Assessment* 54: 236–251.

Blatt, S. J., Bers, S. A. & Schaffer, C. E. (1993). *The Assessment of Self-Descriptions*. Unpublished manual, Yale University, New Haven, CT.

Bleger, J. (1966). Psychoanalysis of the psychoanalytic frame. *International Journal of Psychoanalysis* 48: 511–519.

Bleger, J. (1967a). *Simbiosis y ambigüedad*. [Symbiosis and ambiguity.] Buenos Aires: Paidós.

Bleger, J. (1967b). *Symbiosis and Ambiguity: The Psychoanalysis of Very Early Development*. Trollope, C., trans. London: Free Association Books, 1990.

Bleger, J. (1969). Teoría y práctica en psicoanálisis. La praxis psicoanalítica. *Revista Uruguaya de Psicoanálisis* XI: 287–303.

Bleger, J. (1977). The group as institution and within institutions. *International Journal of Therapeutic Communities* 10: 109–115.

Blum, H. (1991). Affect theory and the theory of technique. *Journal of the American Psychoanalytic Association* 39S: 265–289.

Bodde, D. (1953). Harmony and conflict in Chinese philosophy. In *Studies in Chinese Thought.* Ed. A. F. Wright. Chicago, IL: University of Chicago Press, Midway reprint, 1976.

Bollas, C. (1987). *The Shadow of the Object.* London: Free Association Books.

Borbely, A. F. (1987). Towards a temporal theory of the mind. *Psychoanalysis and Contemporary Thought* 10: 459–487.

Borbely, A. F. (1998). A psychoanalytic concept of metaphor. *International Journal of Psychoanalysis* 79: 923–936.

Borbely, A. F. (2004). Toward a psychodynamic understanding of metaphor and metonymy: Their role in awareness and defense. *Metaphor and Symbol* 19 (2): 91–114.

Borbely, A. F. (2008). Metaphor and psychoanalysis. In R. Gibbs (ed.) *The Cambridge Handbook of Metaphor and Thought.* New York: Cambridge University Press.

Borbely, A. F. (2009). The centrality of metaphor and metonymy in psychoanalytic theory and practice. *Psychoanalytic Inquiry* 29: 58–68.

Borbely, A. F. (2011). Metaphor and metonymy as the basis of a new psychoanalytic language. *Psychoanalytic Inquiry* 31: 159–171.

Bornstein, R. F. (2001). The impending death of psychoanalysis. *Psychoanalytic Psychology* 18: 3–20.

Bornstein, R. F. (2003). Behaviorally referenced experimentation and symptom validation: A paradigm for 21st century personality disorder research. *Journal of Personality Disorders* 17: 1–18.

Bornstein, R. F. (2005). Reconnecting psychoanalysis to mainstream psychology: Opportunities and challenges. *Psychoanalytic Psychology* 22: 323–340.

Bornstein, R. F. (2006). Self-schema priming and desire for test performance feedback: Further evaluation of a cognitive/interactionist model of interpersonal dependency. *Self and Identity* 5: 110–126.

Bornstein, R. F. (2007a). Might the Rorschach be a projective test after all? Social projection of an undesired trait alters Rorschach Oral Dependency scores. *Journal of Personality Assessment* 88: 354–367.

Bornstein, R. F. (2007b). Nomothetic psychoanalysis. *Psychoanalytic Psychology* 24: 590–602.

Bornstein, R. F. (2009). Heisenberg, Kandinsky, and the heteromethod convergence problem: Lessons from within and beyond psychology. *Journal of Personality Assessment* 91: 1–8.

Bornstein, R. F., Bowers, K. S. &. Bonner, S. (1996). Effects of induced mood states on objective and projective dependency scores. *Journal of Personality Assessment* 67: 324–340.

Bornstein, R. F. & Craver-Lemley, C. (2004). The mere exposure effect. In R. Pohl (ed.), *Cognitive illusions* (pp. 215–233). Brighton, UK: Taylor & Francis/Psychology Press.

Bornstein, R. F., Ng, H. M., Gallagher, H. A., Kloss, D. M. & Regier, N. G. (2005). Contrasting effects of self-schema priming on lexical decisions and Interpersonal Stroop Task performance: Evidence for a cognitive/interactionist model of interpersonal dependency. *Journal of Personality* 73: 731–761.

Bornstein, R. & Becker-Matero, N. (2011). Reconnecting psychoanalysis to mainstream psychology: Metaphor as glue. *Psychoanalytic Inquiry* 31: 172–184.

Boston Change Process Study Group (2008). Forms of relational meaning: Issues in the relation between the implicit and reflective verbal domains. *Psychoanalytic Dialogues* 18 (2): 125–148.

Botella, C. & Botella, S. (2001). *La figurabilité psychique.* Paris: Delachaux and Nestlé.

Botella, C. & Botella, S. (2005). *The Work of Psychic Figurability.* New York: Brunner-Routledge.

Brenner, C. (2006). Psychoanalysis or Mind and Meaning.

Bromberg, P. (2008). "Grown-up" words: An interpersonal/relational perspective on unconscious fantasy. *Psychoanalytic Inquiry* 28: 131–150.

Bruner, J. (1986). *Actual Minds, Possible Worlds.* Cambridge, MA: Harvard University Press.

Bruner, J. (1987). *Actual Minds, Possible Worlds.* Cambridge, MA: Harvard University Press.

Bruner, J. (1990). *Acts of Meaning.* Cambridge, MA: Harvard University Press.

Bucci, W. (1997). *Psychoanalysis and cognitive science: A multiple code theory.* Guilford Press.

Bucci, W. (2001). Pathways of emotional communication. *Psychoanalytic Inquiry* 21: 40–70.

Bucci, W. & Maskit, B. (2007). Beneath the surface of the therapeutic interaction: The psychoanalytic method in modern dress. *Journal of the American Psychoanalytic Association* 55: 1355–1397.

Busch, F. (2009). Can you push a camel through the eye of a needle? Reflections on how the unconscious speaks to us and its clinical implications. *International Journal of Psychoanalysis* 90: 53–68.

Butterfield, E. & Siperstein, G. (1974). Influence of contingent auditory stimulation upon non-nutritional suckle. In *Proceedings of the Third Symposium on Oral Sensation and Perception: The Mouth of the Infant*, pp. 313–334. Springfield, IL: Charles C. Thomas.

Carbone, M. (2008) *Proust et les idées sensibles.* Paris: Vrin.

Caruth, E. & Ekstein, R. (1966) Interpretation within the metaphor: Further considerations. *Journal of American Academic Child Psychology* 5: 35-45.

Cassorla, R.M. (2005). From bastion to enactment: The 'non-dream' in the theatre of analysis. *International Journal of Psychoanalysis* 86: 699–719.

Casti, J. (1995). *Complexification: Explaining a Paradoxical World Through the Science of Surprise.* New York: Harper Collins.

Cavell, M. (1993). *The Psychoanalytic Mind.* Cambridge, MA: Harvard University Press.

Chan, W. (1967, 1986). Chinese theory and practice, with special reference to humanism, 11–30; The story of Chinese philosophy, 31–76. Syntheses in Chinese Metaphysics, 132–148. In *The Chinese Mind. Essentials of Chinese Philosophy and Culture* (ed.) C. A. Moore. University of Hawaii, Honolulu.

Chianese, D. (1997). *Constructions and the Analytic Field. History, Scenes and Destiny.* London: Routledge, 2007.

Chinesisch–deutsches Wörterbuch (1985). Shang Wu Yin Shu guan, Beijing.

Chomsky, N. (1980). *Rules and Representations.* New York: Columbia University Press.

Churcher, J. (2008). Some notes on the English translation of The analytic situation as a dynamic field by Willy and Madeleine Baranger. *International Journal of Psychoanalysis* 89: 785–793.

Civitarese, G. (2006). Dreams that mirror the session. *International Journal of Psychoanalysis* 87: 703–723.

Civitarese, G. (2008). *The Intimate Room: Theory and Technique of the Analytic Field.* London: Routledge, 2010.

Civitarese, G. (2010). Towards an ethics of responsibility. On "Bion and his first analyst, John Rickman (1891–1951). A revisitation of their relationship in the light of Rickman's personality and scientific production and of Bion's letters to him (1939–1951)" by Marco Conci. *International Forum Psychoanal.*, in press.

Civitarese, G. (2011, in press). *La violenza delle emozioni. Bion e la psicoanalisi postbioniana.* Milan: Raffaello Cortina.

Clyman, R. (1991). The procedural organization of emotions: a contribution from cognitive science to the psychoanalytic theory of therapeutic action. *Journal of the American Psychoanalytic Association* 39: 349–382.

Coburn, J. (2002). A world of systems: The role of systemic patterns of experience in the therapeutic process. *Psychoanalytic Inquiry* 22: 655–677.

Conci, M. (2010). Comment to "Bion and his first analyst, John Rickman (1891–1951)—A revisitation of their relationship in the light of Rickman's personality and scientific production and of Bion's letters to him (1939–1951)." *International Forum Psychoanal.*, in press.

Condon, W. S. & Sander, L. W. (1974). Neonate movement is synchronized with adult speech: Interactional participation and language acquisition. *Science* 183: 99–101.

Confucius (Kung Fu Tse) (1966). *Confucian Analects (Lun Yü)*. Original Chinese Text, trans. James Legge, Paragon Book Reprint, New York.

Corneille, O., Huart, J., Becquart, E. & Bredart, S. (2004). When memory shifts toward more typical category exemplars: Accentuation effects in the recollection of ethnically ambiguous faces. *Journal of Personality and Social Psychology* 86: 236–250.

Corrao, F. (1986). *Il concetto di campo come modello teorico*. In A. Orme, Vol. II, Milano, Raffaello Cortina, 1998.

Correale, A. (1991). *Il campo istituzionale*. Roma, Borla. *International Journal of Psychoanalysis* 86: 699–719.

Costa, P. T. & McCrae, R. R. (1997). Personality trait structure as a human universal. *American Psychologist* 52: 509–516.

Crews, F. (1996). The verdict on Freud. *Psychological Science* 7: 63–67.

Danto, A. C. (1959). Meaning and theoretical terms in psychoanalysis. In Sidney Hook (ed.) *Psychoanalysis, Scientific Method, and Philosophy,* , New York: New York University Press, pp. 314–318.

Damasio, A. R. (1994). *Descartes' Error: Emotion, Reason, and the Human Brain*. New York: Viking.

Davidson, D. (1978). What metaphors mean. In M. Platts (ed.) *Reference, Truth and Reality*. London: Routledge and Kegan, 1980.

Davis, S. (2002). The Relevance of Gerald Edelman's Theory of Neuronal Group Selection and Nonlinear Dynamic Systems for Psychoanalysis. *Psychoanalytic Inquiry* 22: 814–840.

de León, B. (1993). El sustrato compartido de la interpretación. Imágenes, afectos y palabras en la experiencia analítica. *Revista de Psicoanálisis y Boletin de la A.P.I. (38º Congreso de la A.P.I., Amsterdam, 1993)*: 809–826. Asociación Psicoanalítica Argentina, tomo L, nº 4/5. También publicado en: *Revista Uruguaya de Psicoanálisis* 81: 121–140.

de León, B. (2000). The countertransference: A Latin American view. *International Journal of Psychoanalysis* 81 (2): 331–351.

de León, B. (2003). Discusión del trabajo "La interpretación y el saber en Psicoanálisis." *Revista de Psicoanálisis* TLX. N1, Enero Marzo de 2003, pp. 19–23.

de León, B. (2005). Narrativa y psicoanálisis; alcances y límites de la palabra. *Revista Uruguaya de Psicoanálisis* 100: 170–202.

de León, B. (2008). Introduction to the paper by Madeleine and Willy Baranger: The analytic situation as a dynamic field. *International Journal of Psychoanalysis* 89: 773–784.

de León, B. (2010). La formación psicoanalítica en un cotexto de pluralismo teórico y técnico. [Psychoanalytical training in a context of technical and theoretical pluralism.] *Revista Latinoamericana de Psicoanálisis* 9: 119–138.

Dewey, J. (1971). *Experience and Nature*. La Salle: Open Court.

Dickens, C. (1840–1841, 1972). *The Old Curiosity Shop*. Harmondsworth, Middlesex, UK: Penguin Books.

Dickens, C. (1864–1865, 1971). *Our Mutual Friend*. Harmondsworth, Middlesex, UK: Penguin Books.

Dickens, C. (1870, 1961). *The Mystery of Edwin Drood*. New York: Signet Classic, New American Library.

Dodds, E. R. (1951, 1968). *The Greeks and the Irrational*. Berkeley, CA: University of California Press.

Donnet, J.-L. (2001). From the Fundamental Rule to the Analyzing Situation. *International Journal of Psychoanalysis* 82: 129–140.

Dorpat, T. & Miller, M. (1992). *Clinical Interaction and the Analysis of Meaning.* Hillsdale, NJ: Analytic Press.

Dozois, D. J. A. & Backs-Dermott, R. J. (2000). Sociotropic personality and information processing following imaginal priming. *Canadian Journal of Behavioral Science* 32: 117–126.

Dunn, J. (1995). Intersubjectivity in psicoanálisis: A critical review. *International Journal of Psychoanalysis* 76: 4.

Eagle, M. (2000). Repression, Part I of II. *Psychoanal. Rev.* 87: 1–38.

Eco, U. (1984). *Semiotics and the Philosophy of Language.* Bloomington, IN: Indiana University Press, 1986.

Edelman, G. (1989). *The Remembered Present.* New York: Basic Books.

Edelman, G. (1998). Building a picture of the brain. *Daedalus* 127 (2).

Edelson, J. T. (1983). Freud's use of metaphor. *Psychoanalytic Study of the Child* 38: 17–59.

Ekstein, R. (1954). The space child's time machine: On "reconstruction" in the psychotherapeutic treatment of a schizophrenoid child. *American Journal of Orthopsychiatry* 24: 492–506.

Ekstein, R & Wright, D. (1952). The space child: A note on the psychotherapeutic treatment of a "schizophrenoid" child. *Bulletin of the Menninger Clinic* 16: 211–224.

Elbow, P. (1973). *Writing Without Teachers.* New York: Oxford University Press.

Erikson, E. H. (1963). *Childhood and Society.* New York: W.W. Norton.

Erreich, A. (2003). A modest proposal: (Re)Defining unconscious fantasy. *Psychoanalytic Quarterly* 72 (3): 541–574.

Etchegoyen, R. H. (1986). *The Fundamentals of Psychoanalytic Technique.* London: Karnac, 1991.

Euripides (1964). Trans. A. S. Way. Loeb Classical Library. Cambridge, MA: Harvard University Press.

Exner, J. E. & Erdberg, P. S. (2005). *The Rorschach: A Comprehensive System* (Vol. 2, advanced interpretation). New York: Wiley.

Faimberg, H. (2005). *The Telescoping of Generations: Listening to the Narcissistic Links Between Generations.* London: Routledge.

Faimberg, H. (2006). *El Telescopaje de Generaciones.* Buenos Aires: Amorrortu.

Faimberg, H. (2007). A plea for a broader concept of Nachträglichkeit. *Psychoanalytic Quarterly* 76: 1221–1240.

Feirstein, F. (2009). The man in the BMW: Manifest content, metaphor, and trauma. *Psychoanalytic Review* 96 (1): 85–100.

Feldman, J. & Narayanan, S. (2004). Embodied meaning in a neural theory of language. *Brain and Language* 89: 385–392.

Ferenczi, S. (1932). *The Clinical Diary of Sándor Ferenczi.* Cambridge, MA: Harvard University Press, 1988.

Fernald, A. (1996). The onset of language development. In Paul Bloom, (ed.) *Language Acquisition: Core Readings,* pp. 51–94. Cambridge, MA: MIT Press.

Fernández, A. (1967). Confusión y acting out. Algunos aspectos del análisis de un paciente homosexual. *Revista Uruguaya de Psicoanálisis* 11 (2): 149–200.

Ferro, A. (1992). *La tecnica nella psicoanalisi infantile. Il bambino e l'analista: Dalla relazione al campo emotive.* [The Bi-Personal Field: Experiences in Child Analysis. London and New York: Routledge, 1999.]

Ferro, A. (1996). *In the Analyst's Consulting Room.* P. Slotkin, trans. Hove: Brunner-Routledge.

Ferro, A. (1999a). El diálogo analítico: Mundos posibles y transformaciones en el campo analítico. In L. Kancyper (comp.) *Volviendo a pensar con Willy y Madeleine Baranger,* comp. L. Kancyper, Lumen, Buenos Aires.

Ferro, A. (1999b). *The Bipersonal Field: Experiences in Child Analysis.* New York and London: Routledge.

Ferro, A. (2005a). "Commentary" in *Truth, Reality and the Psychoanalyst: Latin American Contributions*. In S. Lewkowitz & S. Flechner, S. (eds). London: International Psychoanalytic Association, pp. 87–96.

Ferro, A. (2005b). *Psychoanalysis as Therapy and Storytelling*. New York: Routledge.

Ferro, A. (2005c). *Seeds of Illness, Seeds of Recovery*. New York: Brunner-Routledge.

Ferro, A. (2006a). *Mind Works: Technique and Creativity in Psychoanalysis*. Slotkin, P., trans. Hove: Routledge, 2008.

Ferro, A. (2006b). *Psychoanalysis as Therapy and Storytelling*. Slotkin, P., trans. Hove: Routledge.

Ferro, A. (2010). *Tormenti di anime. Passioni, sintomi, sogni*. Milan: Raffaele Cortina.

Ferro, A. & Basile, R. (2008). Countertransference and the characters of the psychoanalytic session. *Scand. Psychoanal. Rev.* 31, 3–10.

Ferro, A. & Basile, R. (2009). *The Analytic Field: A Clinical Concept*. London: Karnac.

Ferro, A., Civitarese, G., Collovà, M., Foresti, G., Molinari, E., Mazzacane, F. & Politi, P. (2007). *Sognare l'analisi. Sviluppi clinici del pensiero di Wilfred R. Bion*. Turin: Boringhieri.

Fingarette, H. (1972). *Confucius—The Secular as Sacred*. New York: Harper Torchbooks.

Finke, R. A. (1989). *Principles of Mental Imagery*. Cambridge, MA: MIT Press.

Fodor, J. (2007). Why pigs don't have wings. *London Review of Books* 29 (20): 19–22.

Fonagy, and Target, M. (2007). *Journal of the American Psychoanalytic Association* 55: 411–455.

Fornaro, M. (1990). *Psicoanalisi tra scienza e mistica. L'opera di Wilfred R. Bion*. Rome: Edizioni Studium.

Fosshage, J. L. (2005). The explicit and implicit domains in psychoanalytic change. *Psychoanalytic Inquiry* 25: 516–539.

Foulkes, S. H. (1948). *Introduction to Group-Analytic Psychotherapy*. London: Maresfield, 1984.

Foulkes, S. H. & Anthony, E. J. (1965). *Group Psychotherapy: The Psychoanalytical Approach* (2nd revised edition). London: Maresfield, 1984.

Freeman, W. J. (1999). *How Brains Make Up Their Minds*. London: Weidenfeld & Nicholson.

Frege, G. (1892). On Sense and reference. In P. Geach and M. Black *Translations from the Philosophical Writings of Gottlob Frege*. Oxford, UK: Basil Blackwell, 1970.

Frenkel-Brunswik, E. (1954). Psychoanalysis and the unity of science. In N. Heiman & J. Grant (eds), *Else Frenkel-Brunswik: Selected Papers* (1974), Journal of Psychological Issues, Monograph 31. New York: International University Press, pp. 161–231.

Freud, S. (1890). Psychical (or mental) treatment. In R. Kossmann & J. Weiss (eds) *Die Gesundheit*. Stuttgart; Berlin; Leipzig: Union Deutsche Verlagsgesellschaft, pp. 368–384.

Freud, S. (1891). *On Aphasia. A Critical Study*. Trans. Erwin Stengel. New York: International University Press, 1953.

Freud, S. (1893–95). Studies on hysteria. *Standard Edition*, 2, London: Hogarth Press, 1961.

Freud, S. (1895). Letter from Freud to Fliess, May 25, 1895. In J. M. Masson (ed.) (1985), *The Complete Letters of Sigmund Freud to Wilhelm Fliess, 1887–1904*. Cambridge, MA: Harvard University Press, pp. 128–131.

Freud, S. (1900). The interpretation of dreams. *Standard Edition*, 4/5. London: Hogarth Press, 1961.

Freud, S. (1901). The psychopathology of everyday life. *Standard Edition*. London: Hogarth Press.

Freud, S. (1904). Freud's psycho-analytic procedure. *Standard Editon* 7: 247–254. London: Hogarth Press, 1953.

Freud, S. (1908). Creative writers and day-dreaming. *Standard Edition* 9: 141–154. London: Hogarth Press, 1959.

Freud, S. (1910). The future prospects of psychoanalytic therapy. *Standard Edition*, 11, London: Hogarth, 1958.

Freud, S. (1912a). A note on the unconscious in psycho-analysis. *Standard Edition* 12: 260–266. London: Hogarth Press, 1958.

Freud, S. (1912b). Recommendations to physicians practicing psychoanalysis, *Standard Edition*, 12. London: Hogarth, 1958.

Freud, S, (1912c) The dynamics of transference, *Standard Edition* 12: 97-108 London: Hogarth Press 1999

Freud, S. (1913a). On beginning the treatment. (Further recommendations on the technique of analysis). *Standard Edition*, 12: 121–144, 1958.

Freud, S. (1913b). Totem and taboo. *Standard Edition* 13: vii–162, London: Hogarth Press, 1961.

Freud, S. (1914a). On the history of the psycho-analytic movement. *Standard Edition*, 14: 1–66, 1957.

Freud, S. (1914b). On narcissism. An introduction. *Standard Edition*, 14: 67–102, 1957.

Freud, S. (1914c). Remembering, repeating and working-through. *Standard Edition*, 12, London, Hogarth.

Freud, S. (1915a). Repression. *Standard Edition* 14: 141–158, London: Hogarth Press, 1961.

Freud, S. (1915b). The unconscious. *Standard Edition* 14: 159–216, London: Hogarth Press, 1961.

Freud, S. (1916). Introductory lectures on psychoanalysis. *Standard Edition*, XV 1915–16: 1–240.

Freud, S. (1919a). Lines of advance in psycho-analytic therapy. *Standard Edition*, 17: 157–168, London: Hogarth Press, 1961.

Freud, S. (1919b). The uncanny. *Standard Edition*, 17: 217–256, London: Hogarth.

Freud, S. (1923a). The ego and the id. *Standard Edition* 19: 1–66. London: Hogarth Press, 1961.

Freud, S. (1923b). Two encyclopaedia articles. *Standard Edition*, XVIII.

Freud, S. (1925). A note upon the "mystic writing-pad." *Standard Edition*, 19: 225–232, 1961.

Freud, S. (1927). Fetishism. *Standard Edition* 21: 149–157, London: Hogarth Press, 1961.

Freud, S. (1933a). The dissection of the psychical personality. *Standard Edition* 22: 57–80. London: Hogarth Press, 1964.

Freud, S. (1933b). New introductory lectures on psychoanalysis. *Standard Edition* 22: 1–267, London: Hogarth Press, 1961.

Freud, S. (1937a). Analysis terminable and interminable. *Standard Edition* 23: 209–253, 1964.

Freud, S. (1937b). Constructions in analysis. *Standard Edition* 23: 255–270. London, Hogarth.

Freud, S. (1939). Moses and monotheism. *Standard Edition*, 23: 1–296. London: Hogarth Press, 1961.

Freud, S. (1940a). An outline of psychoanalysis. *Standard Edition* 23.

Freud, S. (1940b). Some elementary lessons in psycho-analysis. *Standard Edition* 23: 279–286. London: Hogarth Press, 1964.

Freud, S. (1940c). Splitting of the ego in the process of defense. *Standard Edition* 23: 275–278

Freud, S. (1950). Project for a scientific psychology. *Standard Edition* 1: 281–391. London: Hogarth Press, 1966.

Freud, S. (1953a). The interpretation of dreams. In J. Strachey (ed. & trans.), *The Standard Edition of the Complete Psychological Works of Sigmund Freud* (Vols 4/5). London: Hogarth Press. (Original work published 1900.)

Freud, S. (1953b). Three essays on the theory of sexuality. In J. Strachey (ed. & trans.), *The Standard Edition of the Complete Psychological Works of Sigmund Freud* (Vol. 7, pp. 125–243). London: Hogarth Press. (Original work published 1905.)

Freud, S. (1955). Beyond the pleasure principle. In J. Strachey (ed. & trans.), *The Standard Edition of the Complete Psychological Works of Sigmund Freud* (Vol. 18, pp. 3–64). London: Hogarth Press. (Original work published 1910.)

Freud, S. (1957a). Five lectures on psychoanalysis. In J. Strachey (ed. & trans.), *The Standard Edition of the Complete Psychological Works of Sigmund Freud* (Vol. 11, pp. 7–55). London: Hogarth Press. (Original work published 1910.)

Freud, S. (1957b). Repression. In J. Strachey (ed. & trans.), *The Standard Edition of the Complete Psychological Works of Sigmund Freud* (Vol. 14, pp. 141–158). London: Hogarth Press. (Original work published 1915.)

Freud, S. (1959). Inhibitions, symptoms, and anxiety. In J. Strachey (ed. & trans.), *The Standard Edition of the Complete Psychological Works of Sigmund Freud* (Vol. 20, pp. 75–175). London: Hogarth Press. (Original work published 1926.)

Freud, S. (1963). Introductory lectures on psychoanalysis. In J. Strachey (ed. & trans.), *The Standard Edition of the Complete Psychological Works of Sigmund Freud* (Vols. 15 & 16). London: Hogarth Press. (Original work published 1916.)

Friedman, L. (2002). Lawrence Friedman responds. *Journal of the American Psychoanalytic Association* 50: 325–330.

Fung YuLan (1931/1934, trans. 1952/53). A history of Chinese philosophy. Trans. Derk Bodde. Princeton, NJ: Princeton University Press.

Gaburri, E. (1998). Il Campo gruppale e la "non cosa." In G. Rugi & E. Gaburri, *Campo gruppale*. Roma: Borla.

Gadamer, H.-G. (1960). *Verdad y método I.* [Truth and Method I.] Salamanca: Sígueme, 1994.

Gallese, V. (2006). Embodied simulation: From mirror neuron systems to interpersonal relations. In *Empathy and Fairness.* Chichester (Novartis Foundation Symposium): Wiley, pp. 3–19.

Gallese, V., Eagle, M. N. & Migone, P. (2007). Intentional attunement: Mirror neurons and the neural underpinning of interpersonal relations. *Journal of the American Psychoanalytic Association* 55: 131–176.

Gargiulo, G. J. (1998). Meaning and metaphor in psychoanalytic education. *Psychoanalytic Review* 85: 413–422.

Gargiulo, G. J. (2006). Ontology and metaphor: Reflections on the unconscious and the "I" in the therapeutic setting. *Psychoanalytic Psychology* 23: 461–474.

Gazzaniga, M. S. (1995). Consciousness and the cerebral hemispheres. In Michael S. Gazzaniga (ed.) *The Cognitive Neurosciences*, pp. 1391–1400. Cambridge, MA: MIT Press.

Gedo, J. (1984). *Psychoanalysis and Its Discontents.* London: Guilford Press.

Gedo, J. (1991). *The Biology of Clinical Encounters.* Hillsdale, NJ: Analytic Press.

Gedo, J. (1999). *The Evolution of Psychoanalysis.* New York: Other Press.

Ghent, E. (2002). Wish, need, drive: Motive in the light of dynamic systems theory and Edelman's selectionist theory. *Psychoanalytic Dialogues* 12: 763–808.

Gibbs, R. (1994). Figurative thought and figurative language. In M. Gernsbacher (ed.), *Handbook of Psycholinguistics.* New York: Academic Press, pp. 411–463.

Gibbs, R. (2008). Metaphor and thought: The state of the art. In R. Gibbs (ed.), *The Cambridge Handbook of Metaphor and Thought.* Cambridge: Cambridge University Press.

Gill, M. (1976). Metapsychology is not psychology. In M. Gill and P. Holzman, *Psychology Versus Metapsychology, Journal of Psychological Issues.* Monograph 36: 71–105.

Gill, M. (1983). The point of view in psychoanalysis: Energy discharge or person? *Psychoanalysis and Contemporary Thought* 6: 523–551.

Godel, K. (1931). On formally undecidable propositions of *Principia Mathematical* and related systems. In J. van Heijenoort (1970), *Frege and Godel.* Cambridge, MA: Harvard University Press.

Goethe, J. W. v. (1961). *Dtv Gesamtausgabe.* Vol. 32, p. 186. München.

Goldstein, K. (1940). *Human Nature in the Light of Psychopathology.* Cambridge, MA: Harvard University Press.

Grassi, E. (n.d.). *Das heimatliche Unheimliche*. In D. Borchmeyer & T. Heimeran (eds) *Weimar am Pazifik*. Niemeyer, Tübingen.

Green, A. (1972–1986). *On Private Madness*. Colchester: Mark Paterson & Assoc.

Green, A. (1975). The analyst, symbolization and absence in the analytic setting (on changes in analytic practice and analytic experience). *International Journal of Psychoanalysis* 56: 1–22.

Green, A. (1978). Le Credo Du Psychanalyste (Incroyable Mais Vrai). *Nouvelle Revue de Psychanalyse* 18: 263–72.

Green, A. (1998). The primordial mind and the work of the negative. *International Journal of Psychoanalysis* 79: 649–665.

Green, A (1999a). On discriminating and not discriminating between affect and representation. *International Journal of Psychoanalysis* 80: 277–316.

Green, A. (1999b). *The Fabric of Affect in the Psychoanalytic Discourse*. Trans. A. Sheridan. New York: Routledge.

Green, A. (2003). *Idées directrices pour une psychanalyse contemporaine*. Paris: Presses Universitaires de France.

Green, A (2004). Thirdness and psychoanalytic concepts. *Psychoanalytic Quarterly* 73: 99– 135.

Greenberg, J. (1991). *Oedipus and Beyond*. Cambridge, MA: Harvard University Press.

Greenberg, J. & Mitchell, S. (1983). *Object Relations in Psychoanalytic Theory*. Cambridge, MA: Harvard University Press.

Greene, B. (1999). *The Elegant Universe*. New York: W. W. Norton & Co.

Greene, B. (2004). *The Fabric of the Cosmos*. New York: Vintage.

Grinberg, L. (1956). Sobre algunos problemas de técnica psicoanalítica determinados por la identificación y contraidentificación proyectivas. *Revista Psa.*, Buenos Aires, XIII, Nº 4.

Grinberg, L. (1957). Perturbaciones en la interpretación por la contraidentificación proyectiva. *Rev Psicoanál* 14: 23–30.

Grossman, W. I. (1992). Hierarchies, boundaries, and representation in a Freudian model of mental organization. *Journal of the American Psychoanalytic Association* 40: 27–62.

Grossman, W. I. & Simon, B. (1969). Anthropomophism: Motive, meaning, and causability in psychoanalytic theory. *Psychoanalytic Study of the Child* 24: 78–111.

Grotstein, J. (2007). *A Beam of Intense Darkness: Wilfred Bion's Legacy to Psychoanalysis*. London: Karnac.

Grotstein, J. (2009). "The play's the thing wherein I'll catch the conscience of the king!" Psychoanalysis as a passion play. In A. Ferro & R. Basile (eds), *The Anaytic Field*. London: Karnac Books, pp.189–212.

Grunbaum, A. (1984). *The Foundations of Psychoanalysis*. Berkeley, CA: University of California Press.

Guépin, J. P. (1968). *The Tragic Paradox. Myth and Ritual in Greek Tragedy*. Hakkert, Amsterdam.

Hadley, J. (1992). The instincts revisited. *Psychoanalytic Inquiry* 12: 396–418.

Harries, K. (1978). Metaphor and transcendence. *Critical Inquiry*. 73–90.

Hausman, C. (1984). *A Discourse in Novelty and Creation*. Albany, NY: State University of New York Press.

Heidegger, M. (1953). *Being and Time*. Albany, NY: State University of New York Press.

Heidegger, M. (2001). *Zollikon Seminars*. Evanston, IL: Northwestern University Press.

Heimann, P. (1950). On countertransference. *International Journal of Psychoanalysis*, XXXI.

Heiman, N. & Grant, J. (1974). *Else Frenkel-Brunswik: Selected papers*. Journal of Psychological Issues, Monograph 31. New York: International Universities Press.

Hernández-Tubert, R. (2004). Inconsciente y concepción del mundo. [The unconscious and the *Weltanschauung*.] In M. Kolteniuk, J. Casillas & J. de la Parra (eds), *El inconsciente freudiano*. [The Freudian Unconscious.] Mexico City: Editores de Textos Mexicanos, pp. 63–78.

Hernández-Tubert, R. (2005). Baluarte e ideología en la obra de Willy Baranger. [Ideology and the bastion in the work of Willy Baranger.] *Cuadernos de Psicoanálisis* 38 (3–4): 47–54.

Hirsch, I. (1995). Changing conceptions of unconscious. *Contemporary Psychoanalysis* 31: 263–276. 47–54.

Hirsch, I. (2002). Beyond interpretation: Analytic interaction in the interpersonal tradition. *Contemporary Psychoanalysis* 38: 573–587.

Hochschild, J. P. (2001). The semantics of analogy according to Thomas de Vio Cajetan's *De Nominum Analogia*. Dissertation for the Degree of Doctor in Philosophy, Graduate School, University of Notre Dame. Web page of the Institute for Philosophical Research, Hungarian Academy of Sciences: <http://www.phil-inst.hu/~gyula/FILES/Josh-Thesis.pdf > (14 November 2010).

Hoffman, I. (1991). Towards a social-constructivist view of the psychoanalytic situation. *Psychoanalytic Dialogues* 1: 74–105.

Holt, R. (1975). The past and the future of ego psychology. *Psychoanalytic Quarterly* 44: 550–576.

Holt, R. (1989). *Freud Reappraised.* New York: Guilford Press.

Home, H. J. (1966). The concept of mind. *International Journal of Psychoanalysis* 47: 42–49.

Husserl, E. (1930/2004). *Ideas.* London: Taylor & Francis.

Imbasciati, A. (2002). An explanatory theory for psychoanalysis: The unconscious as symbolopoiesis. *International Forum of Psychoanalysis* 11: 173–183.

Imbasciati, A. (2003). Cognitive sciences and psychoanalysis: A possible convergence. *Journal of the American Academy of Psychoanalysis and Dynamic Psychiatry* 31: 627–646.

Imbasciati, A. (2004). A theoretical support for transgenerationality: The theory of the protomental. *Psychoanalytic Psychology* 21: 83–98.

Imbasciati, A. (2006). *Constructing a Mind.* London: Brunner-Routledge.

Isaacs, S. (1948). The nature and function of phantasy. *International Journal of Psychoanalysis* 29: 73–97.

Isaacs, S. (1952). The nature and function of fantasy. *Developments in Psychoanalysis.* London: Hogarth.

Jacobs, T. J. (2011). *Reflections on the Field Theory.* Presentation for the Panel on The Field Theory at the IPA in Mexico City.

Jackendoff, R. (1988). Conceptual semantics. In U. Eco, M. Santambrogio & P. Violi (eds), *Meaning and Mental Representations*, pp. 81–97. Bloomington, IN: Indiana University Press.

Jakobson, R. (1956). Two aspects of language and two types of aphasics disturbances. In *Word and Language.* The Hage Mouton, 1971, pp. 239–259.

Jakobson, R. (1990). The speech event and the function of language. In Linda R. Waugh & Monique Monville-Burston (eds) *On Language*, pp. 69–79. Cambridge, MA: Harvard University Press.

Jakobson, R. (1995). *On Language.* Cambridge, MA: Harvard University Press.

Johnson, M. (1987). *The Body in the Mind: The Bodily Basis of Meaning, Imagination, and Reason.* Chicago, IL: University of Chicago Press.

Joseph, B. (1985). La transferencia como situación total. *Libro Anual de Psicoanálisis Lima*; Ediciones Psicoanalíticas Imago SRL, 1986: 85–92.

Kancyper, L. (comp.). (1999). *Volviendo a pensar con Willy y Madeleine Baranger.* Buenos Aires: Lumen.

Kandel, E. (1998). A new intellectual framework for psychiatry. *American Journal of Psychiatry* 155: 457–469.

Katz, D. (1943). *Gestalt Psychology.* Westport, CT: Greenwood Publishing Group, 1979.

Katz, M. (1985). *Reflections on Meaning Theory.* Doctoral Dissertation.

Katz, M. (2001). The implications for revising Freud's empiricism for drive theory. *Psychoanalysis and Contemporary Thought* 24 (3): 253–272.

Katz, M. (2004). Fantasy and transference. *Free Associations* 11 (2): 226–241.

Katz, M. (2010a). A holistic framework for psychoanalysis. *Psychoanalytic Review* 97: 107–135.

Katz, M. (2010b). Review of *The Analytic Field* by Ferro and Basile. *Psychoanalytic Quarterly.*

Katz, M. (2010c). Review of *The Work of Confluence* by Madeleine and Willy Baranger. *Psychoanalytic Quarterly.*

Katz, M. (2011a). Editor. Metaphoric processes as the common ground for psychoanalytic perspectives. *Psychoanalytic Inquiry* 31 (2).

Katz, M. (2011b). Unconscious metaphoric processes as the basis for an inclusive model of psychoanalytic perspectives. *Psychoanalytic Inquiry* 31: 134–146.

Katz, M. (2012). General psychoanalytic field theory: Its structure and applications to psychoanalytic perspectives. *Psychoanalytic Inquiry*, this issue.

Kernberg, O. (1982). Self, ego, affects, and drives. *Journal of the American Psychoanalytic Association* 30: 893–917.

Kernberg, O. (1984). *Severe Personality Disorders.* New Haven, CT: Yale University Press.

Kernberg, O. (2001). Object relations, affects, and drives: Toward a new synthesis. *Psychoanalytic Inquiry* 21: 604–619.

Kittay, E. (1987). *Metaphor: Its Cognitive Force and Linguistic Structure.* Oxford, UK: Clarendon Press.

Klein, G. S. (1973). Two theories or one? *Bulletin of the Menninger Clinic* 37: 102–132.

Klein, G. S. (1976). *Psychoanalytic Theory. An Exploration of Essentials.* New York: International Universities Press.

Klein, M. (1921). The development of a child. *The Writings of Melanie Klein*, Vol. I.

Klein, M. (1928). The early stages of the Oedipus conflict. *The Writings of Melanie Klein*, Vol. I.

Klein, M. (1930). The importance of symbol-formation in the development of the ego. *International Journal of Psychoanalysis* 11: 24–39.

Klein, M. (1932). Psychoanalysis of children. In P. Heimann, S. Isaacs & J. Rivière (1952), *Developments in Psycho-Analysis.* London: Hogarth.

Klein, M., Heimann, P., Isaacs, S. and Rivière, J. (1952). *Developments in Psycho-Analysis.* London: Hogarth.

Koffka, K. (1935). *Principles of Gestalt Psychology.* New York: Hartcourt, Brace & Co.

Kohut, H. (1971). *The Analysis of the Self. A Systematic Approach to the Psychonanalytic Treatment of Narcisstic Personality Disorders.* New York: International Universities Press. [trans. it. *Narcisismo e analisi del Sé.* Torino: Boringhieri, 1976.]

Kohut, H. (1977). *The Restoration of the Self.* New York: International University Press. [trans. it. *La guarigione del sé.* Torino: Boringhieri, 1980.]

Kojève, A. (1947). *Introduction to the Reading of Hegel.* Bloom A., ed.; Nichols J. H. Jr., trans. New York: Basic Books, 1969.

Kolata, G. (1984). Studying learning in the womb. *Science* 225 (20 July): 302–303.

Kosslyn, S. M. (1994). *Image and Brain: The Resolution of the Imagery Debate.* Cambridge, MA: MIT Press.

Kövecses, Z. (2002). *Metaphor: A Practical Introduction.* New York: Oxford University Press.

Kris, A. (1985) Resistance in convergent and divergent conflicts *Psychoanalytic Quarterly* 54: 537–68.

Kris, A. (1987) Fixation and regression in relation to convergent and divergent conflicts *Bulletin of the Anna Freud Centre* 10: 99–117.

Kris, A. (1988) Some clinical applications of the distinction between convergent and divergent conflicts *International Journal of Psychoanalysis* 69: 431–442.

Kristeva, J. (2000). *Melanie Klein*. Goberman, R., trans. New York: Columbia University Press, 2001.

Kubie, L. S. (1960). Psychoanalysis and the scientific method. *Journal of Nervous and Mental Disease* 131: 495–512.

Kubie, L. S. (1966). A reconsideration of thinking, the dream process, and the "dream." *Psychoanalytic Quarterly* 35: 191–198.

Kubie, L. S. (1978). Symbol and neurosis. Selected Papers. Hgb. H. J. Schlesinger. *Psychol. Issues, Monogr.* 44. New York: International University Press.

Kuhn, T. S. (1962). *The Structure of Scientific Revolutions*. Chicago: University of Chicago Press.

Kuhn, T. (1977). *The Essential Tension*. Chicago, IL: University of Chicago Press.

Lacan, J. (1947). British psychiatry and war. P. Dravers & V. Voruz, trans. In *Psychoanalytical Notebooks of the London Circle*, Spring 2000.

Lacan, J. (1953). *Función y campo de la palabra y del lenguaje en psicoanálisis*. Escrtos I. 59–139. Buenos Aires Siglo XXI, 1972.

Lakoff, G. (2008). The neural theory of metaphor. In R. Gibbs (ed.), *The Cambridge Handbook of Metaphor and Thought*. Cambridge: Cambridge University Press.

Lakoff, G. & Johnson, M. (1980a). *Metaphors We Live By*. Chicago, IL: University of Chicago Press.

Lakoff, G. & Johnson, M. (1980b). *Metáforas de la vida cotidiana*. [The metaphors we live by.] Ediciones Catedra, 1991 España.

Lakoff, G. & Johnson, M. (1999). *Philosophy in the Flesh: The Embodied Mind and its Challenge to Western Thought*. New York: Basic Books.

Langacker, R. (1993). Reference-point construction. *Cognitive Linguistics* 4: 1–38.

Langer, S. (1957). *Philosophy in a New Key*. Cambridge, MA: Harvard University Press.

Laplanche, J. and Pontalis, J.-B. (1967) *The Language of Psychoanalysis*. New York: W. W. Norton.

Lao Tse (Lao Tzu). *Tao Te King*. Trans. into English, Tam C. Gibbs, North Atlantic Books, Richmond Cal. 1981 (with commentary by Manjan Cheng); Wingtsit Chan, in A. Rump, trans. of Wang Pi's commentary, University Pr. Hawaii, 1979; German trans. R. Wilhelm, Diederichs Gelbe Reihe, Köln, 1986; trans. O. Sumitomo, Werner Classen Verlag, Zürich, 1945.

Lecours, S. (2007). Supportive interventions and nonsymbolic mental functioning. *International Journal of Psychoanalysis* 88: 895–915.

Lerner, P. M. (2005). Defense and its assessment: The Lerner Defense Scale. In R. F. Bornstein & J. M. Masling (eds), *Scoring the Rorschach: Seven Validated Systems* (pp. 237–269). Mahwah, NJ: Erlbaum.

Leuzinger-Bohleber, M. & Fischmann, T. (2006). What is conceptual research in psychoanalysis? *International Journal of Psychoanalysis* 87: 1355–1351.

Levenson, J. R. & Schurmann, F. (1969). China: An interpretive history. Berkeley, CA: University California Press.

Levin, F. M. (2009). Metaphor: A fascinating philanthropic puzzle piece with neuro-psychoanalytic (NP) implications. *Psychoanalytic Inquiry* 29: 69–78.

Lewin, B. D. (1970). The train ride: A study of one of Freud's figures of speech. *Psychoanalytic Quarterly* 39: 71–89.

Lewin, B. D. (1971). Metaphor, mind and manikin. *Psychoanalytic Quarterly* 40:6–39.

Lewin, K. (1951). *Field Theory in Social Science; Selected Papers*. D. Cartwright (ed.). New York: Harper and Row.

Lewkowicz, S. & Flechner, S. (2005). *Truth, Reality, and the Psychoanalyst: Latin American Contributions to Psychoanalysis*. London: International Psychoanalytical Association.

Liberman, D. (1970). *Lingüística, Interacción Comunicativa y Proceso Psicoanalítico*. Bs. As: Galerna, 1971.

228

Lichtenberg, J. (1989). *Psychoanalytic Motivation*. Hillsdale, NJ: Analytic Press.

Litowitz, B. (2007). Unconscious fantasy. *Journal of the American Psychoanalytic Association* 55 (1): 199–228.

Little, M. (1960). On basic unity. *International Journal of Psychoanalysis* 41: 377–384.

Llinas, R. R. & Pare, D. (1991). On dreaming and wakefulness. *Neuroscience* 44: 521–535.

Locke, J. (1964). *Essay Concerning Human Understanding*. Oxford, UK: Clarendon Press.

Loewald, H. W. (1951). Ego and reality. *International Journal of Psychoanalysis* 32: 10–18.

Loewald, H. (1960). On the therapeutic action of psycho-analysis. *International Journal of Psychoanalysis* 41: 16–33.

Loewald, H. (1978). Primary process, secondary process, and language. In *Papers on Psychoanalysis*. New Haven, CT: Yale University Press, 1980, pp. 178–206.

López-Corvo, R. E. (2002). *The Dictionary of the Work of W. R. Bion*. L. Morabito Gómez, trans. London: Karnac, 2003.

Lowenstein, R. (1953). *Drives, Affects, Behavior*, Vol. I. New York: International Universities Press.

Mahler, M. S. (1968). *On Human Symbiosis and the Vicissitudes of Individuation*. New York: International Universities Press.

Mann, T. (1933). *Joseph und seine Brüder*. Berlin: S. Fischer.

Matthis, I. (2000). Sketch of a metapsychology of affect. *International Journal of Psychoanalysis* 81: 215–227.

Matte-Blanco, I. (1988). *Thinking, Feeling, and Being*. London: Routledge.

McInerny, R. N. (1971). *The Logic of Analogy: An Interpretation of St. Thomas*. The Hague: Martinus Nijboff.

Meier, B. P. & Robinson, M. D. (2004). Why the sunny side is up: Associations between affect and vertical position. *Psychological Science* 15: 243–247.

Meier, B. P., Robinson, M. D. & Caven, A. J. (2008). Why a Big Mac is a Good Mac: Associations between affect and size. *Basic and Applied Social Psychology* 30: 46–55.

Meier, B. P., Hauser, D. J., Robinson, M. D., Friesen, C. K. & Schjeldahl, K. (2007a). What's "up" with God? Vertical space as a representation of the divine. *Journal of Personality and Social Psychology* 93: 699–710.

Meier, B. P., Robinson, M. D., Crawford, L. E. & Ahlvers, W. J. (2007b). When "light" and "dark" thoughts become light and dark responses: Affect biases brightness judgments. *Emotion* 7: 366–376.

Meissner, W. W. (1993). Self-as-agent in psychoanalysis. *Psychoanalysis and Contemporary Thought* 15: 459–495.

Meissner, W. W. (1997). The self and the body: I. The body self and the body image. *Psychoanalysis and Contemporary Thought* 20: 419–448.

Meissner, W. W. (1998). The self and the body: II. The embodied self—self vs. nonself. *Psychoanalysis and Contemporary Thought* 21 (1): 85–112.

Meissner, W. W. (1999a). The self-as-subject in psychoanalysis: I. The nature of subjectivity. *Psychoanalysis and Contemporary Thought* 22 (1999a): 155–201.

Meissner, W. W. (1999b). The self-as-subject in psychoanalysis: II. The subject in analysis. *Psychoanalysis and Contemporary Thought* 22 (1999b): 383–428.

Meissner, W. W. (2000). The self-as-relational in psychoanalysis. I. Relational aspects of the self. *Psychoanalysis and Contemporary Thought* 23 (2): 177–204.

Meissner, W. W. (2003). Mind, brain and self in psychoanalysis. *Psychoanalysis and Contemporary Thought* 26: 279–386.

Meissner, W. W. (2006). The mind–brain relation and neuroscience foundations. *Bulletin of the Menninger Clinic* 70: 87–124.

Meissner, W.W. (2007). Mind, brain and self in psychoanalysis. *Psychoanalytic Psychology* 24 (2): 333–354.

Melnick, B. A. (2000). Cold hard world/warm soft mommy: The unconscious logic of metaphor. *Annual of Psychoanalysis* 28: 225–244.

Melshon, I. (1989). Sentido. Significacao.Soño e Linguagem: Reflexes sobre as formas do consciencia no proceso analítico. *Rev. Brasileira de Psicoanalisis* 23 (3): 57–58.

Meltzer, D. (1981). The Kleinian expansion of Freud's metapsychology. *International Journal of Psychoanalysis* 62: 177–185.

Meltzer, D. (1983). *Dream-Life: A Re-examination of the Psycho-analytical Theory and Technique*. Pertshire: Clunie Press.

Merleau-Ponty, M. (1942). *The Structure of Behavior*. Pittsburgh, PA: Duquesne University Press, 1989.

Merleau-Ponty, M. (1945). *The Phenomenology of Perception*. C. Smith, trans. London: Routledge & Kegan Paul.

Merleau-Ponty, M. (1964). *The Visible and the Invisible*. Evaston, IL: Northwestern University Press, 1968.

Merleau-Ponty, M. (1975). The child's relations with others. J. Edie ed.; W. Cobb, trans. In *The Primacy of Perception*. Evanston, IL: Northwestern University Press, 1964, pp. 96–155.

Merriam-Webster (2002). *Webster's Third New International Dictionary, Unabridged*. Electronic version: <http://unabridged.merriam-webster.com> (14 November 2010).

Michels, R. (2005). Discussion. *Psychoanalytic Inquiry* 25: 569–575.

Milgram, S. (1963). Behavioral study of obedience. *Journal of Abnormal and Social Psychology* 67: 371–378.

Millon, T. (1996). *Disorders of Personality: DSM-IV and Beyond*. New York: Wiley.

Mitchell, S. (1988). *Relational Concepts in Psychoanalysis*. Cambridge, MA: Harvard University Press.

Modell, A. (1968). *Object Love and Reality*. New York: International Universities Press.

Modell, A. (1971). Metaphor, mind, and manikin. *Psychoanalytic Quarterly* 40: 6–39.

Modell, A. (1978). Affects and the complementarity of biologic and historical meaning. *Annals of Psychoanalysis* 6: 167–80.

Modell, A. (1984). *Psychoanalysis in a New Context*. New York: International Universities Press.

Modell, A. (1990). *Other Times, Other Realities*. Cambridge, MA: Harvard University Press.

Modell, A. (1993). *The Private Self*. Cambridge, MA: Harvard University Press.

Modell, A. (1994). Common ground or divided ground? *Psychoanalytic Inquiry* 14: 201–211.

Modell, A. (1997a). Reflections on metaphor and affects. *Annual of Psychoanalysis* 25: 219–233.

Modell, A. (1997b). The synergy of memory, affects and metaphor. *Journal of Analytical Psychology* 42: 105–117.

Modell, A. (2003). *Imagination and the Meaningful Brain*. Cambridge, MA: MIT Press.

Modell, A. (2005). Emotional memory, metaphor, and meaning. *Psychoanalytic Inquiry* 25: 555–568.

Modell, A. (2007). The body in psychoanalysis and the origin of fantasy. In J. Muller & J. Tillman (eds), *The Embodied Subject*. Northvale, NJ: Jason Aronson.

Modell, A. (2009a). Metaphor—The bridge between feelings and knowledge. *Psychoanalytic Inquiry* 29: 6–11.

Modell, A. (2009b). Response to the discussants. *Psychoanalytic Inquiry* 29: 91–96.

Mortara-Garavelli (2010). *Il parlar figurato. Manualetto di figure retoriche*. Bari: Laterza.

Mowrer, O. H. (1952). Speech development in the young child: 1. The autism theory of speech development. *Journal of Speech and Hearing Disorders* 17: 262–268.

M'Uzan, M. de (1976). Contratransferencia y sistema paradojal. In *Del arte a la muerte,* Icaria, 1978.

M'Uzan, M. de (1994). *La Bouche de l'Inconscient.* Paris: Gallimard.

Neri, C. (1987). *Il compimento dell'analisi: Appunti a proposito del tendere dell'analisi verso il suo fine.* Presentato al panel su "La fine analisi" del Centro Milanese di Psicoanalisi (12–13 giugno 1987).

Neri, C. (1988a). Champ de l'expérience groupale: Un homologue ou un analogue du transfert dans le situation de la cure? *Revue de Psychothérapie Psychanalytique de Groupe,* n. 12–13.

Neri, C. (1988b). *Group.* London: Jessica Kingsley Publishers.

Neri, C. (1993). Campo e fantasie transgenerazionali. *Rivista di Psicoanalisi,* XXXIX (1), pp. 43–64.

Neri, C. (2008). Authenticity as an aim of psychoanalysis. *American Journal of Psychoanalysis* 68: 325–349.

Neri, C. (2009). *The enlarged* notion of *field* in psychoanalysis. In A. Ferro & R. Basile (eds), *The Analytic Field: A Clinical Concept.* London: *Karnac* Books, pp. 45–80.

Neri, C. & Selvaggi, L. (2006). Campo. In F. Barale, M. Bertani, V. Gallese, S. Mistura & A. Zamperini (eds), *Psiche. Dizionario storico di psicologia, psichiatria, psicoanalisi, neuroscienze.* Turin: Einaudi, pp. 180–185.

Nietzsche, F. (l885, 1976). *Jenseits von Gut und Böse.* Kröner, Stuttgart.

Nissim Momigliano, L. (2001). *L'ascolto rispettoso. Scritti psicoanalitici.* Milan: Raffaello Cortina.

Noy, P. (1982). A revision of the psychoanalytic theory of affect. *Annual of Psychoanalysis* 10: 139–186.

Ogden, T. (1979). On projective identification. *International Journal of Psychoanalysis* 60: 357–373.

Ogden, T. (1980). Mathematical intuition. *Proceedings of the Aristotelian Society* 80: 145– 168.

Ogden, T. (1986). Intuition in constructive mathematics. In Butterfield, J. *Language, Mind and Logic.* Cambridge: Cambridge University Press.

Ogden, T. (1992). The dialectically constituted/decentred subject of psychoanalysis. II. The contributions of Klein and Winnicott. *International Journal of Psychoanalysis* 73: 613–626.

Ogden, T. (1994a). The analytic third: Working with intersubjective clinical facts. *International Journal of Psychoanalysis* 75: 3–19.

Ogden, T. (1994b). *Subjects of Analysis.* New York: Jason Aronson.

Ogden, T. (1997). Reverie and metaphor. *International Journal of Psychoanalysis* 78: 719–732.

Ogden, T. (1999). The analytic third: An overview. In S. Mitchell & L. Aron (eds), *Relational Psychoanalysis: The Emergence of a Tradition.* Hillsdale, NJ: Analytic Press.

Ogden, T. (2004a). An introduction to the reading of Bion. *International Journal of Psychoanalysis* 85: 285–300.

Ogden, T. (2004b). The art of psychoanalysis dreaming undreamt dreams and interrupted cries. *International Journal of Psychoanalysis* 85: 857–877.

Ogden, T. (2005). *This Art of Psychoanalysis: Dreaming Undreamt Dreams and Interrupted Cries.* London: Routledge.

Ogden, T. (2008). *Rediscovering Psychoanalysis: Thinking and Dreaming, Learning and Forgetting.* London: Routledge.

Ogden, T. (2009). The analytic third: working with intersubjective clinical facts. In A. Ferro & R. Basile (eds), *The Analytic Field.* London: Karnac Books.

O'Shaughnessy, E. (2005). Whose Bion? *International Journal of Psychoanalysis* 86: 1523–1528.

Ozick, C. (1991). *Metaphor and Memory.* New York: Vintage International.

Pally, R. (1998). Emotional processing: The mind–body connection. *International Journal of Psychoanalysis* 79: 349–362.

Panskepp, (2006). The core emotional systems of the mammalian brain: the fundamental substrates of human emeotions. In J. Corrigall, H. Payne & H. Wilkinson (eds) *About a Body*, London: Routledge, pp. 14–32.

Patton, C. J. (1992). Fear of abandonment and binge eating: A subliminal psychodynamic activation investigation. *Journal of Nervous and Mental Disease* 180: 484–490.

Paulucci, O. & Dujovne, I. (2003). La interpretación y el saber en psicoanálisis. *Rev. De Psicoanálisis,* LX, 1: 14–17.

Pennebaker, J. W. (1997). Writing about emotional experiences as a therapeutic process. *Psychological Science*, 8: 162–166.

Peterfreund, E. (1978). Some critical comments on psychoanalytic conceptualizations of infancy. *International Journal of Psychoanalysis* 59: 427–441.

Piaget, J. (1970). *Genetic Epistemology.* New York: W.W. Norton.

Pichon-Rivière, E. (1955–1972). *Del psicoanálisis a la psicologia social.* Buenos Aires: Galerna.

Pichon-Rivière, E. (1971). *El proceso grupal. Del psicoanálisis a la psicología social* (1). [The group process: From psychoanalysis to social psychology (1).] Buenos Aires: Nueva Visión.

Pichon-Rivière, E. (1998). *Teoría del vínculo.* Buenos Aires: Nueva Visión.

Pincus, D., W. Freeman and Modell, A. (2007). A neurobiological model of perception-considerations for transference. *Psychoanalytic Psychology* 24 (4): 623–640.

Plato. *Platonis Opera* (in 5 volumes), ed. J. Burnet. Oxford Classical Texts. Oxford, UK: Clarendon Press, 1967 [Great Books of the Western World], Vol. 7. Ed. R. M. Hutchins; trans. B. Jowell, J. Harward. Chicago, IL: Encyclopedia Britannica.

Posner, R. (1982). *Rational discourse and poetic communication.* Berlin: Walter de Gruyter.

Prigogine, I. (1997). *The End of Certainty: Time, Chaos, and the New Laws of Nature.* New York: Free.

Quine, W. V. O. (1974). *Roots of Reference.* La Salle: Open Court.

Quintanilla, P. (1999). *La hermenéutica de Davidson: Metáfora y creación conceptual*, pp. 75–100. En Ensayos Sobre Davidson. Fundación de Cultura Universitaria. Montevideo.

Racine, J. (1697). *Phèdre.* Paris: Gallimard, 1950. [English translation: Phaedra. In *Three Plays of Racine.* Chicago, IL: The University of Chicago Press, 1961.]

Racker, H. (1953). A contribution to the problem of countertransference. *International Journal of Psychoanalysis* 34: 313–324.

Racker, H (1957a). The meanings and uses of countertransference. *Psychoanalytic Quarterly* 26: 303–357.

Racker, H. (1957b). *Estudios sobre técnica psicoanalítica.* Paidós, Buenos Aires, 1960.

Racker, H. (1958). Counterresistance and interpretation. *Journal of the American Psychoanalytic Association* 6: 215–221.

Racker, H. (1968). Transference and countertransference. *The International Psycho-Analytical Library*, 73:1-196. London: The Hogarth Press and the Institute of Psycho-Analysis.

Rangell, L. (1963). The scope of intrapsychic conflict. *Psychoanalytic Study of the Child* 18: 75–102.

Rappaport, D. (1950). On the psychoanalytic theory of thinking. *International Journal of Psychoanalysis* 31: 161–170.

Rappaport, D. (1953). On the psychoanalytic theory of affects. *International Journal of Psychoanalysis* 34: 177–198.

Rappaport, D. & Gill, M. (1959). The points of view and assumptions of metapsychology. *International Journal of Psychoanalysis* 40: 153–162.

Rappoport de Aisemberg, E. (2011). *The Theory of the Analytical Field.* Presentation for the Panel on The Field Theory at the IPA in Mexico City.

Rickman, J. (1945). A note on the concept of "dynamic structure" and field theory. In P. King (ed.), *No Ordinary Psychoanalyst: The Exceptional Contributions of John Rickman*. London: Karnac, 2003, pp. 343–348.

Ricoeur, P. (1965). *Freud and Philosophy: An Essay on Interpretation*. New Haven, CT: Yale University Press, 1970.

Ricoeur, P. (1986). *The Rule of Metaphor. Multidisciplinairy Studies of the Creation of Meaning in Language*. London: Routledge and Kegen Paul.

Ricoeur, P. (1987). *The Rule of Metaphor*. Toronto: Toronto University Press.

Ricoeur, P. (2008). *Escritos y conferencias alrededor del psicoanálisis*. [Writings and lectures on psychoanalysis.] México City: Siglo Veintiuno, 2009.

Riemann, B. C. & McNally, R. J. (1995). Cognitive processing of personally relevant information. *Cognition and Emotion* 9: 325–340.

Riolo, F. (1986). Dei soggetti del campo: Un discorso sui limiti. *Gruppo e Funzione Analitica* VII, 3: 195–203.

Rizzuto, A.-M. (1990). The Origins of Freud's Concept of Object Representation ("Objektvorstellung") in His Monograph *On Aphasia*: Its Theoretical and Technical Importance. *International Journal of Psychoanalysis* 71: 241–48.

Rizzuto, A.-M. (1993a). First Person Personal Pronouns and Their Psychic Referents. *International Journal of Psychoanalysis* 74: 535–546.

Rizzuto, A.-M. (1993b). Freud's Speech Apparatus and Spontaneous Speech. *International Journal of Psychoanalysis* 74: 113–127.

Rizzuto, A.-M. (2001). Metaphors of a bodily mind. *Journal of the American Psychoanalytic Association* 49: 535–568.

Rizzuto, A.-M. (2003). Psychoanalysis: The transformation of the subject by the spoken word. *Psychoanalytic Quarterly* 72: 287–323.

Rizzuto, A.-M. (2009). Metaphoric process and metaphor. The dialectics of shared analytic experience. *Psychoanalytic Inquiry* 29: 18–29.

Rizzuto, A.-M. (2011). Discussion. *Psychoanalytic Inquiry* 31: 185–201.

Roheim, G. (1934). *The Riddle of the Sphinx*. London: The Hogarth Press.

Rorty, R. (1989) *Contingency, Irony, and Solidarity*. Cambridge: Cambridge University Press.

Rosch, E. (1978). Principles of categorization. In E. Rosch & B. L. Lloyd (eds.), *Cognition and Categorization* (pp. 27–48). Hillsdale, NJ: Erlbaum.

Rousseau, J.-J. (1765, 1965). *Les Confessions*. Présenté par Jean Guéhenno. Gallimard, Paris.

Sacks, S. (1978). *On Metaphor*. Chicago, IL: University of Chicago Press.

Sandler, J. (1976). Countertransference and role-responsiveness. *The International Review of Psychoanalysis*: 43–48.

Sandler, J. (1983). Reflections on some relations between psychoanalytic concepts and psychoanalytic practice. *International Journal of Psychoanalysis* 69: 335–345.

Sandler, J. & Sandler, A.-M. (1983). The "second censorship," the "three box model," and some technical implications. *International Journal of Psychoanalysis* 64: 413–425.

Schafer, R. (1972). Internalization: Process or fantasy. *Psychoanalytic Study of the Child* 27: 411–436.

Schafer, R. (1973a). Action. Its place in psychoanalytic interpretation and theory. *Annual of Psychoanalysis*, Bd. I, 159–196.

Schafer, R. (1973b). Concepts of self and identity and the experience of separation-individualization in adolescence. *Psychoanalytic Quarterly* 42: 42–59.

Schafer, R. (1975). Psychoanalysis without psychodynamics. *International Journal of Psychoanalysis* 56: 41–55.

Schafer, R. (1976). *A New Language for Psychoanalysis.* New Haven, CT: Yale University Press.

Schafer, R. (1993). The conceptualization of clinical facts. *International Journal of Psychoanalysis* 74: 1023–1030.

Schkolnik, F. (1985). Acerca del concepto de curación. *Revista Uruguaya de Psicoanálisis* 64: 70–80.

Scholem, G. (1957). *Die jüdische Mystik in ihren Hauptströmungen.* RheinVerlag, Zürich.

Searle, J. R. (1992). *The Rediscovery of the Mind.* Cambridge, MA: MIT Press.

Segal, H. (1964). *Introduction to the Work of Melanie Klein.* London: William Heinemann.

Seitz, J. (1991). Composition's misunderstanding of metaphor. *College Composition and Communication* 42: 288–298.

Seitz, J (1999). *Motives for Metaphor: Literacy, Curriculum Reform, and the Teaching of English.* Pittsburgh, PA: University of Pittsburgh Press.

Seligman, S. (2005). Dynamic systems theories as a metaframework for psychoanalysis. *Psychoanalytic Dialogues* 15: 285–319.

Shapiro, T. (2005). Naming the unnamable. *Psychoanalytic Inquiry* 25 (4): 506–515.

Sharpe, E. F. (1940). Psychophysical problems revealed in language: An examination of metaphor. *International Journal of Psychoanalysis* 21: 201–213.

Shope, R. K. (1973). Freud's concepts of meaning. *Psychoanalysis and Contemporary Science* 2: 276–303.

Silverman, M. (2010). *Psychoanalytic Quarterly* 79 (4): 1141–1143.

Slipp, S. (ed.) (2000). Neuroscience and psychoanalysis [special issue]. *Journal of the American Academy of Psychoanalysis* 28: 191–395.

Snow, C. E. (1977). The development of conversations between mothers and babies. *Journal of Child Language* 4: 1–22.

Sodré, I. (2005). As I was walking down the stair, I saw a concept which wasn't there. *International Journal of Psychoanalysis* 86: 7–10.

Solms, M. (1997a). Review of affect regulation and the origin of the self: The neurobiology of emotional development. *Journal of the American Psychoanalytic Association* 45: 964–969.

Solms, M. (1997b). What is consciousness? *Journal of the American Psychoanalytic Association* 45: 681–703.

Solms, M. (1999). Preliminaries for and integration of psychoanalysis and neuroscience. *The Annual of Psychoanalysis* 28: 179–200.

Sontag, S. (1978). *Illness as Metaphor.* New York: Farrar, Straus and Giroux.

Spence, D. (1987). *The Freudian metáphor.* New York. London.

Spezzano, C. (2007). A home for the mind. *Psychoanalytic Quarterly* 76 Supplement: 1563–1583.

Stern, D. (1983). Unformulated experience—from familiar chaos to creative disorder. *Contemporary Psychoanalysis* 19: 71–99.

Stern, D. (1985a). *The Interpersonal World of the Infant. A View from Psychoanalysis and Developmental Psychology.* New York: Basic Books.

Stern, D. (1985b). *El mundo interpersonal del infante una perspectiva desde el psicoanálisis y la psicología evolutiva.* Buenos Aires: Paidos, 1991: 176–192.

Stern, D. (1990). Courting surprise—Unbidden perceptions in clinical practice. *Contemporary Psychoanalysis* 26: 452–478.

Stern, D. (1997). *Unformulated Experience.* Hillsdale, NJ: The Analytic Press.

Stern, J. (2000). *Metaphor in Context.* Cambridge, MA: MIT Press.

Stern, D. (2004). *The Present Moment in Psychotherapy and Every Day Life.* W.W Norton. London.

Stern, D. (2009). Shall the twain meet? Metaphor, dissociation, and co-occurrence. *Psychoanalytic Inquiry* 29: 79–90.

Stolorow, R. & Atwood, G. (1989). The unconscious and unconscious fantasy: An intersubjective-developmental perspective. *Psychoanalytic Inquiry* 9: 364–374.

Stolorow, R. & Atwood, G. (1996). The intersubjective perspective. *Psychoanalytic Review* 83: 181–194.

Strenger, C. (1997). Hedgehogs, foxes, and critical pluralism: The clinician's yearning for unified conceptions. *Psychoanalysis and Contemporary Thought* 20: 111–145.

Sullivan, H. S. (1953). *The Interpersonal Theory of Psychiatry*. New York: Norton.

Sweetser, E. & Fauconnier, G. (1996). Cognitive links and domains: Basic aspects of mental space theory. In G. Fauconnier & E. Sweetser (eds), *Space, Word, and Grammar*. Chicago, IL: University of Chicago Press.

Symington, J. & Symington, N. (1996). *The Clinical Thinking of Wilfred Bion*. New York: Brunner-Routledge.

*Talmud.* (1962/1936). *Talmud: Hebrew/Aramaic edition of the Babylonian Talmud*, ed. Rabbi M. Zioni. Jerusalem: Bne Braq. Trans., ed. I. Epstein. London: Soncino, 1936.

Thelen, E. & Smith, L. D. (1994). *A Dynamic Systems Approach to the Development of Cognition and Action* Cambridge, MA: MIT Press.

Thoma, H. & Kachele, H. (1989). *Teoría y Práctica del Psicoanálisis*. Tomo 1, p. 406. Barcelona: Editorial Herder S.A.

Trevarthen, C. (1979). Communication and cooperation in early infancy: A description of primary intersubjectivity. In Margaret Bullowa (ed.), *Before Speech. The Beginning of Interpersonal Communication*. Cambridge, England: Cambridge University Press, pp. 321–347.

Tronick, E. (2002). A model of infant mood states and Sandarian Affective Waves. *Psychoanalytic Dialogues* 12: 73–99.

Tubert-Oklander, J. (2000). El psicoanálisis ante el nuevo milenio. Reflexiones sobre la epistemología del psicoanálisis. [Psychoanalysis facing the new millennium: Reflections on the epistemology of psychoanalysis.] *Estudios sobre Psicosis y Retardo Mental* 5: 275–295

Tubert-Oklander, J. (2004a). Le Journal clinique de 1932 et la nouvelle clinique psychanalytique. *Le Coq-Héron*, Paris, Vol. 178, September 2004, "Ferenczi le clinicien—2," pp. 19–37.

Tubert-Oklander, J. (2004b). Il "Diario clinico" del 1932 e la sua influenza sulla prassi psicoanalitica. In F. Borgogno (ed.), *Ferenczi oggi* [Ferenczi today]. Turin: Bollati Boringhieri, pp. 47–63.

Tubert-Oklander, J. (2004c). ¿Debemos creer en el inconsciente? [Should we believe in the unconscious?]. In M. Kolteniuk, J. Casillas & J. de la Parra (eds), *El inconsciente freudiano* [The Freudian Unconscious]. Mexico City: Editores de Textos Mexicanos, pp. 101–109.

Tubert-Oklander, J. (2005). El concepto de campo en la obra de Willy Baranger. [The concept of field in the work of Willy Baranger.] *Cuadernos de Psicoanálisis* 38 (3–4): 47–54.

Tubert-Oklander, J. (2006a). *Implicaciones metapsicológicas del enfoque intersubjetivo y relacional de la técnica y la clínica psicoanalíticas.* [Metapsychological implications of the intersubjective and relational approach to psychoanalytic technique and clinical practice.] *Cuadernos de Psicoanálisis* 39 (1–2): 12–25.

Tubert-Oklander, J. (2006b). I, thou, and us: Relationality and the interpretive process in clinical practice. *Psychoanalytic Dialogues* 17: 199–216.

Tubert-Oklander, J. (2007). The whole and the parts: Working in the analytic field. *Psychoanalytic Dialogues* 17: 115–132.

Tubert-Oklander, J. (2008). An inquiry into the alpha function. *Canadian Journal of PsychoanalysisRevue Canadienne de Psychanalyse* 16: 224–245.

Tubert-Oklander, J. (2011). Enrique Pichon-Rivière: The social unconscious in the Latin-American tradition of group analysis. In E. Hopper & H. Weinberg, *The Social Unconscious in Persons, Groups and Societies—Volume 1: Mainly Theory*. London: Karnac.

Tubert-Oklander, J. & Beuchot Puente, M. (2008). *Ciencia mestiza. Hermenéutica analógica y psicoanálisis.* [Hybrid science: Analogical hermeneutics and psychoanalysis.] Mexico City: Torres.

Tubert-Oklander, J. & Hernández-Tubert, R. (2004). *Operative Groups: The Latin-American Approach to Group Analysis.* London: Jessica Kingsley.

Tuggy, D. (1993) Ambiguity, polysemy, and vagueness. *Cognitive Linguistics* 4: 273–290.

Tzermias, P. (1976). *Tourismus und Gastfreundschaft in Griechenland.* Neue Zürcher Zeitung, 20 August 57.

Viderman, S. (1970). *La construction de l'espace analytique.* Paris: Gallimard.

Vivona, J. (2009). Leaping from brain to mind: A critique of mirror neuron explanations of countertransference. *Journal of the American Psychoanalytic Association* 57: 525–550.

Voth, H. M. (1970). The analysis of metaphor. *Journal of the American Psychoanalytic Association* 18: 599–621.

Vrobel, S. (2006). Sheer simultaneity: Fractal time condensation. In *IIAS Conference Proceedings*, Baden-Baden 2006.

Vrobel, S., Roessler, O. & Marks-Tarlow, T. (2008). *Simultaneity: Temporal structures and observer perspectives.* Singapore: World Scientific Publishing.

Vygotsky (1962). *Thought and Language.* Cambridge, MA: MIT Press.

Wachtel, P. L. (2003). The surface and the depths: The metaphor of depth in psychoanalysis and the ways in which it can mislead. *Contemporary Psychoanalysis* 39: 5–26.

Waelder, R. (1934). The problem of freedom in psychoanalysis and the problem of reality testing. *Imago* 20: 467–484.

Wallerstein, R. S. (1988). One psychoanalysis or many? *International Journal of Psychoanalysis* 69: 5–21.

Wallerstein, R. S (1990). Psychoanalysis: The common ground. *International Journal of Psychoanalysis* 71: 3–20.

Wallerstein, R. S (2002a). The growth and transformation of American ego psychology. *Journal of the American Psychoanalytic Association* 50: 135–169.

Wallerstein, R. S. (2002b). The trajectory of psychoanalysis: A prognostication. *International Journal of Psychoanalysis* 83: 1247–1267.

Wallerstein, R. S. (2005). Will psychoanalytic pluralism be an enduring state of our discipline? *International Journal of Psychoanalysis* 86: 623–626.

Wallerstein, R. S. (2011) Metaphor in psychoanalysis: bane or blessing? *Psychoanalytic Inquiry* 31: 90–106.

Weinberger, J. & Hardaway, R. (1990). Separating science from myth in subliminal psychodynamic activation. *Clinical Psychology Review* 10: 727–756.

Wheelwright, P. (1962, 1975). *Metaphor and Reality.* Bloomington, IN: Indiana University Press.

White, R. (2011). The non-verbal unconscious: Collision and collusion of metaphor. *Psychoanalytic Inquiry* 31: 147–158.

Wieger, L. (1927, 1965). *Chinese Characters. Their Origin, Etymology, History, Classification and Signification.* Trans. L. Da vrout. New York: Paragon Book Reprint, Dover.

Wilhelm, R. (1921). *Kung Fu Tse: Gespräche.* Lun Yü. Diederichs, Jena.

Williams, J. M., Matthews, A. & MacLeod, C. (1996). The Emotional Stroop Task and psychopathology. *Psychological Bulletin* 120: 3–24.

Winnicott, D. W. (1960). The theory of the parent–infant relationship. *International Journal of Psychoanalysis* 41: 585–595.

Winnicott, D. W. (1965). *The Maturational Process and the Facilitating Environment.* New York: International Universities Press.

Winnicott, D. W. (1967). *Playing and Reality.* New York: Basic Books, 1971.

Wurmser, L. (1977). A defense of the use of metaphor in analytic theory formation. *Psychoanalytic Quarterly* 46: 466–498.

Wurmser, L. (1981). Is psychoanalysis a separate field of symbolic forms? *Humanities and Society* 4: 263–294. Los Angeles: University of Southern California.

Wurmser, L. (1989). *Die zerbrochene Wirklichkeit: Psychoanalyse als das Studium von Konflikt und Komplementarität.* [Broken reality: Psychoanalysis as the study of conflict and complementarity.] Heidelberg: Springer.

Wurmser, L. (1990). The question of conflict in Chinese thought, specifically in Confucius: Some psychoanalytic considerations. *Journal of the Korean Psychoanalytic Study Group* 1: 115–130.

Wurmser, L. (1991). The question of conflict in Lao Tzu: Some psychoanalytic considerations. *Journal of the Korean Psychoanalytic Study Group* 2: 112–133.

Wurmser, L. (1993, 3rd edn). *Die Maske der Scham: Die Psychoanalyse von Schamaffekten und Schamkonflikten.* [The mask of shame: The psychoanalysis of shame affects and shame conflicts.].Heidelberg: Springer.

Wurmser, L. (2000). *The Power of the Inner Judge.* Northvale, NJ: Aronson.

Wurmser, L. (2001). *Ideen- und Wertewelt des Judentums: Eine psychoanalytische Sicht.* Göttingen: Vandenhoeck & Ruprecht.

Wurmser, L. (2011). Metaphor as conflict, conflict as metaphor. *Psychoanalytic Inquiry* 31: 107–125.

Young-Breuhl, E. & Bethelard, F. (1999). The hidden history of the ego instincts. *Psychoanalytic Review* 86 (6): 823–851.

Zimmer, R. (2010). *Psychoanalytic Quarterly* 79 (4): 1151–1165.

# INDEX